MOON HANDBOOKS®

CANADIAN ROCKIES

© ANDREW HEMPSTEAD

Wedge Pond, Kananaskis Country

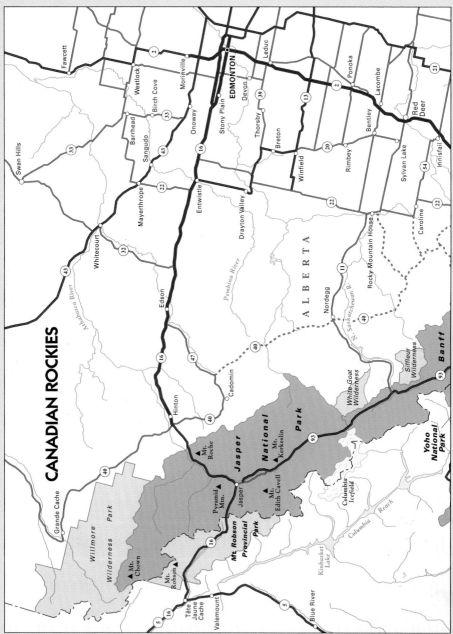

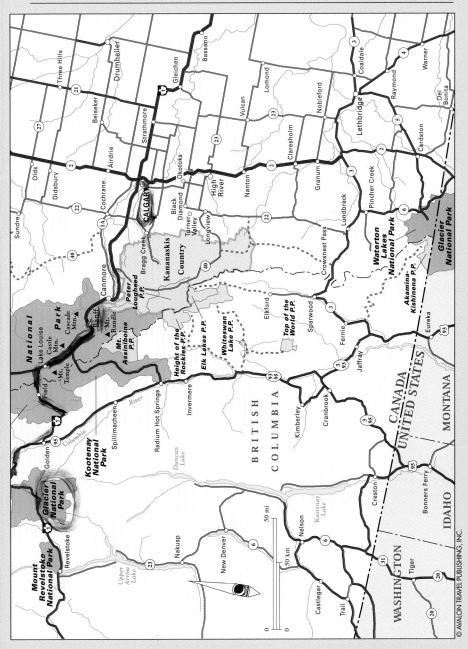

© AVALON TRAVEL PUBLISHING, INC.

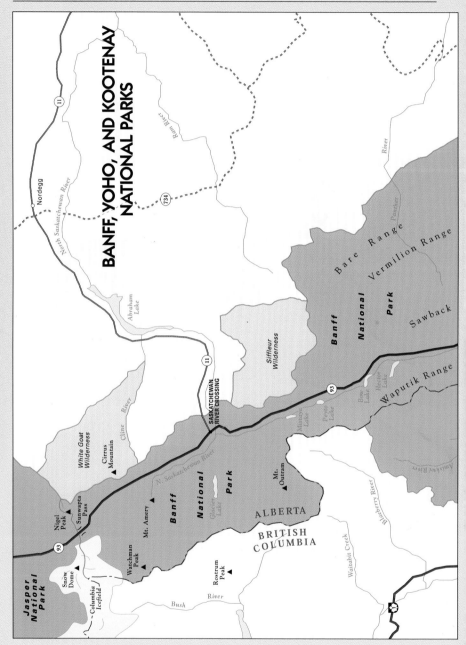

BANFF, YOHO, AND KOOTENAY NATIONAL PARKS

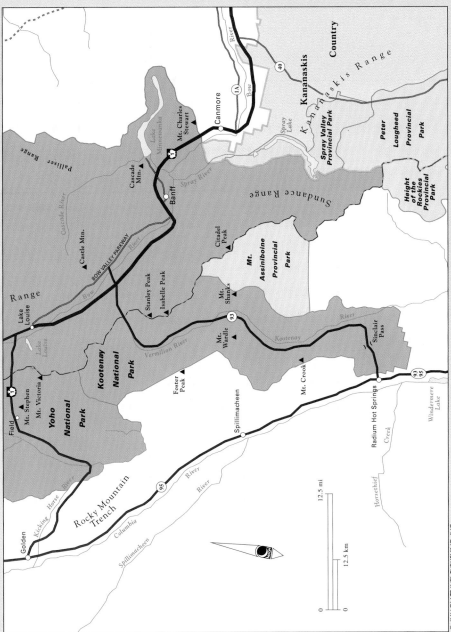

© AVALON TRAVEL PUBLISHING, INC.

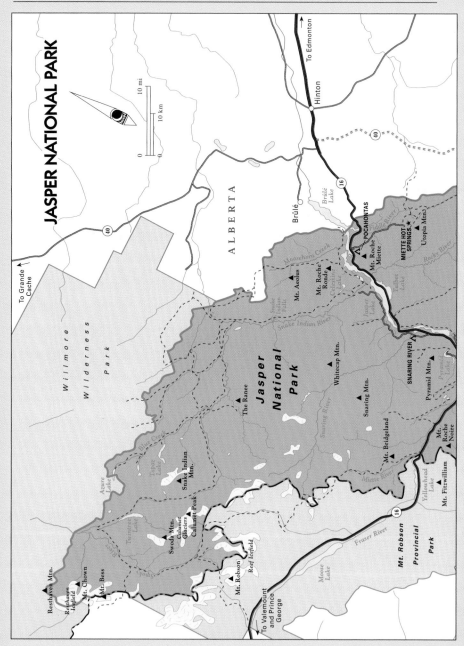

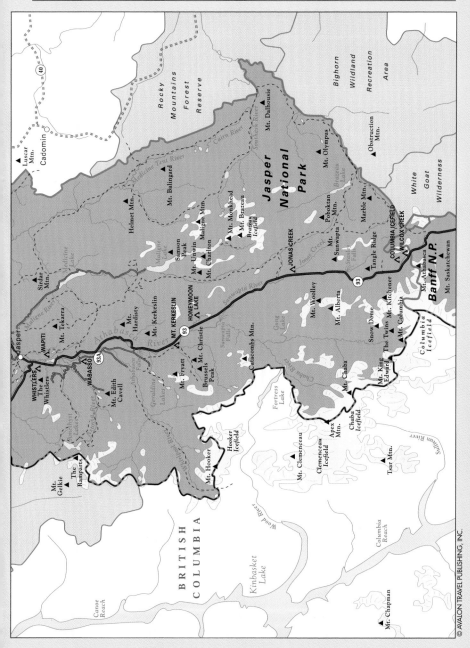

Emerald Lake, Yoho National Park

MOON HANDBOOKS®

CANADIAN ROCKIES

INCLUDING BANFF AND JASPER NATIONAL PARKS

THIRD EDITION

ANDREW HEMPSTEAD

AVALON
TRAVEL

**Moon Handbooks Canadian Rockies
Including Banff and Jasper National Parks
Third Edition**

Andrew Hempstead

Text © 2003 by Andrew Hempstead.
Illustrations and maps © 2003 by
Avalon Travel Publishing, Inc.
All rights reserved.
Photos and some illustrations are used
by permission and are the property of their
original copyright owners.

ISBN: 1-56691-493-0
ISSN: 1522-3477

Please send all comments, corrections,
additions, amendments, and critiques to:

Moon Handbooks Canadian Rockies

Avalon Travel Publishing
1400 65th Street, Suite 250
Emeryville, CA 94608, USA
atpfeedback@avalonpub.com
www.moon.com

Printing History
1st edition—1999
3rd edition—May 2003
5 4 3 2 1

Editor and Series Manager: Kevin McLain
Copy Editor: Ginjer L. Clarke
Graphics and Production Coordinator: Justin Marler
Cover Designer: Kari Gim
Interior Designers: Amber Pirker, Alvaro Villanueva, Kelly Pendragon
Map Editor: Olivia Solís
Cartographers: Mike Morgenfeld, Mark Stroud, Sheryle Veverka
Indexer: Judy Hunt

Front cover photo: © Terry Donnelly

Distributed by Publishers Group West

Printed in the U.S.A. by Worzalla

ABOUT THE AUTHOR
Andrew Hempstead

As a travel writer and photographer, Andrew Hempstead has spent many years exploring, photographing, and writing about Canada. While he spends much of his life on the road, he looks forward to spending every second summer at home in the Canadian Rockies, traveling mountain highways and hiking trails, exploring new places and updating old favorites, and searching out unique photographic opportunities. Rather than having an itinerary laid out for him by local tourism offices or relying on the telephone or internet to update this book, he spends as much time as possible on the road, traveling incognito, experiencing the many and varied delights of the region just as his readers do. The result is the book you hold in front of you, the most comprehensive and up-to-date source of information available for traveling in the Canadian Rockies.

Andrew has been writing since the late 1980s, when he left an established career in advertising and took off for Alaska, linking up with veteran travel writer Deke Castleman to research and update the fourth edition of *Moon Handbooks Alaska–Yukon*. In the ensuing years he produced several guides to Canada, including books on Alberta, British Columbia, Vancouver, the Northwest Territories, and Nunavut. He is also the co-author of *Moon Handbooks Atlantic Canada* and a contributor to *Moon Handbooks San Juan Islands, Road Trip USA, Northwest Best Places,* and *Eyewitness Guide to the USA.* Further afield, Andrew is co-author of *Moon Handbooks Australia* and *Moon Handbooks New Zealand,* and has updated the last three editions of *The Illustrated Guide to New Zealand.* His writing and photographs have appeared in a wide variety of media, including *National Geographic Traveler, Travesias, Where, Interval World,* Microsoft's *Automap,* and on the Alaska Airlines website. Amazingly enough, he has also found the time to travel purely for pleasure, visiting most of the United States, Europe, India, and the South Pacific.

Andrew lives with his wife, Dianne, and their two dogs in Banff, Alberta. When not working on his books, he spends as much time as possible enjoying the sublime landscape he calls home—hiking, fishing, golfing, camping, and skiing. The website www.westerncanadatravel.com showcases Andrew's work, while also providing invaluable planning tips for travelers heading to Canada.

Contents

SPECIAL TOPIC

SPECIAL TOPIC

JASPER NATIONAL PARK 204

The Land; Flora; Fauna; History

SIGHTS AND DRIVES 209
Columbia Icefield; Icefields Parkway; Mount Edith Cavell; Sights in and Around
the Town of Jasper; Maligne Lake and Vicinity; Continuing East along Highway 16

HIKING 219
Hikes around the Town of Jasper; Hiking in the Maligne Lake Area; Hikes Near
Mount Edith Cavell; Hikes along Icefields Parkway

OTHER RECREATION 225
Fair Weather; Wintertime; Arts and Entertainment

ACCOMMODATIONS AND CAMPING 230
In and Around the Town of Jasper; Along the Icefields Parkway; East of the Town
of Jasper; Hinton; Other Lodging Options; Campgrounds

OTHER PRACTICALITIES 238
Food; Transportation; Information and Services

WATERTON LAKES NATIONAL PARK 244

The Land; History

SIGHTS AND RECREATION 249
Scenic Drives; Hiking; Other Recreation

ACCOMMODATIONS AND CAMPING 255
Hotels, Motels, and Lodges; Campgrounds

OTHER PRACTICALITIES 259
Food; Transportation; Information and Services

Maps

MAP SYMBOLS

══════	Divided Highway/Road	▾	Restaurant/Bar
─────	Primary Highway/Road	▪	Other Location
─────	Secondary Highway/Road	○	City/Town
········	Unpaved Road	⋀	Campground
- - - - -	Hiking Trail	▲	Mountain
─┼──┼─	Railroad	⌡	Golf Course
⬢	TransCanada Highway	🎿	Ski Resort
○	Provincial/State Highway	⟍	Mountain Pass
⬭	U.S. Highway	⫶	Waterfall
★	Point of Interest	⬡	Glacier/Icefield
•	Accommodation		

Abbreviations

AB—Alberta
APEX fare—advance-purchase excursion fare
B&B—bed-and-breakfast inn
BC—British Columbia
CPR—Canadian Pacific Railway
d—double occupancy
GPS—global positioning system
GST—Goods and Services Tax
Hwy.—Highway

km—kilometer
kph—kilometers per hour
NWT—Northwest Territories
NWMP—North West Mounted Police
RCMP—Royal Canadian Mounted Police
RV—recreational vehicle
s—single occupancy
UNESCO—United Nations Educational, Scientific, and Cultural Organization

Keeping Current

We have strived to produce the most well-researched and up-to-date travel guide to the Canadian Rockies available, but accommodations and restaurants come and go, others change hands, hiking trails close, and prices rise—and your concerned travel writer loses considerable sleep over it all. You can help. You may notice discrepancies between what's written in this book and what you actually encounter in your travels, or discover wonderful off-the-beaten-track attractions or new accommodations. Letters from tour operators and those in the local tourism industries are also appreciated.

Moon Handbooks Canadian Rockies
Avalon Travel Publishing
1400 65th Street, Suite 250
Emeryville, CA 94608
atpfeedback@avalonpub.com

If we can't export the scenery, we'll import the tourists.

William C. Van Horne, president of the
Canadian Pacific Railway, circa 1885

Introduction

Snowcapped peaks by the hundreds, glaciers and icefields, multihued lakes, rushing rivers, an abundance of wildlife—the awe-inspiring Canadian Rockies are one of North America's premier travel destinations. Mother Nature dealt the original winning hand here, which early governments had the foresight to protect for all time in a string of contiguous parks straddling the British Columbia–Alberta border. **Banff** and **Jasper National Parks,** on the east side of the Continental Divide in the province of Alberta, are the best known of these. Originally conceived as tourist resorts, the bustling towns of Banff and Jasper serve millions of visitors annually and boast championship golf courses, world-class resorts, hundreds of restaurants, and international shopping.

Two more national parks lie just west of Banff and Jasper, across the Continental Divide in the province of British Columbia. This side of the Canadian Rockies is much less crowded but is no less impressive. Here **Kootenay National Park** features hot springs and high concentrations of wildlife, while **Yoho National Park** is famous for multihued Emerald Lake and the superb hiking country around Lake O'Hara. Together, the four national parks make up a complex geological and natural area that has been declared a World Heritage Site by the United Nations Educational, Scientific, and Cultural Organization (UNESCO).

© ANDREW HEMPSTEAD

Moraine Lake, Banff National Park

In addition to these four national parks, several other parks also preserve parts of the Canadian Rockies. On the British Columbia side of the divide, **Mount Assiniboine Provincial Park** is favored by backcountry hikers, while at the northern reach of Jasper National Park lies **Mount Robson Provincial Park,** which surrounds and is named for the highest peak of the Canadian Rockies. In southern Alberta, **Waterton Lakes National Park** is a hidden gem that lacks the crowds of its northern counterparts, and **Kananaskis Country** is a preserve developed as a four-season, multiuse recreation area. Nearby, nestled among the high peaks of the Bow Valley, is **Canmore,** Alberta, the largest population center of the Canadian Rockies, and offering numerous opportunities for hiking and rock climbing.

The Land

The Rocky Mountains rise from the dense forests of central Mexico and run north through the U.S. states of New Mexico, Colorado, Wyoming, and Montana. Continuing north across the 49th parallel (the U.S.–Canada border), the range forms a natural border between the Canadian provinces of British Columbia and Alberta. Mountainous British Columbia is Canada's westernmost province, extending to the Pacific Ocean, while Alberta, to the east, is mostly prairie. The actual provincial boundary is the Continental Divide, an imaginary line that runs along the Rockies' highest peaks. Although it is a subjective matter, perhaps most would agree that this particular stretch of the Rocky Mountains—the Canadian Rockies—is the most spectacular segment anywhere along the entire range. North of British Columbia and Alberta, the Rockies descend to their northern terminus in the boreal forests of northern Canada.

The Canadian Rockies are relatively low compared to other mountain ranges of the world; the highest peak, Mount Robson, tops out at 3,954 meters (12,970 feet). Running parallel to the mountains along their eastern edge is a series of long, rolling ridges known as the foothills. To the west is the Rocky Mountain Trench, a long, wide valley that in turn is bordered to the west by various subranges of the Columbia Mountains.

GEOLOGY

The Rocky Mountains began rising 75 million years ago, making them relatively young compared to the world's major mountain ranges. But to fully appreciate the geology of the Rockies, you must look back many hundreds of millions of years, to the Precambrian era. At this time, about 700 million years ago, the Pacific Ocean covered most of the western provinces and states. The ocean advanced, then receded, several times over the next half billion years. Each time the ocean flooded eastward it deposited layers of silt and sand on its bed—layers that built up with each successive inundation. Starting approximately 550 million years ago, the oceans began to come alive with marine invertebrates and the first crustaceans. As these creatures died and sank to the ocean floor, they added to the layers of sediment. Over time, the ever-increasing sediment load compressed the underlying layers into sandstone, shale, and quartzite.

Birth of the Rockies

Some 200 million years ago, the stability of the ocean floor began wavering along the West Coast of North America, culminating 75 million years ago as two plates of the earth's crust collided. According to plate tectonics theory, the earth's crust is broken into several massive chunks (plates) that are always moving and occasionally bump into each other. This isn't something that happens overnight; a plate may move only a few centimeters over thousands of years. In the case of the Rockies, the Pacific Plate butted into the North American Plate and was forced beneath it. The land at this subduction zone was crumpled and thrust upward, creating the Rocky Mountains. Layers of sediment laid down on the ocean floor over the course of hundreds of millions of

The Front Ranges, between the Continental Divide and the foothills, are the most severely folded and faulted. Mount Kidd (pictured), in Kananaskis Country, is a classic example.

years were folded, twisted, and squeezed; great slabs of rock broke away, and in places older strata were pushed on top of younger. By the beginning of the Tertiary period, around 65 million years ago, the present form of mountain contours was established and the geological framework of the mountains was in place.

The Ice Ages

No one knows why, but around one million years ago the world's climate cooled a few degrees. Ice caps formed in Arctic regions and slowly moved south over North America and Eurasia. These advances, followed by retreats, occurred four times.

The final major glaciation began moving south 35,000 years ago. A sheet of ice up to 2,000 meters (6,560 feet) deep covered all but the highest peaks of the Rocky Mountains. The ice scoured the terrain, destroying all vegetation as it crept slowly forward. In the mountains, these rivers of ice carved hollows, known as *cirques,* into the slopes of the higher peaks. They rounded off lower peaks and reamed out valleys from their preglacier V shape to a trademark, postglacial U shape. The retreat of this ice sheet, beginning

around 12,000 years ago, also radically altered the landscape. Rock and debris that had been picked up by the ice on its march forward melted out during the retreat, creating high ridges known as lateral and terminal *moraines.* Many of these moraines blocked natural drainages, resulting in

FOOTHILLS ERRATICS TRAIN

During the last ice age, a sheet of ice up to 1,000 meters (3,280 feet) thick crept southward across the area that is now Jasper National Park. A landslide deposited hundreds of large quartzite boulders atop the ice, which continued moving south, carrying the boulders with it. Many thousands of years later, as temperatures warmed and the ice melted, the boulders were deposited far from their source, creating an erratics train extending 650 km (400 miles) south through Alberta. The largest of these boulders—the world's largest erratic, weighing an estimated 18,000 tons—lies just beyond the foothills, seven km (4.3 miles) west of Okotoks. The name is difficult to forget; it's called the **Big Rock.**

the formation of lakes. Meltwater drained into rivers and streams, incising deep channels into the sedimentary rock of the plains. Today, the only remnants of this Ice Age are the scattered icefields along the Continental Divide, including the 325-square-km (125-square-mile) **Columbia Icefield.**

Waterways

Water in its various forms has had a profound effect on the appearance of the Canadian Rockies. In addition to the scouring action of the glaciers, flowing water in rivers and streams has, over the millennia, deeply etched the landscape. The process continues today.

The flow of water is directly related to *divides,* or high points of land that dictate the direction of water flow. The dominant divide in the Canadian Rockies, and indeed North America, is the Continental Divide. The natural boundary created by this divide forms the Alberta–British Columbia border, while other, less obvious divides form borders of many parks of the Canadian Rockies. The five national parks are classic examples of this scenario. The divides forming the boundaries of Banff National Park encompass the entire upper watershed of the **Bow River.** The Bow flows southward through the park then heads east out of the mountains and into the Saskatchewan River system, whose waters continue east to Hudson Bay and the Atlantic Ocean. The Bow River is fed by many lakes famed for their beauty, including the **Bow, Louise,** and **Moraine.** To the south, the rivers of Kananaskis Country and Waterton Lakes National Park also drain into the Saskatchewan River system.

The boundary between Jasper and Banff National Parks is an important north–south divide. The **Columbia Icefield,** a remnant of the last Ice Age, lies on either side of this divide. Runoff from the south side of the icefield flows south into the Saskatchewan River system, while runoff from the north side forms the upper headwaters of the **Athabasca River** system. The Athabasca flows north through Jasper National Park and into the Mackenzie

River system, which continues north to the Arctic Ocean. All water draining off the western slopes of the Continental Divide ends up in the Pacific Ocean via two major river systems: the **Columbia** and the **Fraser.** The mighty Columbia makes a wide northern loop before heading south into the U.S. state of Washington and draining into the Pacific Ocean. Along the way it picks up the waters of the **Kootenay River,** which begins high in Kootenay National Park and makes a lazy loop south through Montana and Idaho before joining the Columbia at Castlegar, British Columbia, and the **Kicking Horse River,** which flows down from the divides that form the borders of Yoho National Park. The **Fraser River,** the longest river entirely within British Columbia, begins in the high reaches of Mount Robson Provincial Park.

CLIMATE

More than any other factor, prevailing moisture-laden westerlies blowing across British Columbia from the Pacific Ocean dictate the climate of the Canadian Rockies. The cold heights of the mountain peaks wring the winds dry, making for clear, sunny skies in southern Alberta; Calgary gets up to 350 hours of sunshine in June alone—good news, unless you're a farmer. In winter, the dry winds blasting down the eastern slopes of the Rockies can raise temperatures on the prairies by up to 40°C (72°F) in 24 hours. Called *chinooks,* these desiccating blows are a phenomenon unique to Alberta.

Elevation and, to a lesser degree, latitude are two other factors affecting the climate within the mountain ecosystem. Elevations vary from 800 meters (2,600 feet) above sea level at Radium Hot Springs to 1,500 meters (4,920 feet) at Lake Louise to 3,954 meters (12,970 feet) at the summit of Mount Robson. As a general rule, temperatures fall 5°C (9°F) for every 1,000 meters (3,280 feet) of elevation gained. Another interesting phenomenon occurring in the Canadian Rockies is the *temperature inversion,* in which a layer of warm air

CHINOOK WINDS

On many days in the dead of winter, a distinctive arch of clouds forms in the sky over the southwestern corner of Alberta as a wind peculiar to the Rockies swoops down over the mountains. The warm wind, known as a *chinook* (snow eater), can raise temperatures by up to 20°C (36°F) in an hour and up to 40°C (72°F) in a 24-hour period. The wind's effect on the snowpack is legendary. One story tells of a backcountry skier who spent the better part of a day traversing to the summit of a snow-clad peak on the front range of the Canadian Rockies. As he rested and contemplated skiing down, he realized that the slope had become completely bare!

Chinooks originate over the Pacific Ocean when warm, moist air is pushed eastward by prevailing westerlies. The air pressure of these winds is less than at lower elevations, and, therefore, as the air moves down the front ranges of the Canadian Rockies, it is subjected to increased pressure. This increasing of the air pressure warms the winds, which then fan out across the foothills and prairies. The "chinook arch" is formed as the clear air clashes with the warmer cloud-laden winds. The phenomenon is most common in southern Alberta but occurs to a lesser degree as far north as the Peace River Valley. Pincher Creek, the gateway to Waterton Lakes National Park, experiences about 35 chinooks each winter.

sits on top of a cold air mass. During these inversions, high- and low-country roles are reversed; prairie residents can be shivering and bundling up, while their mountain fellows are sunning themselves in short sleeves.

The Seasons

Summer in the mountains is short, but the days are long. With up to 17 hours of daylight around the summer solstice of June 21, this is an ideal time for travel and camping out. The months on either side of summer are ideal for touring, especially September when rainfall is minimal. Winter is cold, but the skiing and snowboarding are fantastic.

January is usually the coldest month, when Banff's average temperature is –10°C (14°F). In winter, extended spells of –30°C (–22°F) are not uncommon anywhere in the mountains, and temperatures occasionally drop below –40°C (–40°F). The coldest temperature recorded was –52°C (–62°F), in Lake Louise on January 25, 1950. Severe cold weather is often accompanied by sunshine; the cold is a dry cold, unlike the damp cold experienced in coastal regions. Cold temperatures and snow can be expected through mid-March.

Although March, April, and May are, more or less, the official months of spring, snow often falls in May, many lakes may remain frozen until June, and snow cover on higher mountain hiking trails remains until early July. During this period of the year the mountains are often affected by low-pressure weather patterns from the southeast, creating continuous days of rain, especially in the south.

Things warm up in summer. July is the hottest month, with Banff, Jasper, and Canmore's average daytime temperature topping out above 23°C (73°F) and Radium Hot Springs and Golden enjoying average daytime highs of 29°C (84°F) and 27°C (81°F), respectively. On hot days, the temperature can hit 30°C (86°F) along lower elevation valleys. Again, because of the dryness of the air, these temperatures are more bearable here than in coastal regions experiencing the same temperatures.

By late September the mountain air begins to have a distinct chill. October brings the highest temperature variations of the year; the thermometer can hit 30°C (86°F) but also dip as low as –20°C (–4°F). Mild weather can continue until early December, but generally the first snow falls in October, and by mid-November winter has set in.

Flora

Botanists divide the Canadian Rockies into three distinct vegetation zones (also called *biomes*): montane, subalpine, and alpine. The boundaries of these zones are determined by several factors, the most important being altitude. Latitude and exposure are also factors, but less so. Typically, within any 1,500 meters (4,920 feet) of elevation change, you'll pass through each of the three zones. These changes can be seen occurring most abruptly in Waterton Lakes National Park. Conifers (evergreens) predominate in the montane and subalpine, whereas above the treeline, in the alpine, only low-growing hardy species survive.

MONTANE

The foothills, along with most major valleys below an elevation of about 1,500 meters (4,920 feet), are primarily cloaked in montane forest. **Aspen, balsam poplar,** and **white spruce** thrive here. **Lodgepole pine** is the first species to emerge after fire. Its hard seed cones are sealed by a resin that is melted only at high temperatures. When fire races through the forest, the resin melts and the cones release their seeds. The lodgepole is named for its straight, slender trunk, which natives used as a center pole for tepees. On dry, south-facing slopes, **Douglas fir** is the climax species. Where sunlight penetrates the forest, such as along riverbanks, flowers like **lady's slipper, Indian paintbrush,** and **saxifrage** are common. Large tracts of **fescue grassland** are common at lower elevations. The montane forest holds the greatest diversity of life of any vegetation zone and is prime winter habitat for larger mammals. But this is the habitat where most development occurs and therefore is often much changed from its natural state.

SUBALPINE

Subalpine forests occur where temperatures are lower and precipitation higher than in the montane. In the Canadian Rockies, this is generally from 1,500 to 2,200 meters (4,920 to 7,220 feet) above sea level. The upper limit of the subalpine zone is the treeline. Approximately half the flora of the mountains falls within this zone. The climax species are **Engelmann spruce** and **subalpine fir** (recognized by its spirelike crown), although extensive forests of **lodgepole pine** occur in areas that have been scorched by fire in the last 100 years. At higher elevations, stands of **larch** are seen. Larches are deciduous conifers—unlike other evergreens, their needles turn a burnt-orange color each fall, producing a magnificent display for photographers.

ALPINE

The alpine zone extends from the treeline to mountain summits. The upper limit of tree growth in the Canadian Rockies varies between 1,800 and 2,400 meters (5,900–7,900 feet) above sea level, dropping progressively

Fireweed is easily recognized by a long spike of bright pink flowers.

© ANDREW HEMPSTEAD

to the north until it meets the treeless tundra of the Arctic. Vegetation at these high altitudes occurs only where soil has been deposited. Large areas of alpine meadows burst with color for a short period each summer as **lupines, mountain avens, alpine forget-me-nots, avalanche lily, moss campion,** and a variety of **heathers** bloom.

Fauna

One of the biggest attractions of the Canadian Rockies is the abundance of wildlife, especially large mammals such as elk, moose, bighorn sheep, and bears, which are widespread and easily viewed throughout the mountains.

THE DEER FAMILY
Mule Deer and White-Tailed Deer
Mule deer and white-tailed deer are similar in size and appearance. Their color varies with the season but is generally light brown in summer, turning dirty-gray in winter. While both species are considerably smaller than elk, the mule deer is a little stockier than the white-tailed deer. The mule deer has a white rump, a white tail with a dark tip, and large mulelike ears. It inhabits open forests along valley floors. Waterton townsite has a healthy population of mule deer. The white-tailed deer's tail is dark on top, but when the animal runs, it holds its tail erect, revealing an all-white underside. White-tails frequent thickets along the rivers and lakes of the foothills. They are most common on the British Columbia side of the Continental Divide.

Elk
The elk, or *wapiti,* is the most widespread and common of the larger mammals living in the Canadian Rockies. It has a tan body with a dark-brown neck, dark-brown legs, and a white rump. This second-largest member of the deer family weighs 250–450 kg (550–1,000 lbs.) and stands 1.5 meters (five feet) at the shoulder. Beginning

> *One of the biggest attractions of the Canadian Rockies is the abundance of wildlife, especially large mammals such as elk, moose, bighorn sheep, and bears, which are widespread and easily viewed throughout the mountains.*

each spring, stags grow an impressive set of antlers, covered in what is known as velvet. The velvet contains nutrients that stimulate antler growth. By fall, the antlers have reached their full size and the velvet is shed. Rutting season takes place between August and October; listen for the shrill bugles of the stags serenading the females. During the rut, randy males will challenge anything with their antlers and can be dangerous. The stags shed their antlers each spring, but don't relax too much because also in spring, females protecting their young can be equally dangerous. Large herds of elk live in around the towns of Banff and Jasper, often nonchalantly wandering along streets and feeding on tasty plants in residential gardens, and always safe from predators.

Moose
The giant of the deer family is the moose, an awkward-looking mammal that appears to have been designed by a cartoonist. It has the largest antlers of any animal in the world, stands up to 1.8 meters (six feet) at the shoulder, and weighs up to 500 kg (1,100 lbs.). Its body is dark brown, and it has a prominent nose, long spindly legs, small eyes, big ears, and an odd flap of skin called a bell dangling beneath its chin. Apart from all that, it's good-looking. Each spring the bull begins to grow palm-shaped antlers that by August will be fully grown. Moose are solitary animals preferring marshy areas and weedy lakes, but they are known to wander to higher elevations searching out open spaces in summer. They forage in and around ponds on willows, aspen, birch, grasses,

WILDLIFE VIEWING

Where's the best place to view animals? This is probably the most common question posed by visitors to the Canadian Rockies. While a precise answer is impossible—this isn't a zoo after all—noting a couple rules of thumb can make your chances of observation more likely. Spring is the best time for viewing wildlife from the roadside; larger mammals come down into the valleys in winter and stay through spring, moving back up to higher elevations as the snow melts. Mammals are most active at dawn and dusk, which are great times of day for scanning the landscape for movement.

In most cases, all species listed below are widespread in their particular habitat throughout the Canadian Rockies. The single location listed below for each species is simply the one that will give you the best chance of seeing that species.

Beaver: Athabasca River wetlands, Jasper National Park

Bighorn sheep: Mount Norquay Road, Banff National Park

Bison: Buffalo Paddock, Waterton Lakes National Park

Black bear: Icefields Parkway, Banff and Jasper National Parks

Caribou: Bald Hills, Jasper National Park

Cougar: forested valleys around Canmore

Coyote: along Highway 16, east of Jasper townsite, Jasper National Park

Elk: around the outskirts of Banff and Jasper townsites

Grizzly bear (stuffed): Lake Louise Visitor Centre, Banff National Park

Human beings: Banff Avenue, Banff National Park

Lynx: Vermilion Pass, Kootenay National Park

Marmot: end of Stanley Glacier Trail, Kootenay National Park

Moose: Peter Lougheed Provincial Park, Kananaskis Country

Mountain goat: Disaster Point, Jasper National Park

Mule deer: Waterton townsite, Waterton Lakes National Park

Porcupine: Yoho Valley Road, Yoho National Park

White-tailed deer: Sheep River Valley, Kananaskis Country

Wolf: Bow Valley (winter only), Banff National Park

and all aquatic vegetation. They are not particularly common in the Canadian Rockies, numbering around 350. Although they may appear docile, moose will attack humans if they feel threatened.

Caribou

Small populations of caribou inhabit the backcountry of Banff and Jasper National Parks. Native people named the animal *caribou* (hoof scraper) for the way in which they feed in winter, scraping away snow with their hooves. Caribou are smaller than elk and have a dark-brown coat with creamy patches on the neck and rump. Both sexes grow antlers, but those of the females are shorter and have fewer points. On average males weigh 180 kg (400 lbs.), females 115 kg (250 lbs.). Like the elk, they breed in fall, with the males gathering a harem.

BEARS

The two species of bears present in the mountains—black bears and grizzlies—can be differentiated by size and shape. Grizzlies are larger than black bears and have a flatter, dish-shaped face and a distinctive hump of muscle behind their neck. Color is not a reliable way to tell them apart. Black bears are not always black. They can be brown or cinnamon, causing them to be confused with the brown-colored grizzly.

Black Bears

If you spot a bear feeding beside the road, chances are it's a black bear. These mammals are widespread throughout all forested areas of the Canadian Rockies and are good swimmers and climbers. Their weight varies considerably, but males average 150 kg (330 lbs.) and females 100 kg (220 lbs.). Their diet is omnivorous, consisting primarily of grasses and berries but supplemented by small mammals. They are not true hibernators, but in winter they can sleep for up to a month at a time before changing position. During this time, their heartbeat drops to 10 beats per minute, body temperature drops, and they lose up to 30 percent of their body weight. Females reach reproductive maturity after five years; cubs, usually two, are born in late winter, while the mother is still asleep.

Grizzly Bears

Grizzlies, second largest of eight recognized species of bears (only polar bears are larger), have disappeared from most of North America but are widespread throughout the Canadian Rockies, numbering around 300 in the region. Grizzlies are only occasionally seen by casual observers; most sightings occur in alpine and subalpine zones, although sightings at lower elevations are not unusual, especially when snow falls early or late. The bears' color ranges from light brown to almost black, with dark tan being the most common. On average, males weigh 200–350 kg (440–770 lbs.).

The bears eat small and medium-sized mammals, and berries in fall. Like black bears, they sleep through most of the winter. When they emerge in early spring, the bears scavenge carcasses of animals that succumbed to the winter, until the new spring vegetation becomes sufficiently plentiful. Females first give birth at four years old, and then every three years, with cubs remaining with their mother for up to 2–3 years.

WILD DOGS AND CATS
Coyotes

The coyote is often mistaken for a wolf when in fact it is much smaller, weighing up to only 15 kg (33 lbs.). It has a pointed nose and long bushy tail. Its coloring is a mottled mix of brown and gray, with lighter-colored legs and belly. The coyote is a skillful and crafty hunter, preying mainly on rodents. Coyotes have the remarkable ability to hear the movement of small mammals under the snow, allowing them to hunt these animals without actually seeing them. They are often seen patrolling the edges of highways and crossing open meadows in low-lying valleys.

© ANDREW HEMPSTEAD

black bear

Wolves

Wolves that inhabit the Canadian Rockies are larger than coyotes and larger than the wolves of eastern Canada. They weigh up to 60 kg (132 lbs.), stand up to one meter (3.2 feet) high at the shoulder, and resemble large huskies or German shepherds. Their color ranges from snow-white to brown or black; those in the Canadian Rockies are, most often, shades of gray. They usually hunt in packs of up to eight members, traveling, hunting, and resting together, and adhering to a hierarchical social order. As individuals, they are complex and intriguing, capable of expressing happiness, humor, and loneliness.

Once the target of a relentless campaign to exterminate the species, the wolf has made an incredible comeback in the Canadian Rockies; today about 120 wolves roam the region.

Cougars

Rarely encountered by casual hikers, cougars (known in other parts of North America as mountain lions, pumas, or catamounts) measure up to 1.5 meters (five feet) long. The average male weighs 75 kg (165 lbs.) and the female 40–55 kg (90–120 lbs.). Cougars are versatile hunters whose acute vision takes in a peripheral span in excess of 200 degrees. They typically kill a large mammal such as an elk or deer every 12–14 days, eating part of it and caching the rest. Their diet also includes chipmunks, ground squirrels, snowshoe hares, and occasionally porcupines. Their athletic prowess puts Olympians to shame. They can spring forward more than eight meters from a standstill, leap four meters into the air, and safely jump from a height of 20 meters (65 feet).

The cougar is a solitary animal with distinct territorial boundaries. This limits its population density, which in turn means that its overall numbers are low. They are most common in the foothills along the eastern slopes of the Canadian Rockies.

Lynx

The elusive lynx is identifiable by its pointy black ear tufts and an oversized tabby cat appearance. The animal has broad, padded paws that dis-tribute its weight, allowing it to float on the surface of snow. It weighs up to 10 kg (22 lbs.), but appears much larger because of its coat of long, thick fur. The lynx, uncommon but widespread throughout the region, is a solitary creature that prefers the cover of subalpine forests, feeding mostly at night on snowshoe hares and other small mammals.

OTHER LARGE MAMMALS

Mountain Goats

The remarkable rock-climbing ability of these nimble-footed creatures allows them to live on rocky ledges or near-vertical slopes, safe from predators. They also frequent the alpine meadows and open forests of the Canadian Rockies, where they congregate around natural licks of salt. The goats stand one meter at the shoulder and weigh 65–130 kg (140–290 lbs.). Both sexes possess a peculiar beard, or rather, goatee. Both sexes have horns. It is possible to determine the sex by the shape of the horns; those of the female grow straight up before curling slightly backward, whereas those of the male curl back in a single arch. The goats shed their thick coats each summer, making them look ragged, but by fall they've regrown a fine, new white woolen coat.

Bighorn Sheep

Bighorn sheep are some of the most distinctive mammals of the Canadian Rockies. Easily recognized by their impressive horns, they are often seen grazing on grassy mountain slopes or at salt licks beside the road. The color of their coat varies with the season; in summer it's a brownish gray with a cream-colored belly and rump, turning lighter in winter. Fully grown males can weigh up to 120 kg (270 lbs.), while females generally weigh around 80 kg (180 lbs.). Both sexes possess horns, rather than antlers like members of the deer family. Unlike antlers, horns are not shed each year and can grow to astounding sizes. The horns of rams are larger than those of ewes and curve up to 360 degrees. The spiraled horns of an older ram can measure longer than one meter (3.2 feet) and weigh as much as 15 kg (33 lbs.). During the fall

© ANDREW HEMPSTEAD

Bighorn sheep are easily recognized by their long, curled horns.

mating season, a hierarchy is established among the rams for the right to breed ewes. As the males face off against each other to establish dominance, their horns act as both a weapon and a buffer against the head butting of other rams. The skull structure of the bighorn, rams in particular, has become adapted to these head-butting clashes, keeping the animals from being knocked unconscious.

Bighorn sheep are particularly tolerant of humans and often approach parked vehicles; although they are not especially dangerous, as with all mammals, you should not approach or feed them.

Bison

Before the arrival of Europeans, millions of bison roamed the North American plains, with some entering the valleys of the Canadian Rockies to escape harsh winters. Several factors contributed to their decline, including the combined presence of explorers, settlers, and natives. By the 1800s they were wiped out, and since then a couple of attempts at reintroduction have taken place, including the release of a small herd in Jasper National Park. (No one has sighted them for many years.) Today, your best chance of viewing these shaggy beasts is in Waterton Lakes National Park, where a small herd is contained in the buffalo paddock.

SMALL MAMMALS
Beavers

One of the animal kingdom's most industrious mammals is the beaver. Growing to a length of 50 cm (20 inches) and tipping the scales at around 20 kg (44 lbs.), it has a flat, rudderlike tail and webbed back feet that enable it to swim at speeds up to 10 kph (six mph). The exploration of western Canada can be directly attributed to the beaver, whose pelt was in high demand in fashion-conscious Europe in the early 1800s. The beaver was never entirely wiped out from the mountains, and today the animals can be found in almost any forested valley with flowing water. Beavers build their dam walls and lodges of twigs, branches, sticks of felled trees, and mud. They eat the bark and smaller twigs of deciduous plants and store branches under water, near the lodge, as a winter food supply.

WILDLIFE AND YOU

An abundance of wildlife is one of the biggest drawing cards of the Canadian Rockies. To help preserve this precious resource, obey fishing and hunting regulations and use common sense.

Do not feed the animals. Many animals may seem tame, but feeding them endangers yourself, the animal, and other visitors, as animals become aggressive when looking for handouts.

Store food safely. When camping, keep food in your vehicle or out of reach of animals. Just leaving it in a cooler isn't good enough.

Keep your distance. Although it's tempting to get close to animals for a better look or photograph, it disturbs the animal and, in many cases, can be dangerous.

Drive carefully. The most common cause of premature death for larger mammals is being hit by cars.

Squirrels

Several species of squirrel are common in the Canadian Rockies. The **golden-mantled ground squirrel,** found in rocky outcrops of subalpine and alpine regions, has black stripes along its sides and looks like an oversized chipmunk. Most common is the **Columbian ground squirrel,** which lives in burrows, often in open grassland. It is recognizable by its reddish legs, face, and underside, and a flecked, grayish back. The bushy-tailed **red squirrel,** the bold chatterbox of the forest, leaves telltale shelled cones at the base of conifers. Another member of the species, the nocturnal **northern flying fox,** glides through the montane forests of mountain valleys but is rarely seen.

Hoary Marmots

High in the mountains, above the treeline, hoary marmots are often seen sunning themselves on boulders in rocky areas or meadows. They are stocky creatures, weighing 4–9 kg (9–19 lbs.). When danger approaches, these large rodents emit a shrill whistle to warn their colony. Marmots are only active for a few months each summer, spending up to nine months a year in hibernation.

Porcupines

This small, squat animal is easily recognized by its thick coat of quills. It eats roots and leaves but is also known as being destructive around wooden buildings and vehicle tires. Porcupines are common and widespread throughout all forested areas, but they're hard to spy because they feed most often at night.

Other Rodents

Widespread throughout western Canada, **muskrats** make their mountain home in the waterways and wetlands of all low-lying valleys. They are agile swimmers, able to stay submerged for up to 12 minutes. They grow to a length of 35 cm (18 inches), but the best form of identification is the tail, which is black, flat, and scaly. Closely related to muskrats are **voles,** which are often mistaken for mice. They inhabit grassed areas of most valley floors.

Shrews

A member of the insectivore family, the **furry shrew** has a sharp-pointed snout and is closely related to the mole. It must eat almost constantly because it is susceptible to starvation within only a few hours of its last meal. Another variety present throughout the region, the **pygmy shrew,** is the world's smallest mammal; it weighs just four grams (0.1 ounces).

Pikas

Pikas, like rabbits, are lagomorphs, which are distinguished from rodents by a double set of incisors in the upper jaw. The small, grayish pika is a neighbor to the marmot, living among the rubble and boulders of scree slopes above timberline.

Weasels

The weasel family, comprising 70 species worldwide, is large and diverse, but in general, all members have long, slim bodies and short legs, and all are carnivorous and voracious eaters, consuming up to one-third of their body weight each day. Many species can be found in the Canadian Rockies, including the **wolverine,** largest of the weasels worldwide, weighing up to 20 kg (44 lbs.). Known to natives as *carcajou* (evil one), the wolverine is extremely powerful, cunning, and cautious. This solitary creature inhabits forests of the subalpine and lower alpine regions, feeding on any available meat, from small rodents to the carcasses of larger mammals. Rarely sighted by humans, the wolverine is a true symbol of the wilderness.

The **fisher** has the same habitat as the wolverine, but is much smaller, reaching just five kg (11 lbs.) in weight and growing up to 60 cm (24 inches) in length. This nocturnal hunter preys on small birds and rodents, but reports of fishers bringing down small deer have been made. Smaller still is the **marten,** which lives most of its life in the trees of the subalpine forest, preying on birds, squirrels, mice, and voles. Weighing just one kg (2.2 lbs.) is the **mink,** once highly prized for its fur. At home in or out of water, it feeds on muskrats, mice, voles, and fish. Mink numbers in the Canadian Rockies are low.

As well as being home to the largest member of weasel family, the region also holds the smallest—the **least weasel** (the world's smallest carnivore), which grows to a length of just 20 cm (eight inches) and weighs a maximum of 60 grams (two ounces). Chiefly nocturnal, it feeds mostly on mice and lives throughout open wooded areas, but it is not particularly common.

REPTILES AND AMPHIBIANS

Two species of snake, the **wandering garter snake** and the **red-sided garter snake** (North America's northernmost reptile), are found at lower elevations in the Canadian Rockies. **Frogs** are also present; biologists have noted two different species, which are also present at the lower elevations in the Canadian Rockies.

FISH

The lakes and rivers of the Canadian Rockies hold a variety of fish, most of which belong to the trout and salmon family and are classed as cold-water species—that is, they inhabit waters where the temperature ranges 4–18 °C (39–64°F). The predominant species, the **rainbow trout,** is not native to the mountains; it was introduced from more northern Canadian watersheds as a sport fish and is now common throughout lower elevation lakes and rivers. It has an olive-green back and a red strip running along the center of its body. Only three species of trout are native to the mountains. One of these, the **bull trout,** is Alberta's provincial fish. Throughout the mid-1900s, this truly native Canadian trout was perceived as a predator of more favored introduced species, and was mostly removed. Today, what was once the most widespread trout east of the Continental Divide is confined to the headwaters of Canadian Rockies' river systems, and is classed as a threatened species. While the bull trout has adapted to the harsh conditions of its reduced habitat, its continuing struggle for survival can be attributed to many factors, including a scarcity of food and a slow reproductive cycle. Bull trout grow to 70 cm (27 inches) in length and weigh up to 10 kilograms (22 lbs.).

The **lake trout,** which grows to 20 kg (44 lbs.), is native to large, deep lakes throughout the mountains. Identified by a silvery-gray body and irregular white splotches along its back, this species grows slowly, taking up to eight years to reach maturity and living up to 25 years. Named for a bright red dash of color that runs from below the mouth almost to the gills, the **cutthroat trout** is native to southern Alberta's mountain streams, but has been introduced to high-elevation lakes and streams on both sides of the Canadian Rockies. The **brown trout,** introduced from Europe in 1924, is found in the Bow and Red Deer Rivers and some slower streams in the eastern zones of Kananaskis Country. Its body is a golden-brown color, and it is the only trout with both black and red spots. The **brook trout** is a colorful fish identified by a dark green back with pale-colored splotches and purple-sheened sides. It is native to eastern Canada, but was introduced to the mountains as early as 1903 and is now widespread throughout lakes and streams on the Alberta side of the Continental

Divide. **Golden trout** were introduced to a few mountain lakes around 1960 as a sport fish. They are a smallish fish, similar in color to rainbow trout.

The **mountain whitefish** (commonly, but incorrectly, called arctic grayling by Albertan anglers) is a light gray–colored fish that is native to most lower-elevation lakes and rivers of the Canadian Rockies. Also inhabiting the region's waters are **arctic grayling** and **Dolly Varden** (named for a colorful character in a Charles Dickens story).

BIRDS

Bird-watching is popular in the mountains, thanks to the approximately 300 resident bird species and the millions of migratory birds that pass through each year. All it takes is a pair of binoculars, a good book detailing species, and patience. Dense forests hide many species, making them seem less common than they actually are. The Columbia River wetland, between Radium Hot Springs and Golden, lies on the Pacific Flyway and is a major bird-watching area.

Raptors

A wide variety of raptors are present in the Canadian Rockies—some call the mountains home year-round, while others pass through during annual spring and fall migrations. **Golden eagles** migrate across the Canadian Rockies, heading north in spring to Alaska and crossing back over in fall en route to Midwest wintering grounds. Golden eagles—more than 10,000 of them annually—soar high above the mountains on thermal drafts. **Bald eagles** also soar over the Canadian Rockies during annual migrations; mature birds can be distinguished from below by their white head and tail (immature birds resemble the dark brown–colored golden eagle). **Ospreys** spend summers in the region, nesting high up in large dead trees, on telephone poles, or on rocky outcrops, but always overlooking water. They feed on fish, hovering up to 50 meters (160 feet) above water, watching for movement, then diving into the water, thrusting their legs forward and collecting prey in their talons.

Distinct from all previously listed species are a group of raptors that hunt at night. Best known as owls, these birds are rarely seen because of their nocturnal habits but are widespread throughout forested areas of the mountains. Most common is the **great horned owl,** identified by its prominent "horns," which are actually tufts of feathers. Also present is the **snowy owl,** and in the north of the region, the largest of the owls, the **great gray owl,** which grows to a height of 70 cm (2.4 feet).

Others

Bird-watchers will be enthralled by the diversity of eastern and western bird species in the Canadian Rockies. Widespread are **magpies, sparrows, starlings, grouse, ravens,** and **crows. Blackbirds, finches, thrushes, hummingbirds, woodpeckers, flycatchers,** and 28 species of **warblers** are common in forested areas. **Ptarmigan** are common in open meadows above the treeline. The popular campground visitor, the cheeky **gray jay,** is similar in appearance to that of the curious **Clark's nutcracker.**

Clark's nutcracker

History

THE EARLIEST INHABITANTS

Human habitation of the Canadian Rockies began at the end of the last Ice Age, approximately 11,000 years ago. The descendants of the people who migrated from northeast Asia across a land bridge spanning the Bering Strait had fanned out across North America, and as the receding ice cap began to uncover the land north of the 49th parallel, groups of people moved northward with it, in pursuit of large mammals at the edge of the melting ice mass. The mountain landscape then was far different than it is today. Forests were nonexistent; the retreating ice had scoured the land, and most of the lower valleys were carpeted in tundra.

The Kootenay

The Kootenay (other common spellings include Kootenai, Kootenae, and Kutenai) were the first human beings to enter the Canadian Rockies. Once hunters of buffalo on the great American plains, they were pushed westward by fierce enemies. As the ice cap melted, they moved north, up the western edge of the Rocky Mountains. This migration was by no means fast—perhaps only 40 km (25 miles) in each generation—but

about 10,000 years ago the first Kootenay arrived in the Columbia River Valley. They were hunters and gatherers, wintering along the Columbia and Kootenay river valleys, then moving to higher elevations during the warmer months. Over time they developed new skills, learning to fish the salmon-rich rivers using spears, nets, and simple fish weirs. The Kootenay were a serious people with few enemies. They mixed freely with the Shuswap and treated the earliest explorers, such as David Thompson, with respect. They regularly traveled east over the Rockies to hunt—to the wildlife-rich Kootenay Plains or further south to the Great Plains in search of bison. But as the fearsome Blackfoot extended their territory westward to the foothills of present-day Alberta, the Kootenay made fewer trips onto the plains. By the early 1700s, they had been driven permanently back to the west side of the Continental Divide.

The Shuswap

The Shuswap make up only a small chapter in the human history of the Canadian Rockies, although they traveled into the mountains on and off for many thousands of years. They were a tribe of Salish people, who, as the Kootenay did

BANFF INDIAN DAYS

In 1889, the staff at the newly opened Banff Springs Hotel asked the Stoneys from the Morleyville reserve to come to the hotel and entertain guests. About 200 tribe members arrived in Banff, setting up their tepees where the golf course now lies, showing off their horseback-riding skills, dancing, putting on an colorful parade, and inviting hotel guests to inspect their camp. The gathering—called Banff Indian Days—was such a success it became an annual event, attracting the Kootenay from across the mountains, the Sarcee from Calgary, and many thousands of visitors who were able to view customs and traditions of days gone by. As the event got bigger, it moved to a site at the base of Cascade Mountain, with much of the action revolving around a rodeo. But as the years rolled by, times changed. Visitors to the mountains were on tighter schedules than in years past, and park politics and money issues created irremediable problems for the long-running event. As a result, Banff Indian Days was held for the last time in 1978.

farther east, moved north then east with the receding ice cap. By the time the Kootenay had moved into the Kootenay River Valley, the Salish had fanned out across most of southwestern and interior British Columbia, following the salmon upstream as the glacial ice receded. Those who settled along the upper reaches of the Columbia River became known as the Shuswap. They spent summers in the mountains hunting caribou and sheep, put their fishing skills to the test each fall, then wintered in pit houses along the Columbia River Valley. The descendents of these people live on the Kinbasket Shuswap Reserve, just south of Radium Hot Springs.

The Stoney

The movement of humans into the mountains from the east was much more recent. Around 1650, the mighty Sioux nation began splintering, with many thousands moving north into present-day Canada. Although these immigrants called themselves *Nakoda* (people), other tribes called them *Assiniboine* (people who cook with stones) because their traditional cooking method was to heat stones in a fire, place the hot stones in a rawhide or birchbark basket with water, and cook meat and vegetables in the hot water. The white man translated Assiniboine as Stone People, or Stoney for short.

Slowly, generation after generation, smaller groups of the Stoney moved westward along the Saskatchewan River system, allying themselves with the Cree but keeping their own identity. They pushed through the Blackfoot territory of the plains and reached the Rockies' foothills about 200 years ago. There they split into bands, moving north and south along the foothills and penetrating the wide valleys where hunting was productive. They lived in small familylike groups and developed a lifestyle different from that of the Plains Indians, diversifying their skills and becoming less dependent on buffalo. Moving with the seasons, they gathered berries in fall and became excellent hunters of mountain animals. They traveled over the mountains to trade with the Shuswap, but rarely ventured onto the plains, home of the warlike Peigan, Blackfoot, and Blood bands of the Blackfoot Confederacy. The Stoney were a steadfast yet friendly people. Alexander Henry the Younger reported in 1811 that the Stoney, "although the most arrant horse thieves in the world . . . are at the same time the most hospitable to strangers who arrive in their camps."

As the great buffalo herds were decimated, the Stoney were affected less than the Plains Indians, but the effect of white man's intrusion on their lifestyle was still apparent. The missionaries of the day found their teachings had more effect on the mountain people than on those of the plains, so they intensified their efforts on the Stoney. Reverend John McDougall gained their trust and in 1873 built a small mission church by the Bow River at Morleyville. When the Stoney were presented with Treaty 7 in 1877, they chose to locate their reserve around the Morleyville church. Abandoning their nomadic lifestyle, they quickly became adept at farming; unlike the Plains Indians, who relied for their survival on government rations, the Stoney were almost self-sufficient on the reserve.

EUROPEAN EXPLORATION AND SETTLEMENT

In 1670, the British government granted the Hudson's Bay Company the right to govern Rupert's Land, roughly defined by all the land that drained into Hudson Bay. A vast area of western Canada, including present-day Manitoba, Saskatchewan, Alberta, Northwest Territories, and Nunavut, fell under that definition. The land was rich in fur-bearing mammals, which both the British and the French sought to exploit for profit. The Hudson's Bay Company first built forts around Hudson Bay and encouraged Indians to bring furs to the posts. But soon, French fur traders based in Montreal began traveling west to secure furs, forcing their British rivals to do the same. On one such trip, Anthony Henday became the first white man to view the Canadian Rockies when, on September 11, 1754, he climbed a ridge above the Red Deer River near present-day Innisfail. Henday returned to the east the following spring, bringing canoes loaded with furs and providing reports of snowcapped peaks.

DAVID THOMPSON

One of Canada's greatest explorers, David Thompson was a quiet, courageous, and energetic man who drafted the first comprehensive and accurate map of western Canada. He arrived in Canada from England as a 14-year-old apprentice clerk for the Hudson's Bay Company. With an inquisitive nature and a talent for wilderness navigation, he quickly acquired the skills of surveying and mapmaking. Natives called him Koo-koo-sint, which translates as "the man who looks at stars."

Between 1786 and 1812, Thompson led four major expeditions into western Canada—the first for the Hudson's Bay Company and the last three for its rival, the North West Company. The longest and most important one was the last, during which he traveled up and crossed the Continental Divide at **Howse Pass.** After descending into the Co-lumbia River Valley, he established Kootenae House on Lake Windermere, using this outpost for a five-year odyssey of exploration of the entire Columbia River system. In the process, he discovered the **Athabasca Pass,** which for the next 50 years was the main route across the Canadian Rockies to the Pacific Ocean.

In 1813, Thompson began work on a master map covering the entire territory controlled by the North West Company. The map was four meters long and two meters wide, detailing more than 1.5 million square miles. On completion it was hung out of public view in the council hall of a company fort in the east. Years later, after his death in 1857, the map was discovered and Thompson became recognized as one of the world's greatest land geographers.

In 1792, Peter Fidler became the first in a long succession of Europeans to actually enter the mountains. The following year Alexander Mackenzie became the first man to cross the continent, traveling the Peace and Fraser river watersheds to reach the Pacific Ocean. Mackenzie's traverse was long and difficult, so subsequent explorers continued to seek an easier route farther south. In 1807, David Thompson set out from Rocky Mountain House, traveling up the North Saskatchewan River to Howse Pass, where he descended into the Columbia River. He established a small trading post near Windermere Lake, but warring Peigan and Kootenay natives forced him to search out an alternate pass to the north. In 1811, he discovered Athabasca Pass, which was used as the main route west for the next 50 years.

In 1857, with the fur trade in decline, the British government sent Captain John Palliser to investigate the agricultural potential of western Rupert's Land. During his three-year journey he explored many of the watersheds leading into the mountains, including one trip up the Bow River and over Vermilion Pass into the area now encompassed by Kootenay and Yoho National Parks.

The Dominion of Canada

By the 1860s, some of the eastern provinces were tiring of British rule, and a movement was abuzz to push for Canadian independence. The British government, wary of losing Canada as it had lost the United States, passed legislation establishing the Dominion of Canada. At that time, the North-West Territories, as Rupert's Land had become known, was a foreign land to those in eastern Canada; life out west was primitive with no laws, and no outpost held more than a couple of dozen residents. But in an effort to solidify the Dominion, the government bought the North-West Territories back from the Hudson's Bay Company in 1867. In 1871, British Columbia agreed to join the Dominion as well, but only on the condition that the federal government build a railway to link the fledgling province with the rest of the country.

The Coming of the Railway

The idea of a rail line across the continent, replacing canoe and cart routes, was met with scorn by those in the east, who saw it as unnecessary and uneconomical. But the line pushed westward, reaching Winnipeg in 1879 and what was then Fort Calgary in 1883.

© ANDREW HEMPSTEAD

This trestle bridge, which once linked Canmore coal mines to the main rail line, is one of the most visible signs of the Bow Valley's mining history.

Many routes across the Continental Divide were considered by the Canadian Pacific Railway, but Kicking Horse Pass, surveyed by Maj. A.B. Rogers in 1881, got the final nod. The line and its construction camps pushed into the mountains, reaching Siding 29 (known today as Banff) early in the fall of 1883; Laggan (Lake Louise) a couple of months later; then crossing the divide and reaching the Field construction camp in the summer of 1884. The following year, on November 7, 1885, the final spike was laid, opening up the lanes of commerce between British Columbia and the rest of the Canada. In 1914, rival company Grand Trunk Pacific Railway completed a second rail line across the Rockies, at Yellowhead Pass to the north.

PARKS AND TOURISM

The Parks of Today Take Shape

In 1883, three Canadian Pacific Railway (CPR) workers stumbled on hot springs at the base of Sulphur Mountain, near where the town of Banff now lies. This was the height of the Victorian era, when the great spa resorts of Europe were attracting hordes of wealthy clients. With the thought of developing a similar-style resort, the government designated a 2,600-hectare (6,425-acre) reserve around the hot springs, surveyed a townsite, and encouraged the CPR to build a world-class hotel there. In 1887, Rocky Mountains Park was officially created, setting aside 67,300 hectares (166,300 acres) as a "public park and pleasure ground for the benefit, advantage, and enjoyment of the people of Canada." The park was later renamed Banff. It was Canada's first national park and only the third national park in the world.

Across the Continental Divide, the railway passed by a small reserve that had been created around the base of Mount Stephen. This was the core of what would become Yoho National Park, officially dedicated in 1901. In anticipation of a flood of visitors to the mountains along the more northerly Grand Trunk Pacific Railway, Jasper National Park was established in 1907. Kootenay National Park was created to protect an eight-km-wide strip of land either side of the Banff-Windermere Road, which was completed in 1922. Of the five national parks in the Canadian Rockies, Waterton Lakes National Park was the only one created purely for its aesthetic value. It was established after tireless public campaigning by local resident John George "Kootenai" Brown, who also became the park's first superintendent.

The First Tourists Arrive

In the era the parks were created, the Canadian Rockies region was a vast wilderness accessible only by rail. The parks and the landscape they encompassed were seen as economic resources to be exploited rather than as national treasures to be preserved. Logging, hunting, and mining were permitted inside park boundaries; all but Kootenay National Park had mines operating within them for many years (the last mine, in Yoho National Park, closed in 1952). To help finance the rail line, the CPR began encouraging visitors to the mountains by building grand mountain resorts: Mount Stephen House in 1886, the Banff Springs Hotel in 1888, a lodge at Lake Louise in 1890, and Emerald Lake Lodge in 1902. Knowledgeable locals, some of whom had been used as guides and outfitters during railway construction, offered their services to the tourists the railway brought. Tom Wilson, Bill Peyto, Jim and Bill Brewster, the Otto Brothers, and Donald "Curly" Phillips are synonymous with this era, and their names grace everything from pubs to mountain peaks.

Early Mountaineering

Recreational mountaineering has been popular in the Canadian Rockies for more than 100 years. Reports of early climbs on peaks around Lake Louise spread, and by the late 1880s the area had drawn the attention of both European and American alpinists. Many climbers were inexperienced and ill-equipped, but first ascents were nevertheless made on peaks that today are still considered difficult. In 1893, Walter Wilcox and Samuel Allen, two Yale schoolmates, spent the summer climbing in the Lake Louise area, making two unsuccessful attempts to reach the north peak of Mount Victoria. The following

summer they made first ascents of Mount Temple and Mount Aberdeen, extraordinary achievements considering their lack of experience and proper equipment. Accidents were sure to happen, and they did. During the summer of 1896, P.S. Abbot slipped and plunged to his death attempting to climb Mount Lefroy. In doing so, he became North America's first mountaineering fatality. Following this incident, Swiss mountain guides were employed by the CPR to satisfy the climbing needs of wealthy patrons of the railway and make the sport safer. During the period of their employment, successful climbs were made of Mount Victoria, Mount Lefroy, and Mount Balfour.

In 1906, Arthur O. Wheeler organized the Alpine Club of Canada, which was instrumental in the construction of many trails and backcountry huts still in use today. In 1913, Swiss guide Conrad Kain led a group of the club's members on the successful first ascent of Mount Robson, the highest peak in the Canadian Rockies. By 1915, most of the other major peaks in the range had been climbed as well.

Changing Times

One major change that occurred at the park early on was the shift from railroad-based to automobile-based tourism. Until 1913, motorized vehicles were banned from the mountain parks, allowing the CPR a monopoly on tourists. Wealthy visitors to the mountains came in on the train and generally stayed in the CPR's own hotels for weeks on end and often for the entire summer. The burgeoning popularity of the automobile changed all this; the motor-vehicle ban was lifted, and road building went ahead full steam. Many of the trails that had been built for horseback travel were widened to accommodate autos, and new roads were built: from Banff to Lake Louise in 1920, to Radium Hot Springs in 1923, and to Golden in 1930. The Icefields Parkway was finally completed in 1940. Visitor numbers increased, and facilities expanded to keep pace. Dozens of bungalow camps were built specially for those arriving by automobile. Many were built by the CPR, far from their rail line, including in Kootenay National

Park and at Radium Hot Springs. The company also built lodges deep in the backcountry, including at Mount Assiniboine and Lake O'Hara.

Another major change that has occurred over the last 90 years is in the way the complex human–wildlife relationship in the parks has been managed. Should the relationship be managed to provide the visiting public the best viewing experience, or rather to provide the wildlife with the most wild and natural environment possible? Today the trend favors the wildlife, but early in the history of the Canadian Rockies' parks, the operating strategy clearly favored the visitor. The Victorian concept of wildlife was that it was either good or evil. Although an early park directive instructed superintendents to leave nature alone, it also told them to "endeavor to exterminate all those animals which prey upon others." A dusty century-old philosophy, perhaps, but as recently as the 1960s, a predator-

control program led to the slaughter of nearly every wolf in the park. Seventy years ago, you could view a polar bear on display behind the Banff Park Museum. Only 40 years ago, hotels were taking guests to local dumps to watch bears feeding on garbage. Creating a balance between growth and its impact on wildlife is today's most critical issue in the Canadian Rockies. Many high-traffic areas are fenced, with passes built over and under the highway for animal movement. Development in the national park towns of Banff and Jasper is strictly regulated, unlike areas outside the parks, such as Canmore and the Columbia River Valley, where development continues unabated.

Amazingly enough, throughout unsavory sagas of the 20th century and ever-increasing human usage, the Canadian Rockies have remained a prime area for wildlife viewing and will hopefully continue to be so for a long time to come.

On the Road

Recreation

The Canadian Rockies are a four-season playground, their great outdoors offering something for everyone. Hiking grabs first place in the popularity stakes; many thousands of kilometers of trails crisscross the entire region. But you can also enjoy canoeing and kayaking, mountain climbing, golfing, horseback riding, photography, skiing and snowboarding, scuba diving, and everything in between. An overview of available outdoor-recreation opportunities is provided in the following sections, and you'll find more detail in the individual travel chapters.

National Park Passes

Unless you're passing directly through, passes are required for entry into all five national parks covered in this book. Profits raised from these passes goes directly to Parks Canada for park maintenance and improvements.

A National Parks Day Pass is $6 adults, $4.50 seniors, $3 children up to a maximum of $12 ($9 for two or more seniors) per vehicle. It is interchangeable among parks and is valid until 4 P.M. the day following its purchase. An annual National Parks of Canada Pass, good for entry into all of Canada's national parks for one year from the date of purchase, is $38 adults, $29 seniors up to a maximum of $76 per vehicle ($56 for two or more seniors). This

© ANDREW HEMPSTEAD

Icefields Parkway

pass comes with a booklet of discount coupons. Both types of pass can be purchased at park gates (at the entrance to Banff, Kootenay, and Waterton Lakes National Parks), at the tollbooths at either end of the Icefields Parkway, at all park information centers, and at campground fee stations. For more information, check the Parks Canada website, www.parks canada.gc.ca.

HIKING

The Canadian Rockies are a hiker's paradise. Hiking is free, and the mountains offer some of the world's most spectacular scenery. **Banff National Park** holds the greatest variety of trails. Here you can find anything from short interpretive trails with little elevation gain to strenuous slogs up high alpine passes. Trailheads for some of the best hikes are accessible on foot from the town of Banff. Those farther north begin at higher elevations, from which access to the treeline is less arduous. The trails in **Jasper National Park** are oriented more toward the experienced backpacker, offering plentiful routes for long backcountry trips.

Waterton Lakes National Park is small but has a complex trail system geared especially for the day-hiker. Many of the hikes in **Yoho National Park** entail significant elevation gain, but reward your extra effort with spectacular mountain panoramas rivaling those of the more famous parks across the divide. Many less-visited parts of the mountains hold unexpected gems. Examples include Grassi Lakes, near Canmore; Rawson Lake, Kananaskis Country; Fish Lake, Top of the World Provincial Park; and Grande Mountain, near Grande Cache.

With exceptions made for the most popular overnight hikes, all trails detailed in this book are day hikes. Anyone of moderate fitness could complete them in the time allotted. Strong hikers will need less time, and if you stop for lunch it will take you a little longer. Remember, all distances and times are one-way, so allow yourself time at the objective and time to return to the trailhead.

SAFE HIKING

When venturing out on the trails of the Canadian Rockies, using a little common sense will help keep you from getting into trouble. First, don't underestimate the forces of nature; weather can change dramatically anywhere in the mountains at any time. That clear, sunny sky that looked so inviting during breakfast can turn into a driving snowstorm within hours. Go prepared for all climatic conditions (always carry food, a sweater, a waterproof jacket, and matches), and take plenty of water—open slopes can get very hot on sunny days.

All national park visitor centers, as well as those in Kananaskis Country, post daily trail reports and weather forecasts. Check trail conditions before heading out; lingering snow, wildlife closures, or a washed-out trail could ruin your best-laid plans. Also, hikers must register at park information centers for all overnight hikes in national parks.

Topographic maps aren't required for the hikes detailed in this book, but they provide an interesting way to identify natural features. For extended hiking in the backcountry, topo maps are vital. For most hikes, the maps produced by Gem Trek Publishing, www.gemtrek.com, are sufficient. You can purchase them from park information centers, bookstores, gas stations, and other outlets through the region.

Scrambling

The Canadian Rockies hold many peaks that can be reached without ropes or climbing skills, provided you have a good level of fitness and, more important, common sense. Obviously, this type of activity has more inherent dangers than hiking, but these can be minimized by planning ahead. Check weather forecasts; take food, water, and warm clothing; and be aware of the terrain. Routes to the top of the most popular peaks are flagged with tape or marked with rock cairns showing the way, but you should always check with information centers or locals before attempting any ascent. The Bow Valley offers a good selection of well-traveled scrambles. These include

Mount Rundle, Cascade Mountain, and Chinaman's Peak.

Backpacking

Most hikers are just out for the day or a few hours, but staying overnight in the backcountry offers many rewards. Some effort is involved in a backcountry trip—you'll need a backpack, lightweight stove, and tent, among other things—but you'll be traveling through country inaccessible to the casual day hiker, well away from the crowds and far from any road. **Lake O'Hara,** in Yoho National Park, is the trailhead for what is generally considered to be Canada's finest backcountry hiking area. The lake is easily accessible; a shuttle bus runs from the highway up an old fire road to this alpine gem. Unlike other backcountry destinations, visitors to Lake O'Hara not equipped for camping have the option of visiting for just a day. **Mount Assiniboine Provincial Park** is another popular spot far from civilization. Like Lake O'Hara, there's a lodge for hikers not equipped to camp out. Banff and Jasper National Parks also have backcountry lodges. Another option for backcountry accommodations is offered by the **Alpine Club of Canada,** 403/678-3200, www.alpineclubofcanada.ca. The club maintains a series of huts, each generally a full-day hike from the nearest road, throughout the Canadian Rockies.

Heli-Hiking

Heli-hiking is an easy way to appreciate high alpine areas without having to gain the elevation on foot. The day starts with a helicopter ride into the alpine, where short, guided hikes are offered and a picnic lunch is served. For details, contact **Alpine Helicopters,** Canmore, 403/678-4802, www.alpinehelicopter.com, or **Robson Helimagic,** 250/566-4700 or 877/454-4700, www.robsonhelimagic.com, near Mount Robson Provincial Park. Expect to pay from $280

for 30 minutes of flight time, a guided hike, and a mountaintop lunch. Primarily known for their heli-skiing operations, **Canadian Mountain Holidays,** 403/762-7100 or 800/661-0252, www.cmhhike.com, has a summer program of heli-hiking trips, with overnights spent in luxurious backcountry lodges; expect to pay about $600 per person per night, all-inclusive.

CLIMBING AND MOUNTAINEERING

The Canadian Rockies are a mecca for those experienced in climbing and mountaineering, but for those who aren't, instruction is available. **Canmore,** in the Bow Valley, is the self-proclaimed capital of mountain sports. Surrounded by towering peaks of limestone, routes to challenge all levels of ability can be found on the immediate outskirts of town and along narrow canyons that open to the valley. The distinctive south face of Yamnuska, easily recognized to the north of the TransCanada Highway as you enter the Bow Valley from the east, is the most popular climbing spot in the mountains, with dozens of routes up its sheer 350-meter-high (1,150-foot-high) walls. *Bow Valley Rock* (Rocky Mountain Books, 2002) is an indispensable book for Yamnuska-bound climbers. Experienced climbers should also gather as much information as possible before attempting any unfamiliar routes; quiz locals, hang out at climbing stores, and contact park information centers.

The distinctive south face of Yamnuska, easily recognized east of Canmore, is the most popular climbing spot in the mountains, with dozens of routes up its sheer 350-meter-high (1,150-foot-high) walls.

Learning the Ropes

For the inexperienced, the Canadian Rockies are the perfect place to learn to climb. Climbers and mountaineers can't live on past accomplishments alone, so to finance their lifestyle some turn to teaching others the skills of their sport. Canmore is home to many qualified mountain guides who operate both in and out of Banff National Park. One of these—and one of North America's

ON THE ROAD

most respected climbing schools—is **Yamnuska,** 403/678-4164, www.yamnuska.com. Learn basic climbing skills over a weekend ($220 per person), with the option to make a full climb (an extra $190) the following Monday. They also offer guided climbs of peaks throughout the Canadian Rockies, wilderness first-aid classes, and ice-climbing instruction.

ROAD CYCLING AND MOUNTAIN BIKING

The Canadian Rockies are perfect for both road biking and mountain biking. On-road cyclists will appreciate the wide shoulders on all main highways, while those on mountain bikes will enjoy the many designated trails. The most challenging and scenic on-road route is the 290-km (180-mile) **Icefields Parkway** between Lake Louise and Jasper (*Outside* magazine rates it as one of North America's 10 best). Most cyclists allow 4–5 days, but it's easy to spend a lot longer on the parkway. With 11 campgrounds, four hostels, and four lodges along the way, you'll have plenty of accommodation options. An extension of the Icefields Parkway is the **Bow Valley Parkway,** the original route between Banff and Lake Louise, which can easily be cycled in one day.

Backroads, 510/527-1555 or 800/462-2848, www.backroads.com, offers a wide variety of trips through the Canadian Rockies. These trips are designed to suit all levels of fitness and all budgets. An average of six hours is spent cycling each day, but there's also always the option of riding in the support van. There's also the option of camping each night (US$1,100 for six days) or staying in grand mountain lodges (US$2,000 for six days). **VBT,** 800/245-3868, www.vbt.com, offers a seven-day ride through the four contiguous national parks with midrange lodging and all meals included in the price of US$1,400.

Mountain biking is allowed on designated trails throughout the national parks. Park information centers hand out brochures detailing these trails and giving them ratings. The **Canmore Nordic Centre** is home to 70 km (43.5 miles) of biking trails, some steep enough

to hold international downhill competitions each summer. Doug Eastcott's ***Backcountry Biking in the Canadian Rockies*** (Rocky Mountain Books) covers more than 200 routes through the mountains; pick up a copy from local bookstores. Bikes can be rented throughout the national parks and Kananaskis Country. Road and town bikes rent for $5–7 per hour and $22–28 per day. All shops rent front- and full-suspension bikes; expect to pay up to $15 per hour and $45 per day for these.

HORSEBACK RIDING

Horses were used for transportation in the mountains by the earliest explorers. Even after the completion of the railway, horses remained as the most practical way to get deep into the backcountry because crossing unbridged rivers and carrying large amounts of supplies was impossible on foot. The names of early outfitters—Tom Wilson, Jim and Bill Brewster, Bill Peyto, Jimmy Simpson, and Curly Phillips were the best known—crop up again and again through

© ANDREW HEMPSTEAD

Cross Zee, overlooking Canmore, is one of many local horseback riding operations.

the mountains. Another legacy of their trade is that many of the main hiking trails began as horse trails.

The tradition of travel by horseback continues today in the Canadian Rockies; some companies have been operating since before the parks were established. Trail riding is available in Banff, Jasper, Waterton Lakes, and Yoho National Parks as well as in Canmore, Kananaskis Country, Radium Hot Springs, and Grande Cache. Expect to pay around $30 for a one-hour ride (usually covering around three km/1.9 miles), $50 for a two-hour ride, and $70–85 for a ride that includes a meal. If you're an experienced rider, consider heading out of the mountains 40 minutes east of Canmore to **Griffin Valley Ranch,** north of Hwy. 1A, 403/932-7433. This sprawling property is one of the few places in western Canada that allows unguided riding. Horse rentals are similarly priced to trail riding; the only additional cost is an annual membership (simply sign a waiver and pay a $50 fee). Trails lead through the valley and to high viewpoints where the panorama extends back to the Canadian Rockies.

Pack Trips and Guest Ranches

Overnight pack trips consist of up to six hours of riding per day, with nights spent at a remote mountain lodge or a tent camp, usually in a scenic location where you can hike, fish, or ride farther. Rates range $150–210 per person per day, which includes the riding, accommodations, and food. These trips are offered by **Brewster's Kananaskis Guest Ranch,** east of Canmore, 403/762-5454 or 800/691-5085, www.brewsteradventures.com; **Boundary Ranch,** in Kananaskis Valley, 403/591-7171 or 877/591-7177, www.boundaryranch.com; through the south end of Banff National Park by **Warner Guiding and Outfitting,** 403/762-4551 or 800/661-8352,

www.horseback.com; and in Jasper National Park by **Skyline Trail Rides,** 780/852-4215 or 888/852-7787, www.skylinetrail.com; or **Tonquin Valley Adventures,** 780/852-1188, www.tonquinadventures.com. The remote location of Willmore Wilderness Park makes it a popular destination for those on horseback; contact **Wild Rose Outfitting,** 780/693-2296, www.wildroseoutfitting.com.

Guest ranches, where accommodations and meals are included in nightly packages, include **Brewster's Kananaskis Guest Ranch,** east of Canmore, 403/673-3737 or 800/691-5085, www.brewsteradventures.com, and **Black Cat Guest Ranch,** on the northeastern outskirts of Jasper National Park, 780/865-3084 or 800/859-6840, www.blackcatguestranch.ca. Expect to pay $120–150 per person per day for accommodations, meals, and trail riding.

GOLFING

The Canadian Rockies hold special appeal for golfers because some of the world's most scenic courses lie in their midst. All of the best courses are public, lying in national parks or on provincial land, so anyone can play at any time. The scenery alone stands the courses of the Canadian Rockies apart from others, but there are many other reasons that the region is a golf destination in itself. Stanley Thompson, generally regarded as one of the preeminent golf course architects of the early 1900s, designed three courses in the mountains, typified by holes aligned with distant mountains, elevated tee boxes, and fairways following natural contours of the land. (As most of Thompson's work was in Canada, he is still little known in the United States.)

The golfing season is fairly short, from mid-May to early October, depending on snow cover. (The golf courses at Radium Hot Springs and

> *The scenery alone stands the courses of the Canadian Rockies apart from others, but there are many other reasons that the region is a golf destination in itself. Stanley Thompson, generally regarded as one of the preeminent golf course architects of the early 1900s, designed three courses in the mountains.*

ON THE ROAD

Golden are the first to open each spring.) But with the long days of summer, there's plenty of time for golfing. Greens fees range from $25 at the nine-hole layout at Brewster's Kananaskis Guest Ranch to $180 for 18 holes at the Banff course. The greens fee at Kananaskis Country Golf Course ($70) is also worth noting: it is regularly featured in *Golf Digest* as North America's best-value course. At the resort courses, greens fees usually include the use of practice facilities and a cart (complete with global positioning system at SilverTip). The sport's popularity in the mountains is such that tee times need to booked well in advance—up to a month for preferred times at some courses.

The Courses

The jewel in the golfing crown is the **Stanley Thompson 18,** part of a 27-hole layout that graces the grounds of the Fairmont Banff Springs and is rated one of the world's most scenic courses. The **Jasper Park Lodge Golf Course,** a challenging par-73 course surrounded by spectacular mountain scenery, is of the same high standard. The **Kananaskis Country Golf Course,** a 36-hole, Robert Trent Jones–designed course built in the 1980s at a cost of $1 million per hole, was the first of the resort-style courses built in the Canadian Rockies. At Canmore, **SilverTip** set a new standard in golf course difficulty in Canada when it opened in 1998. It promotes itself as an extreme experience, and it is: 7,300 yards long, with elevation changes up to 40 meters (130 feet) on any one hole, and a slope rating of 153—the highest of any Canadian course.

Across the valley from SilverTip, **Stewart Creek** opened in the summer of 2000, bringing the total number of courses in Canmore to three. With two more courses already cut and slated to open by 2006, Canmore is a good base for keen golfers. Other resort courses are **Radium Resort** (36 holes), at Radium Hot Springs, **Greywolf** at Panorama Mountain Village, and **Wintergreen** at Bragg Creek, while the towns of Canmore and Golden offer excellent 18-hole public layouts, as does Waterton Lakes National Park.

ON THE WATER

Canoeing

This traditional form of Canadian transportation is a great way to explore the waterways of the mountains that are otherwise inaccessible—places such as **Vermilion Lakes** in Banff National Park, where beavers, elk, and a great variety of birds can be appreciated from water level. Canoes can be rented on the **Bow River** in the town of Banff, **Lake Louise,** and **Moraine Lake** in Banff National Park; **Pyramid** and **Maligne Lakes** in Jasper National Park; **Cameron Lake** in Waterton Lakes National Park; and **Emerald Lake** in Yoho National Park. Expect to pay around $8–15 per hour, and up to $30 per hour on Lake Louise. The more adventurous visitor can rent a canoe and paddle down the Bow River from Lake Louise to downtown Banff.

White-Water Rafting

The rafting season is relatively short, but the thrill of careening down a river laced with rapids is not easily forgotten. Qualified guides operate on many rivers flowing out of the mountains. The **Kicking Horse River,** which flows through Yoho National Park to Golden, is run by companies based in Golden, Lake Louise, and Banff. This is the most popular river for rafting trips. The **Maligne** and **Sunwapta Rivers** in Jasper National Park are others offering big thrills. For a more sedate river trip, try the **Bow River** in Banff National Park, or the **Athabasca River** in Jasper National Park. Both are run commercially. All companies offer half- and full-day trips, including transportation, wetsuits, and often light snacks.

Scuba Diving

Being landlocked, the Canadian Rockies are not renowned for scuba diving. A few interesting opportunities do exist, however, and rentals are available in Lethbridge, Calgary, and Edmonton. The old townsite of **Minnewanka Landing,** in Banff National Park, has been flooded, and although a relatively deep dive, the site is interesting. **Patricia Lake,** in Jasper National Park, conceals a sunken barge that Winston

© ANDREW HEMPSTEAD

ON THE ROAD

The thrills and spills of white-water rafting can be enjoyed on many local rivers.

Churchill had built as an aircraft carrier that was also capable of functioning as an icebreaker, and due to the high altitude and clear water, visibility is exceptional. Another sunken boat lies at the bottom of **Emerald Bay** in Waterton Lakes National Park, not far from some wagons that fell through the ice many winters ago. For a list of dive shops and sites, contact Alberta Underwater Council, 780/427-9125, www.albertaunderwatercouncil.com.

FISHING

The Canadian Rockies are an angler's delight. Fish are abundant in many lakes and rivers (the exceptions to good fishing are the lakes and rivers fed by glacial runoff, such as Lake Louise), and outfitters provide guiding services throughout the mountains. Many lakes are stocked annually with a variety of trout—most often rainbows— and although stocking was discontinued in the national parks in 1988, populations have been maintained. In Banff National Park, **Lake Minnewanka** is home to the mountains' largest fish—lake trout—as well a variety of other trout and whitefish. This lake, along with **Maligne**

Lake in Jasper National Park, are major fishing centers, with boats and tackle for rent and guides offering their services.

Fish Species

Rainbow trout are the fighting fish of the Canadian Rockies; they are to western Canada what bass are to the United States. Although not native, through stocking they are found in lakes and streams throughout the mountains. The Bow River is considered one of the world's great trout rivers, but most of the action happens downstream of Calgary. Wet flies and small spinners are preferred methods of catching these fish. The largest fish found in the region is the **lake trout,** which grows to 18 kg (40 lbs.). It feeds near the surface after breakup, and then moves to deeper, colder water in summer. Long lines and heavy lures are needed to hook onto these giants. **Brown trout,** introduced from Europe, are found in the Upper Bow River (downstream from Banff) and slow-flowing streams in the foothills of Kananaskis Country. They are most often caught on dry flies, but are finicky feeders, and therefore difficult to hook. **Brook trout** are widespread throughout lower elevation lakes and streams. **Cutthroat trout** inhabit the cold and clear waters of the highest lakes, which generally require a hike to access. Fishing for cutthroat requires using the lightest of tackle because the water is generally very clear; fly-casting is most productive on the still water of lakes, while spinning is the preferred river-fishing method.

Arctic grayling, easily identified by their large dorsal fins, are common in cool, clear streams throughout the far north, but are not native to the Canadian Rockies; Wedge Pond (Kananaskis Country) is stocked with these delicious fish. **Dolly Varden** can be caught in many high-elevation lakes on the British Columbia side of the mountains; Whiteswan Lake is a local favorite. **Whitefish** are a commonly caught fish in lower-elevation lakes and rivers (many anglers in Alberta call whitefish "arctic grayling," but they are in fact two distinct species—and grayling aren't native to the mountains). Hydroelectric dams, such as those east of Canmore and in the Spray Valley Provincial Park, are popular with anglers chasing whitefish.

Note: The **bull trout** is an endangered species and is a catch-and-release fish. Possession of bull trout—a dark-colored fish with light spots—is illegal. The defining difference between the bull trout and the brook trout, with which it is often confused, is that the bull trout has *no black spots on its dorsal fin;* due to its status, correct identification of this species is especially important.

Regulations and Licenses

Three different licenses are in effect in the Canadian Rockies—one license covers all the national parks, another Albertan waters, and a third the freshwaters of British Columbia.

National parks: Licenses are available from park offices and some sport shops; $6 for a seven-day license, $13 for an annual license. The brochure *Fishing Regulations Summary,* available from all park information centers, details limits and closures.

Alberta: Alberta has an automated licensing system, with licenses sold from sporting stores, hardware stores, and gas stations. To use the machines, the vendor needs you to supply a Wildlife Identification Number (WIN) card. These numbers are sold by all license vendors and cost $8 (valid for five years). Once you have your card, it is swiped through a vending machine to purchase a license. An annual license for Canadian residents older than age 16 is $18 (no license required for those 16 years or younger or Albertans older than 64); for nonresidents age 16 and older, it is $36, or $20 for a five-day license.

The *Alberta Guide to Sportfishing Regulations,* which outlines all the open seasons and bag limits, is available from outlets selling licenses and online at the Fish & Wildlife section of the Department of Sustainable Resource Development website, www3.gov.ab.ca. In addition to having the entire regulations online, the site also holds statistics for the provincial stocking program (which lakes, when, and how many fish) and details of Alberta's upcoming mandatory barbless hook rules, which come into effect in 2004. To contact this department by phone, call 780/944-0313.

British Columbia: In British Columbia, the cost of a license varies according to your place of residence. British Columbian residents pay $30 for a one-year license, $17 for an eight-day license, or $8 for a single-day license. Residents of other Canadian provinces pay $40, $25, or $15, respectively, while non-Canadians pay $55, $30, or $15, respectively. For more information, contact the Ministry of Water, Land, and Air Protection, 250/387-4573, www.bcfisheries.bc.ca.

WINTERTIME

Downhill Skiing and Snowboarding

Six world-class winter resorts are perched among the high peaks of the Canadian Rockies. The largest, and Canada's second-largest (only Whistler/Blackcomb is larger), is **Lake Louise,** overlooking the lake of the same name in Banff National Park. The resort boasts 1,700 hectares (4,200 acres) of skiing and boarding on four distinct faces, with wide-open bowls and runs for all abilities. Banff's other two resorts are **Sunshine Village,** sitting on the Continental Divide and accessible only by gondola, and **Ski Banff @ Mount Norquay,** a resort with heart-pounding runs overlooking the town of Banff.

Kananaskis Country is home to **Nakiska,** a resort developed especially for the downhill events of the 1988 Winter Olympic Games in Calgary, and nearby **Fortress Mountain,** in a spectacular location and with runs for all abilities. **Marmot Basin,** in Jasper National Park, has minimal crowds and a maximum variety of terrain. Across the border in British Columbia, near Golden, **Kicking Horse Mountain Resort** is a big hill that has gained an even bigger reputation for its challenging terrain since opening for the 2001–2002 season.

Winter is low season in the mountains, so many accommodations reduce their rates drastically. Lift and lodging package deals at many resorts start around $60 per person per night. Sunshine Village and Fortress Mountain have on-slope lodging, while the other resorts are served by shuttle buses from the nearest towns. Most major resorts open in early December and close in May.

Heli-Skiing

Helicopters are banned in the national parks of the Canadian Rockies, but two surrounding heli-ski operators provide transfers from Banff and Jasper. One such company is **R.K. Heli-Ski,** 250/342-3889 or 800/661-6060, www.rkhelis-ki.com, which is based on the west side of the mountains at Panorama, but provides daily transfers from Banff and Lake Louise for a day's heli-skiing or boarding high in the Purcell Mountains. The cost is $600 per person plus $70 for Banff transfers. The only other company that offers day trips is **Robson Helimagic,** based west of Jasper at Valemont, 250/566-4700, which charges $500 for a day's skiing on the northern boundary of Mount Robson Provincial Park.

Banff is also headquarters for the world's largest heli-skiing operation, **CMH Heli-Skiing,** founded by Hans Gmoser. Seven-day packages in British Columbia's interior mountain ranges begin at around $5,200 per person, rising to more than $8,000 in the high season. For more information, contact CMH at 403/762-7100 or 800/661-0252, www.cmhski.com.

Other Winter Activities

Many hiking trails provide ideal routes for **cross-country skiing,** and many are groomed for that purpose. The largest concentration of groomed trails is in Kananaskis Country. Other areas are Banff, Jasper, Kootenay, Waterton, and Yoho National Parks. The Canmore Nordic Centre was developed for the 1988 Winter Olympic Games and is now a public facility. The townsite in Waterton Lakes National Park all but closes down for winter, but this park is one of the most enjoyable spots for a skiing sojourn. Anywhere you can cross-country ski you can **snowshoe,** a traditional form of winter transportation that is making a comeback. **Sleigh rides** are offered in Banff, Lake Louise, and Jasper.

Winter travel brings its own set of potential hazards, such as hypothermia, avalanche, frostbite, and sunburn. Necessary precautions should be taken. All park information centers can provide information on hazards and advice on current weather conditions.

Dogsledding is a traditional form of transportation that visitors are encouraged to try.

© ANDREW HEMPSTEAD

ON THE ROAD

Accommodations and Food

Following is a summary of the types of accommodations and dining choices you can expect to find throughout the Canadian Rockies. Individual properties are detailed in each travel chapter, along with prices and contact information. Nearly all accommodations now have toll-free numbers and websites, through which you can find out more information about each property and make bookings.

HOTELS AND MOTELS

Hotels and motels throughout the Canadian Rockies range from substandard road motels to sublime resorts such as the famous Fairmont Banff Springs. Bookings throughout the mountains, but especially in Banff, Lake Louise, and Jasper, should be made as far in advance as possible. Finding inexpensive lodging in the mountain national parks is difficult in summer. By late afternoon, the only rooms left will be in the more expensive categories, and by nightfall all

of these will go. Hotel rooms in Banff begin around $150; those in Jasper and Waterton are a little less. Accommodation prices are slashed by as much as 70 percent outside summer. Always ask for the best rate available and check local tourist literature for discount coupons. All rates quoted in this handbook are for the cheapest category of rooms during the most expensive time period (summer). To all rates quoted you must add the 7 percent Goods and Services Tax (GST), which is refundable to nonresidents (keep receipts). Additionally, accommodations in Alberta are subject to a 5 percent Marketing Levy, while those in British Columbia are subject to an 8 percent Hotel Room Tax.

Park-at-your-door, single-story road motels are mostly a thing of the past in the mountains, although Radium Hot Springs, just outside Kootenay National Park, still has many of these motels (one of which proudly boasts "Electric Heat"). In most cases rooms are fine,

© ANDREW HEMPSTEAD

Staying in a self-contained log cabin, like this one at the Post Hotel, is a typical mountain experience.

GET THE BIGGEST BED FOR YOUR BUCK

It can't be stressed enough: the Internet is an invaluable tool for searching out the best accommodation deals.

Rates quoted in this book are for a standard double room throughout the high season, which generally extends from mid-June to mid-September. Almost all accommodations are less expensive outside of these busy months. As a general rule of thumb, the more expensive the property, the steeper the discount. For example, and at different ends of the spectrum, the cost of a dorm bed at the Banff Alpine Centre drops $4 per night on 15 September, while in downtown Banff, already reasonably priced Brewster's Mountain Lodge halves its rates to $110 in winter, with graduated discounts in spring and fall. Plan on traveling a few weeks on either side of the peak season, then use hotel websites to check when individual properties are offering discounts. Most accommodations post seasonal specials on their websites well in advance.

While you have no influence over seasonal pricing fluctuations, *how* you reserve a room *can* make a difference in how much you pay. Book through a central reservations agency or travel agent, or pay for accommodations as part of a tour package, and you'll pay the full published price.

In some years, getting a room in July and August without advance reservations is almost impossible. In others, hotels will be selling rooms well into the night for a fraction of the published rate. Leaving reservations until the last minute is a risky proposition if you're not prepared to be flexible, but it's a good way to save a lot of money.

Don't be afraid to negotiate during slower times. Even if the desk clerk has no control over rates, there's no harm in asking for a bigger room or one with a better view. Just look for a "Vacancy" sign hanging out front.

Most hotels in the Canadian Rockies offer auto association members an automatic 10 percent discount, and whereas senior discounts apply only to those older than 60 or 65 at attractions, most hotels offer discounts to those older than 50. Finally, when it comes to frequent flyer programs, you really do need to be a frequent flyer to achieve free flights, but the various loyalty programs offered by hotel chains often provide benefits simply for signing up.

but check before paying, just to make sure. Most have a few rooms with kitchenettes, but these fill fast. Expect to pay $50–70 s, $50–85 d. You will also find this style of accommodation in Canmore, Waterton townsite, and Golden.

Information and Reservations

For a list of all hotels, motels, lodges, and bed-and-breakfasts in Alberta, pick up a copy of *Alberta Accommodation Guide,* produced by the Alberta Hotel & Lodging Association. The guide is available from tourist information centers or through **Travel Alberta,** 780/427-4321 or 800/661-8888, and is also online at www.explorealberta.com. The same association produces the *Alberta Campground Guide* (also online at www.explorealberta.com). **Tourism British Columbia** produces the *British Columbia Approved Accommodation* brochure, which lists all accommodations and campgrounds in the province. Copies are available from Visitor Information Centres, or direct from Tourism British Columbia, 250/387-1642 or 800/435-5622, www.hellobc.com.

BED-AND-BREAKFASTS

The bed-and-breakfast phenomenon is well entrenched in Canada. Hosts are generally well-informed local people and rooms are cozy. They are usually private residences, with up to four guest rooms, although bylaws are different throughout the region. Rates fluctuate greatly, with the least expensive rooms costing $50 s, $60 d and the most expensive more than $100. Bed-and-breakfasts are located in Banff, Canmore, Bragg Creek, and Jasper. In Jasper National Park, a park bylaw that prevented such establishments from serving breakfast was recently lifted; some have started serving meals, but those that don't are still known as private home accommodations. The best way to find out about individual lodging is from local tourist information centers or from listings in the *Alberta Accommodation Guide* or *British Columbia Approved Accommodation* brochure.

Bed-and-Breakfast Associations and Agencies

The **Western Canada Bed and Breakfast Innkeepers Association,** 604/255-9199, www.wcbbia.com, represents bed-and-breakfasts across the region. They produce an informative brochure with simple descriptions and a color photo of each property, but they don't take the actual bookings. Without the color photos, **Jasper Home Accommodation Association,** website: www.stayinjasper.com, offers the same kind of literature.

Canada-West Accommodations, 604/990-6730 or 800/561-3223, www.b-b.com, does take bookings, along with providing recommendations based on your likes and dislikes.

OTHER LODGING OPTIONS

Seasonal Accommodations

As roads through the mountains were improved in the 1920s, the number of tourists arriving by automobile increased greatly. To cater to this new breed of traveler, many bungalow camps were constructed along the highways. Many remain today, offering a high standard of accommodation away from the hustle and bustle of the towns. Generally they consist of freestanding, self-contained units and are open for the summer only.

Backcountry Huts and Lodges

Scattered throughout the backcountry are 18 huts maintained by the Alpine Club of Canada. The huts are rustic—typically bunkbeds, a woodstove, a wooden dining table, and an outhouse. Rates are $14–24 per person per night. Reservations should be made in advance by contacting the Alpine Club of Canada, 403/678-3200, www.alpineclubofcanada.ca.

Privately operated backcountry lodges are found in Banff, Jasper, and Yoho National Parks, as well as Mount Assiniboine Provincial Park. The best known is **Lake O'Hara Lodge** in Yoho National Park. It lies 11 km (6.8 miles) from the nearest public road—access is on foot or shuttle bus—and is surrounded by some of the finest hiking in all the Canadian Rockies. Banff National Park has two backcountry lodges: **Shadow Lake Lodge,** northwest of Banff, and **Skoki Lodge,** east of Lake Louise. Jasper National Park is home to **Tonquin Amethyst Lake Lodge.** All require some degree of effort to reach—either on foot or on horseback in summer, or on cross-country skis or snowshoes in winter. **Mount Assiniboine Lodge** is farthest from the road system but can be reached by helicopter. Rates at these lodges begin at $140 per person, including three meals. None have television, but all have running water and a congenial atmosphere.

BACKPACKER ACCOMMODATIONS

Throughout the Canadian Rockies, traditional hostels operated by Hostelling International are still the most common form of accommodation for budget travelers, but other options do exist. Banff and Radium Hot Springs have privately run backpacker lodges, and Banff has a YWCA with dormitory accommodation for men and women. Generally, you need to supply your own sleeping bag or linen, but most places supply extra bedding at a minimal cost.

Hostelling International

Hostelling International–Alberta operates 13 hostels in the Canadian Rockies. The curfews and chores are long gone at Hostelling International, a worldwide, 4,500-hostel-strong organization, and you don't even need to be a member to stay. Five of these are in Banff National Park, five in Jasper National Park, and one each in Kananaskis Country, Yoho National Park (British Columbia), and Waterton Lakes National Park. A sheet or sleeping bag is required, although these can usually be rented. All of the hostels are equipped with a kitchen and lounge room, and some have laundries and private rooms. Those in Banff and Lake Louise are world-class, with hundreds of beds as well as libraries and cafés. The five rustic hostels along the Icefields Parkway are evenly spaced, perfect for a bike trip along one of the world's great mountain highways. Rates for members are $13–26 per night, nonmembers $17–30. Staying in hostels is an especially good bargain for skiers and snowboarders; packages including accommodation and a day pass at a local resort start at $55.

Whenever you can, make reservations in advance, especially in summer. Make bookings by calling Central Reservations at 403/521-8421 or 866/762-4122, or online at www.hihostels.ca. It's also possible to make bookings through the International Booking Network, www.hostel-booking.com.

You don't have to be a member of Hostelling International to take advantage of this inexpensive form of accommodation, but membership pays for itself after just a few nights of discounted lodging. Other benefits include discounted tours, car rental, bus and rail travel, and even flights. For Canadians, the membership cost is $35 annually or $175 for a lifetime membership. Call the Canadian head office at 613/237-7884 or sign up online at www.hihostels.ca. In the United States, contact **Hostelling International–American Youth Hostels,** 202/783-6161; website: www.hiayh.org. Other contact addresses include **YHA England and Wales,** tel. 0870/770-8868, www.yha.org.uk; **YHA Australia,** tel. 02/9261-1111, www.yha.com; and **YHA New Zealand,** tel. 03/379-9970 or 0800/278-299, www.yha.co.nz.

CAMPING

Camping is the way to stay cheaply in the Canadian Rockies. Each of the five national parks has excellent campgrounds, which have a combined total of 6,000 sites plus large areas set aside for overflow camping. Many of the campgrounds consist of nothing more than picnic tables, drinking water, pit toilets, and firewood ($6 per site per night), but at least one campground in each park has hot showers and full hookups. Each park

also has an area set aside for winter camping. All national park campgrounds operate on a first-come, first-served basis and often fill by midday in July and August. Check the **Parks Canada** website, www.parkscanada.gc.ca, for details.

Each of the road-accessible provincial parks covered in this book provides camping facilities, usually only with drinking water, picnic tables, and pit toilets. The exceptions are Peter Lougheed and Bow Valley Provincial Parks in Kananaskis Country, where hookups and showers are provided. Campground operations in Kananaskis Country are contracted to private operators, but ultimately come under the auspices of the Ministry of Community Development, www.cd.gov.ab.ca. This department is also in charge of other campgrounds on public lands, including those in provincial recreation areas along the eastern slopes of the Canadian Rockies. BC Parks, website: http://wlap-www.gov.bc.ca/bcparks, manages similar facilities along the other side of the divide; camp fees range $10–18 per night.

Commercial campgrounds operate in Canmore, Radium Hot Springs, at the entrance to Waterton Lakes National Park, in Golden, in Mount Robson Provincial Park, and in Grande Cache. They provide full hookups and have showers, but generally lack the natural surroundings found in national and provincial parks. In Kananaskis Country, the privately operated Mount Kidd RV Park boasts a tennis court, recreation room, spa, and sauna.

Backcountry Camping

Backcountry camping in all national parks is $6 per person per night to a maximum of $30 per person per trip. An annual Wilderness Pass ($42) is valid for unlimited backcountry travel and camping for 12 months from its purchase date. Before heading out, you must register at the respective park information center (regardless of whether you have an annual pass) and pick up a Wilderness Pass (for those without an annual pass, the nightly camping fee multiplied by the number of nights you'll be in the backcountry). Many popular backcountry campgrounds have quotas, with reservations taken up to three months in advance. The reservation fee is $10 per party per trip. Most campgrounds in the backcountry have pit toilets, and some have bear bins for secure food storage. Fires are discouraged, so bring a stove.

FOOD AND DRINK

Although Canada isn't renowned for its culinary delights, there are some dishes to look for. Alberta beef is delicious and is served in most restaurants. Game features prominently in many better restaurants, and although it may seem a little hypocritical to admire wildlife throughout the day and then eat it in local restaurants, you can be assured that meats such as buffalo and venison are farmed, mostly on the grasslands of Alberta. While the mountains are a long way from the ocean, British Columbia is known for its seafood. For a three-course meal in a family-style restaurant, including a steak dish, expect to pay $30 per person—at least double that in the better eateries. Banff holds an astonishing array of restaurants— more than 100 at last count.

The best way to eat cheaply if you're camping is with a campstove (those made by Coleman are the most reliable). Don't rely on an open fire for cooking—fire bans are often in effect. The two largest supermarkets, Safeway and I.G.A., generally have the least expensive groceries, but prices are still marginally higher than in the United States.

The Canadian Rockies are home to two small boutique breweries: Grizzly Paw Brewery and Peak Brewing Company, both in Canmore. Grizzly Paw, on Canmore's main street, has a pub on site. The minimum age for alcohol consumption in both Alberta and British Columbia is 18. From the United States, visitors may bring 1.1 liters of liquor or wine or 24 cans or bottles of beer into Canada free of duty.

Getting There

AIR

The closest city to the Canadian Rockies is **Calgary,** Alberta, 128 km (80 miles) east of Banff. **Vancouver,** British Columbia's largest city, is also a major gateway to the mountains. It lies on Canada's West Coast, 830 km (515 miles) west of Banff. **Edmonton,** 360 km (224 miles) east of Jasper also has an international airport. Even though Vancouver is a lot farther from the Canadian Rockies than Calgary, it is a popular starting point, as the trip across British Columbia by rail, bus, or car is spectacular.

Air Canada

Calgary and Vancouver International Airports are served by many international carriers. In mid-2000, Air Canada took over Canadian Airlines, leaving just one national carrier and a huge network of routings throughout the world. Air Canada is now one of the world's largest airlines, serving five continents. It offers direct

DEPARTURE TAXES

The Canadian government imposes a tax of 7 percent of the ticket price plus $6 up to a maximum of $55 on all flights departing Canada for the United States. For all other international destinations, the departure tax is set at $55. These taxes are generally added to the ticket price at the time of purchase, but it pays to ask when booking.

Additionally, all passengers departing Vancouver and Calgary airports must pay an **Airport Improvement Fee.** In Vancouver, the fee on flights destined for all points within British Columbia and the Yukon is $5, elsewhere in North America it's $10, and for all other international flights it's $15. Pay the fee at the vending machines or at the desk beside the security check. At Calgary, it's a flat fee of $12 for every departing passenger and is usually added to the original ticket price.

CUTTING FLIGHT COSTS

Ticket structuring for international air travel is so complex that often even travel agents have problems coming to grips with it. The first step when planning your trip to the Canadian Rockies is to contact the airlines that fly to Vancouver or Calgary and ask for the best price they have for the time of year you wish to travel. Then shop around the travel agencies—you should be able to save 30–50 percent of the price you were quoted by the airline. Check the Sunday travel section of most newspapers for an idea of current discount prices. The Internet is another good place to start searching out the cheapest fares.

Many cheaper tickets have strict restrictions regarding changes of flight dates, lengths of stay, and cancellations. A general rule is the cheaper the ticket, the more restrictions. Most travelers today fly on APEX (advance-purchase excursion) fares. These are usually the best value, although some (and, occasionally, many) restrictions apply. These might include minimum and maximum stays, and nonchangeable itineraries (or hefty penalties for changes); tickets may also be nonrefundable, once purchased.

Within Canada, **Travel Cuts,** website: www.travelcuts.com, with offices in all major cities, consistently offers the lowest airfares available. In the United States, one of the largest consolidators is **Unitravel,** 800/325-2222, www.unitravel.com. With offices around the world, **Flight Centre** is a reputable company that guarantees to match any quoted airfare. Contacts are: in Canada, 888/967-5331, www.flightcentre.ca; in the United States, 866/967-5364, www.flightcentre.com; in the United Kingdom, tel. 08708/908-099, 1-33, www.flightcentre.com.au; in New Zealand, tel. 0800/24-35-44, www.flightcentre.co.nz. In London, **Trailfinders,** 215 Kensington High Street, Kensington, tel. 020/7937-5400, www.trailfinders.com, always has good deals to Canada and other North American destinations.

When you have found the best fare, open a **frequent flyer** membership with the airline—**Air Canada** has a popular program that makes rewards easily obtainable.

flights to Calgary from all major Canadian cities, as well as from Seattle, Los Angeles, San Francisco, Reno, Las Vegas, Phoenix, Chicago, Boston, Washington D.C., Dallas/Fort Worth, New York, Atlanta, and St. Louis. From Europe, Air Canada flies direct from London to both Calgary and Vancouver, and from Paris, Frankfurt, and Rome to either Calgary or Vancouver via Toronto. From the South Pacific, Air Canada operates flights via Los Angeles from Sydney, Melbourne, and Auckland in alliance with Air New Zealand. Asian cities served by direct flights to Vancouver include Hong Kong, Taipei, Nagoya, Shanghai, Beijing, Tokyo, and Osaka, some on code-sharing agreements with other carriers. Air Canada's flights originating in the South American cities of Santiago, Buenos Aires, Sao Paulo, and Rio de Janeiro are routed through Toronto. For information on Air Canada flights, call 604/688-5515 or 888/247-2262, www.aircanada.ca (www.aircanada.com in the United States).

Other Canadian Airlines

Canada's second-largest airline is **Westjet,** 800/538-5956, www.westjet.com. Based in Calgary, this carrier offers extremely competitive fares between Calgary and Vancouver and eastern cities such as Saskatoon, Regina, Thunder Bay, Hamilton, Ottawa, and as far east as St. Johns.

Air Canada operates several smaller affiliated airlines. **Tango,** 800/315-1390, www.flytango.com, is a no-frills carrier with routes across Canada. **Air Canada Jazz,** 888/247-2262, www.flyjazz.com, links regional centers throughout western Canada and flies between Calgary and Spokane (Washington).

U.S. Airlines

Air Canada (see previous entry) offers the most flights into Calgary and Vancouver from the United States, but one or both of the cities are also served by the following U.S. carriers: **Alaska Airlines,** 800/252-7522, www.alaskaair.com, from Las Vegas, Los Angeles, Palm Springs, Phoenix, and San Francisco; **American Airlines,** 800/433-7300, www.aa.com, from Dallas and St. Louis; **Continental Airlines,** 800/231-0856, www.continental.com, from its Houston hub and New York; **Northwest Airlines,** 800/225-2525, www.nwa.com, from Detroit and Minneapolis; and **United Airlines,** 800/247-2262, www.ual.com, from Chicago, Denver, Los Angeles, San Francisco, and Seattle.

International Airlines

In addition to Air Canada's direct flights to Calgary and Vancouver, **British Airlines,** 800/247-9297, www.britishairlines.com, also flies this route daily. Air Canada flights between continental Europe and western Canada are routed through Toronto, with connections linking this eastern hub to Calgary, Edmonton, and Vancouver. European carriers with direct flights to western Canada are **KLM,** 604/278-3485, www.klm.nl, and **Lufthansa,** 800/563-5954, www.lufthansa.de, which both fly to Vancouver.

Qantas, 800/227-4500, www.qantas.com.au, flies to Vancouver via Honolulu from Sydney, Melbourne, and Brisbane. **Air New Zealand,** 800/663-5494, www.nzair.com, operates in alliance with Air Canada to either Calgary or Vancouver, with a variety of interesting options including stops in South Pacific destinations like Nandi (Fiji). **Air Pacific,** 800/227-4446, www.airpacific.com, offers flights from points throughout the Pacific to Honolulu and then on to Vancouver.

RAIL

The original transcontinental line passed through Banff, crossing the Continental Divide at Kicking Horse Pass and continuing to Vancouver via Rogers Pass. But this form of transportation, which opened up the Canadian Rockies to tourists, began to fade with the advent of efficient air services, and the last scheduled services on this line ended in 1991. Government-run **VIA Rail** provides coast-to-coast rail service using a more northerly route

that passes through Jasper National Park. At Jasper, the westbound transcontinental line divides, with one set of tracks continuing west to Prince Rupert via Prince George and the other heading southwest to Vancouver. Another, more luxurious option, is the privately run **Rocky Mountaineer,** with summer service to Banff and Jasper from Vancouver.

VIA Rail

The *Canadian* is a thrice-weekly service between Toronto and Vancouver via Winnipeg, Saskatoon, Edmonton, Jasper, and Kamloops. Service is provided in two classes of travel: **Economy** features lots of leg room, reading lights, pillows and blankets, and a Skyline Car complete with bar service, while **Silver and Blue** is more luxurious, featuring sleeping rooms, daytime seating, all meals, a lounge and dining car, and shower kits for all passengers. At Jasper the west-

© ANDREW HEMPSTEAD

Rail travel opened up the Canadian Rockies to tourism, and today continues as a popular form of transportation in the mountains.

bound transcontinental line divides, with one set of tracks continuing slightly north to Prince Rupert. Along this route, the **Skeena** makes three trips per week. It is a daytime-only service, with passengers transferred to Prince George accommodations for an overnight stay. It also offers first-class travel, in **Totem Class.**

Discounts of 25–40 percent apply to travel in all classes October–June. Those older than 60 and younger than 25 receive a 10 percent discount that can be combined with other seasonal fares. Students receive a 50 percent discount year-round. Check for advance-purchase restrictions on all discount tickets. The **Canrailpass** allows unlimited travel anywhere on the VIA Rail system for 12 days within any given 30-day period. During high season (June 1–October 15) the pass is $678; the rest of the year it's $423. Even if you plan limited train travel, the pass is an excellent deal; the regular Toronto–Vancouver one-way fare alone is almost $600. In partnership with Amtrak, VIA Rail offers a North America Rail Pass, with all the same seasonal dates and discounts as the Canrailpass. The cost is CDN$1,029 for a high-season pass. (For Amtrak information, call 800/872-7245).

Pick up a train schedule at any VIA Rail station or call 888/842-7245 within western Canada; in other Canadian locations, contact your local VIA Rail Station. In the United States, call any travel agent. The VIA Rail website, www.viarail.ca, provides route, schedule, and fare information as well as links to towns and sights en route.

Rocky Mountaineer

Rocky Mountaineer Rail Tours, 604/606-7245 or 800/665-7245, www.rockymountaineer.com, runs a luxurious rail trip between Vancouver and Banff or Jasper, through the spectacular interior mountain ranges of British Columbia. Travel is during daylight hours only so you don't miss anything. Trains depart in either direction in the morning (every second or third day), overnighting at Kamloops. One-way travel in RedLeaf Service, which includes light meals, nonalcoholic drinks, and three nights' accommodations costs US$949 per person from either Banff or Jasper to Van-

couver and US$959 from Calgary. GoldLeaf Service is the ultimate in luxury. Passengers ride in a two-story glass-domed car, eat in a separate dining area, and stay in Kamloops' most luxurious accommodations. GoldLeaf costs US$1579 per person from Banff or Jasper to Vancouver and $1629 from Calgary. During value season (mid-April to May and the first two weeks of October), fares are reduced US$150–350.

BUS

Greyhound

Greyhound, 403/762-1092 or 800/661-8747, www.greyhound.ca, serves areas throughout Canada and the United States. Travel by Greyhound is simple—just roll up at the depot and buy a ticket. No reservations are necessary. Greyhound bus depots are always close to downtown and generally link up with local public transportation. Always check for any promotional fares that might be available at the time of your travel. Regular-fare tickets are valid for one year and allow unlimited stopovers between paid destinations.

Greyhound's **Discovery Pass** comes in many forms, including passes valid only in Canada, in the western states and provinces, and in all of North America. The Canada Pass is sold in periods of seven days ($264), 10 days ($334), 15 days ($404), 21 days ($444), 30 days ($474), 45 days ($564), and 60 days ($634) and allows unlimited travel west of Montreal. The Domestic Western CanAm Pass, valid for Greyhound travel through western Canada and the western United States is valid for 10 days (US$264) and 21 days (US$364). You can buy the passes at any bus depot. In the United States, the pass can be bought from most travel agents. Outside of North America, it is sold as the **International Canada Pass** with a similar pricing structure except that there is a low season with a 25 percent discount that runs mid-September to mid-June.

From Calgary: Greyhound runs five times daily from their depot at 850 16th Street, Calgary, 403/265-9111, to Canmore and Banff.

From Vancouver: The main Greyhound routes from Vancouver include the TransCanada Highway to Golden, Field, and Banff; a northern route along Hwy. 5 through Jasper to Edmonton and beyond; and a southern route on Hwy. 3, through Cranbrook to Radium Hot Springs and on to Banff. The fare between Vancouver and Banff is around $120 one-way. The bus depot in Vancouver is at 1150 Station Street, 604/482-8747.

From the United States: If you're traveling from the United States, get yourself to Great Falls, Montana, from which regular services continue north to the Coutts/Sweetgrass port of entry. There you change to a Canadian Greyhound bus for Calgary, where you can make connections to Banff.

From Calgary International Airport

This airport, 128 km (80 miles) west of Banff, is the main gateway to the Canadian Rockies. In addition to car rental desks, many shuttles are represented opposite the baggage carousels. The main companies are **Brewster,** 403/762-6767, www.brewster.ca; **Banff Airporter,** 403/762-3396, www.banffairporter.com; and **Rocky Mountain Sky Shuttle,** 403/762-5200, www.rockymountainskyshuttle.com. Brewster is the only one of these services that continues beyond Banff, with buses continuing to Lake Louise and Jasper once daily.

The advantage of traveling with either of the latter two companies is that they offer door-to-door-service for around the same price. Reserve a seat by booking over the phone or online in advance. Expect to pay $40 each way, with slight discounts for booking a round-trip.

Getting Around

BUS

Getting around the Canadian Rockies is easiest with your own vehicle because public transportation is limited. **Brewster,** 403/762-6767, is primarily a tour company, but also runs a scheduled bus service linking Calgary International Airport, Canmore, Banff, and Lake Louise, with a summer-only service between Lake Louise and Jasper. Sample fares are Banff to Lake Louise, $12; Banff to Jasper, $56; Lake Louise to Jasper, $44. **Greyhound,** 403/762-1092, serve the TransCanada Highway, providing a link between Canmore, Banff, Lake Louise, and Golden three times daily. Once daily, buses run through Kootenay National Park, between Banff and Radium Hot Springs.

Hostel Shuttle

Between early June and early September, the **Canadian Rockies Hostel Shuttle** runs between all hostels in the Canadian Rockies every second day. The route begins from the Banff Alpine Centre at 8 A.M., taking five hours to reach Jasper, then returning that same afternoon. Sample fares are Banff to Lake Louise, $12; Lake Louise to Jasper, $46. Book at 780/852-4056 or 888/786-3641, or check the Hostelling International website, www.hihostels.ca, for details.

DRIVING

Driving in Canada

Driver's licenses from all countries are valid in Canada for up to six months. An **International Driving Permit,** available in your home country, is valid in Canada for one year. You should also carry car registration papers or rental contracts. Proof of insurance must be carried, and you must wear seatbelts. If coming from the United States, check that your American insurance covers travel in Canada. All highway signs give distances in kilometers and speeds in kilometers per hour (kph). The speed limit on major highways is 100 kph (62 mph). U.S. motorists are advised to obtain a Canadian Non-resident Inter-provincial Motor Vehicle Liability Insurance Card, available through U.S. insurance companies, which is accepted as evidence of financial responsibility in Canada. Members of the American Automobile Association (AAA) are entitled to services provided by the Canadian Automobile Association, including travel information.

Note: Drunk-driving laws in Canada are tough.

Car and RV Rental

All major car rental agencies have outlets at Calgary and Vancouver International Airports. Car rentals are also available in Banff, Canmore, and Jasper, but it is strongly recommended to rent a vehicle *before* arriving in the Canadian Rockies. Generally, vehicles can be booked through parent companies in the United States. Rates start at $60 per day for a small economy car, $75 for a mid-size car, and $85 for a full-size car. Most major agencies now offer unlimited mileage, but check to make sure. Cheaper cars are available from agencies such as **Rent-A-Wreck,** 800/327-0116, www.rentawreck.ca, but each kilometer driven over 100 km each day will cost 15–30 cents. In all cases insurance is from $15 per day and is compulsory. Rates are often lower outside summer. Charges apply if you need to drop off the car at an agency other than the rental location. All agencies provide free pick-up and drop-off at major city hotels. Major rental agencies include **Avis,** 800/879-2847, www.avis.com; **Budget,** 800/268-8900, www.budgetcanada.com; **Dollar,** 800/800-4000, www.dollar.com; **Enterprise,** 800/325-8007, www.enterprise.com; **Hertz,** 800/263-0600, www.hertz.com; **National,** 800/227-7368, www.nationalcar.com; and **Thrifty,** 800/847-4389, www.thrifty.com.

Camper vans, recreational vehicles, and travel trailers are a great way to get around the Canadian Rockies without having to worry about accommodations each night. The downside is cost. The smallest vans, capable of sleeping two people, start at $150 per day with 100 free kilometers per day. Standard extra charges include insurance, a preparation fee (usually around $50 per rental), a linen/cutlery charge (around $60 per person per trip), and taxes. The major agencies, based in Calgary and Vancouver, are **Cruise Canada,** 403/291-4963 or 800/327-7799, or, in the U.S., 800/327-7778, www.cruisecanada.com; **C.C. Canada Camper,** 604/327-3003, www.Canada-camper.com; and **Go West,** 604/987-5288 or 800/661-8813, www.go-west.com.

TOURS

For those with limited time, an organized tour is the best way to see the Canadian Rockies. **Brewster,** 403/762-6767 or 800/661-1152, www.brewster.ca, offers day tours and overnight tours throughout the mountains, as well as car rental and accommodation packages. Rocky Mountaineer Rail Tours (see "Getting There") offer a wide variety of longer tours in conjunction with rail travel between Vancouver and Banff or Jasper.

On a smaller scale, **Good Earth Travel Adventures** provides one-on-one consultations for all aspects of travel through the Canadian Rockies—from day tours to accommodation reservations. Contact them at 403/678-9358 or 888/979-9797; website: www.goodearthtravel.com. **True North Tours,** 403/912-0407 or 888/464-4842, operate three- and six-day tours between Banff and Jasper, traveling in a 15-seat bus, staying at hostels, and all throwing in a few bucks a day for food. Transportation is $115 and $215, respectively, with hostel accommodation and food extra.

ON THE ROAD

Information and Services

VISAS AND OFFICIALDOM

Entry for U.S. Citizens

Citizens and permanent residents of the United States do not need a passport for entry to Canada. Although photo driver's licenses are acceptable forms of identification for entry, it is advisable to carry extra identification such as a birth certificate, passport, or alien card. (The latter is essential for U.S. resident aliens to re-enter the United States.)

Other Foreign Visitors

Visitors from countries other than the United States must have a valid passport and, in some cases, a visa for entry to Canada. Presently, citizens of the British Commonwealth and Western Europe do not need a visa, but check with the Canadian embassy in your home country. The standard entry permit is valid for six months; proof of onward tickets and/or sufficient funds is required in order to obtain the permit. Extensions are possible from the Employment and Immigration Canada offices in Calgary and Vancouver ($60 per person).

Employment and Study

Anyone wishing to work or study in Canada must obtain authorization *before* entering Canada. Authorization to work will only be granted if no qualified Canadians are available for the work in question. Applications for work and study are available from all Canadian embassies and must be submitted with a nonrefundable processing fee.

The Canadian government has a reciprocal agreement with Australia for a limited number of **holiday work visas** to be issued each year. Australian citizens younger than 30 are eligible; contact your nearest Canadian embassy or consulate for more information.

MONEY

As in the United States, Canadian currency is based on dollars and cents. Coins come in de-nominations of one, five, 10, and 25 cents, and one and two dollars. The one-dollar coin is the 11-sided, gold-colored "loonie," named for the bird featured on it. The unique two-dollar coin, introduced in 1996, is silver with a gold-colored insert. The most common notes are $5, $10, $20, and $50. A $100 bill does exist but is uncommon. Each note features a different bird.

All prices quoted in this book are in Canadian dollars unless otherwise indicated. American dollars are accepted at many tourist areas, but the exchange rate will be more favorable at banks. Traveler's checks are the safest way to carry money, but often a fee is charged to cash them if they're in a currency other than Canadian dollars.

All major credit cards are honored at Canadian banks, gas stations, and most commercial establishments. Credit cards eliminate the necessity of thinking about the exchange rate—the amount and rate of exchange on the day of the transaction will automatically be reflected in the bill from your credit card company.

Costs

The cost of living in the mountains is generally higher than in other parts of Canada, especially when it comes to accommodations. Provincially, the cost of living is lower in Alberta than in British Columbia, but higher than in the United States. By planning ahead, having a tent or joining Hostelling International, and being prepared to cook your own meals, it is possible to get by on $60 per person per day. Gasoline is sold in liters (3.78 liters equals one U.S. gallon) and is generally 70–80 cents per liter for regular unleaded.

Tipping charges are not usually added to your bill. You are expected to add a tip of 15 percent to the total amount for waiters and waitresses, barbers and hairdressers, taxi drivers, and other such service providers. Bellhops, doormen, and porters generally receive $1 per item of baggage.

Taxes

Canada imposes a 7 percent **Goods and Services Tax (GST)** on most consumer purchases. Nonresident visitors can get a rebate for the GST they pay on short-term accommodations and on most consumer goods bought in the country and taken home. Items not included in the GST rebate program include gifts left in Canada, meals and restaurant charges, campground fees, services such as drycleaning and shoe repair, alcoholic beverages, tobacco, automotive fuels, groceries, agricultural and fish products, prescription drugs and medical devices, and used goods that tend to increase in value, such as paintings, jewelry, rare books, and coins.

The rebate is available on services and retail purchases of at least $50 each, that total at least $200, and that were paid for within 60 days before your exit from the country. Rebates can be claimed any time within one year from the date of purchase. You'll need to include with your claim all receipts and vouchers that prove the GST was paid. Most visitors apply for the rebate at duty-free shops (also called Visitor Rebate Centres) when exiting the country. The duty-free shops can rebate up to $500 on the spot. For rebates of $500 or more, you'll need to mail your completed GST rebate form directly to Visitor Rebate Program, Summerside Tax Centre, Canada Customs and Revenue Agency, 275 Pope Road, Suite 104, Summerside, PE C1N 6C6, Canada. You can also submit rebate forms for amounts less than $500 directly to this address. Rebate checks are issued in Canadian funds. For more information, call toll-free from anywhere in Canada 800/668-4748; from outside Canada, phone 902/432-5608; website: www.ccra-adrc.gc.ca.

Provincial Sales Tax applies in British Columbia but not Alberta and ranges 5–12 percent on most goods purchased in shops or restaurants.

HEALTH

Compared to other parts of the world, Canada is a relatively safe place to visit. That said, wherever you are traveling, carry a medical kit that includes bandages, insect repellent, sunscreen, antiseptic, antibiotics, and water-purification tablets. Good first-aid kits are available through most camping shops.

Taking out a travel-insurance policy is a sensible precaution because hospital and medical charges start at around $1,000 per day. Bring copies of your current prescriptions with you to Canada.

Giardia

Giardiasis, also known as beaver fever, is a real concern for those who drink water from backcountry water sources. It's caused by an intestinal parasite, *Giardia lamblia,* that lives in lakes, rivers, and streams. Once ingested, its effects, although not instantaneous, can be dramatic; severe diarrhea, cramps, and nausea are the most common. Preventive measures should always be taken and include boiling all water for at least 10 minutes, treating all water with iodine, or filtering all water using a filter with a small enough pore size to block the *Giardia* cysts.

Winter Travel

Travel through the mountains during winter months should not be undertaken lightly. Before setting out in a vehicle, check antifreeze levels

---

CURRENCY EXCHANGE

The Canadian dollar lost value against the greenback throughout the late 1990s, steadied through 2000–2001, and then dipped slightly again to reach record lows in early 2002. It currently trades at **US$1 per CDN$1.57–1.60.**

Current exchange rates are available on the Internet at **www.xe.com/ucc.** At the time of publication, exchange rates (into CDN$) for other major currencies are:

AUS$1 = $.85
€1 = $1.50
HK$10 = $1.98
NZ$1 = $.70
UK£ = $2.35
¥100 = $1.30

and always carry a spare tire and blankets or sleeping bags. **Frostbite** is a potential hazard, especially when cold temperatures are combined with high winds (a combination known as *windchill*). Most often it leaves a numbing, bruised sensation, and the skin turns white. Exposed areas of skin, especially the nose and ears, are most susceptible.

Hypothermia occurs when the body fails to produce heat as fast as it loses it. It can strike at any time of year but is more common during cooler months. Cold weather, combined with hunger, fatigue, and dampness, creates a recipe for disaster. Symptoms are not always apparent to the victim. The early signs are numbness, shivering, slurring of words, dizzy spells, and, in extreme cases, violent behavior, unconsciousness, and even death. The best way to dress for the cold is in layers, including a waterproof outer layer. Most important, wear headgear. The best treatment is to get the patient out of the cold, replace wet clothing with dry, slowly give hot liquids and sugary foods, and place the victim in a sleeping bag. Warming too quickly can lead to heart attacks.

COMMUNICATIONS AND MEASUREMENTS

All **mail** posted in Canada must have Canadian postage stamps attached. First-class letters and postcards are $.48 to destinations within Canada, $.65 to the United States, and $1.25 to all other destinations.

Alberta and British Columbia have two area codes each. The **area code** for southern Alberta is **403.** The area code for northern Alberta, including Jasper National Park, is **780.** The area code for all of British Columbia except Vancouver and environs is **250.** The area code for Vancouver is **604.** Unless otherwise noted, all numbers must be dialed with this prefix, including long-distance calls made within the province that you are calling from. The country code for Canada is 1, the same as the United States.

INTERNET ACCESS IN THE ROCKIES

It probably will surprise no one that public internet access is available, even in the Rockies. Send and receive email and surf the Internet at the locations listed below. (These locations are also listed in the Banff National Park, Canmore, and Jasper Banff National Park chapters.)

BANFF
Banff Public Library: 101 Bear St., 403/762-2661; Mon.–Thurs. 10 A.M.–8 P.M., Fri. 10 A.M.–6 P.M., Sat. 11 A.M.–6 P.M., and Sun. 1–5 P.M.
Cascade Plaza: lower level, 317 Banff Ave.; 403/762-8484; open daily 7:30 A.M.–10 P.M.
Cyber-web: Sundance Mall, 215 Banff Ave., 403/762-9226; daily 9 A.M.–midnight.

CANMORE
Beamer's Coffee Bar: 1702 Bow Valley Trail, 403/678-3988; daily 7 A.M.–10 P.M.
Café Books: 826 Eighth St., 403/678-0908; Mon.–Sat. 9:30 A.M.–9 P.M., Sun. 10:30 A.M.–5:30 P.M.
Canmore Business Services: 512 Bow Valley Trail, 403/678-1919; Mon.–Fri. 9 A.M.–5:30 P.M.
Canmore Public Library: 700 Ninth St., 403/678-2468; Mon.–Thur. 11 A.M.–8 P.M., Fri.–Sun. 11 A.M.–5 P.M.

JASPER
Digital Den: upstairs at 610 Patricia Street, 780/852-9765; daily 9 A.M.–10 P.M.
Jasper Municipal Library: Elm Ave., 780/852-3652; Mon.–Thur. 11 A.M.–9 P.M., Fri.–Sat. 11 A.M.–5 P.M.
More than Mail: 620 Connaught Dr., 780/852-3151; daily 9 A.M.–10 P.M.
Soft Rock Café: 632 Connaught Dr., 780/852-5850; daily 8 A.M.–10 P.M.

Public phones accept five-, 10-, and 25-cent coins. Local calls cost 35 cents, and most long-distance calls from public phones cost at least $2 for the first minute. Phone cards, available from drug and grocery stores, provide considerable savings for those using public phones.

Electrical voltage is 120 volts, the same as the United States. Canada is officially on the **metric system** (see the "Metric System" chart at the back of this book), although many people talk in miles and supermarket prices are advertised in ounces and pounds.

Alberta is in the **Mountain time zone,** one hour later than Pacific time, two hours earlier than Eastern Standard Time. The mountain time zone extends west into southern British Columbia, which includes Yoho and Kootenay National Parks as well as the towns of Golden and Radium Hot Springs. The rest of British Columbia, including Mount Robson Provincial Park, is in the **Pacific time zone.**

Shops are generally open Monday–Friday 9 A.M.–5 P.M., Saturday 9 A.M.–noon, and are closed on Sunday. Major shopping centers and those in resort towns are often open until 9 P.M. and all weekend. **Banks** are open Monday–Friday 9:30 A.M.–3:30 P.M., and until 4:30 or 5 P.M. on Friday.

MAPS AND INFORMATION

Maps

The best maps of the Canadian Rockies are produced by **Gem Trek Publishing,** based in Cochrane, between Calgary and the mountains, 403/932-4208 or 877/688-6277, www.gemtrek.com. Gem Trek maps of varying scales cover all of the region, using computer-generated "3D Imagery" to clearly define changes in elevation and GPS to plot hiking trails. The backs of maps are filled with trail information as well as tidbits of history. Waterproofing is an added bonus.

Maps are available at bookstores, gas stations, and gift shops throughout the Canadian Rockies. In Calgary, **Map Town,** 640 6th Ave. SW,

403/266-2241, is a specialist map shop worth stopping at as you pass through. In Vancouver, try **International Travel Maps and Books,** 552 Seymour St., 604/687-3320, www.itmb.com. By request they'll send you a catalog of available maps for hiking (topographical maps), camping (road/access maps), and canoeing (river details such as gradients). Topographic maps are for sale at all park information centers, as well as at some sport and outdoor stores.

Park Information

Each of the five national parks has at least one **Park Information Centre.** These are the places to head for interpretive displays, all park-related information, trail reports, weather forecasts, and Wilderness Passes. Individual addresses and websites are listed in the relevant travel chapters. The national parks are managed by **Parks Canada,** website: www.parkscanada.gc.ca. On the Alberta side of the Canadian Rockies, all other parks are managed by the **Department of Community**

ON THE ROAD

HEADING FARTHER AFIELD?

I f your travels take you beyond the Rockies, you may find the following resources helpful:

Alberta Tourism: 403/427-4321 or 800/661-8888, www.travelalberta.com
Tourism British Columbia: 250/387-1642 or 800/435-5622, www.hellobc.com
Tourism Yukon: 867/667-5036; website: www.touryukon.com
Alaska Division of Tourism: 907/465-2017, www.dced.state.ak.us/tourism/
NWT Arctic Tourism: 867/873-7200 or 800/661-0788, www.nwttravel.nt.ca
Nunavut Tourism: 867/979-6551 or 866/686-2888, www.nunavuttourism.com
Tourism Saskatchewan: 306/787-2300 or 877/237-2273, www.sasktourism.com

Development, 780/944-0313, www.cd.ab.ca. British Columbia's provincial parks are managed by **BC Parks,** http://wlapwww.gov.bc.ca/bcparks.

Tourism Information

Begin planning your trip by contacting the government tourist offices of Alberta and British Columbia: **Alberta Tourism,** 403/427-4321 or 800/661-8888, www.travelalberta.com, and **Tourism British Columbia,** 250/387-1642 or 800/435-5622, hellobc.com. Both will fill your mailbox with literature and maps, which can be ordered by phone or through their respective websites.

In Calgary, the main information center is in the **Calgary Tower Centre,** corner of Centre St. and 9th Ave. SW, 403/263-8510 or 800/661-1678. The **Vancouver Visitor Info Centre** is at 200 Burrard St., 604/683-2000. Both Calgary and Vancouver International Airports have information booths. For general tourism information, the towns of Banff, Canmore, Jasper, Radium Hot Springs, and Golden have information centers that provide advice on local attractions, accommodations, and restaurants.

Banff National Park

This 6,641-square-km (2,564-square-mile) national park encompasses some of the world's most magnificent scenery. The snowcapped peaks of the Rocky Mountains form a spectacular backdrop for glacial lakes, fast-flowing rivers, and endless forests. Deer, moose, elk, mountain goats, bighorn sheep, black and grizzly bears, wolves, and cougars inhabit the park's vast wilderness, while the human species is concentrated in the picture-postcard towns of Banff and Lake Louise—two of North America's most famous resorts. Banff is near the park's southeast gate, 128 km (80 miles) west of Calgary. Lake Louise, northwest of Banff along the TransCanada Highway, sits astride its namesake lake, which is regarded as one of the seven natural wonders of the world. The lake is rivaled for sheer beauty only by Moraine Lake, just down the road. Just north of Lake Louise,

the Icefields Parkway begins its spectacular course alongside the Continental Divide to Jasper National Park.

One of Banff's greatest drawing cards is the accessibility of its natural wonders. Most highlights are close to the road system. But adventurous visitors can follow an excellent system of hiking trails to alpine lakes, along glacial valleys, and to spectacular viewpoints where crowds are scarce and human impact has been minimal. Summer in the park is busy. In fact, the park receives nearly half of its four million annual visitors in just two months—July and August. The rest of the year crowds outside the town of Banff are negligible. In winter, three world-class winter resorts—Ski Banff @ Norquay,

Bow Lake

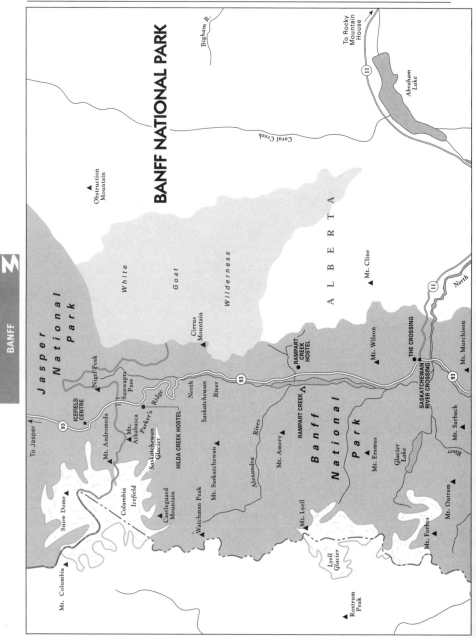

BANFF NATIONAL PARK

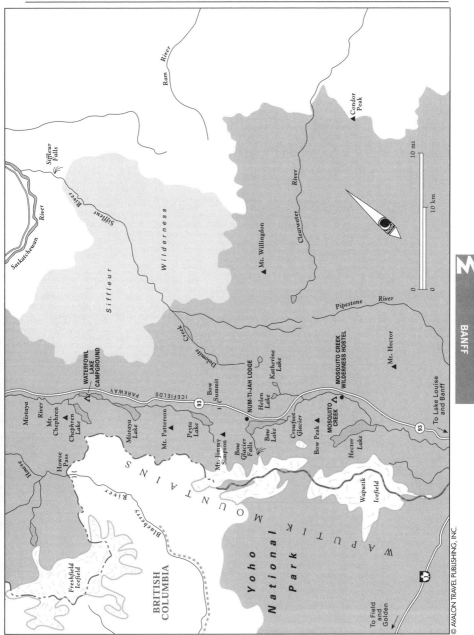

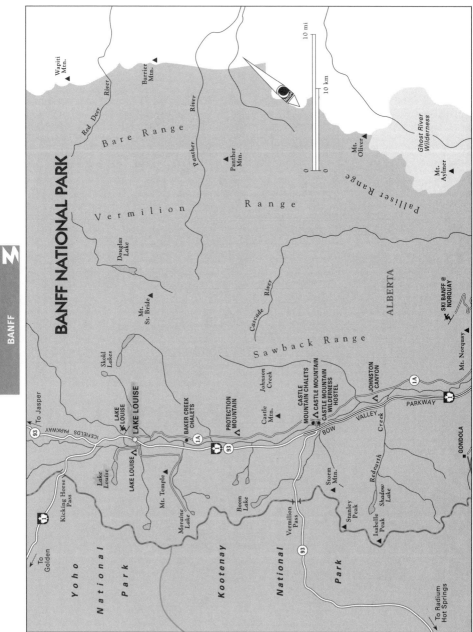

BANFF NATIONAL PARK

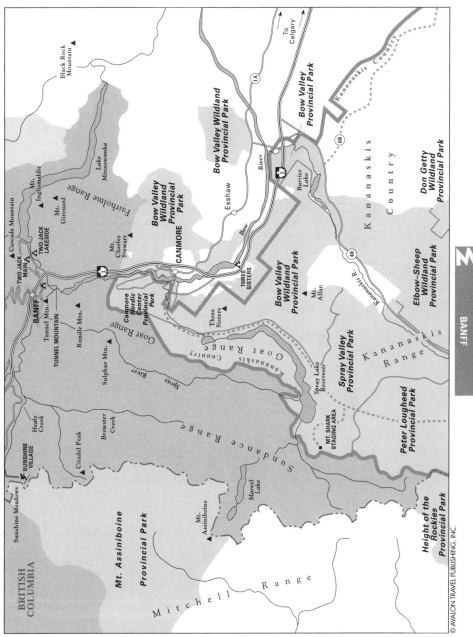

BANFF

© AVALON TRAVEL PUBLISHING, INC.

Sunshine Village, and Lake Louise (Canada's second-largest winter resort)—crank up their lifts. Being low season, hotel rates are reasonable. If you tire of downhill skiing and snowboarding, you can try cross-country skiing, ice-skating, or snowshoeing; take a sleigh ride; soak in a hot spring; or go heli-skiing nearby.

The park is open year-round, although occasional road closures occur on mountain passes along the park's western boundary in winter, due to avalanche-control work and snowstorms.

THE LAND

The park lies within the main and front ranges of the Rocky Mountains, a mountain range that extends the length of the North American continent. Although the mountains are composed of bedrock laid down up to one billion years ago, it wasn't until 100 million years ago that forces below the earth's surface transformed the lowland plain of what is now western Canada into the varied, mountainous topography we see today.

The front ranges lie to the east, bordering the foothills. These geographically complex mountains are made up of younger bedrock that has been folded, faulted, and uplifted. The main ranges are older and higher, with the bedrock lying mainly horizontal and not as severely disturbed as the front ranges. Here the pressures have been most powerful; these mountains are characterized by castlelike buttresses and pinnacles, and warped waves of stratified rock. Most glaciers are found among these lofty peaks. The spine of the main range is the **Continental Divide.** In Canadian latitudes to the east of the divide, all waters flow to the Atlantic Ocean; those to the west flow into the Pacific.

Since rising above the surrounding plains these mountains have been eroding. At least four times in the last million years sheets of ice have covered much of the land. Advancing and retreating back and forth like steel wool across the landscape, they rounded off lower peaks and carved formerly V-shaped valleys into broad U-shaped ones (**Bow Valley** is the most distinctive). Meanwhile, glacial melt-

© ANDREW HEMPSTEAD

Castle Mountain is one of the park's most distinctive peaks, easily recognized while driving north from the town of Banff.

BANFF

PARK ENTRY

Permits are required for entry into Banff National Park. A National Parks Day Pass is $6 adults, $4.50 seniors, $3 children to a maximum of $12 per vehicle ($9 for seniors). It is interchangeable between parks and is valid until 4 P.M. the day following its purchase. An annual National Parks of Canada, good for entry into national parks across Canada, is $38 adults, $29 seniors to a maximum of $75 per vehicle ($56 for two or more seniors). This pass comes with a coupon book, which includes a wide variety of discounts, including to camp fees. Both types of passes can be bought at the eastern park gate on the TransCanada Highway, the park information centers in Banff or Lake Louise, and at campground kiosks. For more information, check online at the Parks Canada website, www.parkscanada.gc.ca.

water continued carving ever-deeper channels into the valleys, and rivers changed course many times.

This long history of powerful and even violent natural events over the eons has left behind the dramatic landscape visitors marvel over today. Now forming the exposed sides of many a mountain peak, layers of drastically altered sediment are visible from miles away, especially when accentuated by a particular angle of sunlight or a light fall of snow. *Cirques,* gouged into the mountains by glacial action, fill with glacial meltwater each spring, creating trademark translucent green lakes that will take your breath away. The wide, sweeping U-shaped valleys scoured out by glaciers past now create magnificent panoramas that will draw you to pull off the road and gasp in awe; open views are easy to come by here, thanks to a climate that keeps the treeline low.

FLORA

Nearly 700 species of plants have been recorded in the park. Each species falls into one of three distinct vegetation zones, based primarily on altitude. Lowest is the montane zone, which covers

the valley floor. Above it, the subalpine zone comprises most of the forested area. Highest of all is the alpine zone, where climate is severe and vegetation cover is limited.

Montane-zone vegetation is usually found at elevations below 1,350 meters (4,430 feet) but can grow at higher elevations on sun-drenched, south-facing slopes. Because fires frequently affect this zone, **lodgepole pine** is the dominant species; its tightly sealed cones only open with the heat of a forest fire, thereby regenerating the species quickly after a blaze. **Douglas fir** is the zone's climax species and is found in open stands, such as on Tunnel Mountain. **Aspen** is common in older burn areas, while **limber pine** thrives on rocky outcrops.

Dense forests of **white spruce** and **Engelmann spruce** typify the subalpine zone. White spruce dominates up to 2,100 meters (6,890 feet); above 2,100 meters (6,890 feet) to 2,400 meters (7,870 feet), Engelmann spruce is dominant. In areas affected by fire, such as west of Castle Junction, lodgepole pine occurs in dense stands. **Subalpine fir** grows above 2,200 meters (7,550 feet) and is often stunted by the high winds experienced at such lofty elevations.

The transition from subalpine to alpine is gradual and usually occurs around 2,300 meters (7,560 feet). The alpine has a severe climate, with temperatures averaging below zero. Low temperatures, strong winds, and a very short summer force alpine plants to adapt by growing low to the ground with long roots. Mosses, mountain avens, saxifrage, and an alpine dandelion all thrive in this environment. The best place to view the brightly colored carpet of **alpine flowers** is at Sunshine Meadows or Parker's Ridge.

FAUNA

Viewing the park's abundant and varied wildlife is one of the most popular visitor activities in Banff. In summer, with the onslaught of the tourist hordes, many of the larger mammals move away from the heavily traveled areas. It then becomes a case of knowing when and where to look for them. Spring and fall are the best times of year for wildlife viewing; the crowds are thinner than in summer, and big-game animals are more likely to be seen at lower elevations. Winter also has its advantages. Although **bears** are hibernating, a large herd of **elk** winters on the outskirts of the town of Banff, **coyotes** are often seen roaming around town, **bighorn sheep** have descended from the heights, and wolf packs can be seen along the Bow Valley Corridor.

Small Mammals

One of the first mammals you're likely to come in contact with is the **Columbian ground squirrel,** seen throughout the park's lower elevations. The **golden-mantled ground squirrel,** similar in size but with a striped back, is common at higher elevations or around rocky outcrops. The one collecting Engelmann spruce cones is the **red squirrel.** The **least chipmunk** is striped, but smaller than the golden-mantled squirrel. It lives in dry, rocky areas throughout the park.

Short-tailed weasels are common, but **long-tailed weasels** are rare. Look for both in higher subalpine forests. **Pikas** (commonly called rock rabbits) and **hoary marmots** (well known for their shrill whistles) live among rock slides near high-country lakes: look for them around Moraine Lake and along Bow Summit Loop.

Porcupines are widespread and are most active at night.

Vermilion Lakes is an excellent place to view the **beaver** at work; the best time is dawn or dusk. **Muskrats** and **mink** are common in all wetlands within the park.

Hoofed Residents

The most common and widespread of the park's hoofed residents are **elk,** which number around 2,800. Starting in 2000, a concerted effort was made to keep them out of Banff's downtown core, but they are still congregating around the outskirts of the town, including up near the Tunnel Mountain campgrounds. They can also be seen along the Bow Valley Parkway. **Moose** were once common around Vermilion Lakes, but competition from an artificially expanded elk population caused their numbers to decline, and now only around 100 live in the park. Look for them at Waterfowl Lakes and along the Icefields Parkway near Rampart Creek.

Mule deer, named for their large ears, are most common in the southern part of the park. Watch for them along the Mount Norquay Road and Bow Valley Parkway. **White-tailed deer** are much less common but are seen occasionally at Saskatchewan River Crossing. A small herd of

THE ELK OF BANFF NATIONAL PARK

Few visitors leave Banff without having seen elk—a large member of the deer family easily distinguished by its white rump. Though the animals have been reported passing through the park for a century, they've never been indigenous. In 1917, 57 elk were moved to Banff from Yellowstone National Park. Two years later 20 more were transplanted and the new herd multiplied rapidly. At that time, coyotes, cougars, and wolves were being slaughtered under a predator-control program, leaving the elk unfettered by nature's population-control mechanisms. The elk proliferated and soon became a problem as they took to wintering in the range of bighorn sheep, deer, moose, and beaver. Between 1941 and 1969, controlled slaughters of elk were conducted in an attempt to reduce the population.

Today, with wolf packs returning to the park, the elk population has stabilized at about 2,800. In summer, look for them in open meadows along the Bow Valley Parkway, along the road to Two Jack Lake, or at Vermilion Lakes.

Each fall, traditionally, hundreds of elk moved into the town itself, but starting in 2000 Parks Canada has been making a concerted effort to keep them away from areas such as the golf course and recreation grounds. The main reason for this is that fall is rutting season, and the libidinal bull elk become dangerous as they gather their harems.

You may still see the odd elk feeding in downtown Central Park or walking proudly down Banff Avenue, but it's more likely you'll spot one on the outskirts of town.

© ANDREW HEMPSTEAD

Elk are common visitors to the local golf course.

around 20 **woodland caribou** remains in the Dolomite Pass area and Upper Pipestone Valley and is rarely seen.

It is estimated that the park is home to around 900 **mountain goats.** These nimble-footed creatures occupy all mountain peaks, living almost the entire year in the higher subalpine and alpine regions. The most accessible place to view these high-altitude hermits is along Parker's Ridge in the far northwestern corner of the park. The park's **bighorn sheep** have for the most part lost their fear of humans and often congregate at certain spots to lick salt from the road. Your best chance of seeing one of the park's 2,000–2,300 bighorn is at the south end of the Bow Valley Parkway, between switchbacks on the Mount Norquay Road, and just beyond Lake Minnewanka along the loop road.

Predators

Coyotes are widespread along the entire Bow River watershed. They are attracted to Vermilion Lakes by an abundance of small game, and many

have permanent dens there. **Wolves** had been driven close to extinction by the early 1950s, but today at least four wolf packs have been reported in the park. One pack winters close to town and is occasionally seen on Vermilion Lakes during that period. The **lynx** population fluctuates greatly; look for them in the backcountry during winter. **Cougars** are shy and number less than 20 in the park. They are occasionally seen along the front ranges behind Cascade Mountain.

Bears

The exhilaration of seeing one of these magnificent creatures in its natural habitat is unforgettable. From the road you're most likely to see **black bears,** which actually range in color from jet black to cinnamon brown and number around 50. Try the Bow Valley Parkway at dawn or late in the afternoon. Farther north they are occasionally seen near the road as it passes Cirrus Mountain. Banff's 60-odd **grizzly bears** spend most of the year in remote valleys, often on south-facing slopes away from the Bow Valley Corridor. During late spring they are occasionally seen in the area of Bow Pass.

The chance of encountering a bear face-to-face in the backcountry is remote. To lessen chances even further, you should take some simple precautions: Never hike alone or at dusk. Make lots of noise when passing through heavy vegetation. Keep a clean camp. Read the pamphlets available at all park visitor centers. At the Banff Visitor Centre, 224 Banff Avenue, daily trail reports list all recent bear sightings. Report any bears you see to the Warden's Office, 403/762-4506.

Reptiles and Amphibians

The **wandering garter snake** is rare and found only near the Cave and Basin, where warm water from the mineral spring flows down a shaded slope into Vermilion Lakes. Amphibians found in the park include the widespread **western toad;** the **wood frog,** commonly found along the Bow River; the rare **spotted frog;** and the **long-toed salamander,** which spawns in shallow ponds and spends summer under logs or rocks in the vicinity of its spawning grounds.

Birds

Although more than 240 species of birds have been recorded in the park, most are shy and live in heavily wooded areas. One species that definitely isn't shy is the fearless **gray jay,** which haunts all campgrounds and picnic areas. Similar in color, but larger, is the **Clark's nutcracker,** which lives in higher, subalpine forests. Another common bird is the black and white **magpie. Ravens** are frequently encountered, especially around campgrounds.

Several species of **woodpecker** live in subalpine forests. Several species of grouse are also in residence. Most common is the **downy ruffed grouse** seen in montane forest. The **blue grouse** and **spruce grouse** are seen at higher elevations, as is the **white-tailed ptarmigan,** which lives above the treeline. (Watch for them in Sunshine Meadows or on the Bow Summit Loop.) A colony of **black swifts** in Johnston Canyon is one of only two in the Canadian Rockies.

Good spots to view **dippers** and migrating waterfowl are Hector Lake, Vermilion Lakes, and the wetland area near Muleshoe Picnic Area. A bird blind has been set up below the Cave and Basin but is only worth visiting at dawn and dusk when the hordes of human visitors aren't around. Part of the nearby marsh stays ice free during winter, attracting **killdeer** and other birds.

Although raptors are not common in the park, **bald eagles** and **golden eagles** are present part of the year, and Alberta's provincial bird, the **great horned owl,** lives in the park year-round.

HISTORY

Although the valleys of the Canadian Rockies became ice free nearly 8,000 years ago and native people periodically have hunted in the area since that time, the story of Banff National Park really began with the arrival of the railroad to the area.

The Coming of the Railway

In 1871, Canadian prime minister John A. MacDonald promised to build a rail line linking British Columbia to the rest of the country as a condition of the new province joining the confederation. It wasn't until early 1883 that the line reached Calgary, pushing through to **Laggan,** now known as Lake Louise, that fall. The rail line was one of the largest and costliest engineering jobs ever undertaken in Canada.

Discovery of the Cave and Basin

On November 8, 1883, three young railway workers—Franklin McCabe and William and Thomas McCardell—went prospecting for gold on their day off. After crossing the Bow River by raft, they came across a warm stream and traced it to its source at a small log-choked basin of warm water that had a distinct smell of sulphur. Nearby they detected the source of the foul smell coming from a hole in the ground. Nervously, one of the three men lowered himself into the hole and came across a subterranean pool of aqua-green warm water. The three men had not found gold, but something just as precious—a hot mineral spring that in time would attract wealthy customers from around the world. Word of the discovery soon got out, and the government encouraged visitors to the Cave and Basin as an ongoing source of revenue to support the new railway.

A 2,500-hectare (6,177-acre) reserve was established around the springs on November 25, 1885, and two years later the reserve was expanded and renamed **Rocky Mountains Park.** It was primarily a business enterprise centered around the unique springs and catering to wealthy patrons of the railway. At the turn of the 20th century, Canada had an abundance of wilderness; it certainly didn't need a park to preserve it. The only goal of Rocky Mountains Park was to generate income for the government and the Canadian Pacific Railway (CPR).

A Town Grows

After the discovery of the Cave and Basin across the Bow River from the railway station (then known as Siding 29), many commercial facilities sprang up along what is now Banff Avenue. The general manager of the CPR (later to become its vice president), William Cornelius Van Horne, was instrumental in creating a hotel business along the rail line. His most recognized achievement was the Banff Springs Hotel, which opened in 1888. It was the world's largest hotel at the time. Enterprising locals soon realized the area's potential and began opening restaurants, offering guided hunting and boating trips, and developing manicured gardens. Banff soon became Canada's best-known tourist resort, attracting visitors from around the world. It was named after Banffshire, the Scottish birthplace of George Stephen, the CPR's first president.

In 1902, the park boundary was again expanded to include 11,440 square km (4,417square miles) of the Canadian Rockies. This dramatic expansion meant that the park became not just a tourist resort but also home to existing coal-mining and logging operations and hydroelectric dams. Government officials saw no conflict of interest, actually stating that the coal mine and township at Bankhead added to the park's many attractions. Many of the forests were logged, providing wood for construction, while other areas were burned to allow clear sightings for surveyors' instruments.

After a restriction on automobiles in the park was lifted in 1916, Canada's best-known tourist resort also became its busiest. More and more commercial facilities sprang up, offering luxury and opulence amid the wilderness of the Canadian Rockies. Calgarians built summer cottages, and the town began advertising itself as a year-round destination. As attitudes began to change, the government set up a Dominion Parks Branch, whose first commissioner, J.B. Hawkins, believed that land set aside for parks should be used for recreation and education. Gradually, resource industries were phased out. Hawkins's work culminated in the National Parks Act of 1930, which in turn led Rocky Mountains Park to be renamed Banff National Park. The park's present boundaries, encompassing 6,641 square km (2,564 square miles), were established in 1964.

Icefields Parkway

Natives and early explorers found the swampy nature of the Bow Valley north of Lake Louise

WILD BILL PEYTO

These words from a friend sum up Bill Peyto—one of Banff's earliest characters and one of the Canadian Rockies' greatest guides: ". . . rarely speaking—his forte was doing things, not talking about them." In 1886, at the tender age of 18, Ebenezer William Peyto left England for Canada. After traveling extensively he settled in Banff and was hired as an apprentice guide for legendary outfitter Tom Wilson. Wearing a tilted sombrero, fringed buckskin coat, cartridge belt, hunting knife, and six-shooter, he looked more like a gunslinger than a mountain man.

As his reputation as a competent guide grew, so did the stories. While guiding clients on one occasion, he led them to his cabin. Before entering, Peyto threw stones in the front door until a loud snap was heard. It was a bear trap that he'd set up to catch a certain trapper who'd been stealing his food. One of the guests commented that if caught, the trapper would surely have died. "You're damned right he would have," Bill replied. "Then I'd have known for sure it was him."

In 1900, Peyto left Banff to fight in the Boer War and was promoted to corporal for bravery. This title was revoked before it became official after the army officials learned he'd "borrowed" an officer's jacket and several bottles of booze for the celebration. Returning to a hero's welcome in Banff, Peyto established an outfitting business and continued prospecting for copper in Simpson Pass. Although his outfitting business thrived, the death of his wife left him despondent. He built a house on Banff Avenue; its name, "Ain't it Hell," summed up his view of life.

In his later years, he became a warden in the Healy Creek–Sunshine district, where his exploits during the 1920s added to his already legendary name. After 20 years of service he retired, and in 1943, at the age of 75, he passed away. One of the park's most beautiful lakes is named after him, as are a glacier and a popular Banff watering hole (**Wild Bill's**—a designation he would have appreciated). His face also adorns the large signs welcoming visitors to Banff.

difficult for foot and horse travel. When heading north, they used instead the Pipestone River Valley to the east. Banff guide Bill Peyto led American explorer Walter Wilcox up the Bow Valley in 1896, to the high peaks along the Continental Divide northeast of Lake Louise. The first complete journey along this route was made by Jim Brewster in 1904. Soon after, A.P. Coleman made the arduous journey, becoming a strong supporter for the route aptly known as The Wonder Trail. During the Great Depression of the 1930s, as part of a relief-work project, construction began on what was to become the Icefields Parkway. The road was completed in 1939, and the first car traveled the route in 1940. In tribute to the excellence of the road's early construction, the original roadbed, when upgraded to its present standard in 1961, was followed nearly the entire way.

Town of Banff

For most of its existence, the town of Banff was run as a service center for park visitors by the Canadian Parks Service in Ottawa, a government department with plenty of economic resources but little idea about how to handle the day-to-day running of a midsized town. Any inconvenience this arrangement caused park residents was offset by cheap rent and subsidized services. In June 1988, Banff's residents voted to sever this tie, and on January 1, 1990, Banff officially became an incorporated town, no different than any other in Alberta (except that Parks Canada controls environmental protection within the town of Banff).

Development and the Future

The town of Banff is the largest urban center in any national park in the world. The official population is quoted as 7,700 full-time residents, but the town hosts 500 times this number of visitors annually. Demand for housing continues to grow faster than development will allow, real estate prices are high, and an ever-increasing number of visitors overload existing facilities. On the surface, Banff's commercialism seems to work against the national park's mandate—visitors park in multistory car parks, shops sell bearskin rugs, and trees are logged for new housing estates—but the situation is admittedly unique, since the park itself has grown from what was originally a money-making exercise.

Another subject of often-heated debate is the high percentage of property in the park owned by foreign interests, principally Japanese. Foreign investors bought into the area heavily in the 1980s and today own around one-third of Banff's hotel industry, including two of the three largest hotels. Non–English-speaking salespeople are common, and over half of all jobs advertised locally require fluent Japanese. These issues of continuing development, housing, and foreign ownership of property here in Canada's first national-park town will be debated well into this new millennium.

Sights and Drives

TOWN OF BANFF

Many visitors planning a trip to the national park don't realize that the town of Banff is a bustling commercial center. The town's location is magnificent. It is spread out along the Bow River, extending to the lower slopes of Sulphur Mountain to the south and Tunnel Mountain to the east. In one direction is the towering face of Mount Rundle, and in the other, framed by the buildings along Banff Avenue, is Cascade Mountain. A strip of hotels and motels lines the north end of Banff Avenue, while a profusion of shops, boutiques, cafés, and restaurants hugs the south end. Also at the south end, just over the Bow River, is the Park Administration Building. Here the road forks—to the right is the historic Cave and Basin Hot Springs, to the left the Fairmont

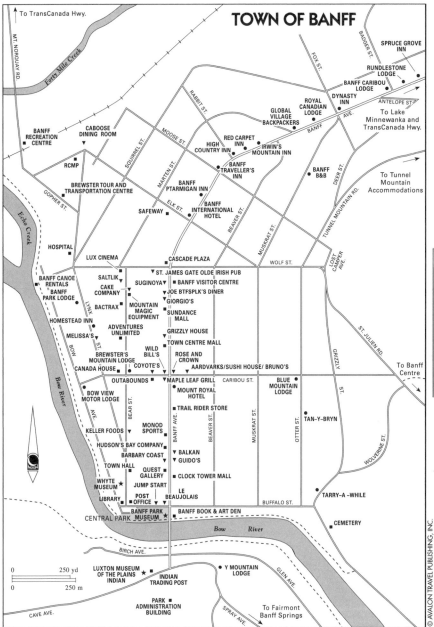

TOWN OF BANFF

To TransCanada Hwy.

MT. NORQUAY RD.

Forty Mile Creek

SPRUCE GROVE INN

RUNDLESTONE LODGE

BANFF CARIBOU LODGE

BADGER ST.

FOX ST.

DYNASTY INN

ANTELOPE ST.

To Lake Minnewanka and TransCanada Hwy.

ROYAL CANADIAN LODGE

GLOBAL VILLAGE BACKPACKERS

RABBIT ST.

BANFF AVE.

DEER ST.

BANFF RECREATION CENTRE

CABOOSE DINING ROOM

MOOSE ST.

HIGH COUNTRY INN

RED CARPET INN

IRWIN'S MOUNTAIN INN

BANFF TRAVELLER'S INN

BANFF B&B

RCMP

SQUIRREL ST.

MARTEN ST.

BANFF PTARMIGAN INN

GOPHER ST.

BREWSTER TOUR AND TRANSPORTATION CENTRE

ELK ST.

SAFEWAY

BANFF INTERNATIONAL HOTEL

BEAVER ST.

MUSKRAT ST.

TUNNEL MOUNTAIN RD.

To Tunnel Mountain Accommodations

Echo Creek

HOSPITAL

LUX CINEMA

CASCADE PLAZA

WOLF ST.

LOST CAMPER AVE.

BANFF CANOE RENTALS

BANFF PARK LODGE

SALTLIK

ST. JAMES GATE OLDE IRISH PUB

SUGINOYA

BANFF VISITOR CENTRE

CAKE COMPANY

JOE BTFSPLK'S DINER

GIORGIO'S

BACTRAX

MOUNTAIN MAGIC EQUIPMENT

SUNDANCE MALL

HOMESTEAD INN

LYNX ST.

ADVENTURES UNLIMITED

GRIZZLY HOUSE

ST. JULIEN RD.

MELISSA'S

BOW AVE.

WILD BILL'S

TOWN CENTRE MALL

ROSE AND CROWN

GRIZZLY ST.

To Banff Centre

BREWSTER'S MOUNTAIN LODGE

COYOTE'S

AARDVARKS/SUSHI HOUSE/ BRUNO'S

CANADA HOUSE

Bow River

OUTABOUNDS

MAPLE LEAF GRILL

CARIBOU ST.

BLUE MOUNTAIN LODGE

BOW VIEW MOTOR LODGE

MOUNT ROYAL HOTEL

BEAR ST.

BANFF AVE.

BEAVER ST.

MUSKRAT ST.

OTTER ST.

WOLVERINE ST.

TRAIL RIDER STORE

TAN-Y-BRYN

KELLER FOODS

MONOD SPORTS

HUDSON'S BAY COMPANY

BARBARY COAST

TOWN HALL

BALKAN

GUIDO'S

QUEST GALLERY

WHYTE MUSEUM

JUMP START

CLOCK TOWER MALL

LIBRARY

POST OFFICE

LE BEAUJOLAIS

TARRY-A-WHILE

BUFFALO ST.

BANFF PARK MUSEUM

CENTRAL PARK

BANFF BOOK & ART DEN

CEMETERY

Bow River

BIRCH AVE.

0   250 yd

0   250 m

LUXTON MUSEUM OF THE PLAINS INDIAN

INDIAN TRADING POST

Y MOUNTAIN LODGE

GLEN AVE.

PARK ADMINISTRATION BUILDING

SPRAY AVE.

To Fairmont Banff Springs

CAVE AVE.

© AVALON TRAVEL PUBLISHING, INC.

N

BANFF

Banff Springs and Banff Gondola. Some people are happy walking along the crowded streets or shopping in a truly unique setting; those more interested in some peace and quiet can easily slip into pristine wilderness just a five-minute walk from town.

Banff Park Museum

Although displays of stuffed animals are not usually associated with national parks, this museum, at 93 Banff Avenue, 403/762-1558, provides an insight into the park's early history. Visitors during the Victorian era were eager to see the park's animals without actually having to venture into the bush. A lack of roads and scarcity of large game resulting from hunting meant that the best places to see animals, stuffed or otherwise, were the game paddock, the zoo, and this museum, which was built in 1903. In its early years, the Banff Zoo and Aviary occupied the grounds behind the museum. The zoo kept more than 60 species of animals, including a polar bear. The museum itself was built before the park had electricity, hence the railroad pagoda design using skylights on all levels.

As times changed, the museum was considered outdated; plans for its demolition were put forward in the 1950s. Fortunately, the museum was spared and later restored for the park's 100th anniversary in 1985. While the exhibits still provide visitors with an insight into the intricate workings of various park ecosystems, they are also an interesting link to the park's past. The museum is open in summer daily 10 A.M.–6 P.M., the rest of the year daily 1–5 P.M. Staff lead a guided tour through the facility Mon.–Fri. at 3 P.M. and Sat.–Sun. at 2:30 P.M.; $4 adults, $3.50 seniors, $3 children. The museum also has a Discovery Room, where touching the displays is encouraged, and a reading room is stocked with books on the park.

Whyte Museum of the Canadian Rockies

The Whyte Foundation was established in the mid-1950s by local artists Peter and Catherine Whyte to help preserve artistic and historical material relating to the Canadian Rockies. Their

The Bow River flows through the heart of Banff.

museum opened in 1968 and has continued to grow ever since. It now houses the world's largest collection of Canadian Rockies literature and art. Included in the archives are more than 4,000 volumes, oral tapes of early pioneers and outfitters, antique postcards, old cameras, manuscripts, and a large photography collection. The highlight is the photography of Byron Harmon, whose black-and-white studies of mountain geography have shown people around the world the beauty of the Canadian Rockies. The downstairs gallery features changing art exhibitions. The museum also houses the library and archives of the Alpine Club of Canada. On the grounds are several heritage homes formerly occupied by local pioneers. The Whyte Museum is beside the library at 111 Bear Street, 403/762-2291. It's open year-round, daily 10 A.M.–5 P.M.; $6 adults, $3.50 seniors and children. Don't miss this one.

The Whyte Museum hosts a variety of interesting walking tours through summer. The most popular of these is the Historic Banff Walk, which departs from the museum daily at 11 A.M. and 3 P.M., taking around 90 minutes.

Natural History Museum

Banff's smallest museum, upstairs in the Clock Tower Mall at 112 Banff Avenue, 403/762-4652, is crammed with exhibits displaying the geological evolution of the Canadian Rockies. Highlights include a replica of Castleguard Cave (one of the largest caves in North America), an interesting slideshow, rock and fossil displays, and a tacky life-size model of Bigfoot—just what you came to Banff for. It's open in summer daily noon–5 P.M., the rest of the year Fri.–Sun. only.

Cascade Gardens

One of the earliest entrepreneurs to take advantage of Banff's hot springs was Dr. R.G. Brett. In 1886, he opened a private spa and hospital that became known as Brett's Sanatorium. It accommodated 90 guests, drawn to Banff by the claimed healing qualities of the hot springs' water. The hotel burned down in 1933 and was replaced in 1936 by the **Park Administration Building** that stands today on the south side of the Bow River. Here you'll have a commanding view along Banff Avenue and of Cascade Mountain. The surrounding gardens are immaculately manicured, making for enjoyable strolling on a sunny day.

Luxton Museum of the Plains Indian

Looking like a stockade, this museum west of the Banff Bridge at 1 Birch Avenue, 403/762-2388, is dedicated to the heritage of the natives who once inhabited the Canadian Rockies and adjacent prairies. It was named for prominent Banff resident Norman Luxton, who had a close relationship with the natives of the area and was involved in the Banff Indian Days (see special topic). He operated a trading post on the site for many years before opening the museum in 1952 with the help of the Glenbow-Alberta Institute. The museum contains memorabilia from Luxton's 60-year relationship with the Stoney, as well as an elaborately decorated tepee, hunting equipment, a few stuffed animals, a realistic diorama of a buffalo jump, peace pipes, and tradi-

tional clothing. The Indian Trading Post is now one of Banff's better gift shops and is definitely worth a browse. The museum is open in summer daily 10 A.M.–6 P.M., the rest of the year 11:30 A.M.–4:30 P.M.; $6 adults, $4 seniors, $2.50 children.

Cave and Basin National Historic Site

At the end of Cave Avenue, this historic site is the birthplace of Banff National Park and of the Canadian National Parks system. Here in 1883, three men employed by the CPR stumbled on the hot springs now known as the Cave and Basin and were soon lounging in the hot water—a real luxury in the Wild West. They built a fence around the springs, constructed a crude cabin, and began the long process of establishing a claim to the site. But the government beat them to it, settling their claims for a few thousand dollars and acquiring the hot springs.

Bathhouses were installed in 1887 and bathers paid 10 cents for a swim. The pools were eventually lined with concrete, and additions were built onto the original structures. Ironically, the soothing minerals in the water that had attracted millions of people to bathe here eventually caused the pools' demise. The minerals, combined with chlorine, produced sediments that ate away at the concrete structure until the pools were deemed unsafe. After closing in 1975, the pools were restored to their original look at a cost of $12 million. They reopened in 1985 only to close again in 1993 for the same reasons, coupled with flagging popularity.

Although the pools are now closed for swimming, the center is still one of Banff's most popular attractions. Interpretive displays describe the hows and whys of the springs. A narrow tunnel winds into the dimly lit cave, and short trails lead from the center to the cave entrance and through a unique environment created by the hot water from the springs. Interpretive tours begin four times daily in summer. The site is open in summer daily 9 A.M.–6 P.M., the rest of the year Mon.–Fri. 11 A.M.–4 P.M., Sat.–Sun. 9:30 A.M.–5 P.M.; $4 adults, $3.50 seniors, $3 children. For more information, call 403/762-1566.

Upper Hot Springs

These springs on Mountain Avenue, toward Banff Mountain Gondola, were first developed in 1901. The present building was completed in 1935, with extensive renovations made in 1996. Water flows out of the bedrock at 47°C and is cooled to 40°C in the main pool. Once considered for privatization, the springs are still run by Parks Canada and are popular throughout the year. Swimming is $7.50 adults, $6.50 seniors and children; lockers and towel rental extra. Within the complex is **Pleiades Massage Therapy & Spa,** offering a wide range of therapeutic treatments including massages from $45 for 30 minutes as well as body wraps, aromatherapy, and hydrotherapy. The facility, 403/762-1515, is open in summer daily 9 A.M.–11 P.M., the rest of the year 10 A.M.–10 P.M.

Banff Gondola

The easiest way to get high above town without breaking a sweat is on this newly renovated gondola, 403/762-2523, which rises 700 meters (2,300 feet) in eight minutes to the summit of 2,285-meter (7,500-foot) **Sulphur Mountain.** From the observation deck at the upper terminal, the breathtaking view includes the town, Bow Valley, Cascade Mountain, Lake Minnewanka, and the Fairholme Range. Bighorn sheep often hang around the upper terminal. The short **Vista Trail** leads along a ridge to a restored weather observatory. Between 1903 and 1931, long before the gondola was built, Norman Sanson was the meteorological observer who collected data at the station. During this period he made more than 1,000 ascents of Sulphur Mountain, all in the line of duty.

The **Summit Restaurant,** 403/762-7486, serves up mediocre food, inexpensive breakfasts, and priceless views. The gondola runs in summer 7:30 A.M.–9 P.M., shorter hours the rest of the year; closed the first two weeks of January; $20 adults, $10 children. From downtown the gondola is three km (1.9 miles) along Mountain Avenue. In summer **Brewster,** 403/762-6717, provides shuttle service to the gondola from downtown hotels ($29 includes gondola ride).

A 5.5-km (3.4-mile) hiking trail to the summit begins from the Upper Hot Springs parking lot. Although it's a long slog, views on the way up are good, and you'll be rewarded with a free gondola ride down—they don't check tickets at the top.

Fairmont Banff Springs

On a terrace above a bend in the Bow River is one of the largest, grandest, and most opulent mountain-resort hotels in the world. What better way to spend a rainy afternoon than to explore this turreted 20th-century castle, seeking out a writing desk overlooking one of the world's most-photographed scenes and penning a long letter to the folks back home?

"The Springs" has grown with the town and is an integral part of local history. William Cornelius Van Horne, vice president of the CPR, decided that the best way of encouraging customers to travel on his newly completed rail line across the Rockies was to build a series of luxurious mountain accommodations. The largest of these was begun in 1886, as close as possible to Banff's newly discovered hot springs. The location chosen had magnificent views and was only a short carriage ride from the train station. Money was no object, and architect Bruce Price began designing a mountain resort the likes of which the world had never seen. At some stage of construction his plans were misinterpreted, and much to Van Horne's shock the building was built back to front. The best guest rooms faced the forested slopes of Sulphur Mountain while the kitchen had panoramic views of the Bow Valley.

On June 1, 1888, it opened, the largest hotel in the world, with 250 rooms beginning at $3.50 per night including meals. Water from the nearby hot springs was piped into the hotel's steam baths. Rumor has it that when the pipes blocked, water from the Bow River was used, secretly supplemented by bags of sulphur-smelling chemicals. Overnight, the quiet community of Banff became a destination resort for wealthy guests from around the world, and the hotel soon became one of North America's most popular accommodations. Every room

© ANDREW HEMPSTEAD

Fairmont Banff Springs is one of the world's great mountain resorts.

BANFF

was booked every day during the short summer seasons. In 1903, a wing was added, doubling the hotel's capacity. The following year a tower was added to each wing. Guest numbers reached 22,000 in 1911, and construction of a new hotel, designed by Walter Painter, began that year. The original design—an 11-story tower joining two wings in a baronial style—was reminiscent of a Scottish castle mixed with a French country chateau. This concrete-and-rock-faced, green-roofed building stood as it did at its completion in 1928 until 1999, when an ambitious multiyear program of renovations commenced. At first, the most obvious change to those who have visited before will be the new lobby, moved to a more accessible location, but all rooms have also been refurbished, and many of the restaurants changed or upgraded. The Canadian Pacific moniker remained part of the Banff Spring's official name until 2000, when the hotel, and all other Canadian Pacific hotels, became part of the Fairmont Hotels and Resorts chain.

Don't let the hotel's opulence keep you from spending time here. Visit the hotel between 11:30 A.M.–1:30 P.M., and enjoy a huge buffet lunch combined with a 30-minute **Historic Castle Tour** for $26.95 per person. Call 403/762-2211 for details. Otherwise wander through on your own, admiring the 5,000 pieces of furniture and antiques (most of those in public areas are reproductions), paintings, prints, tapestries, and rugs. Take in the medieval atmosphere of Mount Stephen Hall with its lime flagstone floor, enormous windows, and large oak beams; take advantage of the luxurious spa facility (see Willow Stream under "Indoor Recreation," later in this chapter), or relax in one of 12 eateries or four lounges.

The hotel is a 15-minute walk southeast of town, either along Spray Avenue or via the trail along the south bank of the Bow River. **Banff Transit** buses leave Banff Avenue for the Springs twice an hour; $1 adults, 50 cents children. Alternatively, horse-drawn buggies take passengers from the Trail Rider Store at 132 Banff Avenue, 403/762-4551, to the Springs for about $70 for two passengers.

Bow Falls

Small but spectacular Bow Falls is below the Fairmont Banff Springs, only a short walk from downtown. The waterfall is the result of a dramatic change in the course of the Bow River brought about by glaciation. At one time the river flowed north of Tunnel Mountain and out of the mountains via the valley of Lake Minnewanka. As the glaciers retreated, they left terminal moraines, forming natural dams and changing the course of the river. Eventually the backed-up water found an outlet here between Tunnel Mountain and the northwest ridge of Mount Rundle. The falls are most spectacular in late spring when runoff from the winter snows fills every river and stream in the Bow Valley watershed.

To get there from town, cross the bridge at the south end of Banff Avenue, scramble down the grassy embankment to the left, and follow a pleasant trail along the Bow River to a point above the falls. This easy walk is one km (0.6 miles); 20 minutes each way. By car, cross the bridge and follow Golf Course signs. From the falls a paved road crosses the Spray River and passes through the golf course.

Banff Centre

On the lower slopes of Tunnel Mountain is Banff Centre, whose surroundings provide inspiration as one of Canada's leading centers for postgraduate students in a variety of disciplines, including Mountain Culture, Arts, and Leadership Development. The Banff Centre opened in the summer of 1933 as a theater school. Since then it has grown to become a prestigious institution attracting artists of many disciplines from throughout Canada. The Centre's **Walter Phillips Gallery,** on St. Julien Road, 403/762-6281, presents changing exhibits of visual arts from throughout the world. Open Tuesday–Sunday noon–5 P.M.

Activities are held on the grounds of the Banff Centre year-round. Highlights include a summer educational program, concerts, displays, live performances, the Playbill Series, the Banff Arts Festival, and Banff Mountain Festivals, to name a few (see "Festivals and Events" section). Call 403/762-6100 for a program, go

© ANDREW HEMPSTEAD

Vermilion Lakes and Mount Rundle

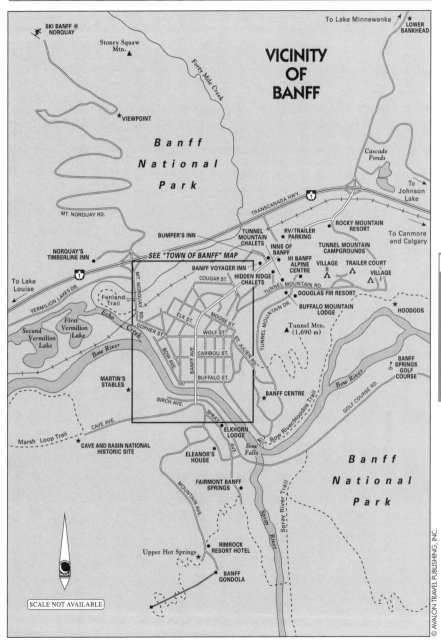

SKI BANFF @ NORQUAY

To Lake Minnewanka

LOWER BANKHEAD

Stoney Squaw Mtn.

VIEWPOINT

VICINITY OF BANFF

Banff

National

Park

Cascade Ponds

To Johnson Lake

TRANSCANADA HWY.

MT. NORQUAY RD.

To Canmore and Calgary

ROCKY MOUNTAIN RESORT

BUMPER'S INN

TUNNEL MOUNTAIN CHALETS

RV/TRAILER PARKING

TUNNEL MOUNTAIN CAMPGROUNDS

INNS OF BANFF

NORQUAY'S TIMBERLINE INN

SEE "TOWN OF BANFF" MAP

HI BANFF ALPINE CENTRE

VILLAGE II

TRAILER COURT

VILLAGE

BANFF VOYAGER INN

COUGAR ST.

HIDDEN RIDGE CHALETS

TUNNEL MOUNTAIN RD.

To Lake Louise

VERMILION LAKES DR.

Fenland Trail

Echo Creek

First Vermilion Lake

DOUGLAS FIR RESORT

BUFFALO MOUNTAIN LODGE

HOODOOS

MT. NORQUAY RD.

GOPHER ST.

ELK ST.

MOOSE ST.

Tunnel Mtn. (1,690 m)

Second Vermilion Lake

WOLF ST.

Bow River

BOW AVE.

BANFF AVE.

CARIBOU ST.

ST. JULIEN RD.

TUNNEL MOUNTAIN DR.

Bow River

BANFF SPRINGS GOLF COURSE

MARTIN'S STABLES

BUFFALO ST.

BIRCH AVE.

BANFF CENTRE

Bow River Hoodoos Trail

GOLF COURSE RD.

Marsh Loop Trail

CAVE AVE.

SPRAY AVE.

ELKHORN LODGE

CAVE AND BASIN NATIONAL HISTORIC SITE

ELEANOR'S HOUSE

Bow Falls

Banff

National

Park

FAIRMONT BANFF SPRINGS

MOUNTAIN AVE.

Spray River

Spray River Trail

Upper Hot Springs

RIMROCK RESORT HOTEL

BANFF GONDOLA

SCALE NOT AVAILABLE

BANFF

© AVALON TRAVEL PUBLISHING, INC.

to the website www.banffcentre.ca, or check the *Crag and Canyon* (published weekly on Wednesday).

VICINITY OF BANFF
Vermilion Lakes

This series of shallow lakes forms an expansive montane wetland supporting a variety of mammals and 238 species of birds. Vermilion Lakes Drive, paralleling the TransCanada Highway immediately west of Banff, provides the easiest access to the area. The level of **First Vermilion Lake** was once controlled by a dam. Since its removal, the level of the lake has dropped. This is the beginning of a long process that will eventually see the area evolve into a floodplain forest such as is found along the Fenland Trail. **Second** and **Third**

Vermilion Lakes have a higher water level that is controlled naturally by beaver dams. Near First Vermilion Lake is an active osprey nest. The entire area is excellent for wildlife viewing, especially in winter when it provides habitat for elk, coyote, and the occasional wolf.

Mount Norquay Road

One of the best views of town accessible by vehicle is on this road, which switchbacks steeply to the base of Ski Banff @ Norquay, the local hangout for skiers and boarders. On the way up are several lookouts, including one near the top where bighorn sheep often graze.

To Lake Minnewanka

Lake Minnewanka Road begins where Banff Avenue ends at the northeast end of town. An

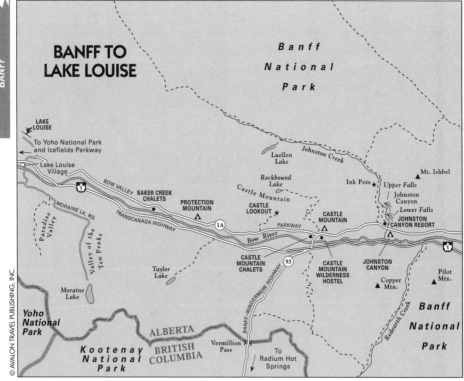

alternative to driving along Banff Avenue is to take Buffalo Street, opposite the Banff Park Museum, and follow it around Tunnel Mountain, passing the hostel, campground, and several viewpoints of the north face of Mount Rundle, rising vertically from the forested valley. This road eventually rejoins Banff Avenue at the Banff Rocky Mountain Resort.

The first road to the right after passing under the TransCanada Highway leads to **Cascade Ponds,** a popular day-use area. The next turnout along this road is at **Lower Bankhead.** During the early 1900s, Bankhead was a booming mining town producing 200,000 tons of coal a year. The poor quality of coal and bitter labor disputes led to the mine's closure in 1922. Soon after, all the buildings were moved or demolished. Although for many years the mine had brought prosperity to the park, peoples' perceptions changed. The National Parks Act of 1930, which prohibited the establishment of mining claims in national parks, was greeted with little animosity.

From the parking lot at Lower Bankhead, a 1.1-km (0.7-mile) interpretive trail leads through the industrial section of the town and past an old mine train. The town's 1,000 residents lived on the other side of the road at what is now known as **Upper Bankhead.** Just before the Upper Bankhead turnoff, the foundation of the Holy Trinity Church can be seen on the side of the hill to the right. Not much remains of Upper Bankhead. It is now a day-use area with picnic tables, kitchen shelters, and firewood. Through the meadow to the west of here are some large slag heaps, concealed mine entrances, and various stone foundations.

Lake Minnewanka

Minnewanka (Lake of the Water Spirit) is the largest body of water in Banff National Park. Mount Inglismaldie (2,964 meters/9,720 feet) and the Fairholme Range form an imposing backdrop. The reservoir was first constructed in 1912, and additional dams were built in 1922 and 1941 to supply hydroelectric power to Banff. **Minnewanka Landing** was a resort village that was submerged when the most recent dam went in. It's now a popular spot for scuba diving.

Lake Minnewanka Boat Tours, 403/762-3473, has a 90-minute cruise to the far reaches of the lake, passing the Devil's Gap formation. It departs from the dock mid-May to the end of September 3–5 times daily (first sailing is 10:30 A.M. and costs $28 adults, $12 children. Brewster, 403/762-6717, offers this cruise combined with a bus tour from Banff for $46 per person. Easy walking trails lead along the western shore. The lake is great for fishing (lake trout to 15 kg/33 lbs) and is the only one in the park where motorboats are allowed. Lake Minnewanka Boat Tours rents aluminum boats with small outboard engines and represents local fishing guides.

From Lake Minnewanka the road continues

BANFF

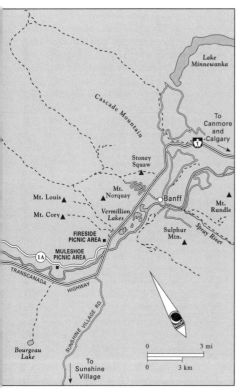

along the reservoir wall, passing a plaque commemorating the Palliser Expedition, to **Johnson Lake,** which has a lakeside trail, good swimming, and picnic facilities with views across to Mount Rundle.

BOW VALLEY PARKWAY

Two roads link Banff to Lake Louise. The Trans Canada Highway is the quicker route, more popular with through traffic. The other is the more scenic 51-km (32-mile) Bow Valley Parkway, which branches off the TransCanada Highway five km (3.1 miles) west of Banff. Cyclists will appreciate this road's two long, divided sections and low speed limit (60 kph/37 mph). Along this route are several impressive viewpoints, interpretive displays, picnic areas, good hiking, great opportunities for viewing wildlife, a hostel, three lodges, campgrounds, and one of the park's best restaurants (see "Accommodations" and "Food"). Between March 1 and late June, the southern end of the parkway (as far north as Johnston Canyon) is closed daily 6 P.M.–9 A.M. for the protection of wildlife.

As you enter the parkway, you pass the quiet, creekside **Fireside** picnic area, where an interpretive display describes how the Bow Valley was formed. At **Backswamp Viewpoint,** you can look upstream to the site of a former dam, now a swampy wetland filled with aquatic vegetation. Farther along the road is another wetland at **Muleshoe.** This wetland consists of oxbow lakes that were formed when the Bow River changed its course and abandoned its meanders for a more direct path. Across the parkway is a one-km (0.6-mile) trail that climbs to a viewpoint overlooking the valley. (The slope around this trail is infested with wood ticks during late spring/early summer, so be sure to check yourself carefully after hiking in this area.) To the east, **Hole-in-the-wall** is visible. This large-mouthed cave was created by the Bow Glacier, which once filled the valley. As the glacier receded, its meltwater dissolved the soft limestone bedrock, creating what is known as a solution cave.

Beyond Muleshoe the road inexplicably divides for a few car lengths. A large white spruce stood on the island until it blew down in 1984. The story goes that while the road was being constructed, a surly foreman was asleep in the shade of the tree, and not daring to rouse him, workers cleared the roadway around him. The road then passes through particularly hilly terrain, part of a massive rockslide that occurred approximately 8,000 years ago.

Continuing down the parkway you'll pass the following sights.

Johnston Canyon

Johnston Creek drops over a series of spectacular waterfalls here, deep within the chasm it has carved into the limestone bedrock. The canyon is not nearly as deep as Maligne Canyon in Jasper National Park—30 meters (100 feet) at its deepest, compared to 50 meters (165 feet) at Maligne—but the catwalk that leads to the lower falls has been built through the depths of the canyon rather than along its lip, making it seem just as spectacular. The lower falls are one km (0.6 miles) from Johnston Canyon Resort, while the equally spectacular upper falls are a further 1.6 km (one mile) upstream. Beyond this point are the **Ink Pots,** mineral springs whose sediments reflect sunlight, producing a brilliant aqua color. While in the canyon, look for nesting great gray owls and black swifts.

Silver City

At the west end of **Moose Meadows,** a small plaque marks the site of Silver City. At its peak this boomtown had a population of 2,000, making it bigger than Calgary at the time. The city was founded by John Healy, who also founded the notorious Fort Whoop-Up in Lethbridge. During its heady days, five mines were operating, extracting not silver but ore rich in copper and lead. The town had a half-dozen hotels, four or five stores, two real-estate offices, and a station on the transcontinental rail line when its demise began. Two men, named Patton and Pettigrew, salted their mine with gold and silver ore to attract investors.

"LAKE OF LITTLE FISHES"

During the summer of 1882, outfitter Tom Wilson was camped near the confluence of the Bow and Pipestone Rivers when he heard the distant rumblings of an avalanche. He questioned Stoney Indian guides and was told the noises originated from "Lake of Little Fishes." The following day Wilson, led by a native guide, hiked to the lake to investigate. He became the first white man to lay eyes on what he named Emerald Lake. Two years later, the name was changed to Lake Louise, honoring Princess Louise Caroline Alberta, daughter of Queen Victoria.

In 1890, as word of the lake's beauty spread, a modest two-bedroom wooden hotel replaced the crude cabin that had been built on the lakeshore. The coming of the transcontinental railroad further increased the lake's popularity. A railway station known as Laggan was built where the rail line passed closest to the lake, six km (3.7 miles) away. (Until a road was completed in 1926, everyone arrived by train.) The station's name was changed to Lake Louise in 1913 to prevent confusion among visitors. The hotel by the lake continued to prosper. After many additions, a disastrous fire, and the construction of a new concrete wing in 1925, the chateau of today took shape.

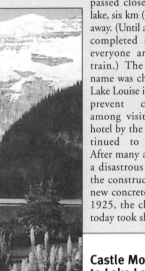

© ANDREW HEMPSTEAD

Lake Louise

After selling 2,000 shares at $5 each, they vanished, leaving investors with a useless mine. Investment in the town ceased, mines closed, and the people left. Only one man refused to leave. His name was James Smith, but he was known to everyone as Joe. In 1887, when Silver City came under the jurisdiction of the National Parks Service, Joe was allowed to remain. He did so and was friendly to everyone, including Stoney Indians, Father Albert Lacombe who occasionally stopped by, well-known Banff guide Tom Wilson, and of course to the animals who grazed around his cabin. By 1926, he was unable to trap or hunt due to failing eyesight, and many people tried to persuade him to leave. It wasn't until 1937 that he finally moved to a Calgary retirement home, where he died soon after.

Castle Mountain to Lake Louise

After leaving the former site of Silver City, the aptly named Castle Mountain comes into view. It's one of the park's most recognizable peaks and most interesting geographical features. The mountain consists of very old rock (approximately 500 million years old) sitting atop much younger rock (a mere 200 million years old). This unusual situation occurred as the mountains were forced upward by pressure below the earth's surface, thrusting the older rock up and over the younger rock in places.

The road skirts the base of the mountain, passes Castle Mountain Village (which has gas, food, and accommodations), and climbs a small hill to Storm Mountain Viewpoint, which provides more stunning views and a picnic area. The next

BANFF

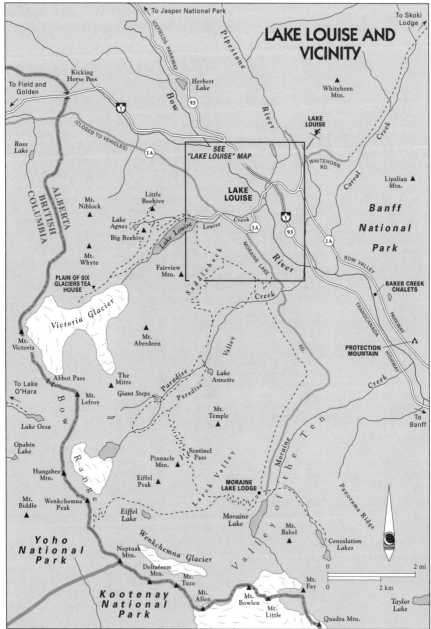

LAKE LOUISE AND VICINITY

commercial facility is **Baker Creek Chalets and Bistro,** an excellent spot for a meal. Then it's on to another viewpoint at Morant's Curve, from where Temple Mountain is visible. After passing another picnic area and a chunk of Precambrian shield, the road rejoins the TransCanada Highway at Lake Louise.

LAKE LOUISE AND VICINITY

When you see the first flush of morning sun hit Victoria Glacier and the impossibly steep northern face of Mount Victoria reflected in the sparkling, emerald-green waters of Lake Louise, you'll understand why this lake is regarded as one of the world's seven natural wonders. Overlooking the magnificent scene, Fairmont Chateau Lake Louise is without a doubt one of the world's most photographed hotels. Apart from staring, photographing, and videotaping, the area has plenty to keep you busy. Nearby you'll find some of the park's best hiking, canoeing, and horseback riding. Only a short distance away is Moraine Lake, not as famous as Lake Louise but rivaling it in beauty.

Lake Louise is 56 km (35 miles) northwest of Banff along the TransCanada Highway, or a little bit longer if you take the quieter Bow Valley Parkway. The hamlet of Lake Louise, composed of a small mall, hotels, and restaurants, is in the Bow Valley, just west of the TransCanada Highway. The lake itself is 200 vertical meters (660 vertical feet) above the valley floor, along a winding four-km (2.5-mile) road. Across the valley is Canada's second-largest winter resort, also called Lake Louise. It's a world-class facility renowned for diverse terrain, abundant snow, and breathtaking views.

From Lake Louise the TransCanada Highway continues west, exiting the park over Kicking Horse Pass (1,647 meters/5,400 feet) and passing through Yoho National Park to Golden. Highway 93, the famous Icefields Parkway, begins one km (0.6 miles) north of the village and heads northwest through the park's northern reaches to Jasper National Park.

Lake Louise

In summer, about 10,000 visitors per day make the journey from the Bow Valley floor up to Lake Louise. By noon the tiered parking lot is often full. An alternative to the road is one of two hiking trails that begin in the village and end at the public parking lot (see "Hiking"). From here several paved trails lead to the lake's eastern shore. From these vantage points the dramatic setting can be fully appreciated. The lake is 2.4 km (1.5 miles) long, 500 meters (1,640 feet) wide, and up to 90 meters (295 feet) deep. Its cold waters reach a maximum temperature of 4°C (39°F) in August.

Fairmont Chateau Lake Louise is a tourist attraction in itself. Built by the CPR to take the pressure off the popular Fairmont Banff Springs, the chateau has seen many changes in the last 100 years, yet it remains one of the world's great mountain resorts. No one minds the hordes of camera-toting tourists who traipse through each day—and there's really no way to avoid them. The immaculately manicured gardens between the chateau and the lake make an interesting foreground for the millions of Lake Louise photographs taken each year. At the lakeshore boathouse, canoes are rented for $30 per hour.

The snow-covered peak at the back of the lake is **Mount Victoria** (3,459 meters/11,350 feet), which sits on the Continental Divide. Amazingly, its base is more than 10 km (6.2 miles) from the eastern end of the lake. Mount Victoria, first climbed in 1897, remains one of the park's most popular peaks for mountaineers. Although the difficult northeast face (facing the chateau) was first successfully ascended in 1922, the most popular and easiest route to the summit is along the southeast ridge, approached from Abbot Pass.

Moraine Lake

Although less than half the size of Lake Louise, Moraine Lake is just as spectacular and worthy of just as much film. It is located up a winding road 13 km (eight miles) off Lake Louise Drive. Its rugged setting, nestled in the Valley of the Ten Peaks among the towering mountains of the main ranges, has provided inspiration for millions of people from around the world since

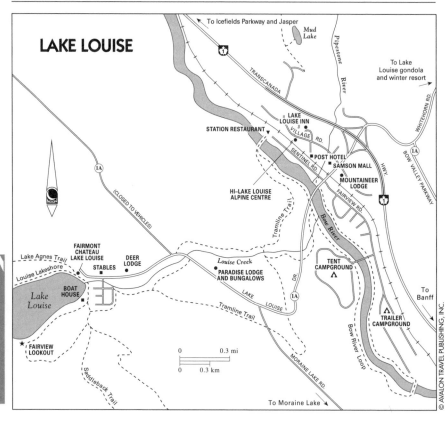

LAKE LOUISE

To Icefields Parkway and Jasper

Mud Lake

Pipestone River

To Lake Louise gondola and winter resort

TRANSCANADA

WHITEHORN RD.

LAKE LOUISE INN

STATION RESTAURANT

VILLAGE RD.

SENTINEL RD.

POST HOTEL

SAMSON MALL

MOUNTAINEER LODGE

FAIRVIEW RD.

HI-LAKE LOUISE ALPINE CENTRE

BOW VALLEY PARKWAY

(CLOSED TO VEHICLES)

Tramline Trail

Bow River

FAIRMONT CHATEAU LAKE LOUISE

Lake Agnes Trail

Louise Lakeshore

STABLES

DEER LODGE

Louise Creek

PARADISE LODGE AND BUNGALOWS

TENT CAMPGROUND

BOAT HOUSE

Lake Louise

LAKE LOUISE DR.

To Banff

Tramline Trail

TRAILER CAMPGROUND

FAIRVIEW LOOKOUT

Saddleback Trail

0   0.3 mi
0   0.3 km

Bow River Loop

MORAINE LAKE RD.

To Moraine Lake

© AVALON TRAVEL PUBLISHING, INC.

BANFF

Walter Wilcox became the first white man to reach its shore in 1899. Wilcox's subsequent writings—such as "no scene has given me an equal impression of inspiring solitude and rugged grandeur"—guaranteed the lake's future popularity. Although Wilcox was a knowledgeable man, he named the lake on the assumption that it was dammed by a glacial moraine deposited by the retreating Wenkchemna Glacier. In fact, the large rock pile that blocks its waters was deposited by major rockfalls from the Tower of Babel to the south. The lake often remains frozen until June, and the access road is closed all winter. A trail leads along the lake's northern shore, and canoes are rented for $25 per hour from the concession below the lodge.

Lake Louise Sightseeing Gondola

During summer the Friendly Giant at Lake Louise winter resort whisks visitors up the face of Mount Whitehorn to Whitehorn Lodge in either open chairs or enclosed gondola cars. The view from the top—at an altitude of more than two km (1.2 miles) above sea level across the Bow Valley, Lake Louise, and the Continental Divide—is among the most spectacular in the Canadian Rockies. Short trails lead through the forests, across open meadows, and, for the energetic, to the summit of Mount Whitehorn, more than 600 vertical meters (1,970 vertical feet) above. Visitors are free to walk these trails, but guided walks are complimentary and leave regularly from the Interpretation Centre. After working up an appetite (and working off breakfast), head to the teahouse in the Whitehorn Lodge, try the outdoor barbecue, or back at the base area, enjoy lunch at the Lodge of the Ten Peaks, the resort's impressive post-and-beam day lodge. The lift operates mid-May to mid-September daily 8:30 A.M.–6 P.M.; $18.95 adults, $16.95 seniors, $8.95 children. Pay an extra $2 per person and have a buffet breakfast (from 7:30 A.M.) included with the gondola ride. For more information, call 403/522-3555. Free shuttles run from Lake Louise accommodations to the day lodge.

ICEFIELDS PARKWAY

The 230-km (143-mile) Icefields Parkway, between Lake Louise and Jasper, is one of the most scenic, exciting, and inspiring mountain roads ever built. From Lake Louise it parallels the Continental Divide, following in the shadow of the highest, most rugged mountains in the Canadian Rockies. The first 122 km (76 miles) to Sunwapta Pass (the boundary between Banff and Jasper National Parks) can be driven in two hours, and the entire parkway in four hours. But it's likely you'll want to spend at least a day, probably more, stopping at each of the 13 viewpoints, hiking the trails, watching the abundant wildlife, and just generally enjoying one of the world's most magnificent landscapes. Along the section within Banff National Park are two lodges, three hostels, three campgrounds, and one gas station.

Although the road is steep and winding in places, it has a wide shoulder, making it ideal for an extended bike trip. Allow seven days to pedal north from Banff to Jasper, staying at hostels or camping along the route. This is the preferable direction to travel by bike because the elevation at the town of Jasper is more than 500 meters (1,640 feet) lower than either Banff or Lake Louise.

The parkway remains open year-round, although winter brings with it some special considerations. The road is often closed for short periods for avalanche control—check road conditions in Banff or Lake Louise before setting

out. And be sure to fill up with gas; no services are available between November and April.

Lake Louise to Crowfoot Glacier

The Icefields Parkway forks right from the Trans Canada Highway just north of Lake Louise. The impressive scenery begins immediately. Just three km (1.9 miles) from the junction is **Herbert Lake,** formed during the last Ice Age, when retreating glaciers deposited a pile of rubble—known as a *moraine*—across a shallow valley and water filled in behind it. The lake is a perfect place for early morning or evening photography, when the Waputik Range and distinctively shaped **Mount Temple** are reflected in its waters.

Traveling north, you'll notice numerous depressions in the steep, shaded slopes of the Waputik Range across the Bow Valley. The cooler climate on these north-facing slopes makes them prone to glaciation. Cirques were cut by small local glaciers. On the opposite side of the road, **Mount Hector** (3,394 meters/11,130 feet), easily recognized by its layered peak, soon comes into view.

Hector Lake Viewpoint is 16 km (10 miles) from the junction. Although the view is partially obscured by trees, the emerald-green waters nestled below a massive wall of limestone form a breathtaking scene. **Bow Peak,** seen looking northward along the highway, is only 2,868 meters (9,410 feet) high but is completely detached from the Waputik Range, making it a popular destination for climbers. As you leave this viewpoint, look across the northeast end of Hector Lake for glimpses of **Mount Balfour** (3,246 meters/10,650) on the distant skyline.

Crowfoot Glacier

The aptly named Crowfoot Glacier can best be appreciated from a viewpoint 17 km (10.6 miles) north of Hector Lake. The glacier sits on a wide ledge near the top of Crowfoot Mountain, from where its glacial claws cling to the mountain's steep slopes. The retreat of this glacier has been dramatic. Only 50 years ago, two of the claws extended to the base of the lower cliff. Today, they are a shadow of their former self, barely reaching over the cliff edge.

Bow Lake

The sparkling, translucent waters of Bow Lake are among the most beautiful that can be seen from the Icefields Parkway. The lake was created when moraines deposited by retreating glaciers dammed subsequent meltwater. On still days, the water reflects the snowy peaks, their sheer cliffs, and the scree slopes that run into the lake. You don't need photography experience to take good pictures here! At the southeast end of the lake, a day-use area offers waterfront picnic tables and a trail to a swampy area at the lake's outlet. At the upper end of the lake, you'll find a historic Num-ti-jah Lodge and the trailhead for a walk to Bow Glacier Falls (see "Hiking").

The road leaves Bow Lake and climbs to **Bow Summit.** Looking back toward the lake, its true color becomes apparent, and the Crowfoot Glacier reveals its unique shape. At an elevation of 2,069 meters (6,790 feet), this pass is one of the highest points crossed by a public road in Canada. It is also the beginning of the Bow River, the one you camped beside at Lake Louise, photographed flowing through the town of Banff, and fished along downstream of Canmore.

Peyto Lake

From the parking lot at Bow Summit, a short paved trail leads to one of the most breathtaking views you could ever imagine. Far below the viewpoint is Peyto Lake, an impossibly intense green lake whose hues change according to season. Before heavy melting of nearby glaciers begins (in June or early July), the lake is dark blue. As summer progresses, meltwater flows across a delta and into the lake. This water is laden with finely ground particles of rock debris known as rock flour, which remains suspended in the water. It is not the mineral content of the rock flour that is responsible for the lake's unique color, but rather the particles reflecting the blue-green sector of the light spectrum. As the amount of suspended rock flour changes, so does the color of the lake.

The lake is one of many park landmarks named for early outfitter Bill Peyto (see special topic). In 1898, Peyto was part of an expedition camped at Bow Lake. Seeking solitude (as he was wont to do), he slipped off during the night to sleep near this lake. Other members of the party coined the name Peyto's Lake, and it stuck.

A farther three km (1.9 miles) along the parkway is a viewpoint from which **Peyto Glacier** is visible at the far end of Peyto Lake Valley. This glacier is part of the extensive **Wapta Icefield,** which straddles the Continental Divide and extends into the northern reaches of **Yoho National Park** in British Columbia.

Beside the Continental Divide

From Bow Pass the parkway descends to a viewpoint directly across the Mistaya River from **Mount Patterson** (3,197 meters/10,490 feet). Snowbird Glacier clings precariously to the mountain's steep northeast face, and the mountain's lower, wooded slopes are heavily scarred where rock and ice slides have swept down the mountainside.

As the parkway continues to descend and crosses Silverhorn Creek, the jagged limestone peaks of the Continental Divide can be seen to the west. **Mistaya Lake** is a three-km-long (1.9-mile-long) body of water that sits at the bottom of the valley between the road and the divide, but it can't be seen from the parkway. The best place to view it is from the Howse Peak Viewpoint at Upper Waterfowl Lake. From here the high ridge that forms the Continental Divide is easily distinguishable. Seven peaks can be seen from here, including **Howse Peak** (3,290 meters/10,790 feet). At no point along this ridge does the elevation drop below 2,750 meters (9,000 feet). From Howse Peak, the Continental Divide makes a 90-degree turn to the west. One dominant peak that can be seen from Bow Pass to north of Saskatchewan River Crossing is **Mount Chephren** (3,268 meters/10,720 feet). Its distinctive shape and position away from the main ridge of the Continental Divide make it easy to distinguish. (Look for it directly north of Howse Peak.)

To Saskatchewan River Crossing

Numerous trails lead around the swampy shores of **Upper** and **Lower Waterfowl Lakes,** providing one of the park's best opportunities to view moose, who feed on the abundant aquatic vegetation that grows in Upper Waterfowl Lake. Rock and other debris that have been carried down nearby valley systems have built up, forming a wide alluvial fan, nearly blocking the Mistaya River and creating Upper Waterfowl Lake.

Continuing north is **Mount Murchison** (3,337 meters/10,950 feet), on the east side of the parkway. Although not one of the park's highest mountains, this gray-and-yellow massif of Cambrian rock comprises 10 individual peaks, covering an area of 3,000 hectares (7,400 acres).

From a parking lot 14 km (8.9 miles) northeast of Waterfowl Lake Campground, a short trail descends into the montane forest to **Mistaya Canyon.** Here the effects of erosion can be appreciated as the Mistaya River leaves the floor of Mistaya Valley, plunging through a narrow-walled canyon into the North Saskatchewan Valley. The area is scarred with potholes where boulders have been whirled around by the action of fast-flowing water, carving deep depressions into the softer limestone bedrock below.

The **North Saskatchewan River** posed a major problem for early travelers and later for the builders of the Icefields Parkway. This swift-ly running river eventually drains into Hudson Bay. In 1989 it was named a Canadian Heritage River. One km (0.6 miles) past the bridge you'll come to a panoramic viewpoint of the entire valley. From here the Howse and Mistaya Rivers can be seen converging with the North Saskatchewan at a silt-laden delta. This is also a junction with Hwy. 11 (also known as David Thompson Hwy.), which follows the North Saskatchewan River to Rocky Mountain House and Red Deer. From this viewpoint numerous peaks can be seen to the west. Two sharp peaks are distinctive: **Mount Outram** (3,254 meters/10,680 feet) is the closer; the farther is **Mount Forbes** (3,630 meters/11,975 feet), the highest peak in Banff National Park (and the sixth-highest in the Canadian Rockies).

To Sunwapta Pass

On the north side of the North Saskatchewan River is the towering hulk of **Mount Wilson** (3,261 meters/10,700 feet), named for Banff outfitter Tom Wilson. The Icefields Parkway passes this massif on its western flanks. A pullout, just past Rampart Creek Campground, offers good views of Mount Amery to the west and Mounts Sarbach, Chephren, and Murchison to the south. Beyond here is the **Weeping Wall,** a long cliff of gray limestone where a series of waterfalls tumbles more than 100 meters (330 feet) down the steep slopes of Cirrus Mountain. In winter this wall of water freezes, becoming a mecca for ice climbers.

After ascending quickly, the road drops again before beginning a long climb to Sunwapta Pass. Halfway up the 360-vertical-meter climb is a viewpoint well worth a stop (cyclists will definitely appreciate a rest). From here views extend down the valley to the slopes of Mount Saskatchewan and, on the other side of the parkway, Cirrus Mountain. Another viewpoint, farther up the road, has the added attraction of a view of Panther Falls across the valley. A cairn at **Sunwapta Pass** (2,023 meters/6,640 feet) marks the boundary between Banff and Jasper National Parks. It also marks the divide between the North Saskatchewan and Sunwapta Rivers, whose waters drain into the Atlantic and Arctic oceans, respectively.

© ANDREW HEMPSTEAD

Peyto Lake

BANFF

Hiking

After experiencing the international thrills of Banff Avenue, most people will want to see the *real* park, which is, after all, the reason that millions of visitors flock here, thousands take low-paying jobs just to stay here, and others become so severely addicted that they start families and live happily ever after here.

Although many landmarks can be seen from the roadside, to really experience the park's personality you'll need to go for a hike. One of the best things about Banff's 80-odd hiking trails is the variety. From short interpretive walks originating in town to easy hikes rewarded by spectacular vistas to a myriad of overnight backcountry opportunities, Banff's trails offer something for everyone.

Before attempting any hikes, you should visit the **Banff Visitor Centre,** 224 Banff Avenue, 403/762-1550, where staff can advise you on the condition of trails and closures. If you are planning an overnight trip into the backcountry, you *must* pick up a Wilderness Pass from either of the park information centers before heading out; $6 per person per night.

HIKES AROUND THE TOWN OF BANFF

Fenland

- Length: 2 km/1.2 miles (30 minutes) round-trip
- Elevation gain: none
- Rating: easy
- Trailhead: Forty Mile Creek Picnic Area, Mount Norquay Road, 300 meters (0.2 miles) north of the rail crossing

If you've just arrived in town, this short interpretive trail provides an excellent introduction to the Bow Valley ecosystem. A brochure, available at the trailhead, explains the various stages in the transition between wetland and floodplain spruce forest, visible as you progress around the loop. This fen environment is prime habitat for many species of birds. The work of beavers can be

Mount Louis, as seen from a high ridge between Cory and Edith Passes

seen along the trail, and elk are here during winter. This trail is also a popular shortcut for joggers and cyclists heading for Vermilion Lakes.

Tunnel Mountain

- Length: 2.3 km/1.4 miles (30–60 minutes) one-way
- Elevation gain: 300 meters/990 feet
- Rating: easy/moderate
- Trailhead: St. Julien Road, 350 meters (0.2 miles) south of Wolf Street

Accessible from town, this short hike is an easy climb to one of the park's lower peaks. It ascends the western flank of Tunnel Mountain through a forest of lodgepole pine, switchbacking past some viewpoints before reaching a ridge just below the summit. Here the trail turns northward, climbing through a forest of Douglas fir to the summit (which is partially treed, preventing 360-degree views).

Bow River/Hoodoos

- Length: 4.8 km/3 miles (60–90 minutes) one-way
- Elevation gain: minimal
- Rating: easy
- Trailhead: Bow River Viewpoint, Tunnel Mountain Drive

From a viewpoint famous for the Fairmont Banff Springs outlook, the trail descends to the Bow River, passing under the sheer east face of Tunnel Mountain. It then follows the river a short distance before climbing into a meadow where deer and elk often graze. From this perspective the north face of Mount Rundle is particularly imposing. As the trail climbs you'll hear the traffic on Tunnel Mountain Road long before you see it. The trail ends at *hoodoos,* strange limestone-and-gravel columns jutting mysteriously out of the forest. An alternative to returning the same way is to catch the **Banff Transit** bus from Tunnel Mountain Campgrounds. It leaves every half-hour; the trip costs $1.

Sundance Canyon

- Length: 4.4 km/2.7 miles (90 minutes) one-way
- Elevation gain: 100 meters/330 feet
- Rating: easy
- Trailhead: Cave and Basin National Historic Site

Sundance Canyon is a rewarding destination across the river from downtown. Unfortunately, the first three km (1.9 miles) are along a paved road that is closed to traffic (but not bikes) and hard on your soles. Occasional glimpses of the Sawback Range are afforded by breaks in the forest. The road ends at a shaded picnic area from where the 2.4-km (1.5-mile) Sundance Loop begins. Sundance Creek was once a larger river whose upper drainage basin was diverted by glacial action. Its powerful waters have eroded into the soft bedrock, forming a spectacular overhanging canyon whose bed is strewn with large boulders that have tumbled in.

Spray River

- Length: 6 km/3.7 miles (two hours) one-way
- Elevation gain: 70 meters/230 feet
- Rating: easy/moderate
- Trailhead: from the Bow Falls parking lot, cross the Spray River, and walk along Golf Course Road to behind the green of the first golf hole on the right-hand side of the road.

This trail follows one of the many fire roads in the park. It is not particularly interesting, but it's accessible from downtown Banff and makes a pleasant way to escape the crowds. From behind the green of the 15th hole on the Stanley Thompson 18, the trail heads uphill into the forest. It follows the Spray River closely—when not in sight the river can always be heard. For those so inclined, a river crossing one km (0.6 miles) from the golf course allows for a shorter loop. Continuing south, the trail climbs a bluff for a good view of the Fairmont Banff Springs and Bow Valley. The return journey is straightforward with occasional views, ending at a locked gate behind the Fairmont Banff Springs, a short walk to Bow Falls.

For serious hikers this trail provides access to the park's rugged and remote southern reaches, but there's another interesting option involving this trail for keen day-hikers. It involves arranging a lift to the trailhead of the Goat Creek hike in Kananaskis Country (see "Hiking" under "Spray Valley Provincial Park" in the Kananaskis Country chapter). From this trailhead, it's 19 km/11.8 miles (six hours) one-way back to Banff down the Spray River watershed on a trail that drops 370 meters (1,210 feet) in elevation. The trail is most popular with mountain bikers and cross-country skiers.

Western Slope of Mount Rundle

- Length: 5.4 km/3.3 miles (two hours) one-way
- Elevation gain: 480 meters/1,755 feet
- Rating: moderate
- Trailhead: from the Bow Falls parking lot, cross the Spray River, and walk along Golf Course

BANFF

Road to behind the green of the first golf hole on the right-hand side of the road.

At 2,950 meters (9,680 feet), Mount Rundle is one of the park's dominant peaks. Climbing to its summit is possible without ropes, but previous scrambling experience is advised. An alternative is to ascend the mountain's western slope along an easy-to-follow trail that ends just over 1,000 vertical meters (3,280 vertical feet) before the summit. The trail follows the Spray River Trail from Golf Course Road, branching off left after 700 meters (0.4 miles). Climbing steadily, it breaks out of the enclosed forest after 2.5 km (1.6 miles). The trail ends in a gully from which the undefined route to the summit begins.

Stoney Squaw

- Length: 2.4-km/1.5-mile loop (50 minutes round-trip)
- Elevation gain: 180 meters/590 feet
- Rating: easy
- Trailhead: top of Mount Norquay Road, six km (3.7 miles) from town

Looking north along Banff Avenue, Stoney Squaw's 1,884-meter (6,180-foot) summit is dwarfed by Cascade Mountain, directly behind it. To get to the trailhead of a trail that leads to its easily reached summit, follow Mount Norquay Road to a parking lot in front of the resort's day lodge. Immediately to the right of the entrance, a small sign marks the trail. The narrow trail passes through a thick forest of lodgepole pine and spruce before breaking out into the open near the summit. The sweeping panorama includes Vermilion Lakes, the Bow Valley, Banff, Spray River Valley, Mount Rundle, Lake Minnewanka, and the imposing face of Cascade Mountain (2,998 meters/9,840 feet). The return trail follows the northwest slope of Stoney Squaw to an old ski run at the opposite end of the parking lot.

Cascade Amphitheatre

- Length: 6.6 km/4.1 miles (2–3 hours) one-way
- Elevation gain: 610 meters/2,000 feet
- Rating: moderate/difficult

- Trailhead: day lodge, top of Mount Norquay Road, six km (3.7 miles) from town

This enormous cirque and the subalpine meadows directly behind Cascade Mountain are one of the most rewarding destinations for hiking in the Banff area. The demanding trail begins by passing the day lodge, then skirting the base of several lifts, and following an old road to the floor of Forty Mile Valley. Keep right at all trail junctions. One km (0.6 miles) after crossing Forty Mile Creek, the trail begins switchbacking up the western flank of Cascade Mountain through a forest of lodgepole pine. Along the way are breathtaking views of Mount Louis's sheer east face. After the trail levels off, it enters a magnificent U-shaped valley and the amphitheater begins to define itself. The trail becomes indistinct in the subalpine meadow, which is carpeted in colorful wildflowers during summer. Farther up the valley, vegetation thins out as boulder-strewn talus slopes cover the ground. If you sit still long enough on these rocks, marmots and pikas will slowly appear, emitting shrill whistles before disappearing again.

The most popular route to the summit of 2,998-meter (9,840-foot) Cascade Mountain is along the southern ridge of the amphitheater wall. It is a long scramble up scree slopes and is made more difficult by a false summit; it should be attempted only by experienced scramblers.

C Level Cirque

- Length: 4 km/2.5 miles (90 minutes) one-way
- Elevation gain: 455 meters/1,500 feet
- Rating: moderate
- Trailhead: Upper Bankhead Picnic Area, Lake Minnewanka Road, 3.5 km (2.2 miles) beyond the TransCanada Highway underpass

From a picnic area that sits on the site of an abandoned mining town, the trail climbs steadily through a forest of lodgepole pine, aspen, and spruce to a pile of tailings and broken-down concrete walls. Soon after is a panoramic view of Lake Minnewanka, then the trail reenters the forest before ending in a small cirque with views down the Bow Valley to Canmore and beyond.

The cirque is carved into the eastern face of Cascade Mountain, where snow often lingers until July. When the snow melts, the lush soil is covered in a carpet of colorful wildflowers.

Aylmer Lookout

- Length: 12 km/7.5 miles (four hours) one-way
- Elevation gain: 810 meters/2,660 feet
- Rating: moderate/difficult
- Trailhead: Lake Minnewanka, Lake Minnewanka Road, 5.5 km (3.4 miles) beyond the TransCanada Highway underpass

The first eight-km (five-mile) stretch of this trail follows the northern shore of Lake Minnewanka from the day-use area to a junction. The right fork leads to a campground, while the left climbs steeply to the site of an old fire tower on top of an exposed ridge. The deep blue waters of Lake Minnewanka are visible, backed by the imposing peaks of Mount Girouard (2,995 meters/9,830 feet) and Mount Inglismaldie (2,964 meters/9,725 feet). Bighorn sheep often graze in this area. From here a trail forks left and continues climbing to the alpine tundra of Aylmer Pass.

HIKES BETWEEN BANFF AND LAKE LOUISE

Cory Pass

- Length: 5.8 km/3.6 miles (2.5 hours) one-way
- Elevation gain: 920 meters/3,020 feet
- Rating: moderate/difficult
- Trailhead: Fireside Picnic Area, Banff end of the Bow Valley Parkway

This strenuous hike has a rewarding objective—a magnificent view of dog-toothed Mount Louis. The towering slab of limestone rises more than 500 meters (1,640 feet) from the valley below. Just over one km (0.6 miles) from the trailhead, the trail divides. The left fork climbs steeply across an open slope to an uneven ridge that it follows before ascending yet another steep slope to Cory Pass—a wild, windy, desolate area surrounded in jagged peaks dominated by Mount Louis. An alternative to returning along the same trail is continuing down into Gargoyle Valley, following the base of Mount Edith before ascending to Edith Pass and returning to the junction one km (0.6 miles) from the picnic area. Total distance for this trip is 13 km (eight miles), a long day considering the steep climbs and descents involved.

Bourgeau Lake

- Length: 7.6 km/4.7 miles (2.5 hours) one-way
- Elevation gain: 730 meters/2,400 feet
- Rating: moderate
- Trailhead: signposted parking lot, TransCanada Highway, three km (1.9 miles) west of Sunshine Village Junction

This trail follows Wolverine Creek to a small subalpine lake nestled at the base of an impressive limestone amphitheater. Although the trail is moderately steep, plenty of distractions along the way are worthy of a stop (and rest). Across the Bow Valley, the Sawback Range is easy to distinguish. As the forest of lodgepole pine turns to spruce, the trail passes under the cliffs of Mount Bourgeau and crosses Wolverine Creek (below a spot where it tumbles photogenically over exposed bedrock). After strenuous switchbacks, the trail climbs into the cirque containing Bourgeau Lake. As you continue around the lake's rocky shore, you'll hear the colonies of noisy pikas, even if you don't see them.

Shadow Lake

- Length: 14.3 km/8.9 miles (4.5 hours) one-way
- Elevation gain: 440 meters/1,445 feet
- Rating: moderate
- Trailhead: Redearth Creek Parking Area, TransCanada Highway, 11 km (6.8 miles) west of Sunshine Village Junction

Shadow is one of the many impressive subalpine lakes along the Continental Divide and a popular base for a great variety of day trips. It follows the old Redearth fire road for 11 km

SUNSHINE MEADOWS

Sunshine Meadows, straddling the Continental Divide, is a unique and beautiful region of the Canadian Rockies. It's best known as home to Sunshine Village, a self-contained alpine resort accessible only by gondola from the valley floor. But for a few short months each summer, the area is clear of snow and becomes a wonderland for hiking. Large amounts of precipitation create a lush cover of vegetation—over 300 species of wildflowers alone have been recorded here.

From Sunshine Village, trails radiate out across the alpine meadow, which is covered in a colorful carpet of fireweed, glacier lilies, mountain avens, white mountain heather, and forget-me-nots (the meadows are in full-bloom late July to mid-August). The most popular destination is **Rock Isle Lake**, an easy 2.5-km (1.6-mile) jaunt from the upper village that crosses the Continental Divide while only gaining 100 meters (330 feet) of elevation. The descent to the lake is nothing short of stunning. On a clear day, Mount Assiniboine (3,618 meters/11,870 feet), known as the "Matterhorn of the Rockies," is visible to the southeast. At the lake itself, an observation area and bench invite quiet contemplation. From this point, a variety of options present themselves, including a loop around Larix Lake and Grizzly Lakes and a traverse along Standish Ridge. If the weather is cooperating, it won't matter which direction you head (so long as it's along a formed trail), you'll experience the Canadian Rockies in all their glory.

Sunshine Village first began promoting summer recreation in 1984 and suddenly, instead of a few hundred adventurous souls willing to hike the six-km (3.7-mile) road up to the meadows, tens of thousands of visitors were whisked onto the fragile alpine tundra by gondola. In 1992 Sunshine Village terminated its summer gondola service and the meadows are quiet once again. Visitors are still able to make the trek on foot, but a more practical alternative is to take the Sunshine Meadows Shuttle along a road closed to public traffic. This service is operated by **White Mountain Adventures,** 403/678-4099 or 800/408-0005; website: www.canadiannatureguides.com. It departs Banff (daily at 8:45 A.M., adult $35, child $20 roundtrip) and the Sunshine Village parking lot (daily at 9:30 A.M., 10:30 A.M., 11:30 A.M., and 1:30 P.M., adult $18, child $10 roundtrip). Advance reservations are required. To get to the base of the gondola from Banff, follow the TransCanada Highway nine km (5.6 miles) west to Sunshine Village Road, which continues a similar distance along Healy Creek to the Sunshine Village parking lot.

(6.8 miles) before forking right and climbing into the forest. The campground is two km (1.2 miles) beyond this junction, and just 500 meters (0.3 miles) farther is **Shadow Lake Lodge** (see "Backcountry Huts and Lodges" in the "Accommodations" section for details). The lake is nearly two km (1.2 miles) long, and from its southern shore trails lead to Ball Pass, Gibbon Pass, and Haiduk Lake.

Castle Lookout

- Length: 3.7 km/2.3 miles (90 minutes) one-way
- Elevation gain: 520 meters/1,700 feet
- Rating: moderate
- Trailhead: Bow Valley Parkway, five km (3.1 miles) northwest of Castle Junction

However you travel through the Bow Valley, you can't help but be impressed by Castle Mountain rising proudly from the forest floor. This trail takes you above the treeline on the mountain's west face to the site of Mount Eisenhower fire lookout, abandoned in the 1970s and burned in the 1980s. From the Bow Valley Parkway, the trail follows a wide pathway for 1.5 km (0.9 miles) to an abandoned cabin in a forest of lodgepole pine and spruce. It then becomes narrower and steeper, switchbacking through a meadow before climbing through a narrow band of rock and leveling off near the lookout site. Magnificent panoramas of the Bow Valley spread out before you in both directions. Storm Mountain can be seen directly across the valley.

Rockbound Lake

- Length: 8.4 km/5.2 miles (2.5 hours) one-way
- Elevation gain: 760 meters/2,500 feet
- Rating: moderate/difficult
- Trailhead: Castle Junction, Bow Valley Parkway, 30 km (18.6 miles) west of Banff

This strenuous hike leads to a delightful little body of water tucked behind Castle Mountain. For the first five km (3.1 miles) the trail follows an old fire road along the southern flanks of Castle Mountain. Early in the season or after heavy rain, this section can be boggy. Glimpses of surrounding peaks ease the pain of the steady climb as the trail narrows. After eight km (five miles) you'll come to Tower Lake, backed by grassed slopes, which the trail skirts to the right before climbing a steep slope. From the ridge, Rockbound Lake comes into view, and the reason for its name immediately becomes apparent. A scramble up any of the nearby slopes will reward you with good views.

HIKES AROUND LAKE LOUISE

The variety of hiking opportunities in the vicinity of Lake Louise and Moraine Lake is surely equal to any area on the face of the earth. The region's potential for outdoor recreation was first realized in the late 1800s, and it soon became the center of hiking activity in the Canadian Rockies. This popularity continues today; trails here are among the most heavily used in the park. Hiking is best early or late in the short summer season. Head out early in the morning to miss the strollers, high heels, dogs, and bear-bells that you'll surely encounter during the busiest periods.

The two main trailheads are at Fairmont Chateau Lake Louise and Moraine Lake. Two trails lead from the village to the chateau (a pleasant alternative to driving the steep and busy Lake Louise Drive). Shortest is the 2.7-km/1.7-mile **Louise Creek Trail.** It begins on the downstream side of the point where Lake Louise Drive crosses the Bow River, crosses Louise Creek three times, and ends at the Lake

Louise parking lot. The other trail, **Tramline,** is 4.5 km (2.8 miles) longer but not as steep. It begins behind the railway station and follows the route of a narrow-gauge railway that once transported guests from the CPR line to Fairmont Chateau Lake Louise.

Bow River Loop

- Length: 7 km/4.3 miles (1.5–2 hours)
- Elevation gain: minimal
- Rating: easy
- Trailheads: various points throughout Lake Louise Village, including behind Samson Mall

This loop follows both banks of the Bow River southeast from the railway station. Used by joggers and cyclists to access various points in the village, the trail also links the station to the Lake Louise Alpine Centre, Post Hotel, Samson Mall, both campgrounds, and the Louise Creek and Tramline trails to Lake Louise. Interpretive signs along its length provide information on the Bow River ecosystem.

Louise Lakeshore

- Length: 2 km/1.2 miles (30 minutes) one-way
- Elevation gain: none
- Rating: easy
- Trailhead: Lake Louise, four km (2.5 miles) from TransCanada Highway

Probably the busiest trail in all of the Canadian Rockies, this one follows the north shore of Lake Louise from in front of the chateau to the west end of the lake. Here numerous braided glacial streams empty their silt-filled waters into Lake Louise. Along the trail's length are benches to sit and ponder what English mountaineer James Outram once described as "a gem of composition and of coloring . . . perhaps unrivalled anywhere."

Plain of the Six Glaciers

- Length: 5.3 km/3.3 miles (90 minutes) one-way
- Elevation gain: 370 meters/1,215 feet
- Rating: easy/moderate
- Trailhead: Lake Louise

looking back at Fairmont Chateau Lake Louise from Louise Lakeshore Trail

Hikers along this trail are rewarded not only with panoramic views of the glaciated peaks of the main range, but also with a rustic trail's-end teahouse serving homemade goodies baked on a wooden stove. For the first two km (1.2 miles), the trail follows Louise Lakeshore Trail to the western end of the lake. From there it begins a steady climb through a forest of spruce and subalpine fir. It enters an open area where an avalanche has come tumbling down (now a colorful carpet of wildflowers), then passes through a forested area into a vast wasteland of moraines produced by the advance and retreat of Victoria Glacier. Views of surrounding peaks continue to improve until the trail enters a stunted forest. After switchbacking up through this forest, the trail arrives at the teahouse.

Built by the CPR at the turn of the 20th century, the teahouse operates the same way now as it did then. Supplies are packed in by horse and all cooking is done in a rustic kitchen. It's open July through early September. After resting, continue one km (0.6 miles) to the end of the trail on the narrow top of a lateral moraine. From here the trail's namesakes are visible. From left to right the glaciers are Aberdeen, Upper Lefroy, Lower Lefroy, Upper Victoria, Lower Victoria, and Pope's. Between Mount Lefroy (3,441 meters/11,290 feet) and Mount Victoria (3,459 meters/11,350 feet) is Abbot Pass, where it's possible to make out Abbot Hut on the skyline. When constructed in 1922, this stone structure was the highest building in Canada. The pass and hut are named for Phillip Abbot, who died attempting to climb Mount Lefroy in 1896.

Lake Agnes

- Length: 3.6 km/2.2 miles (90 minutes) one-way
- Elevation gain: 400 meters/1,312 feet
- Rating: moderate
- Trailhead: Lake Louise

This moderately strenuous hike is one of the park's most popular. It begins in front of the chateau, branching right near the beginning of the Louise Lakeshore Trail. For the first 2.5 km (1.6 miles), the trail climbs steeply, switchbacking through a forest of subalpine fir and Engelmann spruce, crossing a horse trail, passing a lookout, and leveling out at tiny Mirror Lake. Here the old, traditional trail veers right (use it if the ground is wet or snowy), while a more direct route veers left to the Plain of the Six Glaciers. The final elevation gain along both trails is made easier by a flight of steps beside Bridal Veil Falls. The trail ends beside a rustic teahouse overlooking Lake Agnes, a subalpine lake nestled in a hanging valley. The teahouse offers homemade soups, healthy sandwiches, and a wide assortment of teas.

From the teahouse a one-km (0.6-mile) trail leads to Little Beehive and impressive views of the Bow Valley. Another trail leads around the northern shore of Lake Agnes, climbing to Big Beehive (see following entry) or joining to the Plain of the Six Glaciers Trail (see previous entry), just 3.2 km (two miles) from the chateau and 2.1 km (1.3 miles) from the teahouse at the end of that trail.

Big Beehive

- Length: 5 km/3.1 miles (two hours) one-way
- Elevation gain: 520 meters/1,710 feet
- Rating: moderate
- Trailhead: Lake Louise

The lookout atop the larger of the two "beehives" is one of the best places to admire the uniquely colored waters of Lake Louise, more than 500 meters (1,640 feet) directly below. The various trails to the summit have one thing in common—all are steep. But the rewards are worth every drop of sweat along the way. The most popular route follows the Lake Agnes Trail for the first 3.6 km (2.2 miles) to Lake Agnes. From the teahouse, a trail leads to the western end of the lake, then switchbacks steeply up an exposed north-facing ridge. At the crest of the ridge, the trail forks. To the right it descends to the Plain of the Six Glaciers Trail, to the left it continues 300 meters (0.2 miles) to a log gazebo. This trail is not well defined, but scrambling through the large boulders is easy. Across Lake Louise is Fairview Mountain (2,745 meters/9,000 feet), and behind this peak is the distinctive shape of Mount Temple (3,549 meters/11,645 feet). Views also

extend up the lake to Mount Lefroy and northeast to Lake Louise winter resort. Views from the edge of the cliff are spectacular, but be very careful—it's a long, long way down. By returning down the Lake Louise side of the Big Beehive, the loop is 11.5 km (7.1 miles).

Saddleback

- Length: 3.7 km/2.3 miles (90 minutes) one-way
- Elevation gain: 600 meters/1,970 feet
- Rating: moderate
- Trailhead: boathouse, Lake Louise

This trail climbs the lower slopes of Fairview Mountain from beside the boatshed on Lake Louise, ending in an alpine meadow with a view of Mount Temple from across Paradise Valley. Four hundred meters (0.2 miles) from the trailhead, the trail forks. Keep left and follow the steep switchbacks through a forest of Englemann spruce and subalpine fir until reaching the flower-filled meadow. The meadow is actually a pass between Fairview Mountain (to the northwest) and Saddle Mountain (to the southeast). Although most hikers are content with the awesome views from the pass and return along the same trail, it is possible to continue to the summit of Fairview (2,745 meters/9,000 feet), a further climb of 400 vertical meters (1,310 vertical feet). The barely discernible, switchbacking trail to the summit begins near a stand of larch trees above the crest of Saddleback. As you would expect, the view from the top is stupendous; Lake Louise is more than one km (0.6 miles) directly below. This option is for strong, experienced hikers only. From the Saddleback, the trail descends into Sheol Valley, then into Paradise Valley. The entire loop would be 15 km (9.3 miles).

Paradise Valley

- Length: 18 km/11.2 miles (six hours) round-trip
- Elevation gain: 380 meters/1,250 feet
- Rating: moderate
- Trailhead: Moraine Lake Road, 3.5 km (2.2 miles) from Lake Louise Drive

This aptly named trail makes for a long day hike, but it can be broken up by overnighting at the backcountry campground at the far end of the loop. The trail climbs steadily for the first five km (3.1 miles), crossing Paradise Creek numerous times and passing the junction of a trail that climbs the Sheol Valley to Saddleback (see previous entry). After five km (3.1 miles) the trail divides again, following either side of the valley to form a 13-km (eight-mile) loop. **Lake Annette** is 700 meters (0.4 miles) along the left fork. It's a typical subalpine lake in a unique setting—nestled against the near-vertical 1,200-meter (3,940-foot) north face of snow- and ice-capped **Mount Temple** (3,549 meters/11,645 feet), one of the 10 highest peaks in the Canadian Rockies. This difficult face was successfully climbed in 1966, relatively late for mountaineering firsts. The lake is a worthy destination in itself. Allow yourself four hours round-trip from the trailhead. For those completing the entire loop, continue beyond the lake into an open avalanche area that affords views across Paradise Valley. Look and listen for pikas and marmots among the boulders. The trail then passes through Horseshoe Meadow, crosses Paradise Creek, and heads back down the valley. Keep to the left at all trail crossings and you'll quickly arrive at a series of waterfalls known as the Giant Steps. From the base of these falls, it is eight km (five miles) back to the trailhead.

Larch Valley

- Length: 2.9 km/1.8 miles (60 minutes) one-way
- Elevation gain: 400 meters/1,310 feet
- Rating: moderate
- Trailhead: Moraine Lake, 13 km (eight miles) from Lake Louise Drive

In fall, when the larch trees have turned a mag-

In fall, when the larch trees have turned a magnificent gold and the sun is shining, few spots in the Canadian Rockies can match the beauty of Larch Valley, but don't expect to find much solitude.

nificent gold and the sun is shining, few spots in the Canadian Rockies can match the beauty of this valley, but don't expect to find much solitude (and don't be too disappointed if the trail is closed in fall—it often is due to wildlife). Although the most popular time for visiting the valley is fall, it is a worthy destination all summer, when the open meadows are filled with colorful wildflowers. The trail begins just past Moraine Lake Lodge and climbs fairly steeply with occasional glimpses of Moraine Lake below. After reaching the junction of the Eiffel Lake Trail, keep right, passing through an open forest of larch and into the meadow beyond. The range of larch is restricted within the park, and this is one of the few areas where they are prolific. Mount Fay (3,235 meters/10,615 feet) is the dominant peak on the skyline, rising above the other mountains that make up the Valley of the Ten Peaks.

Sentinel Pass

- Length: 5.8 km/3.6 miles (2–3 hours) one-way
- Elevation gain: 725 meters/2,380 feet
- Rating: moderate/difficult
- Trailhead: Moraine Lake

Keen hikers should consider continuing through the open meadows of Larch Valley to Sentinel Pass (2,608 meters/8,560 feet), one of the park's highest trail-accessible passes. The length and elevation gain listed are from Moraine Lake. Once in Larch Valley, you're halfway there and have made over half of the elevation gain. Upon reaching Larch Valley, take the formed trail that winds through the open meadow. From the end of the meadow, the trail switchbacks for 1.2 kilometers (0.7 miles) up a steep scree slope to the pass, sandwiched between Pinnacle Mountain (3,067 meters/10,060 feet) and Mount Temple (3,549 meters/11,645 feet). From the pass most hikers opt to return along the same trail, although with advanced planning it is possible to continue into Paradise Valley and back to the Moraine Lake access road, a total of 17 km (10.6 miles) one way.

Eiffel Lake

- Length: 5.6 km/3.5 miles (two hours) one-way
- Elevation gain: 400 meters/1,310 feet
- Rating: moderate/difficult
- Trailhead: Moraine Lake

Eiffel Lake is small, and looks even smaller in its rugged and desolate setting, surrounded by the famed Valley of the Ten Peaks. For the first 2.4 km (1.5 miles), follow the Larch Valley Trail (see previous entry), then fork left. Most of the elevation gain has already been made, and the trail remains relatively level before emerging onto an open slope from where each of the 10 peaks can be seen, along with Moraine Lake far below. From left to right the peaks are Fay, Little, Bowlen, Perren, Septa, Allen, Tuzo, Deltaform, Neptuak, and Wenkchemna. The final two peaks are divided by Wenkchemna Pass (2,605 meters/8,550 feet), a further four km (2.5 miles) and 360 vertical meters (1,180 vertical feet) above Eiffel Lake. The lake itself soon comes into view. It lies in a depression formed by a rockslide from Neptuak Mountain. The lake is named for **Eiffel Peak** (3,085 meters/10,120 feet), a rock pinnacle behind it, which with a little imagination could be compared to the Eiffel Tower in Paris.

Consolation Lakes

- Length: 3 km/1.9 miles (one hour) one-way
- Elevation gain: 65 meters/213 feet
- Rating: easy/moderate
- Trailhead: beside the restrooms at Moraine Lake parking lot

This short trail begins with a crossing of Moraine Creek at the outlet of Moraine Lake and ends at a pleasant subalpine lake. The first section of the trail traverses a boulder-strewn rock pile—the result of rock slides on the imposing Tower of Babel (3,100 meters/10,170 feet)—before entering a dense forest of Engelmann spruce and

subalpine fir and following Babel Creek to the lower lake. The wide valley affords 360-degree views of the surrounding jagged peaks, including Mount Temple back down the valley and Mts. Bident and Quandra at the far end of the lakes. After eating a picnic lunch (from Laggans, in the Samson Mall) while perched on one of many boulders, you could continue to Upper Consolation Lake by crossing Babel Creek and following a usually wet and muddy trail along the lake's eastern shore.

Skoki Lodge

- Length: 14.4 km/8.9 miles (five hours) one-way
- Elevation gain: 775 meters/2,540 feet
- Rating: moderate/difficult
- Trailhead: end of Fish Creek Road, off Whitehorn Road 1.8 km (1.1 miles) north of Lake Louise interchange

The trail into historic Skoki Lodge is only one of the endless hiking opportunities tucked behind Lake Louise winter resort, across the valley from all hikes detailed previously. The first four km (2.5 miles) of the trail are along a gravel access road leading to Temple Lodge, part of the Lake Louise winter resort. From here, the trail climbs to Boulder Pass, passing a campground and Halfway Hut, above Corral Creek. The pass harbors a large population of pikas and hoary marmots. The trail then follows the north shore of Ptarmigan Lake before climbing again to Deception Pass, named for its false summit. It then descends into Skoki Valley, passing the Skoki Lakes and eventually reaching Skoki Lodge (see "Accommodations"). Just over one km (0.6 miles) beyond the lodge is a campground, an excellent base for exploring the region.

HIKES ALONG ICEFIELDS PARKWAY

Helen Lake

- Length: 6 km/3.7 miles (2.5 hours) one-way
- Elevation gain: 455 meters/1,500 feet
- Rating: moderate
  - Trailhead: across the Icefields Parkway from

Crowfoot Glacier Lookout, 33 km (20 miles) northwest from the junction with the Trans-Canada Highway

The trail to Helen Lake is one of the easiest ways to access a true alpine environment from the southern end of the Icefields Parkway. The trail climbs steadily through a forest of Engelmann spruce and subalpine fir for the first 2.5 km (1.6 miles) to an avalanche slope, reaching the treeline and the first good viewpoint after three km (1.9 miles). The view across the valley is spectacular, with Crowfoot Glacier visible to the southwest. As the trail reaches a ridge, it turns and descends into the glacial cirque where Helen Lake lies. Listen and look for hoary marmots around the scree slopes along the lakeshore.

For those with the time and energy, it's possible to continue an additional three km (1.9 miles) to Dolomite Pass; the trail switchbacks steeply up a further 100 vertical meters (330 vertical feet) in less than one km (0.6 miles), then descends steeply for a further one km (0.6 miles) to Katherine Lake and beyond to the pass.

Bow Glacier Falls

- Length: 3.4 km/2.1 miles (one hour) one-way
- Elevation gain: 130 meters/430 feet
- Rating: easy
- Trailhead: Num-ti-jah Lodge, Bow Lake, 36 km (22.3 miles) northwest from the Trans-Canada Highway

This hike skirts one of the most beautiful lakes in the Canadian Rockies before ending at a narrow but spectacular waterfall. From the parking lot in front of Num-ti-jah Lodge, follow the shore through Willow Flats to a gravel outwash area at the end of the lake. Across the lake are reflected views of Crowfoot Mountain and, farther west, a glimpse of Bow Glacier among the jagged peaks of the Waputik Range. The trail then begins a short but steep climb up the rim of a canyon before leveling out at the edge of a vast moraine of gravel, scree, and boulders. This is the end of the trail, although it's possible to reach the base of Bow Glacier Falls by picking your

way through the 800 meters (0.5 miles) of rough ground that remains.

Peyto Lake

- Length: 1.4 km/0.9 miles (30 minutes) one-way
- Elevation loss: 100 meters/330 feet
- Rating: easy
- Trailhead: unmarked pullout, Icefields Parkway, 2.4 km (1.5 miles) north of Bow Summit

Without doubt the best place to view Peyto Lake is from a popular viewpoint accessible via a short trail from Bow Summit, 41 km (25.5 miles) along the Icefields Parkway from the TransCanada Highway. The easiest way to access the actual shoreline, though, is along this short trail further along the highway. A pebbled beach, strewn with driftwood, is the perfect setting for picnicking, painting, or just admiring the lake's quieter side. Back at the lake lookout, a rough trail drops nearly 300 meters (980 feet) in 2.4 km (1.5 miles) to the lake.

Chephren Lake

- Length: 4 km/2.5 miles (60–90 minutes) one-way
- Elevation gain: 100 meters/330 feet
- Rating: easy
- Trailhead: Waterfowl Lake Campground, Icefields Parkway, 57 km (35 miles) northwest from the TransCanada Highway

This pale-green body of water (pronounced "Kefren") is hidden from the Icefields Parkway but easily reached. The official trailhead is a bridge across the Mistaya River at the back of Waterfowl Lakes Campground (behind site 86). If you're not registered at the campground, park at the end of the unpaved road running along the front of the campground, and walk 300 meters (0.2 miles) down the well-worn path to the river crossing. From across the river, the trail dives headlong into a subalpine forest, reaching a crudely signposted junction after 1.6 km (one mile). Take the right fork. This leads 2.4 km to Chephren Lake, descending steeply at the end (this stretch of trail is often muddy). The lake is nestled under the buttresses of Mount Chephren. To the left—farther up the lake—is Howse Peak.

The trail to smaller **Cirque Lake** (4.5 km/2.8 miles from the trailhead) branches left 1.6 km (one mile) along this trail. It is less heavily used, but this lake is popular with anglers for its healthy population of rainbow trout.

Glacier Lake

- Length: 9 km/5.6 miles (2.5–3 hours) one-way
- Elevation gain: 220 meters/770 feet
- Rating: moderate
- Trailhead: an old gravel pit on the west side of the highway, one km (0.6 miles) west of Saskatchewan River Crossing

This three-km-long (1.9-mile-long) lake is one of the park's largest lakes not accessible by road. Although not as scenic as the more accessible lakes along the parkway, it's a pleasant destination for a full-day or overnight trip. For the first one km (0.6 miles), the trail passes through an open forest of lodgepole pine to a fancy footbridge across the rushing North Saskatchewan River. From

Chephren Lake

© ANDREW HEMPSTEAD

there it climbs gradually to a viewpoint overlooking Howse River and the valley beyond, then turns away from the river for a long slog through dense forest to Glacier Lake. A primitive campground lies just over 300 meters (0.2 miles) from where the trail emerges at the lake.

Saskatchewan Glacier

- Length: 7.3 km/4.5 miles (two hours) one-way
- Elevation gain: 150 meters/490 feet
- Rating: moderate
- Trailhead: small parking lot, 35 km (22 miles) northwest of the Saskatchewan River Crossing (just before the highway begins its "Big Bend" up to Sunwapta Pass)

The Saskatchewan Glacier, a tongue of ice from the great Columbia Icefield, is visible from various points along the Icefields Parkway. This hike will take you right to the toe of the glacier. After crossing an old concrete bridge, the trail disappears into the forest to the right, joining an overgrown road, and continuing up the valley along the south bank of the river. When the toe of the glacier first comes into sight it looks deceptively close, but it's still a long hike away over rough terrain.

Nigel Pass

- Length: 7.4 km/4.6 miles (2.5 hours) one-way
- Elevation gain: 365 meters/1,200 feet
- Rating: moderate
- Trailhead: Icefields Parkway, 2.5 km (1.6 miles) north of the switchback on the "Big Bend"

Park on the east side of the highway and follow the gravel road to a locked gate. Turn right here and cross Nigel Creek on the bridge. The trail is obvious, following open avalanche paths up the east side of the valley. In a stand of Engelmann spruce and subalpine fir two km (1.2 miles) from the trailhead is an old campsite used first by native hunting parties, then by mountaineers exploring the area around the Columbia Icefield. Look for carvings on trees recording these early visitors. From here the trail continues to climb steadily, only increasing in gradient for the last one km (0.6 miles) to the pass. The pass (2,195 meters/7,200 feet) marks the boundary between Banff and Jasper National Parks. For the best view, scramble over the rocks to the left. To the north, the view extends down the Brazeau River Valley, surrounded by a mass of peaks. To the west (left) is Nigel Peak (3,211 meters/10,535 feet), and to the southwest are views of Parker's Ridge and the glaciated peaks of Mount Athabasca.

Parker's Ridge
• Length: 2.4 km/1.5 miles (one hour) one-way
• Elevation gain: 210 meters/690 feet
• Rating: easy/moderate
• Trailhead: Icefields Parkway, four km (2.5 miles) south of Sunwapta Pass

From the trailhead on the west side of the highway, this wide path gains elevation quickly through open meadows and scattered stands of subalpine fir. This fragile environment is easily destroyed, so it's important that you stay on the trail. During the short alpine summer, these meadows are carpeted with red heather, white mountain avens, and blue alpine forget-me-nots. From the summit of the ridge, you look down on the two-km-wide (1.2-mile-wide) Saskatchewan Glacier spreading out below. Beyond is Castleguard Mountain, renowned for its extensive cave system.

Other Recreation

FAIR WEATHER

Mountain Biking
Whether you have your own bike or you rent one from the many bicycle shops in Banff or Lake Louise, cycling in the park is for everyone. The roads to Lake Minnewanka, Mount Norquay, through the golf course, and along the Bow Valley Parkway are all popular routes. Several trails radiating from Banff and ending deep in the backcountry have been designated as bicycle trails. These include Sundance (3.7 km/2.3 miles one-way), Rundle Riverside to Canmore (15 km/9.3 miles one-way), and the Spray River Loop (via Goat Creek; 48 km/30 miles round-trip). Farther afield, other trails are at Redearth Creek, Lake Louise, and in the northeastern reaches of the park near Saskatchewan River Crossing. Before heading into the backcountry, pick up the *Trail Mountain Biking Guide* from the Banff or Lake Louise Visitor Centres. Riders are particularly susceptible to sudden bear encounters. Be alert and make loud noises when passing through heavy vegetation.

Bactrax, 225 Bear Street, 403/762-8177, and **Adventures Unlimited,** 211 Bear Street, 403/762-4554, rent front- and full-suspension mountain bikes for $6–10 per hour and $22–40 per day. Rates include a helmet, lock, and biking map. Bactrax also offers mountain-bike tours, including to Vermilion Lakes and along Sundance Canyon. Tours cost $15 per person per hour. The shop is open daily 8 A.M.–8 P.M.

Horseback Riding
Jim and Bill Brewster led Banff's first paying guests into the backcountry on horseback more than 100 years ago. Today visitors are still able to enjoy the park on this traditional form of transportation.

Warner Guiding & Outfitting, website: www.horseback.com, offers a great variety of trips. Their main office is downtown in the Trail Rider Store at 132 Banff Avenue, 403/762-4551, although trips depart from either **Martin's Stables,** 403/762-2832, behind the recreation grounds on Birch Avenue, or **Banff Springs Corral,** 403/762-2848, along Spray Avenue. One-hour rides are $27, two hours $40, three hours $64. Other day trips include the three-hour **Mountain Morning Breakfast Ride,** featuring a hearty breakfast along the trail (departs 9 A.M.), $61; **Explorer,** a seven-hour ride up the Spray River Valley (departs 9 A.M.), $125; and the **Evening Steak Fry,** a three-hour ride with a steak dinner along the trail (departs 5 P.M.), $67.

BANFF

Overnight trips to established backcountry camps and lodges are also available; rates begin at $359 including all meals, two nights' accommodation at Sundance Lodge, and the horse, of course.

Brewster Lake Louise Stables, 403/522-3511, offers 90-minute rides to the end of Lake Louise for $55, half-day rides to Lake Agnes Teahouse for $70, and all-day rides up Paradise Valley, including lunch, for $130.

White-Water Rafting and Canoeing
Anyone looking for white-water-rafting action will want to run the **Kicking Horse River,** which flows down the western slopes of the Canadian Rockies into British Columbia. Many operators provide transportation from Banff and Lake Louise (see "Sights and Recreation" under "Golden" in the Yoho National Park and Vicinity chapter).

Rocky Mountain Raft Tours, 403/762-3632, offers one-hour ($28) and two-hour ($42) float trips down the Bow River, beginning just below Bow Falls. No rapids are involved, so you'll stay dry.

On a quiet stretch of the Bow River, at the north end of Wolf Street, **Banff Canoe Rentals,** 403/762-3632, rents canoes for use on the river from where it's an easy paddle upstream to the Vermilion Lakes and Forty Mile Creek; $18 per hour or $50 for a full day of paddling. Rentals are available in summer, daily 10 A.M.–7 P.M.

Fishing and Boating
The finest fishing in the park is in Lake Minnewanka, where lake trout as large as 15 kg (33 lbs.) have been caught. One way to ensure a good catch is through **Lake Minnewanka Boat Tours,** 403/762-3473, which offers fishing trips in a heated cabin cruiser; trolling and downrigging are preferred methods of fishing the lake. A half-day's fishing (3.5 hours) is $240 for one or two persons. The company also rents small aluminum fishing boats with outboard motors for $32 for the first hour, then $12 for every extra hour.

The most experienced of local guides is Dan Bell of **Upper Bow Fly Fishing,** 403/760-7668, www.upperbowflyfishing.com. Bell has been fishing and guiding in the Banff area for more than

20 years and has represented Canada as a member of the National Fly-Fishing Team on multiple occasions. His purpose-built drift boats are perfect for chasing brown trout along the Bow River downstream from Banff, with regular stops made for fly-casting from the banks. He'll also take interested anglers to high alpine lakes chasing cutthroat trout. Rates start at $175 per person for a half-day on the river and include guiding, gear, and lessons.

Before fishing anywhere in the park you need a national park fishing license ($6 per week, $13 per year), available from the Banff and Lake Louise visitors centers and sport shops throughout the park.

Golfing
One of the world's most scenic golf courses, the Banff Springs Golf Course, spreads out along the Bow River between Mount Rundle and Tunnel Mountain. The first course was laid out here in 1911, but in 1928 Stanley Thompson was brought in by the CPR to redesign it into 18 holes and to build what was at the time North America's most expensive course. In 1989 the Tunnel Nine opened (along with a new clubhouse), creating today's 27-hole course.

Between 1997 and 1999 no expense was spared in rebuilding the entire original 18 holes and adding longer tees, while also reverting to Thompson's planned sequence of play, known now as the **Stanley Thompson 18.** The course is typically Thompson, taking advantage of natural contours, and featuring elevated tees, wide fairways, treacherous fescue grass rough, and holes aligned to distant mountains. From the back markers it is 7,087 yards and plays to a par of 71. The course is not only breathtakingly beautiful, but it's also challenging for every level of golfer. Pick up a copy of the book *The World's Greatest Golf Holes,* and you'll see a picture of the fourth hole on the Rundle Nine. It's a par three, over Devil's Cauldron 70 meters (230 feet) below, to a small green backed by the sheer face of Mount Rundle rising vertically more than 1,000 meters (3,280 feet) above the putting surface. Another unique feature of the course is the abundance of wildlife: there's always the chance of

© ANDREW HEMPSTEAD

Please rake the bunkers when you've finished.

seeing elk feeding on the fairways, or coyotes, deer, or black bears scurrying across.

Greens fees are $180 for the Stanley Thompson 18 ($150 for Canadian residents). Rates are discounted to $135 in June, and reduced further through the first and last months of operation, May and early October, to $70. The Tunnel 9 offers the same spectacular challenges as Thompson's original layout, but lacks the history; nine holes is $50, or play twice for $75. Free shuttle buses run from the Fairmont Banff Springs to the clubhouse. (The original 1911 clubhouse still stands, but has been replaced by a modern, circular building in the heart of the course.) There you'll find club rentals ($40), three putting greens, a driving range, a pro shop, two chipping greens with surrounding bunkers, and a restaurant. Booking tee times well in advance is essential; call 403/762-6801.

WINTERTIME

From November till May, the entire park transforms itself into a winter playground covered in a blanket of snow. Of Alberta's six world-class

winter resorts, three are in Banff National Park. Ski Banff @ Mount Norquay is a small but steep hill overlooking the town of Banff; Sunshine Village perches high in the mountains on the Continental Divide, catching more than its share of fluffy white powder; and Lake Louise, Canada's second-largest winter resort, spreads over four distinct mountain faces. Apart from an abundance of snow, the resorts have something else in common—spectacular views, which alone are worth the price of a lift ticket.

Other winter activities in the park include cross-country skiing, ice-skating, snowshoeing, dogsledding, or just relaxing. Crowds are nonexistent and hotels reduce rates by up to 70 percent (except Christmas holidays)—reason enough to venture into the mountains. Lift and lodging packages begin at $70 per person.

Ski Banff @ Mount Norquay

The steep eastern slopes of Mount Norquay had been attracting local skiers for 20 years before Canada's first chairlift was installed on its face in 1948. Ever since then, the resort has had an experts-only reputation, mainly because of terrain serviced by the North American Chair (including the famous double-black-diamond Upper Lone Pine run). But an express quad installed in 1990 opened up new intermediate terrain and made the resort a favorite with shredders and cruisers alike. Snowboarders congregate at a half-pipe and terrain park. A magnificent post-and-beam day lodge nestled below the main runs is surrounded on one side by a wide deck that catches the afternoon sun while inside is a cafeteria, restaurant, and bar. Lift tickets are $49 adults, $38 seniors, $16 children; lift, lesson, and rental packages cost about the same. A few runs are lit for night skiing and boarding on Friday evening; $24 adults, $22 seniors, $12 children. A shuttle makes bus pickups from Banff hotels for the short, six-km (3.7-mile) ride up to the resort; $5. For more information on the resort, call 403/762-4421; website: www.banffnorquay.com.

Sunshine Village

The skiing and boarding at Sunshine has lots going for it—more than six meters (20 feet) of snow annually (no need for snowmaking up here), wide-open bowls, a season stretching for nearly 200 days, skiing and boarding in two provinces, and the only slope-side accommodations in the park.

The first people to ski the Sunshine Meadows were two local men, Cliff White and Cyril Paris, who became lost going over Citadel Pass in the spring of 1929 and returned to Banff with stories of deep snow and ideal slopes for skiing. In the following years, a CPR cabin was used as a base for skiing in the area. In 1938 the Canadian National Ski Championships were held here, and in 1942 a portable lift was constructed. The White family was synonymous with the Sunshine area for many years, running the lodge and ski area while Brewster buses negotiated the steep, narrow road that led to the meadows. In 1980 a gondola was installed to whisk skiers and snowboarders six km (3.7 miles) from the parking area to the alpine village. More recently, new high-speed quads have replaced old chairlifts and opened up new terrain, and the original gondola was replaced. One of Canada's most infamous runs, Delirium Dive, off the northeast-facing slope of Lookout Mountain, opened after a 20-year closure for the 1998–1999 season. To ski or board this up-to-50-degree run, you must be equipped with a transceiver, shovel, probe, and partner, but you'll have bragging rights that night at the bar (especially if you've descended the Bre-X line).

Aside from Delirium Dive, the area is best known for its excellent beginner and intermediate terrain, which covers 60 percent of the mountain. The resort is serviced by an eight-person gondola, six high-speed quads, and a variety of surface lifts. The total vertical rise is 1,070 meters (3,510 feet), and the longest run (down to the lower parking lot) is eight km (five miles). Lift tickets are $56 per day for adults, $46 seniors, $20 children, and those younger than six ride free. Two days of skiing or boarding and one night's lodging at slopeside Sunshine Inn costs from $155 per person per day. The inn has a restaurant, lounge, game room, and hot tub. For lodging and general resort information, call 403/762-6500 or 877/542-2633; website: www.skibanff.com. Transportation from Banff, Canmore, or Lake Louise to the resort is $10 round-trip; check the website or inquire at major hotels for the timetable.

Lake Louise

Canada's answer to U.S. mega-resorts such as Vail and Killington is Lake Louise. The nation's second-largest winter resort (behind only Whistler/Blackcomb) comprises 1,700 hectares (4,200 acres) of gentle trails, mogul fields, long cruising runs, steep chutes, and vast bowls filled with famous Rocky Mountain powder.

The resort is made up of four distinct faces. The front side has a vertical drop of 1,000 meters (3,280 feet) and is served by eight lifts, including four high-speed quads, and western Canada's only six-passenger chairlift. Resort statistics are impressive: a 990-meter (3,250-foot) vertical rise, 1,700 hectares (4,200 acres) of patrolled terrain, and more than 100 named runs. The four back bowls are each as big as many midsize resorts and are all well above the tree line. Larch and Ptarmigan faces have a variety of terrain, allowing you to follow the sun as it moves across the sky or escape into trees for protection on windy days. Each of the three day lodges has a restau-

LAKE LOUISE: THE DEVELOPMENT OF A WORLD-CLASS RESORT

The earliest skiing undertaken in the Lake Louise area was in the 1920s, when groups from Banff went backcountry touring in the Skoki Valley. In 1930, Cliff White and Cyril Paris built a small ski chalet in the valley. The location of this chalet, 20 km (12.5 miles) from the nearest road, turned out not to be practical, so a closer one was built on the site of today's Temple Lodge. In 1954, a lift was constructed next to Temple Lodge's back door, opening the slopes of Larch Mountain to the ever-increasing number of downhill enthusiasts in the area.

A young Englishman who had inherited a fortune from his father saw the potential for a world-class alpine resort here and made the completion of his dream a lifelong obsession. Norman Watson, known as the

© ANDREW HEMPSTEAD

"Barmy Baronet," pulled together a group of financiers and constructed a gondola up the slopes of Whitehorn in 1958. More lifts were constructed, and two runs—Olympic Men's Downhill and Olympic Ladies' Downhill—were cut on the south face of Whitehorn in anticipation of a successful bid for the 1968 Winter Olympics. The bid eventually failed because of the opposition of environmentalists (the same reason that the alpine events of the Calgary Winter Olympics were held on a specially built hill outside of the park boundary).

Huge development plans for the base area that included rooms for 6,500 guests were scuttled in 1972, but under the supervision of one-time local mountain guide Charlie Locke, the resort has retained its reputation as one of the world's great winter resorts.

rant and bar. Ski and snowboard rentals, clothing, and souvenirs are available in the Lodge of the Ten Peaks, a magnificent post-and-beam day lodge that overlooks the front face.

Lift tickets are $59 per day adults, $47 seniors, and $15 children younger than 12. Lifts are open from November to early May, 9 A.M.–4 P.M. Free guided tours of the mountain are available three times daily—inquire at customer service. Free shuttle buses run regularly from Lake Louise accommodations to the hill. From Banff you pay $15 round-trip for transportation to Lake Louise. For more information on the resort, call 403/522-3555 or 877/253-6888; website: www.skilouise.com.

Rentals and Sales

Each resort has ski and snowboard rental and sales facilities, but getting your gear down in town is often easier. **Monod Sports,** 129 Banff Avenue, 403/762-4571, has been synonymous with Banff and the ski industry for more than 50 years, and while the **Rude Boys Snowboard Shop,** downstairs in the Sundance Mall, 215 Banff Avenue, 403/762-8480, has only been around since the 1980s, it is *the* snowboarder hangout. Other shops with sales and rentals include **Abominable Ski & Sport,** 229 Banff Avenue, 403/762-2905; **Adventures Unlimited,** 211 Bear Street, 403/762-4554; **Mountain Magic Equipment,** 224 Bear Street, 403/762-2591; **Ski Stop,** in the Fairmont Banff Springs, 403/762-5333; and **Snow Tips,** 225 Bear Street, 403/762-8177. Basic packages—skis, poles, and boots—are $20–25 per day, while high-performance packages range $30–45. Snowboards and boots rent for $20–40 per day.

Switching Gear, 718 10th Street, 403/678-1992, down the valley from Banff in nearby Canmore, has an excellent selection of used ski and snowboard equipment, as well as winter clothing at very reasonable prices.

Cross-Country Skiing

No better way of experiencing the park's winter delights exists than skiing through the landscape on cross-country skis. Many summer hiking trails are groomed for winter travel. The most popular areas are Johnson Lake, Golf Course Road, Spray River, Sundance Canyon, Moraine Lake Road, on Lake Louise, and in Skoki Valley at the back of Lake Louise winter resort. The booklet *Cross-country Skiing—Nordic Trails in Banff National Park* is available for $1 from the Banff and Lake Louise Visitor Centres. Weather forecasts (403/762-2088) are posted at both centers.

Rental packages are available from **Performance Sports,** 208 Bear Street, 403/762-8222; **Snowtips,** 225 Bear Street, 403/762-8177; and **Mountain Magic Equipment,** 224 Bear Street, 403/762-2591. Expect to pay $12–20 per day. **White Mountain Adventures,** 403/678-4099, offer lessons for $50 per person, as well as an ice walk through a frozen Johnston Canyon.

Ice-Skating

Of all the ice-skating rinks in Canada, the one on frozen **Lake Louise,** in front of the chateau, is surely the most spectacular. Spotlights allow skating after dark, and on special occasions hot chocolate is served. Skates are available in the chateau at **Monod Sports,** 403/522-3837; $12 for two hours. Other rinks are at **Banff High School** on Banff Avenue at Wolf Street and on the **Bow River** along Bow Street. Rent skates from **The Ski Stop** in the Fairmont Banff Springs, 403/762-5333; $7.50 per hour.

Sleigh Rides

Warner Guiding and Outfitting offers sleigh rides on the frozen Bow River throughout winter. For reservations, call 403/762-4551 or stop by the Trail Rider Store at 132 Banff Avenue ($18 per person). **Brewster Lake Louise Sleigh Rides,** 403/522-3511, offers rides in traditional horse-drawn sleighs along the shores of Lake Louise beginning from in front of the chateau. Although blankets are supplied, you should still bundle up. The one-hour ride is $18 per person, $12 for children. Reservations are necessary. The rides are scheduled hourly from 11 A.M. on weekends, from 3 P.M. weekdays.

Other Winter Activities

Beside the Fairmont Banff Springs is an unofficial toboggan run; ask at your hotel for sleds or rent them from **The Ski Stop,** in the Fairmont Banff Springs; $5 per hour.

Banff Fishing Unlimited offers ice-fishing trips on nearby lakes, 403/762-4936, while curling bonspiels take place at the Banff Recreation Centre on Mount Norquay Road.

Anyone interested in ice climbing must register at the national park desk in the Banff Visitor Centre or call 403/762-1550. The world-famous (if you're an ice climber) **Terminator** is just outside the park boundary.

If none of these activities appeal to you, head to **Upper Hot Springs,** 403/762-1515, for a relaxing soak; open daily 10 A.M.–10 P.M. ($7.50).

Camping might not be everyone's idea of a winter holiday, but Tunnel Mountain Village II campground remains open year-round.

INDOOR RECREATION

Fitness and Swimming Facilities

Many of Banff's better hotels have fitness rooms and some have indoor pools. A popular place to swim and work out is in the **Sally Borden Recreation Facility,** at the Banff Centre, St. Julien Road, 403/762-6450, which holds a wide range of fitness facilities and a 25-meter-long heated pool. General admission is $9.50, or pay $3.75 to swim only. It's open daily 6:30 A.M.–11 P.M. **Mountain Magic Equipment,** one block off the main drag at 224 Bear Street, 403/762-2591, has climbing and bouldering walls (free) with instruction and gear rentals offered for a reasonable price.

Willow Stream

This luxurious spa facility in the Fairmont Banff Springs, 403/762-2211, is the place to pamper yourself. Opened in 1995 at a cost of $12 million, it sprawls over two levels and 3,000 square meters (0.7 acres) of a private corner of the hotel. The epicenter of the facility is a circular mineral pool capped by a high glass-topped ceiling and ringed by floor-to-ceiling windows on one side and on the other by hot tubs fed by cascading waterfalls of varying temperatures. Other features include outdoor saltwater hot tubs, private solariums, steam rooms, luxurious bathrooms, a café featuring light meals, and separate male and female lounges complete with fireplaces and complimentary drinks and snacks. A great variety of other services are offered, including facials, body wraps, massage therapy, salon services, and hydrotherapy. Entry to Willow Stream is included in some package rates for guests at the hotel. General admission is $50 per day (book in advance), which includes the use of a locker and spa attire, with almost 100 services available at additional cost (most of these include general admission, so, for example, you can spend the day at Willow Stream and receive a one-hour massage for $129). Willow Stream is open daily 6 A.M.–10 P.M.

Other Indoor Recreation

Fairmont Banff Springs, 403/762-2211, has a four-lane, five-pin bowling center; games are $3.75 per person. **King Edward Billiards,** upstairs at 137 Banff Avenue, 403/762-4629, is a large, clean pool hall. Tables are $15 per hour. The **Lux Cinema Centre,** 229 Bear Street, 403/762-8595, shows new releases for $9 ($5 on Tuesday).

Banff's only waterslide is in the **Douglas Fir Resort** on Tunnel Mountain Drive, 403/762-5591. The two slides are indoors, and the admission price of $7.50 (younger than five free) includes use of a hot tub and exercise room. It's open Mon.–Fri. 4–9:30 P.M., Sat.–Sun. 10 A.M.–9:30 P.M.

NIGHTLIFE
Bars and Lounges

Like resort towns around the world, Banff has more than its fair share of bars and nightclubs. **Wild Bill's,** upstairs at 201 Banff Avenue,

403/762-0333, is named for Banff guide Bill Peyto and is truly legendary. Bands usually play a bit of everything, but generally expect alternative music early in the week and rock or country Thursday–Sunday. The food here is excellent. Just as popular is the **Barbary Coast,** 119 Banff Avenue, 403/762-4616, which also serves good food and has live music in a clean, casual atmosphere. Across the road from Wild Bill's is the **Rose and Crown,** 202 Banff Avenue, 403/762-2121, an English-style pub serving British beers and typical pub meals. It also features a rooftop patio and rock-and-roll bands a few nights a week. The **Pump and Tap Tavern,** in the lower level of the Sundance Mall, 215 Banff Avenue, 403/760-6610, features cavelike furnishings befitting its location. It's a popular locals' hangout, with free pool in the afternoon and nightly drink specials. **St. James Gate Old Irish Pub,** 207 Wolf Street, 403/762-9355, is a large Irish-style bar with a reputation for excellent British-style meals and occasional appearances by Celtic bands. Away from busy Banff Avenue is **Melissa's,** 218 Lynx Street, 403/762-5776, which is a long-time favorite drinking hole for locals. It has a small outdoor patio, a long evening happy hour, pool tables, and multiple TVs.

Many Banff hotels have small lounges open to guests and nonguests alike. They are generally quieter than those listed previously and often offer abbreviated menus from adjacent restaurants. The best of these is **Outfitters,** in Brewster's Mountain Lodge, at 208 Caribou Street, 403/762-2900, a casual yet elegant lounge that exudes a stylish Western atmosphere. Another of the more stylish places for a quiet drink is the lounge at **Buffalo Mountain Lodge,** Tunnel Mountain Road, 403/762-2400. The **Mount Royal Hotel,** corner of Banff Avenue and Caribou Street, has a small lounge off the lobby, while below, accessed from farther up Banff Avenue, is the **Buffalo Paddock,** 138 Banff Avenue, 403/762-3331, with pool tables. At the opposite end of the style scale to the hotel bars is the lounge in the **Voyager Inn,** 555 Banff Avenue, 403/762-3301, which is worth listing for the fact that it has the cheapest beer in town and drink specials every night. Just past the Voyager Inn is **Bumpers,** 603 Banff Avenue, 403/762-2622, a steakhouse with a small bar and pool table upstairs.

Nightclubs

Banff has two nightclubs. Cavernous **Aurora,** downstairs in the Clock Tower Mall at 110 Banff Avenue, 403/760-5300, was formerly an infamous gathering place known as Silver City, but after renovations in the late 1990s added some class to Banff's clubbing scene (and is respectable early in the evening), but becomes one obnoxiously loud, overpriced smoky pickup joint after midnight. The other option is **Outabounds,** 137 Banff Avenue (enter from Caribou St.), 403/762-8434.

Police patrol Banff all night, promptly arresting anyone who even looks like trouble, including anyone drunk or drinking on the streets.

In Lake Louise

Hang out with seasonal workers at the smoky **Lake Louise Grill & Bar,** upstairs in Samson Mall, 403/522-3879, or head to **Charlie's Pub** in the Lake Louise Inn, 403/3791, for dancing to recorded music. Although the bar in the Post Hotel doesn't have mountain views, it has light food, a fireplace, and a distinctive mountain atmosphere. In the Fairmont Chateau Lake Louise, 403/522-3511, is **The Glacier Saloon,** where on most summer nights a DJ plays music ranging from pop to western.

SHOPPING

It may seem a little strange, but city folk from Calgary actually drive into Banff National Park to shop for clothes. This reflects the number of clothing shops in Banff rather than a lack of choice in one of Canada's largest cities. About the only clothing store that Banff lacks is an army-surplus outlet.

Canadiana and Clothing

Few companies in the world were as responsible for the development of a country as was the **Hudson's Bay Company** (HBC) in Canada. Founded in 1670, the HBC established trading posts throughout western Canada, many of which attracted settlers, forming the nucleus for towns and cities that survive today, including Alberta's capital, Edmonton. HBC stores continue their traditional role of providing a wide range of goods, in towns big and small across the country. In Banff, the HBC store is at 125 Banff Avenue, 403/762-5525. Another Canadian store, this one famous for its fleeces, sweaters, and leather goods, is **Roots,** 227 Banff Avenue, 403/762-9434. For western clothing and accessories, check out the **Trail Rider Store,** 132 Banff Avenue, 403/762-4551. Pick up your Canadian-made Tilley Hat and other Tilley Endurables from **Piccatilley Square,** on the main floor of the Cascade Plaza at 317 Banff Avenue, 403/762-0302. Also in Cascade Plaza is **Boardwalk,** 403/760-8755, with a good selection of well-priced outdoor clothing. The **Rude Boys** is a snowboard and skate shop downstairs in the Sundance Mall, 215 Banff Avenue, 403/762-8480. Take a look—their T-shirts are hilarious (and, unlike anything along Banff Avenue, original), but don't expect to find anything for your grandparents here.

Camping and Outdoor Gear

Inexpensive camping equipment and supplies can be found in **Home Hardware,** 208 Bear Street, 403/762-2080, and **The Hudson's Bay Company,** 125 Banff Avenue, 403/762-5525 (in the low-ceilinged downstairs section). More specialized needs are catered to at **Mountain Magic Equipment,** 224 Bear Street, 403/762-2591. The store stocks a large range of top-quality outdoor and survival gear (including climbing equipment) and rents tents ($20 per day), sleeping bags ($12), backpacks ($10), and boots ($10). Mountain Magic Equipment also sells and repairs all types of bikes.

One of the best places to shop for outdoor apparel is **Outdoor Access,** 201 Banff Avenue, 403/760-8282; downstairs is a factory outlet with big savings. Other recommended stores are **Monod Sports,** 129 Banff Avenue, 403/762-4571; **Boardwalk,** in Cascade Plaza at 317 Banff Avenue, 403/760-8755; **Columbia Mountain Shop,** 202 Caribou Street, 403/760-2345; and **Helly Hansen,** in the back of Kirby Lane Mall at 119 Banff Avenue, 403/762-5954.

Gifts and Galleries

Banff's numerous galleries display the work of mostly Canadian artists. **Canada House,** 201 Bear Street, 403/762-3757, features a wide selection of Canadian landscape and wildlife works and native art. The **Quest Gallery,** 105 Banff Avenue, 403/762-2722, offers a diverse range of affordable Canadian paintings and crafts as well as more exotic pieces such as mammoth tusks from prehistoric times and Inuit carvings from Nunavut. Across the Bow River from downtown, browse through traditional native arts and crafts at the **Indian Trading Post,** 1 Birch Avenue, 403/762-2456.

FESTIVALS AND EVENTS

Spring

Most of the major spring events take place at local winter resorts, including a variety of snowboard competitions that make for great spectator viewing. At Lake Louise a half pipe and jump are constructed right in front of the day lodge for this specific purpose. One long-running spring event is the **Slush Cup,** which takes place at Sunshine Village in late May. Events include kamikaze skiers and boarders who attempt to jump an ice-cold pit of water. While winter enthusiasts are at higher elevations, swooshing down the slopes of some of North America's latest-closing resorts, late spring sees the Banff Springs golf course open for the season.

During the second week of June, the **Banff Television Festival,** 403/678-9260, www.banfftvfest.com, attracts the world's best television directors, producers, writers, and even actors for meetings, workshops, and awards, with many show screenings open to the public.

Summer

Summer is a time of hiking and camping, so festivals are few and far between. The main event is the **Banff Arts Festival,** a three-week (mid-July to early August) extravaganza presented by professional artists studying at the Banff Centre.

They perform dance, drama, opera, and jazz for the public at locations around town. Look for details in the *Crag and Canyon,* call 403/762-6214 or 800/413-8368, or go to the website, www.banffcentre.ca.

On July 1, Banff celebrates **Canada Day** with a pancake breakfast, a parade down Banff Avenue, and then an afternoon of fun and frivolity in Central Park that includes events such as a stupid pet tricks competition.

Each summer the national park staff presents an extensive **Park Interpretive Program** at locations in town and throughout the park, including downstairs in the visitors center daily at 8:30 P.M. All programs are free and include guided hikes, nature tours, slideshows, campfire talks, and lectures. For details, consult *The Mountain Guide* available at the Banff Visitor Centre, 403/762-1550, or look for postings on campground bulletin boards.

Fall

Fall is the park's quietest season, but busiest in terms of festivals and events. First of the fall events, on the last Saturday in September, **Melissa's Mini-marathon** attracts more than 2,000 runners in 3-, 10-, and 22-km races. The *International Banff Springs Wine and Food Festival* is hosted by the Fairmont Banff Springs at the end of October. To encourage tourism during the quietest time of the year, **Winterstart** (November to mid-December) features cheap lodging and a host of fun events. This coincides with the opening of lifts at the park's three winter resorts beginning in mid-November.

Banff Mountain Festivals

One of the year's biggest events is the **Banff Mountain Film Festival,** held on the first weekend of November. Mountain-adventure filmmakers from around the world submit films to be judged by a select committee. Films are then shown throughout the weekend to an enthusiastic crowd of thousands. Exhibits and seminars are also presented, and top climbers and mountaineers from around the world are invited as guest speakers.

Tickets go on sale one year in advance and sell out in advance. Tickets for daytime shows start at $40 (for up to 10 films). Night shows are from $30, and all-weekend passes cost around $140 (weekend passes with two nights accommodations and breakfasts start at a reasonable $250). Films are shown in the two theaters of the Banff Centre. For more information, call the festival office at 403/762-6675; for tickets, call the Banff Centre box office, 403/762-6301 or 800/413-8368. Tickets can also be purchased online by following the links at www.banffcentre.ab.ca. If you miss the actual festival, it hits the road on the Best of the Festival World Tour. Look for it in your town, or check out the listed website for venues and dates.

Starting in the days leading up to the film festival, then running in conjunction with it, is the **Banff Mountain Book Festival,** which showcases the work of publishers, writers, and photographers whose work revolves around the world's great mountain ranges. Tickets can be bought to individual events ($15–30), as well as a Book Festival Pass and a pass combining both festivals.

Winter

By mid-December lifts at all local winter resorts are open. **Santa Claus** makes an appearance on Banff Avenue at noon on the last Saturday in November; if you miss him there, he usually goes skiing at each of the local resorts on Christmas Day. Events at the resorts continue throughout the long winter season, among them **World Cup Downhill** skiing at Lake Louise in late November. The **Banff/Lake Louise Winter Festival** is a 10-day celebration at the end of January that has been a part of Banff's history since 1917. Look for ice sculpting on the frozen lake in front of the Chateau Lake Louise, the Lake Louise Loppet, barn dancing, and the Town Party, which takes place in the Fairmont Banff Springs.

Accommodations and Camping

Finding a room in Banff National Park in summer is nearly as hard as trying to justify its price. By late afternoon just about every room and campsite in the park will be occupied, and basic hotel rooms begin at around $100. Fortunately, many alternatives are available. Rooms in private homes begin at around $50 s, $60 d. Canmore, just outside the park boundary, has many hotels and motels. Hostelling International–Banff Alpine Centre has dormitory-style accommodations for less than $30 per person per night. Bungalows or cabins can be rented, which can be cost-effective for families or small groups. Approximately 2,400 campsites in 13 campgrounds accommodate campers. Wherever you decide to stay, it is vital to book well ahead during summer and the Christmas holidays. The park's off-season is from October to May, and hotels offer huge rate reductions during this period. Shop around and you'll find many bargains.

All rates quoted are for a standard room in the high season (June–Sept.).

Banff Central Reservations

Banff Central Reservations, 403/705-4020 or 877/542-2633, www.banffreservations.com, is tied in with Sunshine Village, but has been providing an excellent booking and reservation service for many years.

IN AND AROUND THE TOWN OF BANFF

Banff has a few accommodations right downtown, but most are strung out along Banff Avenue, an easy walk from the shopping and dining precinct. Nearby Tunnel Mountain is also home to a cluster of accommodations.

Less Than $50

The only beds in town less than $50 are in dormitories, and therefore, although rates are well less than $50, this is a per-person rate.

Hostelling International–Banff Alpine Centre, 403/762-4122, is just off Tunnel Mountain Road three km (1.9 miles) from downtown.

The central reservations line for the Banff Alpine Centre (and all other Hostelling International properties in the Canadian Rockies) is at 403/760-7580 or 866/762-4122, or book online at www.hihostels.ca. This large, modern hostel sleeps 216 in small two-, four-, and six-bed dormitory rooms. The large lounge area has a fireplace, and other facilities include a recreation room, public Internet access, bike and ski/snowboard workshop, large kitchen, self-service café, and laundry. In summer, members of Hostelling International pay $26 per person per night (nonmembers $30) for a dorm bed or $69 s or d ($77 for nonmembers) in a private room. The rest of the year, dorm beds are $21 (nonmembers $25) and private rooms $58 s or d (nonmembers $66). During July and August reserve at least one month in advance to be assured of a bed. The hostel is open all day, but check-in isn't until 3 P.M. To get there from town, ride the Banff Transit bus ($1), which passes the hostel twice an hour during summer. The rest of the year the only transportation is by cab, about $6 from the bus depot.

A former hospital building, the **Y Mountain Lodge,** 102 Spray Avenue, 403/762-3560 or 800/813-4138, www.ymountainlodge.com, has undergone massive renovations over the last few years and is now an excellent, centrally located choice for budget travelers. Facilities include the casual Sundance Bistro open throughout the day, a laundry facility, and the Great Room, a huge living area where the centerpiece is a massive stone fireplace with writing desks and shelves stocked with books scattered throughout. A bed in the dormitory is $24 per person, a private room that shares bathroom facilities is $58 s or d, and an ensuite is $75–90 s or d. These rates are reduced outside of summer.

Along the main strip of accommodations and a 10-minute walk to downtown is **Global Village Backpackers,** 449 Banff Avenue, 403/762-5521 or 888/844-7875, www.globalbackpackers.com. As converted motel rooms, each small dormitory has its own bathroom. Guest amenities include a hot tub, sauna, communal kitchen, games room with a pool table, TV room, activities desk,

bike rentals, quiet courtyard, and laundry. Dorm beds are $28 per person, with a number of semi-private rooms for $62 s or d.

$50–100

Accommodations in this price range are limited to private rooms at the three backpacker lodges and at a few bed-and-breakfasts. One such establishment is **Tan-Y-Bryn,** 118 Otter Street, 403/762-3696. Mrs. Cowan has been offering budget accommodation at this 1926 residence for many years, and although furnishings are sparse at best and bathrooms shared, the price is unequalled in town: $50–65 s, $55–75 d includes a light breakfast.

Blue Mountain Lodge, 137 Muskrat Street, 403/762-5134, www.bluemtnlodge.com, is a rambling, older-style lodge with 10 guest rooms, each with a private bath, TV, and telephone. Guests have use of shared kitchen facilities, a lounge, and Internet access while enjoying an expansive cold buffet breakfast for $85–110 s, $90–110 d each morning.

$100–150

Most Banff bed-and-breakfasts fall into this price range. The website of the Banff/Lake Louise Tourism Bureau, www.bankflakelouise.com, has detailed listings of all private homes registered to take guests. At the lower end of this price range, **Banff B&B,** 440 Muskrat Street, 403/762-8806, www.banffbb.com, is as good a choice as any. The owners have created a home-away-from-home atmosphere in a modern home set in a residential street yet just a short walk from Banff Avenue. Rates are $100–125 s or d.

Without a doubt, the best bed-and-breakfast in town is **Eleanor's House,** 125 Kootenay Avenue, 403/760-2457, www.bbeleanor.com, a lovely purpose-built guesthouse on a quiet residential street. It has a guest lounge, and each of the two luxuriously furnished rooms has a private bathroom and separate sitting area. Rates are $135 s, $145 d, which includes a gourmet cooked breakfast and evening drinks. Eleanor's is open mid-May to mid-October.

Elkhorn Lodge, 124 Spray Avenue, 403/762-2299 or 877/818-8488, is halfway up the hill to the Fairmont Banff Springs. The four small sleeping rooms are $105 s or d, while larger rooms with fridges are $155.

At the far end of the motel strip, the **Banff Voyager Inn,** 555 Banff Avenue, 403/762-3301 or 800/879-1991, www.banffvoyagerinn.com, offers the least expensive motel rooms in town. It has an outdoor swimming pool, a restaurant, a bar renowned for the cheapest beer in town, and a liquor store; $120–150 s or d.

Similarly priced and back toward downtown, all 52 rooms at the **Red Carpet Inn,** 425 Banff Avenue, 403/762-4184 or 800/563-4609, were recently renovated. Each has one or two queen beds and a full bath; $125–160 s or d.

Bumper's Inn is at the far end of the strip at 603 Banff Avenue, 403/762-3386 or 800/661-3518, www.bumpersinn.com. It's best known for its steakhouse, but behind the restaurant are 39 older-style rooms for $146 s or d (from $85 in winter).

Two blocks off Banff Avenue, the **Homestead Inn,** 217 Lynx Street, 403/762-4471 or 800/661-1021, www.homesteadinnbanff.com, is a fairly basic hostelry with a faux Tudor exterior and 27 guest rooms. High-season rates are $140–150 s or d, discounted well below $100 outside of summer.

$150–200

Dating to 1917, **Tarry-A-While,** 117 Grizzly Street, 403/762-0462, www.tarry.ca, was built for one of the Canadian Rockies' most famous residents, Mary Schäffer, by her outfitter husband Billy Warren. After escaping demolition in the 1980s, the most recent owners have opened the doors to guests, allowing a lucky few to soak up mountain heritage in its most pure form. Guests choose from three rooms, each with its own character. The simply furnished Wild Horse Room upstairs is particularly appealing. It features fir-paneled walls, a solid pine bed, and a clawfoot tub in the ensuite bathroom. Summer rates are $140 s, $150 d (from $90 s, $100 d the rest of the year), which includes an expansive breakfast spread and use of an upstairs sitting room piled high with local literature.

The days of Banff motel rooms less than $100 disappeared in 2001 when bulldozers took to the town's last remaining park-at-your-door motel, the **Spruce Grove Inn,** 545 Banff Avenue, now replaced by a modern mountain-style

The Spruce Grove Inn, which opened in 2002, provides good value among mid-priced lodging.

lodge of the same name. Rooms are spacious and a relatively good value at $160 s or d. At the time of writing, reservations and check-in are made at the adjacent Banff Voyager Inn, 403/762-3301 or 800/879-1991, www.banff voyagerinn.com.

Irwin's Mountain Inn, 429 Banff Avenue, 403/762-4566 or 800/661-1721, www.irwins-mountaininn.com, dates to the 1960s but was last renovated in 1995. It offers 65 rooms in 12 different configurations from $145 s, $155 d ($175 with a separate bedroom). Other amenities include underground parking, a small fitness room, a games room, laundry facilities, and the El Toro Restaurant.

On the same block as Irwin's is the **High Country Inn,** 419 Banff Avenue, 403/762-2236 or 800/661-1244, www.banffhighcoun-tryinn.com, which has a heated indoor pool, spacious hot tubs, a cedar-lined sauna, and the ever-popular Ticino Swiss/Italian restaurant. All rooms are adequately furnished with comfortable beds and a muted brown color scheme. Standard rooms are $155–165 s or d, but compared to similarly priced Banff rooms, the High Country's Honeymoon Suite ($210) is an excellent value; it features a king-size bed, fireplace, jetted tub, and a large balcony with views to Cascade Mountain.

The rooms at the **Dynasty Inn,** 501 Banff Avenue, 403/762-8844 or 800/667-1464, www.banffdynastyinn.com, are more modern, but town is a five-minute walk away. Each of the 99 rooms has a log-trimmed balcony, and the facade is Rundlestone (quarried locally and named for Mount Rundle). Rooms are $165 s or d.

If you have your own transportation, consider **Norquay's Timberline Inn,** away from downtown on the north side of the TransCanada Highway at the base of the Mount Norquay Road, 403/762-2281 or 877/762-2281, www.banfftimberline.com. Brightly decorated standard rooms are $155 s or d; those that face town (Valley View Rooms) are just $10 extra and have a private balcony. An in-house restaurant is open 7 A.M.–10 P.M.

Across a quiet road from the river and three blocks from downtown is the **Bow View Motor Lodge,** 228 Bow Avenue, 403/762-2261 or 800/661-1565, www.bowview.com. Moderately sized rooms are priced $155–180 s or d, including some with filtered river views. Amenities include a heated outdoor pool and a restaurant open for breakfast and lunch.

The **Rundlestone Lodge,** 537 Banff Avenue, 403/762-2201 or 800/661-8630, www.rundle-stone.com, features mountain-style architecture with an abundance of raw stonework and exposed timber inside and out. At street level is a comfortable sitting area centered on a fireplace, as well as an indoor pool, a lounge-style bar, and The Pines, one of Banff's premier restaurants. Furniture and fittings in the 96 rooms are elegant, and many have small balconies and gas fireplaces. Rooms begin at $195; some are wheelchair accessible.

Banff Traveller's Inn, 401 Banff Avenue, 403/762-4401 or 877/866-6660, www.banff-travellersinn.com, has larger rooms, many with mountain views. Summer rates are $190–200 s or d, with a buffet breakfast an additional $12 per person. It's appealing for winter travelers, with underground parking and accommodation/lift/transportation packages for less than $100 per person.

$200–250

More than 100 years since Jim and Bill Brewster guided their first guests through the park, their descendants are still actively involved in the tourist industry, opening Banff's most central and stylish accommodations in 1996. **Brewster's Mountain Lodge,** 208 Caribou Street, 403/762-2900 or 888/762-2900, www.brewsteradventures.com, features an eye-catching log exterior with an equally impressive lobby and adjoining lounge in a prime downtown location. The Western theme is continued in the 71 upstairs rooms. Superior rooms feature two queen-size beds or one king-size bed ($220), deluxe rooms offer a private balcony ($240), and Loft Suites have hot tubs (from $270). All rates include breakfast. Rates here in the off-season are slashed up to 50 percent.

After undergoing a massive renovation program, the **Banff Ptarmigan Inn,** 337 Banff Avenue, 403/762-2207 or 800/661-8310, has reopened as a full-service hotel with tastefully decorated rooms, down comforters on all beds, a restaurant, and a variety of facilities to soothe sore muscles, including a spa, a whirlpool, and a sauna. The 134 rooms start at $220 s or d.

Within easy walking distance of downtown is the **Banff Caribou Lodge,** 521 Banff Avenue, 403/762-5887 or 800/563-8764, www.banff-caribouproperties.com. Its 200 bright, airy rooms featuring handcrafted log furniture go for $220 s or d. Facilities include a guest shuttle bus, a family-style steakhouse, and a whirlpool and sauna. The impressive log entrance is not easily missed.

The **Banff International Hotel,** at 333 Banff Avenue, right at the downtown end of the motel strip, 403/762-5666 or 800/665-5666, www.banffinternational.com, is a sprawling, three-story full-service hotel that underwent extensive renovations inside and out in 1999, including the construction of an impressive cedar and stone lobby. Guests enjoy an abundance of in-room facilities, oak furniture, and marble bathrooms. Standard rooms are $220 s or d; the much larger corner rooms have mountain views and cost $270.

One of Banff's larger hotels, but a 10-minute walk to town, is **Inns of Banff,** 600 Banff Avenue, 403/762-4581 or 800/661-1272, www.innsofbanff.com. Each of the 180 rooms has a mini-bar, fridge, and balcony, while near the lobby are an indoor pool, lounge, bike rental outlet, and two restaurants; $220–285 s or d.

The following three accommodations are on Tunnel Mountain. Although falling in the same price range as many of those on Banff Avenue, all have self-contained units, making them good for families, small groups, or those who want to cook their own meals. Town is a 15-minute walk away.

The **Douglas Fir Resort,** 403/762-5591 or 800/661-9267, www.douglasfir.com, has 133 large condo-style units. Each has a fully equipped kitchen and a lounge with fireplace. Facilities include an indoor pool, two indoor waterslides, a hot tub, an exercise room, squash and tennis courts, a grocery store, and a laundromat. Rates begin at $210 s or d, discounted outside of early June to mid-September.

Across the road is **Tunnel Mountain Chalets,** 403/762-4515 or 800/661-1859, www.tunnel-mountain.com. Each modern unit has a kitchenette, fireplace, and two TVs; some have a whirlpool. One-bedroom units go for $208, two bedrooms $249.

Hidden Ridge Chalets, 403/762-3544 or 800/661-1372, www.banffhiddenridge.com, is just that, hidden, with 83 self-contained cabins spread among stands of Douglas fir and spruce, behind Tunnel Mountain Chalets. Each has a kitchen and wood-burning fireplace; $205 per night, $235 for larger chalets on the ridge.

$250–300

In the heart of downtown Banff, the venerable **Mount Royal Hotel,** 138 Banff Avenue, 403/762-3331 or 800/267-3035, www.mountroyalhotel.com, first opened in 1908. Since its purchase by the Brewster Transport Company in 1912, this distinctive red-brick building has seen various expansions and a disastrous fire in 1967, which destroyed the original wing. Today guests are offered 60 tastefully decorated rooms with high-speed Internet access and the use of a large health club with hot tub. Also on the premises are a restaurant and small lounge. Rates are from $260 s or d, but are discounted as low as $110 in the shoulder seasons.

With more than 200 rooms, two blocks from the heart of downtown Banff is the **Banff Park Lodge,** 222 Lynx Street, 403/762-4433 or 800/661-9266, www.banffparklodge.com, a modern, full-service luxury hotel that offers 24-hour room service, an indoor saltwater pool, two restaurants, and a string of boutique shops. The 211 rooms are smartly furnished and each has a balcony; standard rooms have two queen or one king bed for $259 s or d. Use the website to search out these same rooms for well less than $100 outside of summer.

One of Banff's newest hotels is the **Royal Canadian Lodge,** 459 Banff Avenue, 403/762-3307 or 800/661-1225, www.charltonresorts.com, which opened in the summer of 2000. It features 99 luxuriously appointed rooms, heated underground parking, a lounge

M

BANFF

and restaurant, a large spa-pool complex, and a landscaped courtyard. Rates start at $290 s or d.

The first things you'll notice at **Buffalo Mountain Lodge,** a 15-minute walk from town on Tunnel Mountain Road, 403/762-2400 or 800/661-1367, www.crmr/bml, is the impressive timber-frame construction, the hand-hewn construction of the lobby, with its vaulted ceiling and eye-catching fieldstone fireplace. The rooms, chalets, and bungalows all have fireplaces, balconies, large bathrooms, and comfortable beds topped by feather-filled duvets; many have kitchens. And you won't need to go to town to eat—one of Banff's best restaurants, Cilantro Mountain Café, is adjacent to the main lodge. Rooms start at $295 s or d. (The lodge takes its name from Tunnel Mountain, which early park visitors called Buffalo Mountain, for its shape.)

On Mountain Avenue, a short walk from the Upper Hot Springs, is **Rimrock Resort Hotel,** 403/762-3356 or 800/661-1587, www.rimrockresort.com. The original hotel was constructed in 1903 but was fully rebuilt and opened as a full-service luxury resort in the mid-1990s. Guest amenities include two restaurants, a health club, an outdoor patio, and underground heated parking. Each of 345 well-appointed rooms is decorated with earthy tones offset by brightly colored fabrics. They also feature picture windows, a king-size bed, a comfortable armchair, a writing desk, two phones, a mini-bar, and a hair dryer. This hotel caters to disabled persons as well as any in the park. Since it's set high above the Bow Valley, views for the most part are excellent. Prices range from $280 to $385 depending solely on the views. Regular shuttle buses make the short run to town during summer.

Also away from the main strip of accommodations is the **Banff Rocky Mountain Resort,** at the northeast end of Banff Avenue on the corner of Tunnel Mountain Road, 403/762-5531 or 800/661-9563, www.rockymountainresort.com. This property is an ideal alternative for groups or families. More than 170 spacious units are spread out across the well-manicured grounds, while the main building holds a lounge, café, restaurant, pool, and exercise room. Tennis courts are available for guest use, and cross-country ski trails are set during winter. Many of the one- and two-bedroom suites have kitchens, and all have fireplaces; $255 and $315, respectively. A free shuttle runs into town from the resort each hour.

More Than $300

The **Fairmont Banff Springs,** one of the world's great mountain resort hotels, has undergone massive renovations in recent years, cementing its position as Banff's premier accommodation. More than $30,000 has been spent installing air-conditioning, updating furnishings, and replacing beds in each of the 770 rooms. Other major changes include moving the lobby to a more accessible side of the hotel, reopening the old lobby as a cavernous lounge area, and changing many of the in-house dining facilities. Throughout the massive changes, the hotel came under the ownership of Fairmont Hotels and Resorts, losing its century-old tag as a Canadian Pacific hotel and in the process its ties to the historic railway company that constructed the original hotel back in 1888.

Even though the rooms have been modernized, many date to the 1920s, and as is common in older establishments, these accommodations are small. But room size is only a minor consideration when staying in this historic gem. With 12 eateries, a luxurious spa facility, a huge indoor pool, an elegant library, a 27-hole golf course, tennis courts, horseback riding, and enough twisting, turning hallways, boardwalks, towers, and shops to warrant a detailed map, you'll not be wanting to spend much time in your room. Unless, of course, you are in the presidential suite, located in the central tower. It has eight rooms, a canopy bed, a hot tub, a baby grand piano, a private pool, and your own private elevator linking each of the three floors.

In the process of changing ownership and undergoing the renovations, the way rooms are charged has also changed. Staying at the Banff Springs is now *very* expensive through summer, as rooms are charged as part of a package. Guests have a choice of two packages—the **Castle Experience** and the **Canadian Rockies Experience.** The Castle Experience is the less expensive of the two and includes golfing and golf lessons, horseback riding, guided hiking and climbing, tennis, mountain bike rental, canoeing, unlimited entry to Willow Stream spa facilities and one spa treatment, tennis, and three meals daily in any of hotel restaurants. This package taken in a Fairmont room costs $1,039 d, but these rooms are fairly small, and for an extra $100 you can stay in a much larger Fairmont Deluxe room. The Canadian Rockies Experience includes all that the Castle Experience does, as well as guided fishing, white-water rafting, and all Brewster tours. This package starts at $1,179 d with accommodations in the smallest rooms. (You may not want to take full advantage of all the activities offered. But if, for example, you decide to take a golf lesson and follow it up with a round on the hotel's course, go for an afternoon horseback ride, spend an evening at the spa, and dine in the hotel, the actual cost of the room will work out to about $300 for the night.) Between mid-September and mid-June, rooms are sold separately, or on a bed-and-breakfast basis, and prices start at $240 s, $280 d, but you may find cheaper deals at the Fairmont website. The hotel is at the end of Spray Avenue. To contact the hotel, call 403/762-2211. For reservations call 506/863-6310 or 800/257-7544, or click on the relevant link at www.fairmont.com.

ALONG THE BOW VALLEY PARKWAY

The Bow Valley Parkway is the original route between Banff and Lake Louise. It is a beautiful drive in all seasons, and along its length are four accommodations, each a viable alternative to staying in Banff.

Less Than $50

Thirty-two kilometers (20 miles) from Banff along the Bow Valley Parkway, **Hostelling International–Castle Mountain Wilderness Hostel** is near several interesting hikes and across the road from a general store with basic supplies. This hostel sleeps 28 and has a kitchen, common room, hot showers, and bike rentals. Members of Hostelling International pay $18, nonmembers $22. Make bookings through the association's reservation line, 403/760-7580 or 866/762-4122, or book online at www.hihostels.ca.

$100–150

Johnston Canyon Resort, 403/762-2971 or 888/378-1720, www.johnstoncanyon.com, is 26 km (16 miles) west of Banff at the beginning of a short trail that leads to the famous canyon. The rustic cabins are older, and some have kitchenettes. On the grounds are tennis courts, a barbecue area, and a general store. Resort dining options are as varied as munching on a burger and fries at the counter of an old-time cafeteria to enjoying oriental-style Chilean sea bass in a dining room that oozes alpine charm. Basic two-person cabins are $119, two-person cabins with a fireplace are $159, and they go up in price all the way to $268 for a Classic cabin complete with cooking facilities and luxurious heritage-style furnishings. It's open mid-May to early October.

$150–200

Baker Creek Chalets, 403/522-3761, www.bakercreek.com, lies along the Bow Valley Parkway 40 km (25 miles) northwest of Banff and just 10 km (6.2 miles) from Lake Louise. Each of the 25 log cabins has a kitchenette, fireplace, and outside deck (complete with cute woodcarvings of bears climbing over the railings). Basic one-room cabins are $165 for two; one-bedroom cabins with loft (sleeps six) are $185; two-bedroom cabins (sleeps six) are $240. A newer lodge wing has eight luxurious suites, each with richly accented log work, a deck, a microwave and fridge, and a deluxe bathroom; $195 s or d, $215 with a double-jetted tub, and $275 with a loft. (Check the website for great off-season deals.) The restaurant here is highly recommended.

More Than $200

At Castle Junction, 32 km (20 miles) northwest of Banff, is **Castle Mountain Chalets,** 403/762-3868, www.castlemountain.com. Set on 1.5 hectares (four acres), this resort is home to 21 magnificent log chalets. Each has high ceilings, beautifully handcrafted log interiors, at least two beds, a stone fireplace, a full kitchen with dishwasher, a bathroom with hot tub, and satellite TV. Rates range $250–330 s or d. At the back of the grounds are several of the resort's original

BANFF

cabins. They can't be booked and are simply available to those who inquire at the front desk. They range $125–175 s or d and are only rented May–October. Part of the complex is a grocery store, barbeque area, library, and the only gas between Banff and Lake Louise. The nearest restaurants are located at Baker Creek and Johnson Canyon (see previous entries).

LAKE LOUISE

In summer, accommodations at Lake Louise are even harder to come by than in Banff, so it's essential to make reservations well in advance. Any rooms not taken by early afternoon will be the expensive ones.

Less Than $50

With beds for $100 less than anyplace else in the village, the **Hostelling International–Lake Louise Alpine Centre** is understandably popular. Of log construction, with large windows and high vaulted ceilings, the lodge is a joint venture between the Alpine Club of Canada and the Southern Alberta Hostelling Association. It opened early in the summer of 1992, and extensions in 1995 brought the total number of beds to 150. Downstairs are a large reception area and **Bill Peyto's Cafe,** the least expensive place to eat in Lake Louise. Upstairs are a large lounge area and guide's room—a quiet place to plan your next hike or browse through the large collection of mountain literature. Members of Hostelling International pay $26 per person per night (nonmembers $30) for a dorm bed or $64 s or d ($72 for nonmembers) in a private room. Rates are discounted to $21 for a dorm and $54 s or d for a private room ($25 and $62, respectively, for nonmembers) outside of summer, including throughout the extremely busy winter season. The hostel is open year-round, with check-in after 3 P.M. In summer and on weekends during the winter season, advance bookings (up to six months) are essential. The hostel is on Village Road, less than one km (0.6 miles) from Samson Mall, 403/522-2200. For reservations, call 403/760-7580 or 866/762-4122, or book online at www.hihostels.ca.

Lake Louise's Post Hotel enjoys a central riverside location.

$150–200

Not right in the village, but a good deal for families, small groups, and those who like privacy, **Paradise Lodge and Bungalows,** 403/522-3595, www.paradiselodge.com, provides excellent value in a wonderfully tranquil setting. Spread out around well-manicured gardens are 21 attractive cabins. Each has a rustic, yet warm and inviting interior, with comfortable beds, separate sitting areas, and well-appointed bathrooms. The least expensive cabins are $165, or pay just $10 extra for a one-bedroom cabin with a fully equipped kitchen ($185 for two bedrooms). A self-contained two-room bungalow, with a large balcony and views across the Bow Valley, is $195. Twenty-four newly built suites, each with a fireplace, TV, one or two bedrooms, and fabulous mountain views, start at $235, or $255 with a kitchen. The Honeymoon Suite, with all of the above as well as a large hot tub, is $285. The lodge is open mid-May to mid-October. To get there from the valley floor, follow Lake Louise Drive toward the Fairmont Chateau Lake Louise for three km (1.9 miles); the lake itself is just one km (0.6 miles) farther up the hill.

Historic **Deer Lodge,** 403/609-6150 or 800/661-1595, www.crmr.com/dl, began life in 1921 as a teahouse, with rooms added in 1925. Facilities include a rooftop hot tub, games room, restaurant, and bar. The least expensive rooms ($165 s or d) are small and don't have phones. Rooms in the $200–250 range are considerably larger, or pay $260 for a heritage-themed Tower Room. It's along Lake Louise Drive, up the hill from the village, and just a five-minute walk from the lake itself.

Aside from the Chateau, the **Lake Louise Inn,** 210 Village Rd., 403/522-3791 or 800/661-9237, www.lakelouiseinn.com, is the village's largest lodging, with more than 200 units spread throughout five buildings. Beyond the lobby, in the main lodge, is an activities desk, a pizzeria, a restaurant, a bar, a gift shop, and a large indoor pool. Standard rooms are $160 s or d, rising well above $200 for a suite with a fireplace.

Mountaineer Lodge, close to everything at 101 Village Road, 403/522-3844, www.mountaineerlodge.com, charges from $160 s, $170 d for large, functional guest rooms, each with separate sleeping areas and most with mountain views. It's only open May–October, with rates halved during the first and last months of the operating season.

More Than $200

Originally called Lake Louise Ski Lodge, the **Post Hotel,** 403/522-3989 or 800/661-1586, www.posthotel.com, is bordered to the east and south by the Pipestone River. It may lack views of Lake Louise, but it is as elegant, in a modern, woodsy way, as the Chateau. Each bungalow-style room is furnished with Canadian pine and has a balcony. Many rooms have whirlpools and fireplaces, while some have kitchens. Other facilities include an indoor pool, steam room, and library. High tea is served in the lobby each afternoon. The hotel has 17 different room types, with 26 different rates depending on the view. Rates start at $310 s or d per night. Between the main lodge and the Pipestone River are a row

of attractive cabins, each with a wood-burning fireplace; $360–600 s or d.

At the lake for which it's named, 16 km (10 miles) from the valley floor, is luxurious **Moraine Lake Lodge,** 403/522-3733 or 800/661-8340, www.morainelake.com. Designed by renowned architect Arthur Erickson, the lodge is a bastion of understated charm, partially obscured from the masses of day-trippers who visit the lake and yet taking full advantage of its location beside one of the world's most-photographed lakes. The décor reflects the wilderness location, with an abundance of polished log work and solid, practical furnishings in heritage-themed rooms. The rooms have no TVs or phones; instead guests take guided nature walks, have unlimited use of canoes, and are pampered with complimentary afternoon tea and evening liqueurs. It's only open June–September, with rooms starting at $435.

The **Fairmont Chateau Lake Louise,** a historic 500-room hotel on the shore of Lake Louise, has views equal to any mountain resort in the world, but all this historic charm and mountain scenery comes at a price. During the summer season (late June to mid-October), rooms must be booked as a Canadian Rockies Experience package, costing from $600 per person for accommodations, a wide range of activities, and all meals. This rate is for a standard room, with the cost rising exponentially for lakeside rooms and suites. Official rates drop as low as $200 s, $250 d outside of summer, with accommodation and lift packages often advertised for around $200 d. Children younger than 17 sharing with parents are free, but if you bring a pet it'll be an extra $25. For reservations—and you'll need one—call 506/863-6310 or 800/257-7544, www.fairmont.com.

ALONG THE ICEFIELDS PARKWAY

Less Than $50

North of Lake Louise, four hostels are spread along the Icefields Parkway, two in Banff and two in Jasper National Park. Facilities are limited, and beds should be reserved as far in advance as possible. For reservations, call 403/760-7580 or

M

BANFF

866/762-4122, or book online at www.hihostels.ca. The first, 24 km (15 miles) from Lake Louise, is **Mosquito Creek Wilderness Hostel,** which is near good hiking and offers accommodations for 32 in four cabins. Facilities include a kitchen, wood-heated sauna, and a large common room with fireplace. Rates are $18 per night for members of Hostelling International; nonmembers pay $22. Check-in is 5–10 P.M., and it's open year-round.

Hostelling International–Rampart Creek Wilderness Hostel, a further 64 km (40 miles) along the parkway, is nestled below the snow-capped peak of Mount Wilson, with views across the North Saskatchewan River to even higher peaks along the Continental Divide. Like Mosquito Creek, it's near good hiking and has a kitchen and sauna. Its two cabins hold 30 people. Members pay $18 per night, nonmembers $22. It's open nightly mid-May to mid-October and weekends only mid-December to mid-May (closed the rest of the year). Check-in is 5–11 P.M.

Note: In 2002, a fire destroyed much of **Hostelling International–Hilda Creek Wilderness Hostel**—for many years a welcome sight for cyclists after the long climb up to Sunwapta Pass from Rampart Creek—and the facility is closed indefinitely. Its closure has left a 55-km (34-mile) gap between hostels at Rampart Creek in the south and Beauty Creek (Jasper National Park) in the north.

$50–100

The Crossing, 403/761-7000, www.thecrossingresort.com, is a large complex 87 km (54 miles) north of Lake Louise and 45 km (28 miles) south of Columbia Icefield. It's also one km (0.6 miles) north of Saskatchewan River Crossing, where Highway 11 spurs east along Abraham Lake to Rocky Mountain House and Red Deer. The rooms offer a good combination of size and value, but lack the charm of those at Num-ti-jah to the south and the views enjoyed by those at the Columbia Icefield Centre to the north. Each of 66 units has a phone and television. They range $95–110 s or d, and are heavily discounted outside of June–September. In addition to overnight rooms, The Cross-

ing has the only gas between Lake Louise and Jasper, a self-serve cafeteria, a restaurant, a pub, and a large gift shop. It's open mid-March to November.

More Than $100

Pioneer guide and outfitter Jimmy Simpson built **Simpson's Num-ti-jah Lodge,** 403/522-2167, www.num-ti-jah.com, on the north shore of Bow Lake, 40 km (25 miles) north of Lake Louise, as a base for his outfitting operation in 1920. In those days, the route north from Lake Louise was nothing more than a horse trail. The desire to build a large structure when only short timbers were available led to the unusual octagonal shape of the main lodge. Simpson remained at Bow Lake, a living legend, until his death in 1972 at the age of 95. With a rustic mountain ambience that has changed little since Simpson's passing, an overnight stay at Num-ti-jah is a memorable experience. Just don't expect the conveniences of a regular motel. Under the distinctively red, steep-pitched roof of the main lodge are 25 rooms, some that share bathrooms, and there's not a TV or phone in sight. Downstairs, guests soak up the warmth of a roaring log fire while mingling in a comfortable library filled with historic mountain literature. A dining room lined with historic memorabilia is open throughout the day, serving up a breakfast buffet and evening delicacies such as shellfish fettuccini ($20). Rates are $165–180 s or d for a room with shared bath, $180–240 s or d for an ensuite. It's open year-round (except November), with rates reduced 40 percent outside of summer.

BACKCOUNTRY HUTS AND LODGES

Alpine Club of Canada Huts

Throughout the backcountry of the national park is an extensive system of 18 rustic huts managed by the Alpine Club of Canada. Due to their locations around favorite climbing areas, they are most often used by mountaineers as an overnight stop before assaulting some of the park's highest peaks, but they are available to anyone who wishes to take advantage of their remote location. Their accessibility ranges from the Elizabeth Parker Hut (Yoho National Park), which can be reached by bus, to the Neil Colgan Hut, Canada's highest habitable structure, 2,960 meters (9,700 feet) from sea level on a windswept ledge above Moraine Lake. Often of historical significance, each of the huts has a stove, lantern, kitchen utensils, and foam mattresses. Rates range $14–24 per person per night. For locations and reservations, contact the club at 403/678-3200, www.alpineclubofcanada.ca.

Shadow Lake Lodge

Shadow Lake Lodge, 403/762-0116, www.shadowlakelodge.com, is 14 km (8.7 miles) from the nearest road. Access is on foot or, in winter, on skis. The lodge is near picturesque Shadow Lake, and many hiking trails are nearby. Dating to 1928, the oldest structure has been restored as a rustic yet welcoming dining area, with a wood stove in the kitchen. Guests overnight in 12 newer, comfortable cabins. The daily rate, including three meals served buffet-style and afternoon tea, is $160 s, $140 d per person per day. The trailhead is along the TransCanada Highway, 19 km (12 miles) from Banff, at the Redearth Creek parking area. The summer season is mid-June to September.

Skoki Lodge

Skoki is a rustic lodge, deep in the backcountry north of Lake Louise winter resort. Getting there requires an 11-km (6.8-mile) hike or ski, depending on the season. The lodge is an excellent base for exploring nearby valleys and mountains. It dates to 1930, when it operated as a lodge for local Banff skiers, and is now a National Historic Site. Today it comprises a main lodge, three cabins, and a wood-fired sauna. Accommodations are rustic—no electricity or indoor plumbing—but comfortable, and the lodge has a reputation for excellent meals, which are included in the nightly rate of $120–150 per person per night. For information and reservations, call 403/522-3555 (1–5 P.M.), www.skokilodge.com.

CAMPGROUNDS

Within the park are 12 campgrounds that hold more than 2,000 sites. All campgrounds are filled on a first-come, first served basis. The official checkout time is 11 A.M., but you should plan on arriving at your campground of choice earlier in the day than this to ensure getting a site. At more popular locations, a lineup forms, waiting for sites to become vacant. This is especially true at the Banff and Lake Louise campgrounds, which offer powered sites. When these main campgrounds fill, those unable to secure a site will be directed to an overflow area. These provide few facilities and no hookups, but cost less. Open fires are permitted in designated areas throughout all campgrounds, but you must purchase a Firewood Permit ($6 per site per night) to burn wood, which is provided at no cost. For general camping information, stop at the Banff Visitor Centre at 224 Banff Avenue, 403/762-1550, or go the Parks Canada website, www.parkscanada.gc.ca/banff, and follow the camping links.

Near the Town of Banff

Although Banff has five campgrounds with more than 1,500 sites in its immediate vicinity, all fill by early afternoon. The three largest campgrounds are strung out over 1.5 km (0.9 miles) along Tunnel Mountain Road, with the nearest sites 2.5 km (1.6 miles) from town.

Closest to town are **Tunnel Mountain Village II** and **Tunnel Mountain Trailer Court.** The former has electrical hookups and is the only campground near Banff open year-round. The latter has full hookups and is open mid-May to September. Both have hot showers but little privacy between sites. Sites are $23–26 and no tents are allowed (except when Tunnel Mountain Village I is closed).

Less than one km (0.6 miles) farther along Tunnel Mountain Road is the park's largest campground (622 sites), **Tunnel Mountain Village I,** which is open mid-May to early September. Each site has a fire ring and picnic table, while other amenities include drinking water, hot showers, and kitchen shelters, but no hookups. Sites are $19.

Along the Lake Minnewanka Road northeast of town are two campgrounds offering fewer services than the others, but with sites that offer more privacy. The pick of the two is **Two Jack Lakeside Campground,** with 80 sites tucked into trees at the south end of Two Jack Lake, an extension of Lake Minnewanka. Facilities include hot showers, kitchen shelters, drinking water, and flush toilets. All sites are $17. Open June to mid-September. It's just over six km (3.7 miles) from the TransCanada Highway underpass. The much larger **Two Jack Main Campground** is a short distance further along the road, with 381 sites spread throughout a shallow valley. It offers the same facilities as Two Jack Lakeside, but has no showers; $15 per night. Open mid-June to mid-September. The overflow camping area for these and the three Tunnel Mountain campgrounds is at the beginning of the Lake Minnewanka Road loop, a short walk along Cascade River from a picturesque picnic area.

Bow Valley Parkway

Along Bow Valley Parkway between the town of Banff and Lake Louise are three campgrounds. Closest to Banff is **Johnston Canyon Campground,** between the road and the rail line 26 km (16 miles) west of Banff. It is the largest of the three campgrounds, with 140 sites, and has hot showers but no hookups. Almost directly opposite is Johnston Canyon Resort, with groceries and a restaurant, and the beginning of a trail to the park's best-known waterfalls. It's open early June to mid-September; $19 per night.

Continuing eight km (five miles) toward Lake Louise, **Castle Mountain Campground** is also within walking distance of a grocery store (no restaurant), but has just 44 sites and no showers. Services are limited to flush toilets, drinking water, and kitchen shelters. Sites are $15 and it's open from early June until the first weekend of September.

Protection Mountain Campground, a further 14 km (8.7 miles) west and just over 20 km (12.5 miles) from Lake Louise, opens as demand dictates, usually by late June. It offers 89 sites, along with flush toilets, drinking water, and stove-equipped kitchen shelters; $15 per site.

Lake Louise

Exit the TransCanada Highway at the Lake Louise interchange, 56 km (35 miles) northwest of Banff, and take the first left beyond Samson Mall and under the railway bridge to reach **Lake Louise Campground,** within easy walking distance of the village. The campground is divided into two sections by the Bow River, but linked by bridge. Individual sites throughout are close together, but some privacy and shade are provided by towering lodgepole pines. Just under 200 serviced (powered) sites are grouped together at the end of the road. In addition to hookups, this section has showers and flush toilets; $23. Across the river are 216 unserviced sites, each with a fire ring and picnic table. Other amenities include kitchen shelters and a modern bathroom complex complete with hot showers. These cost $19 per night. A dump station is located near the entrance to the campground ($6 per use). An interpretive program runs throughout summer, nightly at 9 P.M. (except Tuesday) in the outdoor theater. The serviced section of this campground is open year-round, the unserviced section mid-May to September.

From the campground, the Bow River Loop hiking trail leads into the village along either side of the Bow River, crossing at the southern end of the serviced sites and again behind Samson Mall.

Along the Icefields Parkway

Beyond Lake Louise, the first camping along the Icefields Parkway is at **Mosquito Creek Campground,** 24 km (15 miles) from the Trans-Canada Highway. Don't be perturbed by the name, though, the bugs here are no worse than anywhere else. The 32 sites are nestled in the forest, with a tumbling creek separating the campground from a hostel. Each site has a picnic table and fire ring, while other amenities include pump water, pit toilets, and a kitchen shelter with an old-fashioned woodstove. It's open year-round and all sites are $12. (If you're camping at Mosquito Creek and want a break from the usual camp fare, consider traveling a further 17 km/10.6 miles up the highway to the convivial dining room at Num-ti-jah Lodge, 403/522-2167, to feast on delights such as a tasty vegetable puree soup followed by rack of venison smothered in cranberry sauce.)

Waterfowl Lake Campground is 33 km (20 miles) north along the Icefields Parkway from Mosquito Creek. It features 116 sites between Upper and Lower Waterfowl Lakes, with a few sites in view of the lower lake. Facilities include pump water, flush toilets, and kitchen shelters with wood-burning stoves. Rise early to watch the first rays of sun hit Mount Chephren from the shoreline of the lower lake, then plan on hiking the four-km (2.5-mile) trail to Chephren Lake—

you'll be first on the trail and back in time for a late breakfast. Waterfowl Lake is open late-June–mid-September, and all sites are $15.

Continuing toward Jasper, the Icefields Parkway passes The Crossing, a good place to gas up and buy last-minute groceries before reaching **Rampart Creek Campground,** 31 km (19 miles) beyond Waterfowl Lake and 88 km (55 miles) from Lake Louise. With just 50 sites, this campground fills early. Facilities include kitchen shelters, pit toilets, and pump water. All sites are $12 per night, and it is open late June to early September.

Food

Banff alone has more than 100 restaurants. That's more per capita than any town or city across Canada. From lobster to linguini, alligator to à la carte, and fajitas to fudge, anyone who spends time in the park will find something that suits his or her taste and budget. Many of the town's restaurants have been around for decades and attract diners from as far away as Calgary (some of whom have been known to stay overnight just to eat at their favorite haunt). An eclectic mix of restaurants lines Banff Avenue; most have menus posted out front. The less adventurous can try one of the eateries at the major hotels; the Fairmont Banff Springs tops the list with a choice of 12 different dining options. In July and August, the most popular restaurants don't take reservations, and you can expect a wait. Various dining guides are available throughout town.

BANFF
Groceries
Banff has two major grocery stores. In addition to a wide selection of basic groceries, **Keller Foods,** 122 Bear Street, 403/762-3663, has a good deli with premade salads and sandwiches, preheated soup, and hot chickens. It's open in summer 7 A.M.–10 P.M.; shorter hours the rest of the year. At the other end of downtown, **Safeway,** 318 Marten Street, 403/762-5329, is open 8 A.M.–11 P.M.

Budget Stretchers
The best place to begin looking for cheap eats is the Food Court in the lower level of Cascade Plaza at 317 Banff Avenue. Here you'll find a juice bar, a small café, and **Banff Edo,** which sells simple Japanese dishes for around $7.50, including a drink. **Café Alpenglow,** in the Banff Alpine Centre, Tunnel Mountain

Busy Banff Avenue is lined with restaurants.
© ANDREW HEMPSTEAD

BREAKFAST FAVORITES

All of Banff's coffee shops and cafés open early for coffee and muffins, but for something more substantial to start the day, any one of the following will get you off on the right track.

Outfitter's, in Brewster's Mountain Lodge, 208 Caribou St., 403/762-5454, is a stylish lounge that opens each morning between 7–10 A.M. for a delicious breakfast buffet, which includes everything from mouth-watering omelets to gourmet yogurts; $14.50. The Rimrock Resort Hotel's **Primrose Restaurant,** Mountain Ave., 403/762-3356, is an elegant dining room with mountain views and well-spread tables giving a certain amount of pri-

vacy. This isn't your usual setting for a buffet, but the breakfast spread here through winter is one of the best in the valley; $18. **The Pines,** Rundlestone Lodge, 537 Banff Ave., 403/760-6690, serves up a continental breakfast buffet for $9.50, $14 with hot dishes, daily 7–10:30 A.M.

Melissa's, 218 Lynx St., 403/762-5511, is renowned for hotcakes, piled high on your plate, for $5.50. Or try the bran muffins made from scratch each morning. For traditional diner-style cooked breakfasts, head down to **Craig's Way Station,** 461 Banff Ave., 403/762-4660; open daily from 6:30 A.M. Cooked breakfasts are all less than $8.50.

Rd., 403/762-4122, features all the usual café-style dishes, such as a pile of nachos for $7; no entrée is more than $10. A local bylaw prohibiting obtrusive signs and neon lights means that the fast-food chains are easily missed. For the most expensive Big Macs this side of Toronto's SkyDome, head to **McDonald's,** 116 Banff Avenue. **KFC** is at 202 Caribou St. **Aardvarks,** 304 Caribou Street, 403/762-5500, is a late-night pizza hangout open until 4 A.M.

Cafés and Coffee Shops

The **Cake Company,** 220 Bear St., 403/762-2330, serves great coffee, as well as a delicious range of pastries, muffins, and cakes baked daily on the premises. Another Cake Company outlet is on the lower level of Cascade Plaza; a muffin and coffee is $2.50. **Evelyn's Coffee Bar,** on Banff Avenue in the Town Centre Mall, 403/762-0352, has good coffee and huge sandwiches. The few outside tables—on the busiest stretch of the busiest street in town—are perfect for people watching. **Jump Start,** opposite Central Park at 206 Buffalo Street, 403/762-0332, has a wide range of coffee concoctions as well as delicious homemade soups (from $5.50) and sandwiches ($7).

Family-Style Dining

In the Banff Caribou Lodge is **The Keg,** 521 Banff Avenue, 403/762-4442, part of a restaurant chain that began in Vancouver, which is

noted for its consistently good steak, seafood, and chicken dishes at reasonable prices. It also known for upbeat, well-presented servers. All entrées include a 60-item salad bar. The Keg is open daily 7 A.M.–2 A.M. Another Keg location is downtown at 117 Banff Avenue, 403/760-3030. **Earl's,** upstairs in the heart of the action at 229 Banff Avenue, 403/762-4414, has more of the same at slightly higher prices. This Alberta-born chain has a reputation for a menu of fusion cuisine that follows food trends, employs bright young servers, and offers a fun atmosphere.

The **Old Spaghetti Factory,** upstairs in the Cascade Plaza on Banff Avenue, 403/760-2779, is a family favorite, with a casual rustic décor, stained-glass windows, and a few tables spread along a balcony. Sort through a maze of combinations and specials, and the most you'll pay for a meal is $20, which includes soup or salad, a side of bread, dessert, and coffee. Open daily from 11:30 A.M. to late.

Joe Btfsplk's Diner (pronounced "bi-tif-splik's") is a modern 1950s-style diner, complete with a jukebox, a counter along the kitchen, and a range of tacky souvenirs. The menu is similarly themed, with daily specials for around $10 at lunch, $15 at dinner, and everything from Caesar salad to meatloaf on the regular menu. It's at 221 Banff Avenue., 403/762-5529, and is open daily for breakfast, lunch, and dinner.

Steak

Alberta beef is mostly raised on ranchland not far from the park and features prominently on menus throughout town. Finely marbled AAA beef is used in most restaurants and is unequalled in its tender, juicy qualities.

Even though **Bumper's,** 603 Banff Avenue, 403/762-2622, is away from the center of Banff, it's worth leaving the shopping strip and heading out to this popular steakhouse. Large cuts of Alberta beef, an informal atmosphere, efficient service, and great prices keep people coming back. Favorite choices are the slabs of Roast Prime Rib of Beef, in four sized cuts and cooked to order. Prices range from $18 for the Ladies cut to $29 for the Man Mountain cut, which includes unlimited trips to a small salad bar. Upstairs is the **Loft Lounge,** a good place to wait for a table or relax afterward with an inexpensive drink. It's open 4:30–10 P.M.

Offering tremendous views back across the highway to Mount Rundle and up the Spray Valley is the **Big Horn Steakhouse,** in Norquay's Timberline Inn, 403/762-2285. A cut of prime Alberta beef ranges $20–35, and while the food is good, the views will make you drool here. This restaurant is open daily 7 A.M.–10 P.M., with a sun deck open in summer.

Banff's most fashionable steakhouse is **Saltlik,** 221 Bear Street, 403/762-2467. It's big and bold and the perfect choice for serious carnivores with cash to spare. The concrete and steel split-level interior is complemented with modish wood furnishings. Facing the street, glass doors fold back to a terrace for warm-weather dining. The specialty is AAA Alberta beef, finished with grain feeding to enhance the flavor, then flash-seared at 650°C (1,200°F) to seal in the juices, and served with a side platter of seasonal vegetables. Entrées are priced comparable to a city steakhouse ($18–35), but the cost creeps up as you add side dishes. Open daily from 11 A.M.

Casually Canadian

Of the many Banff drinking holes that offer predictable pub-style menus, **Wild Bill's,** 201 Banff Avenue, 403/762-0333, is a standout. Named for one of Banff's most famed mountain men, the décor is suitably Western, with a menu to match. The Nachos Grande ($9.50) with a side of guacamole ($3) is perfect to share. Later in the day, steaks and spit-roasted chicken are traditional favorites ($15–30). Wild Bill's is open daily from 11 A.M. until well after midnight, but plan on dining before 9 P.M.

A town favorite that has faithfully served locals for many years is **Melissa's,** 218 Lynx Street, 403/762-5511, housed in a log building that dates from 1928 (the original Homestead Inn). Lunch and dinner are casual affairs—choose from a wide variety of generously sized burgers, freshly prepared salads, and mouthwatering Alberta beef. Melissa's also features an outside patio and rustic bar with well-priced drinks. Open daily 7:30 A.M.–10 P.M.

Bruno's Café & Grill, 304 Caribou Street, 403/762-8115, named for Bruno Engler, renowned photographer, ski instructor, and mountain man, is a cozy little café with a great mountain ambience and comfortable couches. It's open daily 7 A.M.–10 P.M.

© ANDREW HEMPSTEAD

Banff is undeniably busy, but escaping the crowds is possible. Head to the deli at Keller's on Bear Street, pick up a pre-made sandwich or freshly prepared salad, then search out an empty picnic table at Two Jack Lake along the Minnewanka Loop Road.

Classically Canadian

Occupying the prime position on one of Banff's busiest corners is the **Maple Leaf Grill,** 137 Banff Avenue, 403/760-7680. Take in the dramatic Canadian-themed décor—exposed river stone, polished log work, a two-story interior waterfall, and moose heads—then decide which section takes your fancy. The cooking uses modern styles with an abundance of Canadian game and produce. The lunch menu has beer-battered halibut and chips, along with lots of lighter salads and stir-frys ($9–15). Some of Canada's finest ingredients appear on the dinner menu: pan-seared arctic char cooked in an apple and wild sage butter and the apple-crusted pork tenderloin are standouts. Treat yourself to a glass of Canadian ice wine to accompany dessert. The Maple Leaf is open 11 A.M.–11 P.M.

The romantic era of the railway is relived in the **Caboose Dining Room,** in the historic railway station at the corner of Elk and Lynx Streets, 403/762-3622. Although not the original station, kings, queens, and millions of other visitors have passed through the building. The walls are lined with railway memorabilia, and the elegant atmosphere makes for a memorable dining experience. Alberta beef and a variety of seafood tops the menu out at $35, but dining here needn't be that expensive—a nut-crusted chicken breast marinated in garlic and lime and smothered in maple syrup is just $15. All meals include the self-service salad cart that is wheeled to your table. The Caboose is open daily 5–10 P.M.

The **Buffalo Mountain Lodge Restaurant,** at a lodge of the same name on Tunnel Mountain Road, 403/762-2400, offers the perfect setting for a moderate splurge. It features a distinctive interior of hand-hewn cedar beams and Old World elegance—complete with stone fireplace and a chandelier made entirely from elk antlers—along with large windows that frame the surrounding forest. The featured cuisine is referred to as Rocky Mountain, reflecting an abundance of Canadian game and seafood combined with native berries and fruits. The least expensive way to dine on this uniquely Canadian fare is by visiting at lunch and ordering the Rocky Mountain Game Platter, costing $20 for two people. Dinner entrées range $24–33 and include fare like elk sirloin that's given an exotic touch with accompanying quince compote. The restaurant is open daily 7 A.M.–10 P.M.

Canadian Contemporary

A hotel restaurant with an excellent reputation is **The Pines,** out of sight in the Rundlestone Lodge, 537 Banff Avenue, 403/760-6690. The setting is contemporary and unexceptional except for local artwork, but the menu shines and the service is excellent. Share a plate of mussels, steamed open with apple cider ($8) to start, then move on to honey-glazed salmon served on wild rice ($24) or one of many other varied mains highlighted by Canadian roots and low-fat cooking. The Pines is open daily for breakfast and for dinner from 5:30 P.M.

Banff's original bistro-style restaurant, which opened in the early 1990s, is **Coyote's,** 206 Caribou Street, 403/762-3963. Meals are prepared in full view of diners, and the menu emphasizes fresh, health-conscious cooking, with just a hint of Southwestern style. To start, it's hard to go past the sweet potato and corn chowder ($6), then chose from mains as varied as a simple Mediterranean-influenced pasta and a flank steak marinated in Cajun spices and topped with a generous dab of corn and tomato salsa. Entrées range $13–24.50. Coyote's is open daily 7:30 A.M.–10 P.M.

Italian

Banff is blessed with fine Italian restaurants. Bright and casual **Guido's,** upstairs at 116 Banff Ave., 403/762-4002, is known for its homemade pasta, which is cooked to perfection in a variety of classic Italian sauces that appeal to all tastes and diets. Entrées are $11–21, including an inexpensive spaghetti carbonara made with real bacon. It's open daily from 5:30 P.M.

More trendy (reflected in the prices) is **Giorgio's,** 219 Banff Avenue, 403/762-5114, which has a stylish décor and a casual Old World atmosphere. Its chefs prepare as many as 400 meals each afternoon, and the lineup for tables is ever present. Pasta dishes begin at $13. Giorgio's is open from 4:30 P.M.

If you are staying up on Tunnel Mountain (or even if you're not), **Cilantro Mountain Café,** housed in a log cabin in front of Buffalo Mountain Lodge, 403/760-3008, is well worth trying. The menu is limited to a few Italian-style dishes, which change as seasonal produce becomes available, and pizza is prepared in a wood-fired oven in full view of diners. The atmosphere is typical mountain dining: casual and elegantly rustic. The outside deck is perfect for those hot summer nights. Appetizers such as tiger prawns on a slice of sweet corn cake are $8, gourmet pizza (the best in town) is $15, and entrées average $25. It's open in summer, daily 11 A.M.–11 P.M., the rest of the year, Wed.–Sun. 5–10 P.M.

Swiss-Italian

Once one of Banff's busiest restaurants, **Ticino** is in the Homestead Inn at 415 Banff Avenue, 403/762-3848. This Banff institution reflects the heritage of Banff's early mountain guides, with solid timber furnishings, lots of peeled and polished log work, and old wooden skis, huge cowbells, and an alpenhorn decorating the walls. It's named for the southern province of Switzerland, where the cuisine has a distinctive Italian influence. The Swiss chef is best known for a wild mushroom soup, unique to the region, his beef and cheese fondues ($16–24 per person), and juicy cuts of Alberta beef. I couldn't fault the pork tenderloin, baked with Gruyere cheese and an apricot paste ($22). Ticino is open daily from 7 A.M. for a hot and cold buffet breakfast and daily for dinner 5–11 P.M.

Greek

The **Balkan,** 120 Banff Avenue, 403/762-3454, is run by a Greek family, but the menu blends their heritage with the cuisines of Italy, China, and Canada. Select from Greek ribs (pork ribs with a lemon sauce) for $15.95, the Greek chow mein (stir-fried vegetables, fried rice, and your choice of meat) for $11.50, or Greek spaghetti for $9.50. But the most popular dishes are souvlaki ($13.95) and an enormous Greek platter for two ($39). The Balkan is open daily 11 A.M.–11 P.M.

French

You'll think you've swapped continents when you step into **Le Beaujolais,** 212 Buffalo Street (at Banff Avenue), 403/762-2712, a Canadian leader in French cuisine. With crisp white linens, old-style stately décor, and immaculate service, this elegant room has been one of Banff's most popular fine-dining restaurants for 20 years. Its second-floor location ensures great views of Banff, especially from window tables. The dishes feature mainly Canadian produce, prepared and served with a traditional French flair. Entrées such as braised caribou with blueberries and wild mushrooms begin at $31, but the extent of your final tab depends on whether you choose à la carte items or one of the three- to six-course table d'hôte menus ($55–85)—and also on how much wine you consume. Nationalism shows through in the 10,000-bottle cellar, with lots of reds from the Bordeaux and Burgundy regions of France. The restaurant is open daily from 6 P.M.; reservations are necessary.

Japanese

The large number of Japanese visitors in Banff has created the need for good Japanese restaurants. **Shiki Japanese Restaurant,** in the back of the Clock Tower Mall, 110 Banff Avenue, 403/762-0527, has a choice of *donburi,* various meat cakes, teriyaki, and sushi. Dishes are $5–10 each. It's a casual, café-type place with only a few tables and is popular for lunch (eat in or take-out). Hours are 11 A.M.–9 P.M. daily. **Sushi House Banff,** 304 Caribou Street, 403/762-2971, is a tiny restaurant with stools set around a moving miniature railway that has diners picking sushi and other delicacies from a train as it circles the chef, loading the carriages as quickly as they empty.

More expensive is **Suginoya,** 225 Banff Avenue, 403/762-4773, which has a relaxed atmosphere. Choose from the sushi bar, *ozashiki* booths, or regular tables. Traditional *shabu-shabu* and seafood teriyaki are popular. The number of Japanese diners here is indicative of the quality. Expect to pay at least $13 for entrées, $19–25 for one of the combination dinners. Suginoya is open daily 11 A.M.–10:30 P.M., with lots of specials outside of summer.

Banff's best Japanese restaurant is the **Samurai,** in the Fairmont Banff Springs (see following entry).

Grizzly House

This unique fondue restaurant at 207 Banff Avenue, 403/762-4055, provides Banff's most unusual dining experience. The décor is, to say the least, eclectic (many say eccentric). Each table has a phone for across-table conversation, or you can call your waiter, the bar, a cab, diners in the private booth, or even those who spend too long in the bathroom. Through all this, the food is good and the service as professional as anywhere in town. The menu hasn't changed in decades, and this doesn't displease anyone. Most dining revolves around traditional Swiss fondues, but with nontraditional dipping meats such as buffalo, rattlesnake, alligator, shark, ostrich, venison, and shrimp. Four-course table d'hôte fondue dinners are $32–48 per person, which includes soup or salad, followed by a cheese fondue, one of six meat or seafood fondue choices, and dessert. The Grizzly House is also open at lunch, when you can sample Canadian game at reduced prices; an Alberta-farmed buffalo burger is $10, and a smoked duck breast salad is $11. Open 11:30 A.M.–midnight.

Fairmont Banff Springs

Whether guests or not, most visitors to Banff drop by to see one of the town's biggest tourist attractions, and a meal here might not be as expensive as you think. The hotel itself has more eateries than most small towns—from a deli serving slices of pizza to the finest of fine dining in the Banffshire Club.

If you are in the mood for a snack such as chili and bread or sandwiches to go, head to the Lobby Level and the **Castle Pantry,** which is open 24 hours daily.

Impressive buffets are the main drawcard at the **Bow Valley Grill,** a pleasantly laid-out dining room that seats 275. Each morning from 6:30 A.M. an expansive buffet of hot and cold delicacies, including freshly baked bread and seasonal fruits, is laid out for the masses ($26 per person). Lunch is served 11:30 A.M.–5:30 P.M., with a wide-ranging menu featuring everything from salads to seafood. Through the busiest months of summer, a buffet lunch is offered 11:30 A.M.–1:30 P.M., with a free Historic Castle Tour included in the rate of $26.95 per person. Dinner is served nightly until 10 P.M., with mains running $15–28.50. The hotel's Sunday brunch, served in the Bow Valley Grill, is legendary, with chefs working at numerous stations scattered around the dining area, and an enormous spread not equaled for variety anywhere in the mountains ($35 per person). Reservations are required for Sunday brunch (as far in advance as possible) and dinner.

Throughout recent hotel renovations, the **Alhambra Dining Room** retained its Old World atmosphere and reputation as an elegant yet casual dining choice. The à la carte dinner menu features a wide variety of beef and seafood dishes. In July and August, this restaurant features Van Horne's Grand Buffet, with chef-attended dining stations offering dishes prepared to order from around the world. Open nightly from 6 P.M. for dinner, **Castello Ristorante** serves pasta at good prices while also offering a wide range of other Italian specialties and a mouthwatering antipasto bar. The **Samurai Restaurant** is the most expensive of Banff's many Japanese restaurants, but it is also the most traditional (and busiest); open for dinner only.

Two restaurants lie within the grounds surrounding the hotel, and both are worthy of consideration. Originally the golf course clubhouse, the **Waldhaus Restaurant** is nestled in a forested area of lodgepole pine directly below the hotel. Open daily 6–10 P.M., it features German specialties, with mains from $17. Below this restaurant is a pub of the same name, with a pub-style dinner menu offered in a casual atmosphere. The **Clubhouse Dining Room** is a seasonal restaurant on the golf course proper that serves light breakfasts, casual lunches, and more formal dinners. A shuttle bus runs every 30 minutes between the main lobby and the clubhouse.

The **Rundle Lounge** is a long, narrow piano bar, where most tables offer views down the

Bow Valley. It's open midday–midnight, with an à la carte menu on offer. Smoke-free **Grapes** is an intimate yet casual wine bar noted for its fine cheeses and pâtés. More substantial meals such as fondues are also offered. It's open for lunch and dinner.

The hotel's most acclaimed restaurant is the **Banffshire Club,** which seats just 76 diners. Like its predecessor, the Rob Roy Room, this fine-dining restaurant is a bastion of elegance, which begins as a harp player serenades you through a gated entrance. Inside, extravagantly rich wood furnishings, perfectly presented table settings, muted lighting, and kilted staff create an atmosphere as far removed from the surrounding wilderness as is imaginable. Most diners choose one of four table d'hôte menus, which range from $75 per person for two courses to $175 for nine courses accompanied by specially selected wines. It's open daily 6–10 P.M., and a jacket is required.

For all Fairmont Banff Springs dining reservations, call 403/662-6860, or after 5 P.M., call 403/762-2211. During the summer months a desk in the main lobby has all menus posted and takes reservations.

BOW VALLEY PARKWAY

Along the Bow Valley Parkway toward Lake Louise are two excellent restaurants, both part of lodgings detailed previously.

Bridges
The first is at Johnston Canyon Resort, 26 km (16 miles) from Banff, 403/762-2971. The resort, which has grown from a 1920s teahouse, has always had a restaurant, but in the past it had only opened as a courtesy to resort guests. This changed when, after extensive renovations, Bridges, with a historic atmosphere and views out to the creek, opened in 2000. It opens nightly at 6 P.M. for a wide-ranging menu that includes a jambalaya pasta served with a generous quantity of shrimp ($13–21).

Baker Creek Bistro
A further 14 km (8.7 miles) along the parkway is Baker Creek Bistro, at Baker Creek Chalets, 403/522-2182. Dining is in a small room that characterizes the term "mountain hideaway," in an adjacent lounge bar, or out on a small deck decorated with pots of colorful flowers. Cooked

© ANDREW HEMPSTEAD

BANFF

Baker Creek Bistro is well worth the drive from town.

breakfasts are served in summer from 8 A.M., but the evening menu draws the biggest raves. The menu isn't large, but dishes feature lots of Canadian game and produce, with favorites like medallions of venison served with an orange and gin sauce ($29) and roasted duck breast with a cream-based cranberry sauce ($24). It's open in summer daily 8 A.M.–9:30 P.M., the rest of the year, Wed.–Sun. 5–9:30 P.M. (closed April); reservations are recommended for dinner.

LAKE LOUISE

Breakfast

Waking up on your first morning in Lake Louise and knowing that the entire village exists just to serve travelers may have you wondering whether getting a hearty, well-priced breakfast will be a problem. Surprisingly, it isn't—there are some excellent options to start your day on the right track.

Laggan's Mountain Bakery, in Samson Mall, 403/552-2017, is *the* place to hang out with a coffee and one of their delicious freshly baked breakfast croissants, pastries, cakes, or muffins. If the tables are full and you manage to somehow reach the cake cabinet, order take-out and enjoy your feast on the grassy bank behind the mall. The chocolate brownie ($1.50) is delicious. Order two slices to save having to line up again. Laggan's is open daily 6 A.M.–8 P.M.

Across the TransCanada Highway, the **Lodge of the Ten Peaks,** at the base of Lake Louise winter resort, 403/522-3555, is open in summer daily from 7:30 A.M. for a large and varied breakfast buffet. It's a casual affair—eat all you can for $16, or eat and ride the gondola for $21, a good deal considering the gondola ride alone is $19.

If you made the effort to rise early and experienced the early-morning tranquility of Moraine Lake, the perfect place to sit back and watch the tour bus crowds pour in is from the dining room of **Moraine Lake Lodge,** 403/522-3733. Staying overnight at the lodge may be an extravagant splurge, but breakfast isn't. A simple, well-presented Continental buffet is just $12.50, while the hot version is a reasonable $15. The lodge is open June–September only, with the dining room opening daily at 7:30 A.M. through the summer season.

Samson Mall and Surrounds

In the center of the action, Samson Mall is a hive of activity each afternoon as campers descend on a single grocery store to stock up on supplies for the evening meal. Prices are high, and by the end of the day stocks are low. The mall is also home to Laggan's (see previous entry), a take-out fast-food place, and a liquor store. Upstairs in the mall is the **Lake Louise Village Grill & Bar,** 403/522-3879. The tiled entrance looks like a public washroom and the food's ordinary. For a casual meal, much better is **Bill Peyto's Cafe** in the Lake Louise Alpine Centre on Village Road, 403/522-2200. The food is consistent and well priced. A huge portion of nachos is $7, pasta is $9–12, and stir-frys range $10–14. Open daily 7 A.M.–9 P.M.

Lake Louise Station Restaurant

One hundred years ago visitors departing trains at Laggan Station were keen to get to the Chateau Lake Louise as quickly as possible to begin their adventure. Today guests from the Chateau, other hotels, and even people from as far away as Banff are returning to dine in the restored station or in the adjacent railcars. Although the menu is not extensive, it puts an emphasis on creating imaginative dishes with a combination of Canadian produce and Asian ingredients. For starters, the seared shrimp and scallops with a mild Indonesian orange cream sauce ($10) is typical. As an entrée, the leek and cranberry–crusted baked sea bass is memorable, with all mains ranging $12–28. Lighter lunches include a Caesar salad topped with roasted garlic dressing, perfect for those planning an afternoon hike. Open for lunch from 11:30 A.M. and dinner from 6 P.M., it's at 200 Sentinel Road, 403/522-2600.

Fairmont Chateau Lake Louise

Within this famous hotel are a choice of eateries and an ice-cream shop. The **Poppy Brasserie** has obscured lake views and is the most casual place for a meal. Breakfasts are offered buffet-style, either Continental ($18) or cooked ($25), from 7 A.M. Lunch and dinner is à la carte. It's open until 8:30 P.M. **Walliser Stube** is an elegant two-story wine bar decorated with rich wood paneling and solid oak furniture. It offers a simple menu of German dishes from $17.95 as well as cheese fondue. The **Lakeside Lounge** is along floor-to-ceiling windows with magnificent lake views. Light meals are served from 4 p.m. daily. The **Victoria Room** enjoys excellent views across the lake to the mountain for which it's named. It's a relaxed but stylish restaurant open for breakfast, a buffet lunch, and evening dining with choices that range from traditional British dishes to innovative Pacific Northwest fare. The **Fairview Dining Room** has a lot more than just a fair view. As the chateau's signature dining room, it enjoys the best views and offers the most elegant setting. Appetizers start at $7, while entrées combine Canadian produce with contemporary cooking styles ($24–37). For all reservations, call 403/522-3511.

Post Hotel

In 1987, the Post Hotel was expanded to include a luxurious new wing. The original log building was renovated as a rustic, timbered dining room, linked to the rest of the hotel by an intimate bar. Although the dining room isn't cheap, it's a favorite of locals and visitors alike. The chef specializes in European cuisine, preparing several Swiss dishes (such as veal zurichois) to make owner George Schwarz feel less homesick. But he's also renowned for his presentation of Alberta beef, Pacific salmon, and Peking duck. Main meals start at $25. The restaurant is open daily 11:30 A.M.–2 P.M. and 6–8:30 P.M. Reservations are essential for dinner; call 403/522-3989.

Practicalities

GETTING THERE

Calgary International Airport, 128 km (80 miles) east, is the closest airport to Banff National Park. **Brewster,** 403/762-6767, www.brewster.ca, is one of many companies offering shuttles between the airport and Banff National Park. Their service leaves the airport three times daily, stopping at Banff then continuing to Lake Louise. Calgary to Banff is $40, Calgary to Lake Louise is $47. This shuttle stops at all major Banff hotels as well as the park's main bus terminal, the **Brewster Tour and Transportation Centre,** a five-minute walk from downtown Banff at 100 Gopher Street. The depot has a ticket office, lockers, a café, and a gift shop. It's open daily 7:30 A.M.–10:45 P.M. Other airporter buses are **Banff Airporter,** 403/762-3396, www.banff airporter.com, and **Rocky Mountain Sky Shuttle,** 403/762-5200, www.rockymountainskyshuttle.com. The advantage of traveling with these two companies is that they offer door-to-door-service for around the same price.

Adjacent desks at the airport's Arrivals level take bookings, but reserve a seat by booking over the phone or online in advance. The earliest service back to the airport departs Lake Louise at 5 A.M. and Banff at 6:30 A.M.

Greyhound, 403/762-1092 or 800/661-8747, www.greyhound.ca, offers scheduled service from the Calgary bus depot at 877 Greyhound Way SW, five times daily to the Brewster Tour and Transportation Centre at 100 Gopher Street and Samson Mall, Lake Louise. Greyhound buses also leave Vancouver from the depot at 1150 Station Street, three times daily for the scenic 14-hour ride to the park.

Between Banff and Jasper

Brewster, 403/762-6717 or 877/791-5500, is the only company with a public bus service between Banff and Jasper. From Jasper, Brewster offers an express service to Banff, for $54, departing the railway station on Connaught Drive May to mid-October daily at 1:30 P.M. A longer alternative is the nine-hour Jasper-to-Banff tour, which stops at the Columbia Icefield and Lake

THE BREWSTER BOYS

Few guides in Banff were as well known as Jim and Bill Brewster. In 1892, at ages 10 and 12, respectively, they were hired by the Banff Springs Hotel to take guests to local landmarks. As their reputation as guides grew, they built a thriving business. By 1900, they had their own livery and outfitting company, and soon thereafter they expanded operations to Lake Louise. Their other early business interests included a trading post, the original Mount Royal Hotel, the first ski lodge in the Sunshine Meadows, and the hotel at the Columbia Icefield.

Today, a legacy of the boys' savvy, **Brewster,** a transportation and tour company, has grown to become an integral part of many tourists' stays. The company operates some of the world's most advanced sightseeing vehicles, including a fleet of Snocoaches on Athabasca Glacier.

Louise; $95 one-way, $133 round-trip. In spring and fall the fare is $67 one-way, $89 round-trip.

The **Canadian Rockies Hostel Shuttle** links the Banff Alpine Centre with major Hostelling International properties at Lake Louise and Jasper as well as all those in between. It's a summer-only service that runs daily in each direction until early September. Sample fares are Banff to Lake Louise, $12; Banff to Jasper, $51, Lake Louise to Jasper $46. Reservations can be made through Hostelling International, www.hihostels.ca, or through Sun Dog Tour Co., 780/852-4056 or 888/786-3641.

No bus service runs between Banff and Jasper in winter.

GETTING AROUND
Banff

Most of the sights and many trailheads are within walking distance of town. **Banff Transit,** 403/760-8294, operates bus service along two routes through the Town of Banff: one from the Fairmont Banff Springs to the RV and trailer parking area at the north end of Banff Avenue; the other from the Fairmont Banff Springs to the Tunnel Mountain Campgrounds. Mid-May to September,

buses run twice an hour between 7 A.M. and midnight. From October to December, the two routes are merged as one, with buses running hourly midday to midnight. No local buses run the rest of the year. Travel costs $1 per sector.

Cabs around Banff and Lake Louise are reasonably priced—flag drop is $3, then it's $1.65 per km. From the Banff bus depot to Tunnel Mountain accommodations will run around $7, same to the Fairmont Banff Springs, more after midnight. Companies are **Banff Taxi,** 403/762-4444; **Legion Taxi,** 403/762-3353; and **Taxi Taxi,** 403/762-8000.

The days when a row of horse-drawn buggies eagerly awaited the arrival of wealthy visitors at the CPR Station have long since passed, but the **Trail Rider Store,** 132 Banff Avenue, 403/762-4551, offers visitors rides around town in a beautifully restored carriage ($11 per person for 15 minutes). Expect to pay $22 per carriage for a short loop along the Bow River.

Plan on renting a vehicle before you reach the park. In addition to high pricing for walk-in customers, the main catch is that no local companies offer unlimited mileage. The most you'll get is a free 150 km, and then expect to pay $.25 cents per km. **Banff Rent-a-car,** 230 Lynx Street, 403/762-3352, rents used cars for $60 per day with 150 free km. Other agencies are **Avis,** 403/762-3222 or 800/879-2847; **Budget,** 403/762-4565 or 800/268-8900; **Hertz,** 403/762-2027 or 800/263-0600; and **National,** 403/762-2688 or 800/227-7368. Reservations for cars in Banff should be made well in advance.

Lake Louise

Samson Mall is the commercial heart of Lake Louise village. If the parking lot out front is full, consider leaving your vehicle across the road behind the ESSO gas station, where one area is set aside for large RVs. The campground, alpine center, and hotels are all within easy walking distance of Samson Mall. Fairmont Chateau Lake Louise is a 2.7-km (1.7-mile) walk from the valley floor. The only car rental agency in the village is **National,** 403/522-3870 or 800/227-7368. The agency doesn't have many vehicles; you'd be better off picking one up at Calgary International

Airport. **Lake Louise Taxi & Tours,** in Samson Mall, 403/522-2020, charges $2.50 for flag drop, then $1.60 per km. From the mall to Fairmont Chateau Lake Louise runs around $11, to Moraine Lake $20, and to Banff $110. **Wilson Mountain Sports,** in Samson Mall, 403/522-3636, has mountain bikes for rent from $15 per hour or $35 per day (includes a helmet, bike lock, and water bottle). Inquire here about canoe rentals for float trips along the Bow River to Banff.

Persons with Disabilities

The Banff and Lake Louise Visitor Centres are wheelchair accessible—restrooms, information desks, and theater are all barrier free. Once inside, use the handy Touchsource monitors for a full listing of all barrier-free services within the park. An all-terrain wheelchair is available at the Cave and Basin National Historic Site for use on park trails. To reserve, call 403/762-1566.

Tours

Brewster, 403/762-6717 or 877/791-5500, is the dominant tour company in the area. Their three-hour Discover Banff bus tour takes in downtown Banff, Tunnel Mountain Drive, the hoodoos, the Cave and Basin, and Banff Gondola (gondola fare not included). This tour runs in summer only and departs from the bus depot daily at 8:30 A.M.; call for hotel pick-up times. Adult fare is $43, children half price.

Brewster also runs several other tours. A nine-hour tour to Lake Louise departs select Banff hotels daily; $72. In winter this tour departs Tuesday and Friday morning, runs five hours, and includes Banff sights; $51.

During summer, the company offers tours from Banff to Upper Hot Springs ($21; includes pool admission), Banff Gondola ($29; includes gondola ride), Lake Minnewanka ($46; includes two-hour boat cruise), and Columbia Icefield ($95; Snocoach extra).

Discover Banff Tours, Sundance Mall, 215 Banff Avenue, 403/760-1299 or 877/565-9372, is a smaller company, with smaller buses and more personalized service. Their tour routes are similar to Brewster: a three-hour Discover Banff tour visits Lake Minnewanka,

the Cave and Basin, and the hoodoos for $45 adults, $25 children; a full-day trip to the Columbia Icefield is $90 adults, $50 children; and a two-hour evening Wildlife Safari is $35 adults, $20 children.

SERVICES
Banff

The **post office** is on the corner of Buffalo and Bear streets opposite Central Park; open Mon.–Fri. 9 A.M.–5:30 P.M. The general-delivery service here is probably among the busiest in the country, with the thousands of seasonal workers in the area, and no home mail-delivery service. A window is set aside for general delivery pick-ups, speeding things up considerably. For all other postal services, try the small and friendly full-service postal outlet in **Cascade Plaza Drug,** in the far corner of the lower level of Cascade Plaza at 317 Banff Avenue.

Major banks can be found along Banff Avenue and are generally open 9 A.M.–4 P.M. The **Bank of Montreal,** 107 Banff Avenue, allows cash advances with MasterCard, while the **C.I.B.C.,** 98 Banff Avenue, accepts Visa. **Freya's Currency Exchange** is in the Clock Tower Mall at 108 Banff Avenue, 403/762-5111.

Downtown laundromats are **Cascade Coin Laundry,** on the lower level of the Cascade Plaza, open daily 7:30 A.M.–10 P.M. Chalet Coin Laundry is on Tunnel Mountain Road at the Douglas Fir Resort, within walking distance of all Tunnel Mountain accommodations; open daily 8 a.m.–10 p.m.

Along Banff Avenue you'll find a handful of one-hour photo places; check around for the cheapest because many have special offers. The most competitive and reliable is the **Film Lab** at 202 Banff Avenue, 403/762-2126, and up at the Fairmont Banff Springs, 403/762-2011.

Mineral Springs Hospital is at 301 Lynx Street, 403/762-2222. **Cascade Plaza Drug,** on the lower level of the Cascade Plaza at 317 Banff Avenue, 403/762-2245, is open until 9 P.M. **Gourlay's Pharmacy,** 229 Bear St., is open until 8 P.M. For the **Royal Canadian Mounted Police (RCMP),** call 403/762-2226.

Lake Louise

A small postal outlet in Samson Mall also serves as a bus depot and car rental agency. Although Lake Louise has no banks, there's a currency exchange in the Fairmont Chateau Lake Louise and a cash machine in the grocery store. The mall also holds a busy laundromat open in summer, daily 8 A.M.–8 P.M., shorter hours the rest of the year. Camping supplies and bike rentals are available from **Wilson Mountain Sports,** 403/522-3636; open 9 A.M.–9 P.M. Open daily 9 A.M.–7 P.M., **Pipestone Photo,** 403/522-3617, has a range of photographic supplies unequaled in all of the Canadian Rockies. It's relatively well priced and has one-hour photo developing. The closest **hospital** is in Banff, 403/762-2222. For the local **RCMP,** call 403/522-3811.

BOOKS AND BOOKSTORES

The Canadian Rockies are one of the most written about, and definitely the most photographed, regions in Canada. As a walk along Banff Avenue will confirm, there is definitely no lack of postcards, calendars, and books about the area. For general reading, the guides and coffee-table books published by **Altitude Publishing** are the best. Look for **Gem Trek** maps at bookstores and gift shops throughout Banff National Park.

Banff Public Library

Banff's library is opposite Central Park at 101 Bear Street, 403/762-2661. The extensive collection of nonfiction books, many about the park and its environs, makes it an excellent rainy-day hangout. It also has a large collection of magazines and newspapers. Internet access is free, but book ahead. Hours are Mon.–Thur. 10 A.M.–8 P.M., Fri. 10 A.M.–6 P.M., Sat. 11 A.M.–6 P.M., and Sun. 1–5 P.M.

Bookstores

Banff Book & Art Den, 94 Banff Avenue, 403/762-3919, www.banffbooks.com, is the largest bookstore in the Canadian Rockies, with reading material spread over a split-level hardwood floor. It stocks a large collection of park literature, wilderness guides, coffee-table books, travel guides, and the entire range of Gem Trek maps. Open in summer daily 10 A.M.–9 P.M., the rest of the year until 7 P.M. Another bookstore is **Cascade Mountain Books,** downstairs in the Cascade Plaza, 403/762-8508.

Lake Louise Bookstores

In Lake Louise, **Woodruff & Blum,** in the Samson Mall, 403/522-3842, offers an excellent selection of books on the natural and human history of the park, as well as animal field guides, hiking guides, and general western Canadiana. It's open daily 9 A.M.–10 P.M. In the Fairmont Chateau Lake Louise, **Mountain Lights,** 403/522-3734, has a similar albeit smaller collection.

Internet Access

Send and receive email and surf the Internet at the following Banff locations:

Banff Public Library: 101 Bear St., 403/762-2661; Mon.–Thurs. 10 A.M.–8 P.M., Fri. 10 A.M.–6 P.M., Sat. 11 A.M.–6 P.M., and Sun. 1–5 P.M.

Cascade Plaza: lower level, 317 Banff Ave.; 403/762-8484; open daily 7:30 A.M.–10 P.M.

Cyber-web: Sundance Mall, 215 Banff Ave., 403/762-9226; daily 9 A.M.–midnight.

Newspapers

Look for the *Crag and Canyon* each Wednesday. It's been keeping residents and visitors informed about park issues and town gossip for more than 90 years. The *Rocky Mountain Outlook* is a free weekly newspaper (Thursday) that offers coverage of mountain life and upcoming events; it's available on stands at businesses throughout the park.

INFORMATION

Many sources of information are available on the park and its commercial facilities. Once you've arrived, the best place to make your first stop is the **Banff Visitor Centre.** This large complex at 224 Banff Avenue houses information desks for **Parks Canada,** 403/762-1550, and the **Banff/Lake Louise Tourism**

Bureau, 403/762-0270, as well as a Friends of Banff National Park shop, which stocks a good variety of park-related literature. The center is open mid-June to August daily 8 A.M.–8 P.M., mid-May to mid-June and September daily 8 A.M.–6 P.M., the rest of the year daily 9 A.M.–5 P.M.

National Park Information

On the righthand side of the Banff Visitor Centre is a row of desks staffed by Parks Canada employees. They will answer all of your queries regarding Banff's natural wonders and advise you of trail closures. Anyone planning an overnight backcountry trip should register here and obtain a Wilderness Pass ($6 per person per night). Also here, you can pick up the brochure *Banff and Vicinity Drives and Walks* (a compact guide to things to see and do around Banff), view a free slideshow, and watch videos about the park. All questions pertaining to the national park itself can be answered here, or check out the park's website, www.parkscanada.gc.ca/banff.

The park's **Warden's Office** is in the industrial park, 403/762-1470 or 762-4506. The **weather office,** 403/762-2088, offers updated forecasts. A full weather synopsis is available by calling 403/762-3091. Tune into 101 on the FM band to listen to Parks Radio.

Tourism Information

In the Banff Visitor Centre, across the floor from Parks Canada, is a desk for the Banff/Lake Louise Tourism Bureau. This organization represents businesses and commercial establishments in the park. Here you can find out about accommodations and restaurants and have any other questions answered. To answer the most frequently asked question, the restrooms are downstairs. For general tourism information, write the Banff/Lake Louise Tourism Bureau, P.O. Box 1298, Banff, AB T1L 1B3; 403/762-8421; website: www.banfflakelouise.com. Another good website is www.banff.com, with good general information on the park and links to accommodations and commercial operators.

Lake Louise Visitor Centre

The Lake Louise Visitor Centre, 403/522-3833, is beside Samson Mall on Village Road. This excellent Parks Canada facility has interpretive displays, slide and video displays, and staff on hand to answer questions, recommend hikes suited to your ability, and issue Wilderness Passes to those heading out into the backcountry. Look for the stuffed (literally) female grizzly and read her fascinating, but sad, story. It's open mid-June to August daily 8 A.M.–8 P.M., mid-May to mid-June and September daily 8 A.M.–6 P.M., the rest of the year daily 9 A.M.–4 P.M.

"The lakes are such marvelous colors. What kind of chemicals do you use?"

—ANONYMOUS, Lake Louise Visitor Centre

M

BANFF

Canmore

Canmore (pop. 11,000) lies in the wide Bow Valley, 103 km (64 miles) west of Calgary, 28 km (17 miles) southeast of Banff, and on the northern edge of Kananaskis Country. Long perceived as a gateway to the mountain national parks, the town is very much a destination in itself these days. Its ideal mountain location and the freedom it enjoys from the strict development restrictions that apply in the nearby parks have made Canmore the fastest-growing town in Canada, with the population having tripled in the last 20 years.

The surrounding mountains provide Canmore's best recreation opportunities. Hiking is excellent on trails that lace the valley and mountainside slopes, with many high viewpoints easily reached. Flowing though town, the Bow River offers great fishing, kayaking, and rafting;

golfers flock to three scenic courses; and nearby Mount Yamnuska has become the most developed rock-climbing site in the Canadian Rockies. Canmore also hosted the nordic events of the 1988 Winter Olympic Games and is the home of the Alpine Club of Canada.

THE LAND

Canmore lies in the Bow Valley, flanked by mountains rising up to 1,000 meters (3,280 feet) above the valley floor. To the south and west are the distinctive peaks of the Three Sisters, Mount Lawrence Grassi, impressive Chinaman's Peak, and the southeastern extent of Mount Rundle. Across the valley are the Fairholme Range, Mount Lady Macdonald, and Grotto Mountain. Like the rest of the Canadian Rockies, these mountains

Three Sisters

© ANDREW HEMPSTEAD

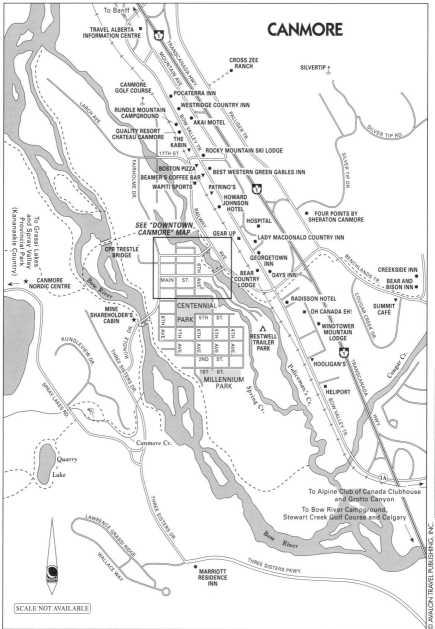

CANMORE

To Banff

TRAVEL ALBERTA INFORMATION CENTRE

CROSS ZEE RANCH

SILVERTIP

TRANSCANADA HWY

MOUNTAIN AVE.

CANMORE GOLF COURSE

POCATERRA INN

WESTRIDGE COUNTRY INN

RUNDLE MOUNTAIN CAMPGROUND

AKAI MOTEL

SILVER TIP RD.

QUALITY RESORT CHATEAU CANMORE

THE KABIN

LARCH AVE.

BOW VALLEY TR.

PALLISER TR.

SILVER TIP DR.

17TH ST.

ROCKY MOUNTAIN SKI LODGE

FAIRHOLME DR.

BOSTON PIZZA

BEAMER'S COFFEE BAR

WAPITI SPORTS

BEST WESTERN GREEN GABLES INN

PATRINO'S

HOWARD JOHNSON HOTEL

FOUR POINTS BY SHERATON CANMORE

HOSPITAL

RAILWAY

SEE "DOWNTOWN CANMORE" MAP

GEAR UP

LADY MACDONALD COUNTRY INN

CPR TRESTLE BRIDGE

AVE.

6TH AVE.

GEORGETOWN INN

BENCHLANDS TR.

CREEKSIDE INN

To Grassi Lakes and Spray Valley Provincial Park (Kanaskaskis Country)

CANMORE NORDIC CENTRE

Bow River

MAIN ST.

BEAR COUNTRY LODGE

DAYS INN

BEAR AND BISON INN

COUGAR CREEK DR.

RUNDLEVIEW DR.

MINE SHAREHOLDER'S CABIN

CENTENNIAL PARK

8TH AVE.

7TH AVE.

5TH ST.

6TH AVE.

5TH AVE.

4TH AVE.

RADISSON HOTEL

OH CANADA EH!

WINDTOWER MOUNTAIN LODGE

SUMMIT CAFÉ

Cougar Cr.

THREE SISTERS DR.

RUNDLE DR.

2ND ST.

RESTWELL TRAILER PARK

Spring Cr.

HOOLIGAN'S

Policeman's Cr.

BOW VALLEY TR.

TRANSCANADA HWY

SPRAY LAKES RD.

1ST ST.

MILLENNIUM PARK

HELIPORT

Canmore Cr.

Quarry Lake

1A

THREE SISTERS DR.

To Alpine Club of Canada Clubhouse and Grotto Canyon

To Bow River Campground, Stewart Creek Golf Course and Calgary

LAWRENCE GRASSI RIDGE

WALLACE WAY

MARRIOTT RESIDENCE INN

THREE SISTERS PKWY.

Bow River

SCALE NOT AVAILABLE

© AVALON TRAVEL PUBLISHING, INC.

CANMORE

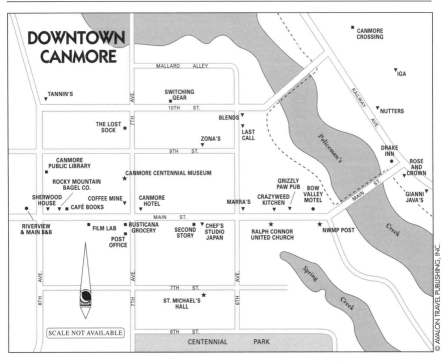

began as layers of sedimentary rock laid down on the bed of an ancient sea. The seabed was forced upward over millions of years to create today's lofty peaks, whose sedimentary layers give them a distinct appearance. Through the valley flows the braided Bow River, heading eastward and into the Saskatchewan River system. At the north end of town, the river divides in two, leaving downtown Canmore on a low-lying island that is protected from annual spring flooding by dikes of large boulders.

Flora and Fauna

Even though much of the valley floor is developed, large tracts of land are protected by Bow Valley Wildland Provincial Park, making the surrounding area a delight for nature lovers. Lowlands on either side of the Bow River are lined with stands of poplar, while the drier mountainsides support extensive stands of **Douglas fir, Engelmann spruce,** and **lodgepole pine.**

The forested valley floor provides habitat for many larger mammals, including around 100 **elk,** most often sighted on the Canmore Golf Course and along the west side of the Bow River. Other larger mammals present include **white-tailed deer, coyotes, black bears,** and **grizzly bears,** all of which are regularly sighted within town limits. **Bighorn sheep** are common on rocky outcrops above Spray Lakes Road. **Cougars** inhabit the surrounding wilderness but are rarely sighted.

Smaller mammals present in Bow River and its adjacent sloughs include a healthy population of **beaver,** as well as **muskrat** and **mink. Red** and **Columbian ground squirrels** and **least chipmunks** inhabit the forests around town, while at higher elevations **golden-mantled ground squirrels** and **pikas** find a home. **Wild rabbits** thrive around the residential streets east of Centennial Park.

Bird life around Canmore is prolific. **Mallard ducks** are a popular attraction on Policeman's

Creek in downtown Canmore. Several active **osprey** nests can be seen along the banks of the Bow River; other permanent residents include **great horned owls, jays,** and **ravens.**

HISTORY

The Hudson's Bay Company explored the Bow Valley corridor and attempted, without success, to establish a fur trade with Stoney natives for most of the 1840s. In 1858, an expedition from the east, led by Captain John Palliser, sent back discouraging reports about the climate and prospects of agriculture in the valley. A few decades later the Canadian Pacific Railway (CPR) chose the Bow Valley Corridor as the route through the mountains, and the first divisional point west of Calgary was established in 1883. It was named Canmore for the 11th-century Scottish king, Malcolm of Canmore.

Coal Mining

The CPR was delighted to discover that the valley was rich with coal, which it could use in the

© ANDREW HEMPSTEAD

The North West Mounted Police built this "temporary" post in 1892. It makes an ideal starting point for exploring the town.

steam engines. Mining on the lower slopes of the Three Sisters and Mount Rundle commenced in 1886, attracting hundreds of miners and their families. Within a few years numerous mines operated around Canmore. In 1899 the CPR moved its divisional point to Laggan (now Lake Louise), but the mines continued to operate, with the most productive mine located on Canmore Creek. Hotels and businesses were established, and a hospital, North West Mounted Police (NWMP) post, and opera house were built. The Canmore Opera House—reputed to be the only log movie house in the world—still stands and has been relocated to Calgary's Heritage Park.

Many British and European miners were attracted to the area, and the population continued to increase. A small contingent of Chinese miners also lived in Canmore. They didn't stay long, but their memory lives on in the name Chinaman's Peak. A Chinese cook, Ha Ling, was bet $50 that he couldn't climb the peak and return to Canmore in less than six hours. He did, and it's been known as Chinaman's Peak ever since. In 1912, the Canadian Anthracite Coal Company relocated its operation from near present-day Banff to the west side of the Bow River, five km (3.1 miles) from the rail line. **Georgetown,** a bustling little village, sprang up beside the mine. Workers enjoyed electricity and running water in cozy cabins along with their own company store, post office, and a school for the kids. Three short years later, markets dried up and the Anthracite mine closed. Georgetown was abandoned, and the buildings were barged downstream to Canmore.

Recent Times

A little more than 100 years after mining commenced and less than 20 years after the last mine closed, Canmore experienced its second boom—tourism—which today shows no sign of slowing. When the last of Canmore's mines closed in 1979, the population stood at 3,500; today that number has tripled. Half the current residents have lived in town for less than five years. There seems no end to the boom, and the population is estimated to reach 20,000 some time in the next 20 years. Resort and residential projects costing more than $2 billion have been planned for the next two decades, and the town's population is estimated to reach 20,000 by the end of that period. The largest and most controversial development is **Three Sisters Mountain Village.** When completed, the 840-hectare (2,080-acre) project will include 3,600 residential units, 500 hotel rooms, and three golf courses—all in an environmentally sensi-tive area along an 11-km (6.8-mile) stretch of the Bow River, between Pigeon Mountain and Chinaman's Peak.

Canmore is a popular spot for moviemakers; recent big-budget movies filmed in and around town have included *Shanghai Noon, Grizzly Falls, Mystery Alaska, The Edge, Wild America, The Last of the Dogmen, Legends of the Fall, Snow Dogs,* and the 2003 Kevin Costner film *Open Range.*

Sights and Recreation

Canmore sprawls across both sides of the Trans-Canada Highway, with downtown Canmore oc-cupying an island in the middle of the Bow River. Although development sprawls in all directions, large tracts of forest remain intact, including along the river, where you'll finding paths leading be-yond built-up areas and into natural areas. The most expansive of these is 32,600-hectare (80,550-acre) **Bow Valley Wildland Provincial Park,** which has been designated in pockets along the valley floor as well as most of the surrounding mountain slopes along both sides of the valley.

SIGHTS

Through booming times, the original core of Canmore, on the southwestern side of the Trans-Canada Highway, has managed to retain much of its original charm. Many historical buildings line the downtown streets, while other buildings from the coal-mining days are being preserved at their original locations around town. The best way to get downtown from the TransCanada Highway is to take Railway Avenue from High-way 1A and drive down 8th Street, the main drag (parking is easiest one street back along 7th Street, where one parking lot—at 6th Av-enue—is designated for RVs).

Downtown

The first building of interest at the east end of 8th Street is Canmore's original NWMP post, built in 1892. It is one of the few such posts still in its original position, even though at the time of its construction the building was de-signed as a temporary structure to serve the newly born coal-mining town. The interior is decorated with period furnishings, while out back is a thriving garden filled with the same food crops planted by the post's original in-habitants. It's open in summer, daily 9 A.M.–6 P.M., the rest of year Mon.–Fri. noon–4 P.M. Admission is free; 403/678-1955. The post sits across from Policeman's Creek, a shallow body of water alive with ducks. Ralph Connor United Church, a little farther down 8th Street, was built in 1890 and is now a Provincial Historic Site. The church is named for its first reverend, Charles Gordon, who used the pen-name Ralph Connor for the 35 books he authored. Can-more Hotel, on the corner of 8th Street and 7th Avenue, was built in 1891 (at a time when three hotels already operated) and is still open for thirsty townsfolk and travelers alike.

Around the corner from the hotel, Canmore Museum and Geoscience Centre, 801 7th Ave., 403/678-2462, highlights the region's rich ge-ological history and its importance to the growth of the town and related industries. Ge-ological formations along three local hikes are described, which along with a small fossil dis-play, microscopes, and computer resources make this facility an interesting rainy-day di-version. It's open in summer, daily 9 A.M.–6 P.M.; the rest of the year Wed.–Sun. 10 A.M.–5 P.M. Admission is by donation.

West of Downtown

Several scenic and historic sights lie across the Bow River from downtown, including the remains of various mining operations. To get there, walk south along 8th Avenue for 500 meters (0.3 miles) to the Bow River. With a pedestrian-only bridge and paved paths on both sides of the river leading in either direction, this is a good point to stop and orient yourself. A pleasant loop can be made by walking north and crossing the river at the old **CPR trestle bridge,** which once served local mines. Follow the trail back downstream, past the **Mine Shareholders' Cabin,** a log structure built in 1914.

In the same vicinity, a trail leads off from Three Sisters Drive up Canmore Creek, passing the remains of a mine site that was first worked in 1891. Beyond the visible coal seam and crumbling concrete foundations is a picturesque waterfall tucked below residential development. Backtrack 300 meters (0.2 miles) from the end of the trail and climb the wooden steps, crossing Spray Lakes Road to **Quarry Lake.** This small lake lies in an open meadow and is a popular sunbathing and swimming spot.

HIKING

The hiking trails around Canmore are usually passed by in favor of those of its famous neighbors, but some interesting trails do exist. Paved paths around town are suitable for walking, bicycling, and, in winter, skiing. They link Policeman's Creek with the golf course, nordic center, and Riverview Park on the Bow River.

Grassi Lakes

- Length: 2 km/1.2 miles (40 minutes) one-way
- Elevation gain: 300 meters/980 feet
- Rating: easy/moderate
- Trailhead: Spray Village, beyond the Nordic center, six km (3.7 miles) west of downtown off Spray Lakes Road

This historical trail climbs to two small lakes below Chinaman's Peak. From the parking lot

just off Spray Lakes Road, take the left fork 150 meters (0.1 miles) along the trail. It climbs steadily to stairs cut into a cliff face before leading up to a bridge over Canmore Creek and to the lakes. Interpretive signs along the trail point out interesting aspects of the Bow Valley and detail the life of Lawrence Grassi, who built the trail in the early 1920s. With Chinaman's Peak as a backdrop, these gin-clear, spring-fed lakes are a particularly rewarding destination. Behind the upper lake, an easy scramble up a scree slope leads to four pictographs (native rock paintings) of human figures. They are on the first large boulder in the gorge. An alternate return route is down a rough access road between the hiking trail and Spray Lakes Road, passing a broken-down log cabin along the way.

Chinaman's Peak

- Length: 2.2 km/1.4 miles (90 minutes) one-way
- Elevation gain: 740 meters/2,430 feet
- Rating: moderate/difficult
- Trailhead: Goat Creek parking lot, Spray Lakes Road, nine km (5.6 miles) west of Canmore

Chinaman's Peak is the impressive pinnacle of rock that rises high above Canmore to the southwest. While the sheer eastern face is visible from town, this trail winds up the backside of the mountain and ends with stunning views across the Bow Valley. Leaving your vehicle at the Goat Creek Trailhead, cross the road, then walk up to and over the canal to search out the trail, which begins from behind a small workshed. The trail climbs steadily through subalpine forest of Engelmann spruce before breaking out above the treeline, where views north extend down the glacially carved Goat Creek Valley. The trail then forks; the left fork climbs unforgivingly to Chinaman's Peak, but hikers are rewarded with views no less spectacular by continuing to the right along a lightly marked trail that ends at a saddle. On a clear day, the panorama afforded from this viewpoint

Chinaman's Peak is the impressive pinnacle of rock that rises high above Canmore to the southwest. On a clear day, the panorama afforded from this viewpoint is worth every painful step.

is worth every painful step. Take care on the return journey; stay high and to the right and watch for rock cairns and colored flagging to ensure you enter the trees at the right spot.

Cougar Creek

- Length: 9.5 km/6 miles (four hours) one-way
- Elevation gain: 550 meters/1,800 feet
- Rating: moderate
- Trailhead: corner Benchlands Trail and Elk Run Boulevard, east side of TransCanada Highway

This unofficial trail follows a valley carved deeply into the Fairholme Range by Cougar Creek. The previously listed length and elevation gain is to a high ridge on the boundary of Banff National Park. Few hikers reach this point, with most content to turn around within an hour's travel. The first section of trail runs alongside a manmade channel that acts as a conduit for runoff in years of high snowfall. It's dry most of summer, but extra care should be taken in spring. Cross just before the mouth of the canyon. From this point the rough trail crosses the creekbed 10 times in the first three km (1.9 km) to a major fork. Stay within the left valley, continuing up and around the base of Mount Charles Stewart. From this point, the valley walls close in and it's a steep climb up to the boundary of Banff National Park. On the return journey, continue beyond the parking lot to the Summit Café, where you can relax on the patio with a cool drink.

Mount Lady Macdonald

- Length: 3.5 km/2.1 miles (90 minutes) one-way
- Elevation gain: 850 meters/2,790 feet
- Rating: moderate/difficult
- Trailhead: corner Benchlands Trail and Elk Run Boulevard, east side of TransCanada Highway

Named for the wife of Canada's first prime minister, this peak lies immediately north of Canmore. Follow Cougar Creek to where the canyon begins, and look for a faint trail winding up a grassy bank to the left. Once on the trail, take the steepest option at every fork, then a sharp right 300 meters (0.2 miles) after the trail bursts out into a cleared area. This section is steep, climbing through a rock band to the mountain's southern ridge, which you'll follow the rest of the way. The distance and elevation listed previously are to a disused helipad below the main summit. It's a steep, unrelenting slog, but views across the Bow Valley are stunning. From this point, the true summit is another 275 vertical meters (900 vertical feet) away, along an extremely narrow ridge that drops away precipitously to the east.

Grotto Canyon

- Length: 2 km/1.2 miles (40 minutes) one-way
- Elevation gain: 60 meters/200 feet
- Rating: easy
- Trailhead: Grotto Pond, Highway 1A, 12 km (7.5 miles) east of Canmore

This is one of the most interesting trails around Canmore. From Grotto Pond, this trail first follows a powerline road behind the Baymag plant. Then at a signed intersection it takes off through the woods to the mouth of the canyon. No official trail traverses the canyon; hikers simply follow the creekbed through the towering canyon walls. Around 300 meters (0.2 miles) into the canyon, look for pictographs to the left. At the two-km (1.2-mile) mark, the canyon makes a sharp left turn at Illusion Rock, where water cascades through a narrow chasm and into the main canyon. Many hikers return from this point, but through the next section of canyon, the valley opens up, passing hoodoos and a cave. It's 6.5 km (four miles) from the trailhead to the end of the valley, with most of the 680 meters (2,230 feet) of elevation gained in the last two km (1.2 miles).

Heart Creek

- Length: 2 km/1.2 miles (40 minutes) one-way
- Elevation gain: 80 meters/260 feet
- Rating: easy
- Trailhead: Lac des Arcs interchange, TransCanada Highway, 15 km (9.3 miles) east of Canmore

This well-formed trail is signposted from the Lac des Arcs interchange, 15 km (9.3 miles) east of Canmore along the TransCanada Highway. The trail parallels the highway eastward until reaching a fork. The trail to the right follows Heart Creek for just over one km (0.6 miles), crossing the creek seven times on narrow log bridges. It ends at a cleared area below a spot where Heart Creek is forced through a narrow cleft. Those tempted to continue further can cross the creek, scramble up a steep, forested ridge, then descend the other side to link up with the creek upstream of the gorge. Cross the creek again for views of another narrow chasm.

Heli-Hiking

Heli-hiking is the summer alternative to heli-skiing—a helicopter does the hard work, and you get to hike in a remote, alpine region that would usually entail a long, steep hike to access. **Alpine Helicopters,** 403/678-4802, offers a variety of options starting at $240 per person, which includes 15 minutes of flight time and 3–4 hours of hiking. The company is flexible, with ground-time and destinations chosen by the clients. Flight-seeing (no landing) costs $135 for 25 minutes of airtime. The heliport is along Highway 1A south of downtown. (Try and book ahead for these trips; they're very popular with travelers staying in Banff, where there is no flight-seeing.)

OTHER RECREATION

Canmore Nordic Centre

This remarkable complex was built at a cost of $15 million for the 1988 Winter Olympic Games in Calgary. The cross-country skiing and biathlon (combined cross-country skiing and rifle shooting) events were held here, and today the center remains a world-class training ground for Canadian athletes. The operation was privatized in 1997 and pronounced a provincial park in 2000. Even in summer, long after the snow has melted, the place is worth a visit. An interpretive trail leads down to and along the west bank of the Bow River to the barely visible remains of Georgetown, a once-bustling coal-mining town.

Many other trails lead around the grounds, and it's possible to hike or bike along the way to the Fairmont Banff Springs. Mountain biking is extremely popular on 70 km (43.5 miles) of trails. Bike rentals are available at **Trail Sports,** below the day lodge, 403/678-6764; $8 per hour and $30 per day for a front-suspension bike. The day lodge has lockers, a lounge area, a café (open daily 10 A.M.–4 P.M.), and an information desk. It's open daily 8 A.M.–4:30 P.M. For more information, call 403/678-2400.

Fishing

The **Bow River** has good fishing for brown and brook trout, including right downtown. Follow Highway 1A east from town to access the best river fishing, as well as **Gap Lake** and **Grotto Pond;** the latter is stocked with rainbow trout. The Bow River is renowned for its rainbow trout fishing. This occurs downstream of Canmore toward Calgary and beyond **Ghost Lake,** which holds healthy populations of lake, rainbow, and brown trout. For all your fishing needs, head to **Wapiti Sports,** 1506 Railway Ave., 403/678-5550, which stocks bait and tackle and sells licenses.

Golfing

Canmore has three golf courses, including two that have opened in the last few years. As with golfing elsewhere in the Canadian Rockies, book all tee times well in advance. The golfing season in Canmore runs from mid-May to late September, with discounted rates at the latter two courses at the beginning and end of each season.

Canmore Golf Course, built in 1929 as a nine-hole course at the north end of 8th Avenue, has developed into an 18-hole course with a modern clubhouse and a practice facility that includes a driving range and chipping greens. It is an interesting layout, with scenic panoramas and water on many holes. Greens fees are $50, a cart is $28; for tee times, call 403/678-4784.

SilverTip, 403/678-1600 or 877/877-5444, www.silvertipresort.com, opened in summer 1998 on a series of wide benches between the valley floor and the lower slopes of Mount Lady

© ANDREW HEMPSTEAD

The fairways at SilverTip serve up magnificent mountain vistas. But don't look now, it's also Canada's most difficult golf course.

Macdonald. It was quickly recognized as one of Canada's finest resort courses, but more tellingly, it boasts a Slope Rating of 153, the highest of any course in mainland North America. Needless to say, the layout is challenging, with the most distinct feature being elevation changes of up to 40 meters (130 feet) on any one hole, and a total 200-meter (656-foot) elevation difference between the lowest and highest points on the course. Adding to this challenge are narrow, sloping, tree-lined fairways, numerous water hazards, 74 bunkers, and a course length of a frightening 7,300 yards from the back markers. Greens fees are $125 Mon.–Wed., $140 Thur.–Sun., which includes a mandatory cart (each cart has GPS to help golfers judge distances). Five hours before sunset, greens fees drop to $90.

Stewart Creek Golf Club, 403/609-6099 or 877/993-4653, www.stewartcreekgolf.com, another new layout, lies across the valley in the Three Sisters Mountain Village development. It is shorter than SilverTip but still measures more than 7,000 yards from the back tees. The fairways are relatively wide, but positioning of tee shots is important, and the course is made more interesting by hanging greens, greenside exposed rock, and historic mine shafts. Greens fees are $135, with twilight rates of $85. These rates include use of a power cart and practice facility.

Horseback Riding

Nestled on a wide bench on the northeastern side of town, **Cross Zee Ranch,** 403/678-4171, has been guiding visitors through the valley since the 1950s. From expansive stables, riders are presented with a variety of options that pass through thickly wooded areas, colorful meadows, and to high lookouts. Options include Ranger Ridge and Bone Gully (one hour; $25 per person), Sunny Bench (90 minutes; $36), and the Great Aspens ride (two hours; $44).

Climbing

Hundreds of climbing routes have been laid out around Canmore. **Mount Yamnuska,** which rises 900 meters (2,950 feet) above the valley floor east of town along Highway 1A, is the most developed site. Climbers also flock to **Chinaman's Peak, Cougar Creek,** the area

ALPINE CLUB OF CANADA

The Alpine Club of Canada (ACC), like similar clubs in the United States and Great Britain, is a nonprofit mountaineering organization whose objectives include encouraging mountaineering through educational programs, exploring and studying alpine and glacial regions, and preserving mountain flora and fauna.

The club was formed in 1906, mainly through the tireless campaign of its first president, Arthur Wheeler. A list of early members reads like a Who's Who of the Canadian Rockies—Bill Peyto, Tom Wilson, Byron Harmon, Mary Schäffer—names familiar to all Canadian mountaineers. Today the club membership includes 3,000 alpinists from throughout Canada.

The original clubhouse was near the Banff Springs Hotel, but in 1980 a new clubhouse was built on benchland at the edge of Canmore to serve as the association's headquarters. The club's ongoing projects include operating the Canadian Alpine Centre (Lake Louise Hostel), maintaining a system of 20 huts throughout the backcountry of the Canadian Rockies, and publishing the annual *Canadian Alpine Journal*—the country's only record of mountaineering accomplishments. A reference library of the club's history is kept at the Whyte Museum of the Canadian Rockies in Banff.

For further information and membership details, contact the Alpine Club of Canada, 403/678-3200, www.alpineclubofcanada.ca.

---

behind **Grassi Lakes,** and **Grotto Canyon.** Canmore is home to many qualified mountain guides. **Yamnuska,** 403/678-4164, www.yamnuska.com, offers basic rock-climbing courses, as well as instruction for all ability levels on ice climbing, mountaineering, and trekking. A good introduction to rock climbing is the weekend-long Basic Rock course, which costs $225. Unique to the company are three-month-long courses that take in all aspects of mountain-oriented skills.

ARTS AND ENTERTAINMENT
Drinking and Dancing

Canmore doesn't have anywhere near the number of bars that nearby Banff is so famous for, but no one ever seems to go thirsty. The **Sherwood House,** 838 8th St., 403/678-5211, has a beer garden that catches the afternoon sun and is especially busy on weekends. One block north, **Tannin's,** 838 10th St., 403/609-9200, best known as a restaurant, has a small lounge bar with comfortable armchairs, a pool table, reading material, and a menu of dishes less than $10. It's open Tues.–Sun. from 4:30 P.M., with happy hour specials until 8 P.M. At the other end of the main street is the **Drake Inn,** 909 Railway Ave., 403/678-5131, with a small

outdoor patio and a nonsmoking section with comfortable lounges. Across the road, at the **Rose and Crown,** 749 Railway Ave., 403/678-5168, you'll find a beer garden. All these bars have midweek drink specials and a couple of pool tables.

The **Grizzly Paw Brewing Company,** 622 8th St., 403/678-9983, brews its own beer, with six ales produced in-house (look for special winter brews around Christmas). Most are heavy, English-style beers, but the lighter Grumpy Bear Honey Wheat Ale suits most tastes. Away from downtown, **Creekside's Fine Food & Drink,** 1005 Cougar Creek Dr., 403/609-2345, provides a relaxed, friendly atmosphere with a wide selection of local and imported beer. Wondering where the cheapest beer in town is? Head to the **Last Call,** 637 10th St., 403/678-3934, where you'll find $2 bottled beer on Thursday nights. The rest of the week, it's happy hour 4–8 P.M., daily drink specials, and a bunch of pool-playing locals.

Canmore's only nightclub is **Hooligan's,** south of downtown along the Bow Valley Trail, 403/609-2662, and there's live music somewhere in town every weekend. The Drake Inn has a band playing Wed.–Sat. nights, as does the Rose and Crown, and the Sherwood House has an occasional Sunday afternoon jam session.

CANMORE

Check out the large wine selection at **Alberta Spirits,** in the Canmore Crossing complex on Railway Avenue, 403/678-2451.

Oh Canada Eh!

Popularized across the country at Niagara Falls, this musical dinner show provides a rip-roaring evening of fun and food in a modern building decorated as a cavernous log cabin. It's unashamedly cheesy, but the parade of costumed Canadian characters—such as lumberjacks, natives, Mounties, and even Anne of Green Gables—will keep you laughing as they sing and dance across the floor. The food is surprisingly good, with Canadian favorites such as Alberta beef, salmon, and maple chocolate cake served buffet-style. Performances are nightly through summer at 6:30 P.M., the rest of the year Friday and Saturday only. It's at 125 Kananaskis Way (off Bow Valley Trail), 403/609-0004 or 800/773-0004.

Festivals and Events

Canmore's small-town pride lives on through a busy schedule of festivals and events, which are nearly always accompanied by parades of flag-waving kids, free downtown pancake breakfasts, and an evening shindig somewhere in town.

Throughout the winter months, locals play **hockey** on ponds and rinks scattered throughout the valley. Things get a little more serious at home games of the **Canmore Eagles,** held at the recreation center along 8th Avenue. Canmore's annual **Winter Carnival** is a two-week celebration including ice-sculpting and kid-and-mutt races. The highlight is the **Sled Dog Classic** held at Canmore Nordic Centre, where up to 100 teams of four, six, eight, and 10 dogs are harnessed up and compete in various heats. (Organizers are always looking for volunteers;

Canmore's small-town pride lives on through a busy schedule of festivals and events, which are nearly always accompanied by parades of flag-waving kids, free downtown pancake breakfasts, and an evening shindig somewhere in town.

ask around if you'd like to help). The festival takes place the last two weeks of January. In early March, the **International Canmore Ice-Climbing Festival** is hosted at venues throughout town, including at a 20-meter-high (66-foot-high) manmade wall of ice beside Bow Valley Trail at 17th Street.

Canada Day is celebrated with a pancake breakfast, parade, various activities in Centennial Park, and 11 P.M. fireworks. Canmore Nordic Centre hosts a variety of mountain-biking events each summer, highlighted by a stop on the **24 Hours of Adrenalin** tour, in which racers complete as many laps as they can in a 24-hour period. For a full listing of mountain bike races, contact the nordic center at 403/678-2400. On the Heritage Day long weekend, the first weekend of August, Canmore hosts a **Folk Music Festival,** 403/678-2524, which starts on Sunday and runs through Monday evening. This event, which attracts more than 10,000 fans, features national and international acts performing in Centennial Park, musical workshops, and a free pancake breakfast beside the post office on Heritage Day.

The first Sunday of September is the **Canmore Highland Games,** 403/678-9454, a day of dancing, eating, and caber tossing, culminating in a spectacular and noisy parade of pipe bands throughout the grounds of Centennial Park that attracts more than 10,000 spectators. On the Sunday evening, a *ceilidh,* a traditional Scottish celebration involving beer-drinking, foot-stomping music, takes place under a massive tent set up in the park for the occasion.

Fall's major gathering is for the **Festival of the Eagles,** on the third weekend of October and coinciding with the southbound migration of golden eagles. It features talks, slideshows, and field trips.

Accommodations and Camping

Canmore's population boom has been mirrored by the construction of new hotels and motels. Most of the new lodgings are on Bow Valley Trail (Hwy. 1A), the traditional strip. As with all resort towns in the Canadian Rockies, reservations should be made as far in advance as possible in summer.

More than 40 bed-and-breakfasts operate in Canmore. They are all small, family-run affairs, with only one or two rooms (a local town bylaw limits the number of guest rooms in private homes to just two). During summer, they fill every night. For a full list of B&Bs, check the website of the **Canmore/Bow Valley Bed and Breakfast Association,** www.bbcanmore.com, for one that suits your needs.

As you raise your eyebrows over hotel pricing in Canmore, consider two things: (1) many hotels discount rooms year-round, so use the listed websites to find current deals and packages; and (2) room rates in Canmore are a bargain compared to Banff, just down the road.

Outside the busiest summer period (mid-June to mid-September), room rates are slashed considerably (especially at the more expensive accommodations); with a little bit of searching, expect to find rates that include two lift tickets (at either the Banff or Kananaskis alpine resorts) for the same price as the room-only rate during summer.

IN AND AROUND TOWN

Less Than $50

The **Canmore Clubhouse** of the Alpine Club of Canada is an excellent hostel-style accommodation at the base of Grotto Mountain. This headquarters for the national mountaineering club overlooks the Bow Valley and can sleep 30 in seven rooms. It has a kitchen, an excellent library, a laundry room, a bar, a sauna, and a lounge area with a fireplace. Rates are $17 per night for Alpine Club members, $21 otherwise. Club member-

ship is inexpensive and includes a discount at the Lake Louise Alpine Centre. For reservations and more information, call 403/678-3200, www.alpineclubofcanada.ca. To get there from downtown, follow Bow Valley Trail southeast; it's signposted to the left, 500 meters (0.3 miles) after passing under the TransCanada Highway.

$50–100

The **Akai Motel,** 1717 Mountain Ave., 403/678-4664 or 877/900-2524, is a little old-fashioned, but each room is air-conditioned and has a small kitchenette, TV, and telephone; $80 s, $90 d. This is Canmore's least expensive motel.

The only other accommodations that fall in this price range are bed-and-breakfasts, although rooms less than $100 are limited. With around $100 budgeted for a room, it's hard to go past **Riverview and Main,** centrally located half a block beyond the end of the downtown core at 918 8th Street, 403/678-9777, www.riverviewandmain.com. The rooms are decently sized and brightly decorated and each has access to a deck. The guest lounge centers on a riverstone, wood-burning fireplace. Rates of $85–120 s or d include a selection of hot and cold breakfast items.

$100–150

Many accommodations fall into this price range; the first three detailed as follows are the pick of the bunch in terms of value for money.

Named for one of the valley's original coal-mining communities, the **Georgetown Inn,** 1101 Bow Valley Trail, 403/678-3439 or 800/657-5955, www.georgetowninn.ab.ca, is run by a friendly English couple who have set the place up as a country inn of times gone by, complete with a private guest-only lounge bar. Each of the 25 rooms has its own individual charm, with a modern twist on décor that features lots of English antiques. The best value are Superior Rooms, each with a separate sitting area and electric fireplace ($149). Complimentary nonalcoholic drinks and a delicious cooked breakfast are included in rates ranging $129–189 s or d (from $89 in winter).

Opening in 2002, **Windtower Mountain Lodge,** 160 Kananaskis Way, 403/609-6600 or 866/609-6600, www.windtowermountainlodge.com, provides hotel and suite accommodation in a much larger condominium development. Complex facilities include a picnic and barbeque area, a fitness center, an outdoor hot tub, a café, and underground parking. Hotel-style rooms range $109–149, depending on size, while suites feature separate bedrooms as well as a full kitchen, private balcony, laundry room, and large well-equipped living area for $179–279 s or d. Either way—and not taking into account perpetually discounted rooms advertised on the website—this is an excellent value.

Also a good value in this price range is the centrally located **Drake Inn,** 909 Railway Ave., 403/678-5131 or 800/461-8730, www.drakeinn.com, at the end of Canmore's main street. It offers bright and cheerfully decorated standard rooms for $99 s, $109 d. Well worth an extra $10 are Creekside Rooms, featuring a private balcony overlooking Policeman's Creek. The adjoining bar opens daily at 7 A.M. for the best-value breakfast in town.

Across the creek from the Drake Inn is the **Bow Valley Motel,** 610 8th St., 403/678-5085 or 800/665-8189, www.bowvalleymotel.com, offering 25 rooms right on the main shopping strip. The rooms are far from the cutting edge of modern style, but the location and price is right, $100–110 s or d, kitchenettes an extra $10. On site is an outdoor hot tub and coin-operated laundry facilities.

The **Rocky Mountain Ski Lodge,** 1711 Bow Valley Trail, 403/678-5445 or 800/665-6111, www.rockymtnskilodge.com, is a sprawling complex of 82 large but standard motel rooms and self-contained one- and two-bedroom units, some with loft bedrooms. Also on the property is a playground, barbecue and picnic area, and a laundromat. The motel rooms are $130 s or d, while the suites cost from $160.

At the top end of this price category is the **Howard Johnson Hotel,** 1402 Bow Valley Trail,

403/609-4656 or 800/678-4656. It is an elongated complex of 202 rooms with a small indoor pool and waterslide, and a restaurant; $145 s or d. Check the Howard Johnson website, www.hojo.com, as far in advance as possible to get the best rates.

$150–200

The quality of accommodations in this category far exceeds that of similarly priced options elsewhere in the Canadian Rockies. With up to $200 (around US$130) per night to spend on accommodations, I strongly recommend you consider the first two options, each offering a unique mountain ambiance impossible to find in a regular hotel.

Lady Macdonald Country Inn, 1201 Bow Valley Trail, 403/678-3665 or 800/567-3919, www.ladymacdonald.com, exudes a welcoming atmosphere and personalized service not experienced in the larger properties. Its 12 rooms are all individually furnished, with the smallest, the Palliser Room, featuring elegant décor and a magnificent wrought iron bed. The largest of the rooms is the Three Sisters, which has bright, welcoming décor, a king bed, two-way gas fireplace, hot tub, and uninterrupted views of its namesake. Rates range $155–225 s or d, which includes a hearty hot breakfast.

Creekside Country Inn, 709 Benchlands Trail, 403/609-5522 or 866/609-552, www.creeksidecountryinn.com, is a modern, mountain-style lodge featuring lots of exposed timber. The 12 rooms are elegant in their simplicity; eight have lofts. Facilities include a lounge with roaring log fire, a small exercise room, a whirlpool, and a steam room. Rates are $159–179 ($79–129 outside of summer), which includes a gourmet Continental breakfast that will set you up for the day.

Along the same strip as Lady Macdonald, the **Days Inn,** 815 Bow Valley Trail, 403/609-0075 or 877/609-6266, www.canmoredaysinn.com, provides a higher standard of accommodation than is usually associated with this chain. This is reflected in the pricing of rooms, but it's still a good value within this price range. Even standard rooms ($159 s or d) have king-sized beds, and each is air-conditioned and well equipped

© ANDREW HEMPSTEAD

Creekside Country Inn

with an array of amenities. The extra space, private balcony, and sleek contemporary styling of the suites is worth the slightly higher cost.

Diagonally opposite the Days Inn is the 30-room **Bear Country Lodge,** 1002 Bow Valley Trail, 403/678-1000 or 888/678-1008, www.bearcountrylodge.com, another of Canmore's many new hotels. It features eye-catching timber and riverstone styling outside and throughout an impressive lobby, but stops short of continuing to the standard rooms, which are unremarkable; $129 s or d, $149 with a kitchenette. King Deluxe rooms, however, reflect the décor of the public areas, with pine log furnishings, gas fireplaces, and hot tubs; $189 s or d. Rates include a Continental breakfast buffet in a pleasant downstairs dining room. The Bear Country kicks off the trend of more expensive hotels that heavily discount rooms outside of summer, with rates from just $69.

Dominated by exposed log work, the **Westridge Country Inn,** 1719 Bow Valley Trail, 403/678-5221 or 800/268-0935, www.westridgecountryinn.com., has new, comfortable air-conditioned rooms, each with a balcony and fireplace. Summer rates of $159–199

include a light breakfast, while in winter rooms start at $100.

The **Best Western Green Gables Inn,** 1602 2nd Ave., 403/678-5488 or 800/661-2133, www.bestwestern.com, offers a whirlpool in many of the 61 spacious pastel-colored rooms, private balconies, fireplaces, and a fine-dining French restaurant. Rooms are $159–199 s or d, and winter packages start at $95 per person.

Farther north along the Bow Valley Trail is another Best Western property, the **Pocaterra Inn,** 1725 Bow Valley Trail, 403/678-4334 or 888/678-6786, www.pocaterrainn.com. It features a large indoor pool, a fitness room, a sauna, and 83 elegant guest rooms, each with a gas fireplace and microwave. Summer rates for a standard room are $170 s or d. Suites provide an excellent value for those looking for accommodations in the $200–250 price range.

With 224 guest rooms, the **Radisson Hotel,** 511 Bow Valley Trail, 403/678-3625 or 800/333-3333, www.radisson.ca/canmore, is Canmore's largest accommodation. Set around landscaped gardens, this complex also features an excellent restaurant (the Sunday brunch here is one of the best in the valley), an in-

BREWSTER'S KANANASKIS GUEST RANCH

Built in 1923, this historic lodge located 28 km (17.4 miles) east of Canmore along Highway 1A has been owned and operated by five generations of the Brewster family, a name synonymous with tourism in the Canadian Rockies. The property is located on a magnificent 800-hectare (2,000-acre) tract of land, alongside the Bow River and below the distinctive peak of Mount Yamnuska.

A traditional Western atmosphere prevails, with the emphasis on horseback riding ($55 for a half-day ride). Guests also enjoy a well-maintained nine-hole golf course ($22), fishing, rafting, and canoeing. The lodge itself overlooks a small lake. Amenities include an indoor hot tub, a cocktail lounge, a pool table, a dining room, and a lounge. Chalets and cabins are basic but comfortable. Rates are $89–105 per person per day, which includes breakfast and dinner. For more information, call 403/673-3737 or 800/691-5085, www.brewster-adventures.com.

door pool, a fitness facility, the town's only car rental agency, and a gift shop. Rooms range $159–209 s or d.

Similarly priced, and of the same high standard, is the **Quality Resort Chateau Canmore,** 1720 Bow Valley Trail, 403/678-6699 or 800/228-5151, www.chateaucanmore.com. Standard rooms are $175 s or d; much more spacious loft suites have kitchenettes and gas fireplaces for around $200. The one- and two-bedroom suites also have a fireplace, as well as a full kitchen and separate living area; $205 s or d. Other facilities include a medium-sized fitness facility with an indoor pool, a bar, and a Swiss restaurant.

$200–250

The **Bear and Bison,** 705 Benchlands Trail, 403/678-2058, www.bearandbison.com, which opened in summer 2002, is an elegant lodging with nine guest rooms in three different themes. Timber and stone surroundings are complemented by rich heritage tones throughout. Each room has a king-sized four-poster bed, a jetted tub, a fireplace, and a private balcony or patio. The lounge has a high vaulted ceiling, a welcoming open fire, and panoramic picture windows. Guests also enjoy an inviting library and a private garden complete with an oversized hot tub. Rates of $245 s or d include baked goods on arrival, predinner drinks, and a gourmet breakfast. Outside of summer, rates run $160–245.

At the base of SilverTip Resort, across the TransCanada Highway from downtown, is **Four Points by Sheraton Canmore,** 1 Silvertip Trail, 403/609-4422 or 888/609-4422, www.fourpoints.com/canmore, Canmore's most luxurious hotel lodging. It is a full-service hotel, complete with 99 contemporary guest rooms, a fitness center, a casual Italian restaurant and adjacent bar, a gift store, and a complimentary shuttle to downtown Canmore and Banff. Rates start at $205 s or d.

In Three Sisters Mountain Village, across the Bow River from downtown, is the **Marriott Residence Inn,** 91 Three Sisters Dr., 403/678-3400 or 877/335-8800, www.canmoremarriott.com. Canmore's only all-suite accommodation, each of 119 units is characterized by bright, contemporary furnishings, a well-equipped kitchen, a separate living area, and a full bathroom. Studio units are $199 s, $209 d; one-bedroom units $229 d; two-bedroom units $269 d. Out front is a small heated pool that is open year-round.

HARVEY HEIGHTS

Lodging in Harvey Heights, eight km (five miles) west of Canmore and less than one km (0.6 miles) from the entrance to Banff National Park, may seem a little more pricey than Canmore, but most units are self-contained.

$50–100

The least expensive option at Harvey Heights are standard motel rooms at the **Gateway Inn,**

403/678-5396 or 877/678-1810, www.gate-wayinn.ca, which range $75–89 s or d. Self-contained cabins, each with a kitchenette and adjacent firepit, are $89–159 s or d, with the more expensive ones having three bedrooms.

$100–150

Rundle Ridge Chalets, 403/678-5387 or 800/332-1299, www.chalets.ab.ca, is one of the mountains' original bungalow camps, with 37 self-contained log cabins scattered around a pleasant two-hectare (five-acre) property. Summer rates range $109–164. The cabins are winterized, and rates drop as low as $69 midweek in the depths of January.

Next door to Rundle Ridge, **The Stockade,** 403/678-5212 or 800/330-3824, www.stockadecabins.com, is smaller but similarly set up. The least expensive option is to stay in one of six bright, cheery log cabins. Seven more modern, kitchen-equipped chalets maintain a distinct mountain atmosphere. All units have wood-burning fireplaces. Rates range $109–225 s or d.

$150–200

The **Banff Boundary Lodge,** 403/678-9555 or 877/678-9555, www.banffboundarylodge.com, is newer than the three previously listed properties. The 42 units each have one or two bedrooms, a comfortable lounge area with TV/VCR, and a full kitchen. In summer, units are $199–229 per night, but the rest of the year rates drop as low as $100, an excellent value.

DEADMAN'S FLATS

Deadman's Flats, seven km (4.3 miles) east of Canmore along the TransCanada Highway, is little more than a truck stop, but it has motels, a bed-and-breakfast, and 24-hour dining at a Husky gas station.

$50–100

The best value of the bunch is the **Big Horn Motel,** 403/678-2290 or 800/892-9908, www.bighornmotel.com. It offers 27 surprising-ly modern, mostly nonsmoking rooms. All have televisions and phones, some have kitchens and balconies, and a couple are wheelchair-accessible. Summer rates range $79–99, while in the off-season you can get a nonsmoking kitchenette for just $50.

The other two motel choices are the **Pigeon Mountain Motel,** 403/678-5756, which charges $80 s or d, and the **Green Acres Motel,** 403/678-5344 or 800/820-5344, decorated with colorful flowers each summer, and offering spacious rooms for $79 s, $89 d.

$100–150

In an alpine-style, two-story chalet, the **Kiska Inn,** 110 1st Ave., 403/678-4041 or 866/678-4041, offers six guest rooms. Each is spacious and features subtly themed rooms (the Canmore Room is particularly appealing). Guest amenities include a shard kitchen, a comfortable lounge room, a barbeque area, and Internet access. Summer rates are a reasonable $105–120 s or d including breakfast.

CAMPGROUNDS

Commercial Campgrounds

The **Restwell Trailer Park** enjoys a great creekside location off 8th Street in downtown Canmore, 403/678-5111, www.restwelltrailerpark.com. It's mostly filled with permanent residents and doesn't try to be anything it's not. Overnight travelers are welcomed, with the best sites situated along a stretch of grass that parallels Policeman's Creek. Unserviced sites are $24, hookups $27–37, self-contained cabins $130 s or d.

Along the Bow Valley Trail toward Banff is the **Rundle Mountain Campground,** opposite the motel of the same name, 403/678-2131 or 866/678-2267. Like Restwell, it offers showers, laundry facilities, and hookups. Sites range $20–25.

Other Campgrounds

East of Canmore are three government campgrounds operated by Bow Valley Campgrounds, 403/673-2163, www.bowvalleycampgrounds.com. Each has pit toilets, kitchen shelters, and firewood

A few campsites at Restwell Trailer Park enjoy a creekside setting.

for sale at $6 per bundle. The **Bow River Campground** is three km (1.9 miles) east of Canmore at the Three Sisters Parkway overpass; **Three Sisters Campground** is accessed from Deadman's Flats, a further four km (2.5 miles) east, but has a pleasant treed setting, while **Lac des Arcs Campground** slopes down to the edge of a large lake of the same name a further seven km (4.3 miles) toward Calgary. These campgrounds are open May to mid-September, and all sites are $17. Reservations are taken from April 1.

Practicalities

FOOD

The restaurant scene has come a long way in Canmore in the last few years. While you can still get inexpensive bar meals at each of the many pubs, other choices run the gamut, from the lively atmosphere of dining in the front yard of a converted residence to an upmarket French restaurant.

Groceries

IGA is a large supermarket on Railway Avenue; especially good are the Chicken Pot Pies, which come heated and ready to eat for $4. It also has an in-house bakery, butcher, and deli, along with a wide selection of seafood. In summer, it's open daily 7 A.M.–10 P.M.; shorter hours the rest of the year. Downtown, **Marra's**, 638 8th St., is a locally owned supermarket open until 8 P.M.

Gourmet Goodies

In front of IGA, **Nutter's**, 900 Railway Ave., 403/678-3335, is chock-full of bulk bins—a great place to stock up for hiking trips. Downtown, **Bella Crusta**, 702 6th Ave., 403/609-3366, are purveyors of the best gourmet pizza in the Bow Valley. Heated slices to go are $5, or pay $12–15 for a family-sized version and heat it yourself, on a barbeque as the friendly staff recommend; closed Sunday. Away from the downtown core, **JK Bakery**, 1514 Railway Ave., 403/678-4232, supply regular and European-style breads to shops and restaurants throughout the Canadian Rockies. A small café out front serves up a variety of sandwiches and pastries, as well as selling gourmet breads over the counter.

Tucked away in an industrial park beyond the south end of Bow Valley Trail is **Valbella Meats,** 104 Elk Run Blvd., 403/678-4109. Mainly supplying gourmet meats to Bow Valley restaurants and grocery stores, head to Valbella for Canadian specialties such as buffalo, venison, and salmon; fresh cuts of marinated Alberta beef, lamb, chicken, and pork; and cured sausages. Finally, we can't forget our four-legged friends in this epicurean tour of town: **Mountain Bones,** produced locally and available in many Canmore outlets, will have your pooch pawing for more.

Cafés and Coffee Shops

Open daily 6:30 A.M.–11 P.M., the **Rocky Mountain Bagel Company,** 830 8th St., 403/678-9978, is a popular early-morning gathering spot. With a central location, it's always busy but manages to maintain an inviting atmosphere. It's the perfect place to start the day with a good strong coffee and fruit-filled muffin. Around the corner, the **Coffee Mine,** 802 8th St., 403/678-2241, is a small café with a large local following and a sunny outlook; open daily at 6:30 A.M. One block from the main street, the pace is more relaxed at **Blends,** 637 10th St., 403/678-2688, which opens weekdays at 8 A.M. and on Saturday at 9:30 A.M.

Gianni Java's, 743 Railway Ave., 403/609-4362, features a funky Greek-inspired interior and tables set outside on an elevated terrace. Coffee is roasted in-house and is the perfect accompaniment to a range of tempting desserts. Out on the Bow Valley Trail (between Dairy Queen and Boston Pizza) is **Beamer's Coffee Bar,** 403/678-3988. Always busy, this place has a huge following through great coffee, a friendly owner, and a long comfortable couch wrapped around a fireplace—the perfect place to relax with one of Beamer's complimentary daily papers. It's open daily at 7 A.M.

The **Crazyweed Kitchen,** downtown at 626 8th St., 403/609-2530, dishes up creative culinary fare daily 11 A.M.–7 P.M. Behind the glass counter are a wide choice of freshly made dishes, which may include Thai chicken wraps or curried seafood. Healthy portions are served at tables inside or out, or packed to go.

Away from downtown, near where Cougar Creek enters Canmore from the Fairholme Range, is the **Summit Café,** 1001 Cougar Creek Dr., 403/609-2120. It features a health-conscious menu including lots of salads, but many people come just to soak up the sun on the outside deck or relax with the daily paper and a cup of coffee. Open for breakfast, lunch, and dinner.

Downtown

Tucked away behind the main street is **Zona's,** 710 9th St., 403/609-2000, a great little bistro with a laidback atmosphere. Earthy tones, hardwood floors, rustic furniture, bamboo blinds, and kiln-fired clay crockery create an inviting ambience unequaled in Canmore. The menu takes its roots from around the world, with an emphasis on healthy eating and freshly prepared Canadian produce. Choose from dishes such as Moroccan Molasses Lamb Curry ($14) or a filet of salmon baked and smothered in a maple and whiskey sauce ($18). It also serves homemade lemonade and a wide selection of slightly overpriced wines and beers. A large deck provides much-needed extra seating in summer. Open daily 11 A.M.–2 A.M.

Best known as a bar with the busiest deck in town, the **Sherwood House,** 838 8th St., 403/678-5211, is also home to a fine restaurant that oozes historic mountain charm. Set in a re-creation of an early-1900s cabin that once stood on the same site, it features log walls adorned with historic mountain memorabilia, timber furniture, and a roaring log fire. It's open daily from 7 A.M., but dinner draws the biggest raves. Creative appetizers are all $10, and Rocky Mountain specialties such as buffalo rib steak, scalloped venison, nut-crusted salmon, and char-broiled Alberta beef are all in the $15–29 price range. Leave room for a generous slice of mixed berry cheesecake.

Two blocks north of the Sherwood House is **Tannin's,** 838 10th St., 403/609-9200, a city-style wine bar with a laid-back mountain ambience. Choices change with the season but usually include a cheese fondue and seafood choices such as blackened red snapper topped with a dollop of cilantro salsa for a reasonable $15. It's open Tues.–Sun. from 4:30 P.M.

Duck down the alleyway at 708 Eighth St. to **Chef's Studio Japan,** 403/609-8383, a Japanese restaurant open daily for lunch and dinner. Seating is at a sushi counter or at regular tables, all within view of an adjacent art gallery, separated from the dining room by a waist-high partition. The cuisine is not overly inventive, but portions are generous and tempura—always a good litmus test—is light and delicate. Educate yourself in the variety of Japanese cooking styles by ordering one of the hot and cold platters designed for sharing between two.

Bow Valley Trail

The Kabin, 1712 Bow Valley Trail, 403/678-4878, is a two-story log structure at the eastern end of a strip of motels. The menu is small but varied. Expect to pay $15–20 for a main meal. The restaurant also offers an appetizing brunch buffet on Sunday, 10:30 A.M.–2 P.M.; $16.95, including dessert.

Nearby, in the Best Western Green Gables Inn, is **Chez Francois,** 1064 Bow Valley Trail, 403/678-6111, a stylish French restaurant that is hidden by a rather nondescript motel facade. At breakfast (from 6:30 A.M.), there's no need to look further than Eggs Benedict—with a choice of Valbella back bacon or smoked salmon—and smothered in a perfectly formed hollandaise sauce ($8.50). Dinner is highlighted by well-priced table d'hôte menus that feature Canadian game and produce, prepared in traditional French flair.

Patrino's, 1602 Bow Valley Trail, 403/678-4060, is a longtime local favorite, especially renowned for its steaks. The casual, family-style restaurant section has a few outdoor tables and a menu of entrées ranging $11–22. The bar area features the same menu, as well as an abbreviated menu of snacks and an extremely popular 20-cent Wing Night every Thursday. They make good pizza, eat-in or take-out, from $14 for a medium.

TRANSPORTATION

Getting There

The following companies stop in Canmore on routes that link Calgary International Airport and Banff: **Brewster,** 403/762-6767, www.brewster.ca; **Banff Airporter,** 403/762-3330, www.banffairporter.com; and **Rocky Mountain Sky Shuttle,** 403/762-5200, www.rockymountainskyshuttle.com. The latter two companies operate door-to-door-services, and all three charge $40–45 one-way. Adjacent desks at the airport's Arrivals level take bookings, but reserve a seat by booking over the phone or online in advance.

Greyhound stops behind Rusticana Grocery, 801 8th St., 403/678-4465, and offers regular services to Calgary, Banff, and beyond.

Getting Around

The most enjoyable way to get around Canmore is on foot or bike, on the extensive trail network winding throughout the town. **Gear Up,** 1302 Bow Valley Trail, 403/678-1636, rents front- and full-suspension mountain bikes, as well as canoes and kayaks. For a cab, call **Apex,** 403/609-0030. **Hertz,** based at the Radisson Hotel, 511 Bow Valley Trail, 403/678-1630, is Canmore's only rental car outlet.

INFORMATION AND SERVICES

The **post office** is on 7th Avenue, beside Rusticana Grocery. **The Lost Sock** laundromat, open 8 A.M.–9:30 P.M., is in the small mall on 7th Avenue at 10th Street. **Canmore Hospital** is along Bow Valley Trail, 403/678-5536. For the **RCMP,** call 403/678-5516.

The **Film Lab,** 801 8th St., 403/678-6066, provides one-hour photo finishing and basic photography supplies. **Switching Gear,** 718 10th St., 403/678-1992, is a consignment store for a wide range of new and used, winter and summer sporting equipment.

Books and Bookstores

Canmore Public Library, 700 9th St., 403/678-2468, is open Mon.–Thur. 11 A.M.–8 P.M., Fri.–Sun. 11 A.M.–5 P.M.

At the top end of the main street, **Café Books,** 826 Main St., 403/678-0908, stocks an excellent selection of Canadiana, including hiking guides, coffee-table-style pictorials, Rocky Mountain cookbooks, and calendars, as well as nonfiction by local authors. Café Books is open Mon.–Sat. 9:30 A.M.–9 P.M., Sun. 10:30 A.M.–5:30 P.M. With a huge collection of used books, **Second Story,** 713 8th St., 403/609-2368, hasn't been on the second floor since the weight of the books forced a move

© ANDREW HEMPSTEAD

Quarry Lake, a scenic locale on the western edge of Canmore

downstairs to the basement of the same address. Second Story's selection of nonfiction Canadiana is particularly strong.

Internet Access

In addition to major hotels, send and receive email and surf the Internet at the following Canmore locations:

Beamer's Coffee Bar: 1702 Bow Valley Trail, 403/678-3988; daily 7 A.M.–10 P.M.

Café Books: 826 Eighth St., 403/678-0908; Mon.–Sat. 9:30 A.M.–9 P.M., Sun. 10:30 A.M.–5:30 P.M.

Canmore Business Services: 512 Bow Valley Trail, 403/678-1919; Mon.–Fri. 9 A.M.–5:30 P.M.

Canmore Public Library: 700 Ninth St., 403/678-2468; Mon.–Thur. 11 A.M.–8 P.M., Fri.–Sun. 11 A.M.–5 P.M.

Information

The best source of pretrip information (apart from this book, of course) is the **Tourism Canmore** website, www.tourismcanmore.com. A **Travel Alberta Information Centre** on the west side of town, 403/678-5277, just off the Trans-Canada Highway, provides plenty of information about Canmore and Banff. Open May–Sept. 8 A.M.–8 P.M., and Oct. 9 A.M.–6 P.M.

The *Rocky Mountain Outlook* is a weekly (Thursday) newspaper filled with news on local issues; it's available free on stands throughout the valley.

Kananaskis Country

Lying along the east side of the Continental Divide south of Banff National Park and less than one hour's drive from Calgary, this sprawling 4,250-square-km (1,640-square-mile) area of the Canadian Rockies (pronounced Can-AN-a-skiss) has been extraordinarily successful in balancing the needs of the 2.4 million outdoor enthusiasts that visit annually while keeping the region in a relatively natural state. Although the area lacks the famous lakes and glaciated peaks of Banff and Jasper National Parks, the landscape rivals those parks in many ways. As well as the areas set aside for recreation, large tracts of land give full protection to wildlife. Throughout Kananaskis Country, wildlife is abundant and

opportunities for observation of larger mammals are superb.

Kananaskis Country encompasses seven provincial parks, 1,300 km (800 miles) of hiking trails, a complex network of bike paths, areas for horseback riding (and some for ATVs), a world-class 36-hole golf course, boat and bike rentals, and 30 lakes stocked annually with more than 150,000 fish. The downhill-skiing events of the 1988 Winter Olympic Games were held here at the specially developed Nakiska alpine resort, which is now open to the public. Deeper in the mountains, Fortress Mountain provides more downhill skiing and boarding. Meanwhile, nordic skiers can glide

Mount Yamnuska as seen from Bow Valley Provincial Park

© ANDREW HEMPSTEAD

over hundreds of cross-country skiing trails in the region.

Geographically, Kananaskis Country can be divided into eight areas, each with its own distinct character. They include Bow Valley Provincial Park, a small park between the TransCanada Highway and Bow River; Kananaskis Valley, home to a golf course, ski resort, and the accommodations of Kananaskis Village; Peter Lougheed Provincial Park, which rises from fish-filled lakes to the glaciated peaks of the Continental Divide; Spray Valley Provincial Park, named for a massive body of water nestled below the Continental Divide; Sibbald, an integrated recreation area where horseback riding is permitted; Elbow River Valley and adjacent Sheep River Valley, sections of the foothills that rise to Elbow-Sheep Wildland Provincial Park; and in the far south Highwood/Cataract Creek areas, where the rugged landscape ranges from forested valleys to snowcapped peaks.

Although the area lacks the famous lakes and glaciated peaks of Banff and Jasper National Parks, the landscape rivals those parks in many ways. Throughout Kananaskis Country, wildlife is abundant and opportunities for observation of larger mammals are superb.

The accommodations and restaurants of **Kananaskis Village** are the centerpiece of Kananaskis Country's facility area, but also contained within the region are two other lodges, 31 frontcountry campgrounds holding 2,300 sites, 15 backcountry campgrounds, and five information centers. In addition to Canmore, at the northern entrance to Kananaskis Country, the foothills to the east hold many well-established towns, such as Bragg Creek, with interesting histories, quaint teahouses, holiday ranches, and sprawling properties that enjoy the inspiring Canadian Rockies as a backdrop.

THE LAND

Within Kananaskis Country are two distinct ecosystems: the high peaks of the Continental Divide to the west and the lower, rolling foothills to the east. The glacier-carved **Kananaskis Valley** separates the two. The Elbow and Sheep river valleys rise in the west to Front Ranges, which formed around 85 million years ago, and have eroded to half their original height. The Main Ranges, which form part of the Continental Divide, are composed of older, erosion-resistant quartzite and limestone, giving them a more jagged appearance.

Flora and Fauna

Kananaskis Country occupies a transition zone between foothills and mountains, and as a result it harbors a wide variety of plant species. In the east, the relatively low-lying Sheep, Elbow, and Sibbald valleys are dominated by stands of **aspen,** interspersed with open meadows. Climbing gradually to the west, you'll pass through the montane zone, with its forests of **Douglas fir, lodgepole pine, white spruce,** and **balsam poplar,** then enter the subalpine zone, where stands of **Engelmann spruce, subalpine fir,** and occasionally **larch** lead up to the treeline. Above the treeline, which here occurs at around 2,300 meters (7,550 feet), lie the open meadows of the alpine zone. These meadows lie under a deep cover of snow for most of the year but come alive with color during July when wildflowers bloom. Highwood Pass, along Highway 40, is one of the most accessible areas of alpine terrain in the Canadian Rockies; look for **forget-me-nots, Indian paintbrush,** and **western anemone** along the interpretive trail.

These hills, valleys, and forests are home to an abundance of wildlife, including large populations of **moose, mule deer, white-tailed deer, elk, black bear, bighorn sheep,** and **mountain goat.** Also present, but less likely to be seen, are **wolves, grizzly bears,** and **cougars.**

HISTORY

In 1858, Captain John Palliser bestowed the name Kananaskis on the valley, a pass, and two

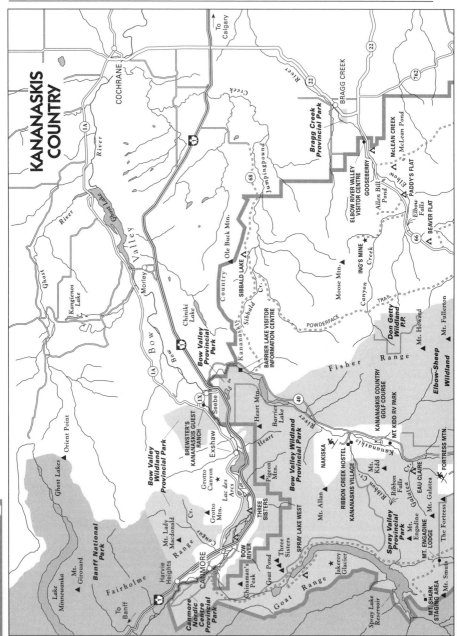

KANANASKIS COUNTRY

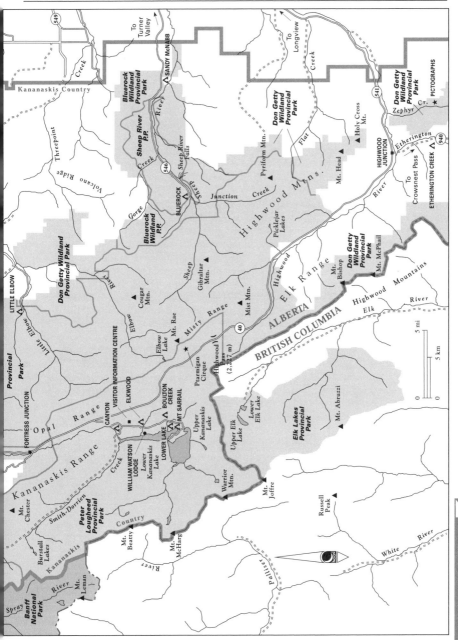

lakes. Kananaskis was a native who, legend had it, suffered a vicious blow to the head by an enemy but survived. The word itself is thought to mean "the meeting of the water." Aside from Palliser, the region was visited by many names synonymous with exploration of the Canadian Rockies: David Thompson in 1787 and 1800, Peter Fidler in 1792, and James Sinclair leading Scottish settlers to the Oregon Territory in 1841. Throughout these times, and until recent times, the valley remained mostly uninhabited. Logging took place from 1883, mostly in the foothill valleys of the Elbow and Sheep Rivers. Coal was mined at various sites, including Ribbon Creek, by Kananaskis Village, but never on a large scale. To serve these industries, roads were built, including the Forestry Trunk Road (Hwy. 40), which traverses the entire foothills parallel to the Continental Divide.

1970s to the Present

During Alberta's oil-and-gas boom of the 1970s, oil revenues collected by the provincial government were placed into the Heritage Savings Trust Fund, from where they were channeled into various projects aimed at improving the lifestyle of Albertans. One lasting legacy of the fund is Kananaskis Country, officially designated by premier Peter Lougheed in 1977 as Kananaskis Country Provincial Recreational Area. The mandate was to accommodate a multitude of uses, including primarily recreational pursuits, but Kananaskis Country also holds 21 active oil and gas leases, 14 grazing permits, timber leases, and a hydroelectric station on the Kananaskis River. Since 1977, the provincial government has pumped more than $250 million into Kananaskis Country, with private investors spending a little more than $60 million in that same period. Kananaskis Village was developed in the early 1980s in anticipation of the 1988 Winter Olympic Games.

The first major boundary change since 1977 occurred in early 1996 when Elbow-Sheep Wildland Provincial Park was established; at 76,900

hectares (190,000 acres) it is Alberta's largest provincial park. User demand for more facilities led to the 1999 Kananaskis Country Recreation Policy, but this was roundly rejected by Albertans, and there is currently a development moratorium, which has put on hold grand plans for a ski area, more golf courses, and boat cruises on Spray Lake. The latest area of Kananaskis Country to be declared a provincial park is the Spray Valley, which has created a continuous stretch of protection for the Canadian Rockies from Willmore Wildness Park in the north to Peter Lougheed Provincial Park in the south.

PRACTICALITIES

Services within Kananaskis Country include an information center at each of the main entrances, high-class accommodations in **Kananaskis Village,** 2,300 campsites in 31 campgrounds, and accommodations for the physically challenged at William Watson Lodge. Gas is available at Fortress Junction and Highwood Junction. For more information, contact the regional Parks and Protected Areas division of the provincial government, in the Provincial Building at 800 Railway Ave., Canmore, AB T1W 1P1; call 403/678-5508, or surf the Internet to www.cd.gov.ab.ca, and click on the "Preserving Alberta" link. Another good source of information is **Friends of Kananaskis Country,** website: www.kananaskis.org, a nonprofit organization that promotes educational programs, is involved in a variety of hands-on projects, and promotes Kananaskis Country in partnership with the government

Access to Kananaskis Country

The main highway through Kananaskis Country is **Highway 40,** which branches off the Trans-Canada Highway 76 km (47 miles) west of Calgary. Other points of access are south of Canmore through the Spray Valley; at Bragg Creek on the region's northeast border; west from Millarville, Turner Valley, and Longview in the southeast; or along the Forestry Trunk Road from the south.

Bow Valley Provincial Park

This provincial park at the north end of Kananaskis Country straddles the TransCanada Highway just west of the Highway 40 junction and extends south to take in a stretch of the Kananaskis River as far south as, and including, Barrier Lake. Most facilities, including two campgrounds and an information center, lie between the TransCanada Highway and the Bow River, at the confluence of the Kananaskis River. The main access point is Highway 1X, which branches north from the TransCanada Highway 80 km (50 miles) west of Calgary and 26 km (16 miles) east of Canmore.

The park protects a small section of the Bow Valley, which was gouged by glaciers during a succession of ice ages, leaving the typical U-shaped glacial valley surrounded by towering peaks. Three vegetation zones are found within the park, but evergreen and aspen forest predominates. The park was originally within the area protected by Banff National Park, but the boundary was moved westward in 1930 to allow development in the Canmore area. The park of today was originally created in 1959 and expanded in 2000.

To the casual motorist driving along the highway, the park seems fairly unspectacular (and is easily missed), but more than 300 species of plants have been recorded and 60 species of birds are known to nest within its boundaries. The abundance of wildflowers, birds, elk, and smaller mammals can be enjoyed along short interpretive trails. Other popular activities in the park include fishing for brown and brook trout and whitefish in the Bow River, bicycling along the paved trail system, and attending interpretive programs presented by park staff. The main road through the park terminates 12 km (7.5 miles) beyond the information center at a picnic area beside the Bow River.

HIKING
Montane Trail
- Length: 2.2 km/1.4 miles (30 minutes) round-trip
- Elevation gain: minimal
- Rating: easy
- Trailhead: Visitor Information Centre off Hwy. 1X

The Montane Trail begins from behind the main information center and, as the name suggests, it traverses montane forest of aspen and towering Douglas fir, as well as skirting an open meadow and several *eskers,* low ridges left behind by retreating glaciers during the last Ice Age.

Many Springs Trail
- Length: 2.8 km/1.7 miles (40 minutes) round-trip
- Elevation gain: minimal
- Rating: easy
- Trailhead: Elk Flats day-use area

From the trailhead, this well-formed trail makes a loop around a wetland fed by underground springs. The spring water is relatively warm, creating a microclimate that attracts birds and mammals year-round. Look for orchids around damp areas.

Flowing Water Interpretive Trail
- Length: 1.4 km/ (30 minutes) round-trip
- Elevation gain: minimal
- Rating: easy
- Trailhead: Willow Rock Campground, eastern side of Highway 1X

This trail traverses montane forest along a bench above the Kananaskis River and passes a beaver pond. Interpretive panels along the way explain the importance of water and its relationship to the ecosystem.

PRACTICALITIES
Campgrounds
Facilities at the two campgrounds within the park, **Bow Valley** and **Willow Rock,** are as good as any in the Canadian Rockies. Both have showers,

flush toilets, firewood sales ($6 per bundle), and kitchen shelters. Continue beyond the information center to reach Bow Valley Campground, which has a grocery store, bike rentals, sites with power and water, and a nightly interpretive program. It's open 1 May to mid-October. Willow Rock has a few powered sites (but these are open to the elements), a coin laundry, and is open May 1 to late October. Unserviced sites are $17, powered sites $20, and sites with both power and water are $23. For more information, or for reservations at Bow Valley, contact **Bow Valley Campgrounds,** 403/673-2163, www.bowvalleycampgrounds.com.

Information

A **Visitor Information Centre** at the park entrance on Highway 1X, 403/673-3663, offers general information on the park and Kananaskis Country, as well as interpretive displays. The short Montane Trail (see previous listing) begins here. The center is open in summer Mon.–Fri. 8 A.M.–8 P.M.; the rest of the year Mon.–Fri. 8:15 A.M.–4:30 P.M.

Kananaskis Valley

This is the most developed area of Kananaskis Country, yet summer crowds are minimal compared to Banff. Highway 40 follows the Kananaskis River through the valley between the TransCanada Highway and Peter Lougheed Provincial Park.

SIGHTS

The following sights are along Highway 40 and are detailed from the TransCanada Highway in the north to Peter Lougheed Provincial Park in the south.

Canoe Meadows

From the TransCanada Highway 76 km (47 miles) west of Calgary, Highway 40 branches south across open rangeland, entering Kananaskis Country beyond the boundary of the Stoney native reserve. The first worthwhile stop along this route is Canoe Meadows, a large day-use area situated above the sparkling Kananaskis River. Below the picnic area, whitewater enthusiasts use a short stretch of river as a slalom course. Manmade obstacles and gates challenge recreational and racing kayakers, while upstream (around the first bend), the manmade Green Tongue creates a steep wave, allowing kayakers to remain in one spot, spinning and twisting while water rushes past them.

Barrier Lake and Vicinity

South from Canoe Meadows, stop at the **Barrier Lake Visitor Information Centre,** 403/673-3985, open June to mid-September, daily 9 A.M.–6 P.M., the rest of the year daily 9 A.M.–4 P.M. Nestled between Highway 40 and the Kananaskis River, riverside trails lead in both directions, including two km (1.2 miles) downstream to Canoe Meadows. Across the road is Tim Horton's Children's Ranch, set up by a Canadian hockey great to help underprivileged kids enjoy summer camp.

The first main body of water Highway 40 passes is **Barrier Lake,** dominated to the south by the impressive peak of Mount Baldy (2,212 meters/7,257 feet). The lake is manmade but still a picture of beauty. From a picnic area at its northern end, an official trail leads across the dam, but just as enjoyable is to walk along the southern lakeshore below the highway. Along its length are stretches of sandy beach, small streams, piles of driftwood, and at the end of the lake a massive scree slope that disappears into the lake.

Opposite Barrier Lake is a **University of Calgary** forestry research station, which has been in use since the 1930s. A cabin from this early era still stands, along with a guard's tower put in place during World War II when the facility was used as an internment camp. The cabin is open for inspection in summer, Sat.–Sun.

10 A.M.–4 P.M. It's also the starting point for the Forestry Management Interpretive Trail, comprising two interconnected loops that describe the forest and forestry practices.

Continuing South to Kananaskis Village and Beyond

After passing a second, lesser used picnic area at the south end of Barrier Lake, Highway 40 continues south around the base of Mount Baldy and crosses **Wasootch Creek** and another picnic area. The next stop of interest, especially for anglers, is **Mount Lorette Ponds,** a string of five shallow lakes stocked annually with rainbow trout. Originally an oxbow in the Kananaskis River, these lakes were artificially deepened when the construction of Highway 40 cut them off from the main flow of the Kananaskis River. Paved paths lead to and around the ponds, passing quiet picnic spots and wheelchair-accessible fishing platforms. **Kananaskis Village** lies just off Highway 40 four km (2.5 miles) south of the ponds. The village

© ANDREW HEMPSTEAD

The shallow waters of Mount Lorette Ponds are stocked annually with rainbow trout.

was the epicenter of action during the 1988 Winter Olympic Games. Developed specially for the games, the village sits on a high bench below Nakiska—where the downhill events of the games were held—and overlooks a golf course. The village comprises two hotels, restaurants, and other service shops set around a paved courtyard complete with waterfalls and trout-stocked ponds.

From the village, it's 15 km (9.3 miles) farther south to the border of Peter Lougheed Provincial Park. Just beyond the village is **Wedge Pond.** Originally dug as a gravel pit during golf course construction, it is now filled with water and encircled by a one-km (0.6-mile) trail offering fantastic views across the river to towering 2,958-meter (9,700-foot) Mount Kidd.

HIKING
Prairie View
- Length: 6.5 km/4 miles (2–2.5 hours) one-way
- Elevation gain: 420 meters/1,380 feet
- Rating: moderate
- Trailhead: north end of Barrier Lake, Highway 40

This trail provides a variety of options; the most straightforward leads to a high viewpoint atop McConnell Ridge. To get started, cross the Barrier Dam, take the right fork at the first junction, and go left at the second. From this point the trail climbs steadily along an old fire lookout road to the summit, where views extend south across Barrier Lake to Mount Baldy. The actual site of the fire lookout is a further one km (0.6 miles) and 80 vertical meters (260 vertical feet) from the main trail along the ridge. The additional climb to the lookout is well worth the effort; you'll be rewarded with views across Bow Valley to Mount Yamnuska and east across the prairies to Calgary. Back on the main trail, at the 6.5-km (four-mile) mark, you'll come to Jewell Pass, a major trail junction. The options from this point are to descend along Jewell Creek to the shore of Barrier Lake, passing picturesque Jewell Falls (14 km/8.7 miles round-trip from the parking lot; allow four hours) or continue north into the Quaite Valley and to the Heart Creek trail-head in the Bow Valley (a further eight km/five miles one-way).

Baldy Pass
- Length: 4.5 km/2.8 miles (1.5–2 hours) one-way
- Elevation gain: 520 meters/1,710 feet
- Rating: moderate
- Trailhead: Highway 40, three km (1.9 miles) south of Barrier Lake

This trail traverses Elbow-Sheep Wildland Provincial Park to a 1,990-meter (6,530-foot) divide separating the Kananaskis River and Jumpingpound Creek watersheds. Cross Highway 40 from the unmarked parking lot, entering the woods at the marked trailhead. After 500 meters (0.3 miles), at a marked intersection, the trail enters a usually dry watercourse, which it follows the entire way to the pass. Only the last 500 meters (0.3 miles) are particularly steep, across an avalanche slope. An even better view than that afforded at the pass can be had by following the northern ridge from the pass. It's a steep scramble, though, gaining as much elevation in one km (0.6 miles) as the whole trail gains between the trailhead and pass.

Ribbon Falls
- Length: 9 km/5.6 miles (three hours) one-way
- Elevation gain: 335 meters/1,100 feet
- Rating: moderate
- Trailhead: upper parking lot at Ribbon Creek, off Kananaskis Village access road

Moderate elevation gain and a well-formed trail make this one of the more popular day hikes in the Kananaskis Valley. Following Ribbon Creek through a narrow valley between Mount Kidd and Ribbon Peak, it passes chunks of iron from an old logging camp and the remains of two abandoned log cabins. Beyond the second cabin, the trail enters Dipper Canyon, dotted with pools of water, then climbs across an avalanche slope to a lookout over Ribbon Falls.

Two km (1.2 miles) beyond the falls is Ribbon Lake, but reaching it requires some rock-climb-

ing skills. From the falls, the trail switchbacks up a scree slope to a sheer cliff face. Three lengths of chain and a series of narrow ledges need to be negotiated to reach the clifftop, then it's a straightforward hike through a subalpine forest to the lake.

Mount Allan (Centennial Ridge)
- Length: 11 km/6.8 miles (4–5 hours) one-way
- Elevation gain: 1,350 meters/4,430 feet
- Rating: difficult
- Trailhead: upper parking lot at Ribbon Creek

This is the highest maintained trail in the Canadian Rockies and one of the few that actually reaches a mountaintop. Its final destination is the summit of Mount Allan, on whose slopes the Nakiska ski area lies. From the marked trailhead, it branches to the right, through the Hidden Ski Trail, then left through an open meadow that was the site of the Ribbon Creek Coal Mine. Then the fun starts—the trail gains 610 meters (2,000 feet) of elevation in the next two km (1.2 miles). At the end of this climb the trail arrives atop Centennial Ridge and at the top of the Olympic Platter, starting point for the Men's Downhill at the 1988 Winter Olympic Games. It follows the ridge past a group of intriguing 25-meter-high (82-foot-high) hoodoos known as the Rock Garden, passes a false summit, and then, finally, reaches the top of 2,990-meter (9,810-foot) Mount Allan.

Galatea Creek
- Length: 5.9 km/3.7 miles (two hours) one-way
- Elevation gain: 425 meters/1,390 feet
- Rating: moderate
- Trailhead: Highway 40, 10 km (6.2 miles) south of Mount Kidd RV Park

Galatea Creek flows from high in the Kananaskis Range through a narrow valley bordered to the north by Mount Kidd and to the south by Fortress Ridge. From Highway 40, the trail descends to the Kananaskis River, crossing via a long suspension bridge. Take the left fork once across the river. The trail is easy to follow as it parallels the north bank of Galatea Creek beneath the sheer southern wall of Mount Kidd. It traverses a wide avalanche slope before reaching the final steep ascent to tree-encircled Lillian Lake, which is stocked with rainbow trout. Behind the lake's backcountry campground, a trail continues a further two km (1.2 miles) to Upper Galatea Lake.

Fortress Lake

- Length: 5 km/3.1 miles (1.5 hours) one-way
- Elevation gain: 280 meters/920 feet
- Rating: easy/moderate
- Trailhead: Fortress Mountain winter resort, 18 km (11 miles) from Fortress Junction

This trail is unmarked but easy enough to follow. From the parking lot at Fortress Mountain—the unofficial trailhead is the cat track—it descends to Aussie Creek. Once across the creek, the trail begins the ascent to the lake, crossing under a T-bar and continuing up to Fortress Ridge. From the upper terminal of Farside chairlift, go left at the fork to reach the lake, a deep blue body of water nestled under the cliff for which the ski area is named. The right fork at the top of the chairlift leads along Fortress Ridge, climbing above the treeline for panoramic views across the Kananaskis Valley. The high point of the ridge is 5.5 km (3.4 miles) from the parking lot, with a more strenuous elevation gain of 530 meters (1,740 feet).

OTHER RECREATION

In Kananaskis Village, **Peregrine Sports,** 403/591-7453, rents a wide variety of sporting equipment including mountain bikes (from $8 per hour, $34 per day), fishing rods ($10 per day), canoes ($40 per day), and various downhill and cross-country skiing equipment. Canmore-based **Mirage Adventure Tours,** 403/678-4919 or 888/312-7238, runs rafting trips on the Kananaskis River below Barrier Dam for $59 per person.

Kananaskis Country Golf Course

Regularly voted "Best Value in North America" by *Golf Digest,* this 36-hole layout is bisected by the Kananaskis River and surrounded by magnificent mountain peaks. It comprises two 18-

Golfing in Kananaskis Country is a spectacular experience.

hole courses: **Mount Kidd,** featuring undulating terrain and an island green on the 197-yard fourth hole, and the shorter (which is a relative term—both courses measure more than 7,000 yards from the back markers) **Mount Lorette.** The course opened in 1983 at a cost of almost $1 million per hole. The bunkers alone—filled with pure-white silica from British Columbia—cost $350,000. Renowned golf-course architect Robert Trent Jones, who designed the layout, described the Kananaskis River Valley as "the best spot I have ever seen for a golf course." After marveling at the surrounding mountains, few will disagree with his statement. Just don't let the 142 sand traps, water that comes into play on more than half the holes, or the large rolling greens distract you. Greens fees are $70 (Albertan residents pay $55) and a cart is an additional $14 per person. Golfers enjoy complimentary valet parking and use of the driving range, as well as a restaurant and bar with awesome mountain views, and a well-stocked golf shop. For tee times, call 403/591-7272 or 877/591-2525; website: www.kananaskisgolf.com.

WINTERTIME

Nakiska

This state-of-the-art alpine resort was built on Mount Allan to host the alpine skiing events of the 1988 Winter Olympic Games. Originally the Olympic events were to be held on existing ski slopes in Banff National Park. Environmentalists succeeded in keeping the games out of the park, but their victory soon turned sour when alternate plans were unveiled to spend $25.3 million creating a new Olympic hill on the slopes of Mount Allan.

The project was controversial right from the start, but environmental politics wasn't the only problem faced here. Anyone familiar with these mountains knows the devastating effect the area's warm, dry chinook winds have on the snow cover—the idea of building a ski hill here seemed ludicrous. The answer was snowmaking. A computerized snowmaking system covering 85 percent of the runs was installed at a cost of $5 million. With 40 km (25 miles) of piping and 343 hydrants, the system is capable of pumping 24 million liters of water a day. So who needs Mother Nature?

In the end, the Olympics came off without a glitch, and Nakiska is now open to the public. Great cruising and fast fall-line skiing on runs cut specially for racing will satisfy the intermediate-to-advanced crowd. The Bronze Chairlift accesses a novice area below the main area. The area has a total of 28 runs and a vertical rise of 735 meters (2,410 feet). Lift tickets are $46 adults, $36 seniors and students, $15 children. Kids five and younger ski free. Packages are offered in adjacent Kananaskis Village, as well as Canmore, 56 km (35 miles) to the northwest, and linked by shuttle Tuesday and Friday through the winter season.

For more ski resort information, call 403/591-7777; website: www.skinakiska.com. For accommodation reservations, call 800/258-7669.

Fortress Mountain

Fortress is a sleeping giant as alpine resorts go. It's a 30-minute drive farther into Kananaskis Country than Nakiska, but the rewards are uncrowded slopes, more snow, on-hill accommodations, a longer season, and spectacular views. The resort has had a checkered history since opening as Snowridge Ski Area in 1969, but since coming under the umbrella of Resorts of the Canadian Rockies, it is much improved. Runs are short and predominantly intermediate, but with skiing and boarding on three distinct faces there's something for everyone. With a little hiking, experienced powderhounds can ski untracked snow days after a storm. Facilities include three chairlifts and three T-bars serving a vertical rise of 329 meters (1,080 feet), and a large day lodge with cafeteria, restaurant, and bar. Lift tickets are $35 adults per day or $27 for the afternoon; $25 seniors and students ($20 after noon). For more information, call 403/264-5825 or the Snowphone at 403/244-6665; website: www.ski-fortress.com. On-hill lodging is at **Fortress Lodge,** 403/591-7108 or 800/258-7669. Package deals in the height of the season start at $140 for two nights' accommodation in a motel-style room and two lift tickets. The latest addition to the base area is a string of comfortable, self-contained three-bedroom chalets.

Cross-Country Skiing

The most accessible of Kananaskis Country's 200 km (124 miles) of cross-country trails are in the Ribbon Creek area. Most heavily used are those radiating from Kananaskis Village and those around the base of Nakiska. Most trails are easy to intermediate, including a five-km (3.1-mile) track up Ribbon Creek. Rentals are available in the Village Trading Post in Kananaskis Village.

KANANASKIS VILLAGE

This modern mountain village 90 km (56 miles) from Calgary was built for the 1988 Winter Olympic Games. It was again in the world spotlight when eight of the world's most politically powerful men met here during the G8 Summit in June 2002. In an attempt to prevent anarchy experienced at previous summits, the Canadian government decided on a wilderness destination, the first time the summit had ever taken place outside of a city. The actual summit was accompanied by Canada's largest-ever security operation, leaving world leaders to discuss economic growth, global poverty, sustainable development, and peace and security without interruption. The bulletproof Suburbans and circling fighter planes have long since disappeared, leaving the village to those who want to experience the wilds of Kananaskis Country while still enjoying the comforts of hotels and fine restaurants.

Accommodations

The village is home to two resortlike hotels, both open year-round. Don't be too perturbed by the rates listed as follows; check the websites for packages and deals offering discounts of up to 50 percent.

The 321-room **Delta Lodge at Kananaskis,** 403/591-7711 or 800/268-1133, www.deltahotels.com, is part of an upmarket, 40-property Canadian hotel chain. It offers two distinctly different types of rooms. In the main lodge are 251 moderately large Delta Rooms, many with mountain views, balconies, and fireplaces. Connected by a covered walkway are 70 Signature Club (a Delta designation) rooms, each boasting elegant Victorian-era charm, a mountain view, a luxurious bathroom complete with bathrobes, extra large beds, and many extras, such as CD players. Guests in this wing also enjoy a private lounge and Continental breakfast. All guests have use of the Summit Spa and Fitness Centre, which comprises a full-facility health club, an indoor swimming pool, whirlpool, steam room, sauna, and a beauty salon with tanning beds. Summer rates for Delta Rooms are $210 s or d, while Signature Club rooms start at $305.

The other accommodation in the Village is the more intimate **Kananaskis Mountain Lodge,** 403/591-7500 or 888/591-7501, www.kananaskismountainlodge.com. Some of the recently upgraded rooms are bedroom lofts with gas fireplaces, kitchenettes, large bathrooms, and sitting rooms ($290 s or d); the others are standard hotel rooms that begin at $230. The inn also offers the Mountain Spa facility, a fitness center, an indoor pool, and a restaurant and pub.

Food

The Delta Lodge contains four restaurants and two bars. For a warm, relaxed atmosphere, head to the **Bighorn Lounge,** near the arcade's main entrance. It features a warm, relaxed atmosphere and a bistro-style menu highlighted by a wide variety of appetizers perfect for sharing, such as cheese platters. It's open daily from 11 A.M. and offers occasional live evening entertainment. **Obsessions Deli** serves up light snacks, including healthy sandwiches and rich, handmade truffles. Also in the arcade is the **Fireweed Grill** (open daily 6 A.M.–10 P.M.), with a casual Western-style atmosphere, floor-to-ceiling windows, and an adjoining outdoor patio used during summer. It's open daily 6 A.M.–10 P.M., with a buffet breakfast offered until 10 A.M. The country-style **Brady's Market** features seasonal produce prepared in traditional European dishes. **Seasons Dining Room,** in the Signature Club wing, is the village's most elegant restaurant. French-Canadian cuisine is served on sterling silver, as a pianist plays in the background. It's open for dinner only; expect to pay $18–30 for an entrée. For reservations, call 403/591-7711.

Food is also available at Wildflowers Restaurant, at Kananaskis Mountain Lodge, or at the golf course, where the restaurant offers a casual atmosphere and stunning valley views. Near the entrance to the village is the **Village Trading Post,** a post office, and an information center (open in summer daily 9 A.M.–5 P.M.).

OTHER ACCOMMODATIONS AND INFORMATION
Sundance Lodges

This privately owned facility sits along Highway 40 beside the Kananaskis River, 22 km (13.7 miles) south of the TransCanada Highway. It combines regular campsites ($19) with the uniquely Western option of spending the night in a colorful, hand-painted canvas tepee. Each tepee has a wooden floor, mattress, heater, and lantern, and there's a picnic table and fire pit out front ($44–56). A larger Trapper Tent is also available for rent ($59). Other facilities include communal bathrooms with hot showers and basic grocery supplies. Linen and cooking utensils can be rented for those not fully equipped. It's open mid-May to early September. For more information call 403/591-7122; website: www.sundancelodges.com

Hostel

Originally the schoolhouse for the short-lived coal-mining town of Kovach, **Kananaskis Wilderness Hostel** lies alongside Ribbon Creek, just off the access road to nearby Kananaskis Village, 403/521-8421 or 866/762-4122, www.hihostels.ca. The 47-bed hostel has hot showers, a kitchen, family rooms, a lounge room with fireplace, an outdoor barbecue, and a laundry room. Cost to members is $18 (nonmembers $17) for a dorm bed, or pay $48 d (nonmembers $56) for a private room. Check-in is between 5 P.M. and 11 P.M.

Campgrounds

Mount Kidd RV Park, 403/591-7700, www.mountkiddrv.com, is arguably the finest RV park in Canada. It's nestled below the sheer eastern face of Mount Kidd in a forest of spruce and lodgepole pine, along Highway 40 south of Kananaskis Village and the golf course and 26 km (16 miles) from the TransCanada Highway. The campground's showpiece is the Campers Center (yes, the American spelling). Inside is the main registration area and all the usual bathroom facilities as well as whirlpools, saunas, a wading pool, a

game room, a lounge, groceries, a concession area, and a laundry room. Outside are two tennis courts, picnic areas by the river, and many paved biking and hiking trails. Most of the 229 campsites are hookups, but the few tenting sites are a good value at $20 per night. Powered sites are $26, with power and water costs $28, and full hookups are $32. It's open year-round, with reservations for less than four nights taken from 8 A.M. up to one calendar month in advance.

Those who can survive without such luxuries should continue 6.5 km (four miles) beyond Mount Kidd RV Park to **Eau Claire Campground,** operated by Kananaskis Camping, 403/591-7226, www.kananaskiscamping.com. Facilities are limited to 51 sites (those on the outside of the loop afford the most privacy), each with a picnic table and firepit, along with pump water, pit toilets, and a playground. No reservations are taken, but the website posts up-to-date vacancy numbers. It's open late June to mid-September and all sites are $17. Other options for campers are to continue south along Highway 40 into Peter Lougheed Provincial Park or take Highway 68 east from Barrier Lake to Sibbald Lake.

Information

A short distance along Highway 40 from Highway 1 (but north of Barrier Lake), **Barrier Lake Visitor Information Centre,** 403/673-3985, is a good place to start your trip into Kananaskis Country. It's open in summer daily 9 A.M.–6 P.M., the rest of the year daily 9 A.M.–4 P.M. A small information booth operates in Kananaskis Village through the months of summer.

KANANASKIS

Peter Lougheed Provincial Park

This park is a southern extension of the Kananaskis Valley and protects the upper watershed of the Kananaskis River. It is contained within a high mountain valley and dominated by two magnificent bodies of water: **Upper** and **Lower Kananaskis Lakes.** To the west and south is the Continental Divide and British Columbia, while to the north is Spray Valley Provincial Park and the east is Elbow-Sheep Wildland Provincial Park. Originally named Kananaskis Provincial Park, it was renamed in 1986 after Peter Lougheed (pronounced LAW-heed). Lougheed was the Albertan premier who, with the help of oil-money–based Heritage Savings Trust Fund, began the development of Kananaskis Country as a multiuse recreation area. The 500-square-km (193-square-mile) wilderness area is the second-largest provincial park in Alberta. Captain John Palliser passed by the Kananaskis Lakes in 1858, summing up the beauty of the lakes by writing "We came upon a magnificent lake, hemmed in by mountains, and studded by numerous islets, very thickly wooded. This lake, about four miles long and one-and-a-half miles wide, receives water from the glacier above, and is a favorite place of resort to the Kootenie Indians."

Highway 40 is the main route through the park. The most important intersection to make note of is five km (3.1 miles) along Highway 40 from the park's north boundary. At this point, Kananaskis Lakes Road branches off to the west, accessing Upper and Lower Kananaskis Lakes. These two lakes are the center of boating and fishing in the park, and opportunities abound for hiking and camping nearby.

Highwood Pass

In the southeastern corner of the park, Highway 40 climbs to Highwood Pass (2,227 meters/7,310 feet), the highest road pass in Canada. On the way up to the pass, a pleasant detour is Valley View Trail, a five-km (3.1 miles) paved road whose route higher up the slopes of the Opal Range allows views across the entire park to the Continental Divide. The pass itself is right at the treeline, making it one of the most accessible alpine areas in all of the Canadian Rockies. Simply step out of your vehicle and follow the interpretive trails through the **Highwood Meadows.** In the vicinity, the **Rock Glacier Trail,** two km (1.2 miles) north of Highwood Pass, leads 150 meters (0.1 miles) to a unique formation of moraine rock.

From the pass, Highway 40 descends into the Highwood/Cataract Creek areas of Kananaskis Country (Highwood Junction is 35 km/22 miles from the pass). Highwood Pass is in a critical wildlife habitat and is closed December 1–June 15.

HIKING

The park offers several interesting interpretive trails and more strenuous hikes. Most trailheads are located along Kananaskis Lakes Road, a paved road that leads off Highway 40 to Upper and Lower Kananaskis lakes. Many trails feature interpretive signs; others require an interpretive booklet available from the Visitor Information Centre. **Rockwall Trail,** from the Visitor Information Centre, and **Marl Lake Trail,** from Elkwood Campground, are wheelchair accessible and barrier-free, respectively. Below are some of the park's more popular interpretive and day hikes.

Boulton Creek

- Length: 4.9 km/3 miles (90 minutes) round-trip
- Elevation gain: minimal
- Rating: easy
- Trailhead: Boulton Bridge, Kananaskis Lakes Road, 10 km (6.2 miles) from Highway 40

A booklet, available at the trailhead or at the Visitor Information Centre, corresponds with numbered posts along this interpretive trail. The highlighted stops emphasize the valley's human history. After a short climb from a riverside parking lot below the Boulton Creek

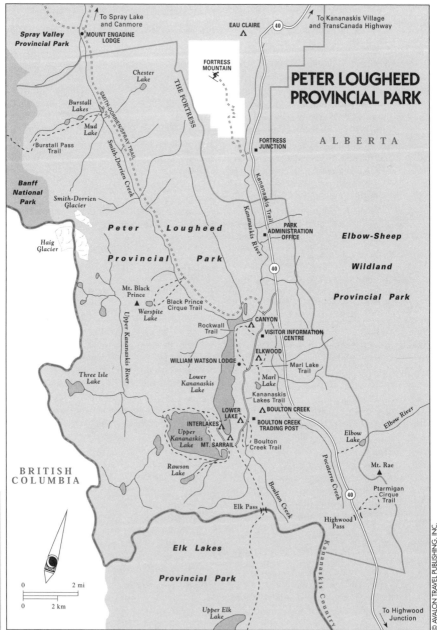

To Spray Lake and Canmore

EAU CLAIRE

To Kananaskis Village and TransCanada Highway

40

Spray Valley Provincial Park

MOUNT ENGADINE LODGE

FORTRESS MOUNTAIN

PETER LOUGHEED PROVINCIAL PARK

Chester Lake

THE FORTRESS

Burstall Lakes

Mud Lake

Burstall Pass Trail

FORTRESS JUNCTION

ALBERTA

Banff National Park

Smith-Dorrien Glacier

Peter   Lougheed

Haig Glacier

Provincial   Park

Kananaskis River

PARK ADMINISTRATION OFFICE

Elbow-Sheep

Wildland

Provincial   Park

40

Mt. Black Prince

Warspite Lake

Black Prince Cirque Trail

Rockwall Trail

CANYON

VISITOR INFORMATION CENTRE

Upper Kananaskis River

ELKWOOD

Marl Lake Trail

WILLIAM WATSON LODGE

Lower Kananaskis Lake

Marl Lake

Three Isle Lake

Kananaskis Lakes Trail

BOULTON CREEK

LOWER LAKE

INTERLAKES

Upper Kananaskis Lake

MT. SARRAIL

BOULTON CREEK TRADING POST

Boulton Creek Trail

Elbow Lake

Mt. Rae

BRITISH COLUMBIA

Rawson Lake

Elk Pass

Boulton Creek

Ptarmigan Cirque Trail

40

Highwood Pass

Elk   Lakes

Provincial   Park

0   2 mi

0   2 km

Upper Elk Lake

Pacaterra Creek

Elbow River

Kananaskis Country

To Highwood Junction

© AVALON TRAVEL PUBLISHING, INC.

KANANASKIS

Trading Post, the trail reaches a cabin built in the 1930s as a stopover for forest-ranger patrols. The trail then follows a high ridge and loops back along the other side of the creek to the trailhead.

Rawson Lake

- Length: 3.5 km/2.2 miles (1.5 hours) one-way
- Elevation gain: 305 meters/1,000 feet
- Rating: moderate
- Trailhead: Upper Lake day-use area, Kananaskis Lakes Road, 13 km (eight miles) from Highway 40

This picturesque subalpine lake is one of the most rewarding half-day hiking destinations in Kananaskis Country. Sitting in a high cirque and backed by a towering yet magnificently symmetrical headwall, it's easy to spend an hour or two soaking up your surroundings once you reach the end of the trail. Snow lies along the trail well into July, and the lake doesn't open for fishing until July 15, but it is nevertheless a popular destination throughout summer.

Make your way to the farthest parking lot at Upper Lake (through the middle of the main parking lot) and begin the trek by taking the Upper Kananaskis Lake Circuit Trail. Sarrail Creek Falls is passed at the one-km (0.6-mile) mark, 150 meters (0.1 miles) before the Rawson Lake cutoff. Taking the uphill option, you're faced with almost two km (1.2 miles) of switchbacks. The trail then levels out, with boardwalks constructed over boggy sections of trail, suddenly emerging at the lake's outlet. Continue around the southern shore, passed an intriguing elevated outhouse, to small meadows and slopes of scree that disappear into the lake.

Elbow Lake

- Length: 1.3 km/0.8 miles (30 minutes) one-way
- Elevation gain: 135 meters/440 feet
- Rating: easy
- Trailhead: Elbow Pass day-use area, Highway 40, 13 km (eight miles) south of Kananaskis Lakes Road

A hiker enjoys the solitude of Rawson Lake.

© ANDREW HEMPSTEAD

The official trail is a wide road that climbs quickly into the bowl holding shallow Elbow Lake. The lake is a popular spot, especially for summer picnics; campsites are spread around the south shore. An interesting side trip is to Rae Glacier, a small glacier on the north face of Mount Rae. The trail starts on the east shore of the lake, gaining 400 meters (1,310 feet) of elevation in just over two km (1.2 miles).

Elbow Lake is the source of the Elbow River, which flows eastward through Elbow-Sheep Wildland Provincial Park and into the foothills. The short hiking trail from Highway 40 up to the lake is part of a much longer historic route that ran between the two valleys and is still passable for backcountry adventurers.

Ptarmigan Cirque

- Length: 5.6 km/3.5 miles (two hours) round-trip
- Elevation gain: 230 meters/750 feet
- Rating: moderate
- Trailhead: Highwood Pass, Highway 40, 17 km (10.5 miles) south of Kananaskis Lakes Road

KANANASKIS

The trailhead for this steep interpretive walk is across the road from the parking lot at Highwood Pass. A booklet, available at the trailhead or at the Visitor Information Centre, corresponds with numbered posts along the trail. As you climb into the alpine zone, magnificent panoramas unfold. Along the trail you are likely to see numerous small mammals. Columbian ground squirrels, pikas, least chipmunks, and hoary marmots are all common. At higher elevations the meadows are home to bighorn sheep, mountain goats, and grizzly bears.

Warspite Lake

- Length: 2.1 km/1.3 miles (40 minutes) one-way
- Elevation gain: 100 meters/330 feet
- Rating: easy
- Trailhead: Mount Black Prince day-use area, Smith-Dorrien/Spray Trail, eight km (five miles) from Kananaskis Lakes Road.

This easily reached lake is away from the busiest part of the park, making it an uncrowded yet worthwhile jaunt (also known as the **Black Prince Cirque Trail,** although officially ending well before the actual cirque). Numbered posts along the trail correspond to a booklet available at the trailhead or at the Visitor Information Centre. The trail begins by climbing steadily to an area that was logged in the early 1970s. It then winds up through a forest of Engelmann spruce and subalpine fir, crossing Warspite Creek, and emerging at the forest-encircled lake. An unmarked route continues along the north shoreline, then climbs unrelentingly before entering Black Prince Cirque, which was formed by ancient glacial action. Each spring the cirque fills with water, forming small, emerald-green lakes. It's an additional three km (1.9 miles) each way from Warspite Lake to the cirque.

Burstall Pass

- Length: 7.4 km/4.6 miles (2.5 hours) one-way
- Elevation gain: 480 meters/1,575 feet
- Rating: moderate/difficult
- Trailhead: Mud Lake, Smith-Dorrien/Spray Trail, 20 km (12.5 miles) from Kananaskis Lakes Road

From Mud Lake (a popular fishing hole), this trail begins with a three-km (1.9-mile) climb up an old logging road to Burstall Lakes. After traversing some willow flats, it begins climbing again through heavy forest and across avalanche paths to a large cirque. The final ascent to the pass is a real slog, but the view across the Upper Spray Valley (which is in Banff National Park) is worth it. From the pass it is possible to continue to Palliser Pass (two days one-way) and Banff townsite (three days one-way).

OTHER RECREATION

Hiking is the most popular activity in the park but by no means the only one. The **Bike Trail,** a 20-km (12.5-mile) paved trail designed especially for bicycles, begins behind the Visitor Information Centre and follows Lower Kananaskis Lake all the way to the Mount Sarrail Campground. Many other trails are designated for mountain-bike use; inquire at the Visitor Information Centre, 403/591-6344. **Boulton Creek Trading Post,** 403/591-7678, rents mountain bikes; $8 per hour, $32 per day.

Fishing is fair in Upper and Lower Kananaskis Lakes, where a variety of trout and whitefish tease anglers. A nightly interpretive program takes place in campground amphitheaters throughout the park. Look for schedules posted on bulletin boards or check with the Visitor Information Centre.

In winter and spring Highwood Pass is closed to traffic, but Highway 40 entering the park from the north is cleared, and cross-country skiing is excellent.

PRACTICALITIES
William Watson Lodge

This special facility by Lower Kananaskis Lake is available to disabled persons and Alberta seniors. It provides a wide range of barrier-free facilities, including hiking trails, a picnic area, and a stocked trout pond. Guests stay in either a campground or one of 22 barrier-free cabins, and they must supply their own bedding and food. The main lodge has a kitchen, lounge, library, laundry room, and a sundeck with gas barbecues. Disabled guests may bring up to three family members or friends. The cost is $5–15 per person per night. Reservations are essential and can be made up to four months in advance by Albertans and up to two months in advance by non-Albertans. Write William Watson Lodge, Peter Lougheed Provincial Park, P.O. Box 130, Kananaskis Village, AB T0L 2H0, or call 403/591-7227.

Campgrounds

Within the park are six auto-accessible campgrounds that hold a total of 507 sites. They're linked by bicycle and hiking trails. Firewood is available at each campground for $6 per bundle. All campgrounds in Peter Lougheed Provincial Park are operated by Kananaskis Camping Inc., 403/591-7226, www.kananaskiscamping.com (this website is a wealth of information and includes vacancy reports, updated daily at 10 A.M.).

The following campgrounds are listed from north to south along Kananaskis Lakes Road, from Highway 40 to the end of the road.

Canyon Campground comprises two distinct types of camping at the northern end of Lower Kananaskis Lake just over four km (2.5 miles) along Kananaskis Lakes Road from Highway 40. An open meadow provides pull-through sites suited to RVs and trailers (Loop B), while up the hill off to the right, sites are protected by a forest of spruce and fir. Between the two loops is the trailhead for a 1.2-km (0.7-mile) hiking path that traverses the Kananaskis Canyon. Another trail leads across Kananaskis Lakes Road to the nearby information center (the trailhead is beside Site 37). Each of 50 sites has a picnic table and firepit, which along with pit toilets and tap water are the limit of facilities. Canyon is open mid-June to the first weekend of September; $17 per night.

Just over one km (0.6 miles) south of the information center (and on the same side of the road), **Elkwood Campground** is the largest of the park's campgrounds with 130 sites. It offers showers ($1 for five minutes) along each of four loops, flush toilets, a playground, and an interpretive amphitheater. All sites are $17 and it's open mid-May to early September.

Boulton Creek Campground has coin-operated showers just beyond the registration gate (complete with rack for those who have a bike), flush toilets, a few of 118 sites with power, an interpretive amphitheater, and is within walking distance of a restaurant and grocery store; $17 per night. Boulton Creek is the only campground that takes reservations; open May–October.

Immediately beyond Boulton Creek Campground, turn right to access **Lower Lake Campground,** with 104 sites spread along three loops. Some sites (along Loop B) come

BEAT THE CAMPING CROWD

Every weekend throughout summer, thousands of Calgarians flee the city for the mountains. Kananaskis Country—and Peter Lougheed Provincial Park in particular—is the most popular destination. With little more than 500 campsites—most offered on a first-come, first-served basis—the park's six campgrounds fill fast. This isn't usually a problem during the week, but by lunchtime Friday, keen Calgarians are busy setting up camp for the weekend, and by mid-afternoon all sites will be filled. (Some folks head out on *Thursday,* stake a spot by paying for three night's camping, head back to Calgary, then return after work on Fri-

day). The official checkout time is 11 A.M., but plan on arriving earlier than this to secure a site. When every campground is full, a sign at the junction of Highway 40 and Kananaskis Lakes Road directs campers to the Pocaterra day-use area, where overflow camping costs $8. Another option is to continue up and over the Highwood Pass to the more remote campgrounds detailed under Highwood/Cataract Creek.

Reservations are taken for some sites at Boulton Creek Campground. Use the website www. kananaskiscamping.com and have your credit card at hand.

close to the lake, but are not within sight. Each private site has a picnic table and fire pit, while campers share pit toilets and two playgrounds. Eight sites are set away from the road—perfect for tent campers who don't mind a short walk. Boulton Creek Trading Post is a short walk up and over Kananaskis Lakes Road from Loop A. This campground is open mid-May to mid-October; $17 per night.

Mount Sarrail Campground, at the southern end of Upper Kananaskis Lake, 2.5 km (1.6 miles) beyond Lower Lake Campground, is for tenters only. It's described as a walk-in campground, but some sites are right by the main parking lot. It has pit toilets, pump water, and bearproof food caches. Sites are $15 per night, and it's open mid-June to the first weekend of September.

Finally, where Kananaskis Lakes Road branches left to the upper lake and right to the lower lake is an unpaved one-way road through **Interlakes Campground,** which loops back along the shore of Lower Kananaskis Lake before rejoining Kananaskis Lakes Road. It has 48 sites, many with lake views and some accessible enough to pull through a large RV or trailer. Facilities are basic: pump water, picnic tables, firepits, and pit toilets, but if you score one of the lakeside sites, you'll be in prime position for a magnificent sunrise. It's open mid-May to mid-October, and all sites are $17 per night.

Boulton Creek Trading Post

Located along Kananaskis Lakes Road, 10 km (6.2 miles) south of Highway 40, this busy hub is the park's only commercial center. It sells groceries, basic camping supplies, fishing tackle and licenses, propane, and firewood. The store also rents bikes. It's open mid-May to mid-October 9 A.M.–6 P.M. extended to 10 P.M. in July and August. Next door is an unremarkable family-style restaurant serving up pasta, burgers, and the like. A cooked breakfast is $8 (although it's not open until 9 A.M.). It also has an ice-cream window and serves coffee.

Information

At the excellent **Visitor Information Centre,** four km (2.5 miles) along Kananaskis Lakes Road from Highway 40, 403/591-6322, exhibits catalogue the natural and cultural history of the park through photographs, videos, and hands-on displays, and a great display opened in 2000 telling the story about the bears of Kananaskis Country. The knowledgeable staff hides hordes of literature under the desk, but you have to ask for it. Also ask them to put a movie or slideshow on in the theater; most revolve around the park. The movie *Bears and Man* is a classic 1970s flick dealing with public attitude toward bears—one of the first documentaries to do so. A large lounge area that overlooks the valley to the Opal Range is used mainly in winter by cross-country skiers but is always open for trip planning or relaxing. It's open in summer daily 9 A.M.–7 P.M., the rest of the year Mon.–Fri. 9 A.M.–5 P.M. and Sat.–Sun. 9 A.M.–5 P.M.

Spray Valley Provincial Park

The creation of 35,800-hectare (88,460-acre) Spray Valley Provincial Park in 2001 provided the final link in continuous protection between bordering Peter Lougheed Provincial Park in the south and Willmore Wilderness Park beyond the northern reaches of Jasper National Park in the north. To the west lies the remote and rarely traveled south end of Banff National Park, while to the north is the Bow Valley and Canmore. The park's dominant feature is **Spray Lake Reservoir,** a 16-km-long (10-mile-long) body of water that is an integral part of a massive hydroelectric scheme. The Spray Development began in 1948 with construction of a road between Canmore and the Spray River. The next stage was damming the river, creating a reservoir of approximately 2,000 hectares (5,000 acres), then diverting its course through Whiteman's Pass and using the water flow as it drops into the Bow River to generate hydroelectric power. The water drops a total of 300 vertical meters (1,000 vertical feet) and passes through three power plants, which combined generate enough electricity to power a city of 100,000.

Smith-Dorrien/Spray Trail

The Smith-Dorrien/Spray Trail (known as Spray Lakes Road from the Canmore end) is the only road through the park. This 60-km (37-mile) unpaved (and often dusty) road links Peter Lougheed Provincial Park in the south to Canmore in the north. From the south, the road climbs up the Smith-Dorrien Creek watershed, passing Mud Lake and entering the Spray Valley Provincial Park just south of Mount Engadine Lodge. Around three km (1.9 miles) further north is **Buller Pond** (on the west side of the road), from where the distinctive "Matterhorn" peak of Mount Assiniboine can be seen on a clear day. The road then parallels the eastern shoreline of Spray Lake for more than 20 km (12.5 miles), passing three lakefront picnic areas. The mountains that rise steeply to the east are the same ones visible to the *west* driving along the Kananaskis Valley. They rise to a highpoint of 3,121 meters (10,240 feet) at **Mount Sparrowhawk** (opposite the picnic area of the same name), which was roundly recommended as having better slopes than the barely adequate Mount Allan for hosting the downhill-skiing events of the 1988 Winter Olympics. In the end, its remote location killed the idea and any development was spared, except for a few lakeside picnic tables across the road. Beyond the north end of Spray Lake, the road passes **Goat Pond** and the Goat Creek trailhead, then descends steeply into the Bow Valley and Canmore.

The obvious loop—south from the TransCanada Highway along Highway 40 to Peter Lougheed Provincial Park, then north through Spray Valley Provincial Park to Canmore and back along the TransCanada Highway to Highway 40—is a total distance of 150 km (93 miles), but you should allow at least three hours for the entire loop.

HIKING

Watridge Lake

- Length: 3.5 km/2.2 miles (one hour) one-way
- Elevation gain: 50 meters/165 feet
- Rating: easy
- Trailhead: follow the Smith-Dorrien/Spray Trail 40 km (25 miles) west then south from Canmore, then head five km (3.1 miles) west to the Mount Shark staging area.

Most of the hiking in Spray Valley Provincial Park requires some route finding; Watridge Lake is the exception and is open to mountain bikes. The trail begins from behind the information board at the entrance to the main parking lot, skirting a maze of cross-country ski trails and quickly reaching the muddy shoreline of the lake, which is known for excellent cutthroat trout fishing. Dedicated anglers stop here; most other hikers cross the lake's outlet and continue 900 meters/0.6 miles (allow 20 minutes one-way) to a delightful spring that bursts from the forested slopes of Mount Shark and flows along a riverbed carpeted in moss.

Jakeroy Glacier

- Length: 4 km/2.5 miles (1.5–2 hours) one-way
- Elevation gain: 600 meters/1,970 feet
- Rating: moderate/difficult
- Trailhead: Spray Lake West Campground

This small, hidden glacier is nestled in the shadow of the Goat Range. Reaching it entails some route finding, but the rewards are ample. To get to the trailhead, follow the campground access road for 1.5 km (0.9 miles) beyond the end of the dam wall and park where it crosses a small creek (opposite Site 17). At the No Camping sign on the upstream side of the road, search out the trail that disappears into a forest of lodgepole pine. The trail parallels the creek for much of the way—making a minimal elevation gain through a moss-carpeted valley—until emerging in an open area where the creek flows through a willow-choked meadow. The headwall and hanging valley are now in clear view straight ahead. Continue a little farther, crossing the creek below a waterfall. From this point onward, the trail becomes indistinct, climbing steeply up the scree slope between the cliff face and the treeline. Most of the elevation gain is made in this last one km (0.6 miles). The final steep pitch is through a forest of Engelmann spruce and larch into a hanging valley. A moraine running along the left side of the valley affords the best views of the glacier.

Small, hidden Jakeroy Glacier is nestled in the shadow of the Goat Range. Reaching it entails some route finding, but the rewards are ample.

Goat Creek

- Length: 19 km/11.8 miles (six hours) one-way
- Elevation loss: 370 meters/1,210 feet
- Rating: easy/moderate
- Trailhead: Smith-Dorrien/Spray Trail, nine km (5.6 miles) west of Canmore

With prearranged transportation, this is an easy trail that gives hikers a real sense of achievement—walking from Kananaskis Country to downtown Banff. Beginning from the north end of the Spray Valley Provincial Park, the trail closely parallels Goat Creek for nine km (5.6 miles) to the confluence of the Spray River, which it then follows all the way to the grounds of the famous Fairmont Banff Springs. This is also a good trail for mountain biking or cross-country skiing. It's downhill all the way.

PRACTICALITIES

The Spray Valley had long been the target of developers, but the creation of a park put an end to proposed heli-skiing and boat tour operations. Existing facilities for visitors include a lodge, a campground, three picnic areas, and a heli-pad used as a staging area for flights into nearby Mount Assiniboine Provincial Park (see the Lesser-Traveled Parks of the Canadian Rockies chapter).

Mount Engadine Lodge

This small lodge comprises 12 rooms in the main lodge and two cabins set on a ridge overlooking an open meadow and small creek. The main lodge has a dining room, a comfortable lounge area, and a beautiful sundeck holding a hot tub. Breakfast is served buffet style, lunch can be taken at the lodge or packed for a picnic, and dinner is served in multiple courses of European specialties. Rates for lodge rooms range from $115 per person for a room with a shared bathroom to $140 for a private bathroom and fireplace. Cabins are $125 per person. All meals are included in these nightly rates. The lodge is open mid-June to mid-October and early February to mid-April (discounted to $95–120 per person). Mount Engadine Lodge is 40 km (25 miles) southwest of Canmore, at the turn-off to the Mount Shark staging area, 403/678-4080, www.mountengadine.com.

Campground

As the name suggests, **Spray Lake West Campground,** the only campground in the park, spreads out along the western shoreline of Spray Lake. Many of the 50-odd sites are private, but facilities are limited to picnic tables, fire pits, and pit toilets. Sites cost $14 per night with firewood an additional $6 per bundle. It's open from when the snow clears (usually late May) to early September.

Sibbald

This small area in the north of Kananaskis Country protects the rolling foothills that descend to the rich grazing land west of Calgary. Access is along partly paved Highway 68, which branches south off the TransCanada Highway 17 km (10.6 miles) west of the Cochrane intersection. Access is also possible from the west, off Highway 40 two km (1.2 miles) south of the Barrier Lake Visitor Information Centre. From the east, Highway 68 climbs through the Jumpingpound Creek watershed to **Jumpingpound Demonstration Forest,** 18 km (11.2 miles) from the highway. The forest is circled by a 10-km (6.2-mile) driving tour, with signs identifying species in surrounding forest. It also passes a portable sawmill, a small picnic area, and a wetland.

Meanwhile, Highway 68 continues westward, passing a turn-off to **Sibbald Lake,** the two hiking trails detailed as follows, a picnic area, and a campground. It then crosses a low divide (look for impressive beaver ponds on the south side of the road) and descends through a narrow valley to Highway 40, the main route through Kananaskis Country. The only other road in Sibbald is the 35-km (22-mile) Powderface Trail, a rough, unsealed road (usually passable by two-wheel drive) that leads south from west of Sibbald Lake to Highway 66 through the Elbow River Valley.

Fishing is a popular activity in Sibbald. Sibbald Lake is stocked with rainbow trout and gets busy. To the west, **Sibbald Meadows Pond** is a quieter body of water, also stocked and surrounded by reeds.

HIKING

Ole Buck Loop

- Length: 4.4 km/2.7 miles (90 minutes) round-trip
- Elevation gain: 170 meters/560 feet
- Rating: easy/moderate
- Trailhead: Sibbald Lake day-use area

This trail makes a loop around the south-facing slopes of Ole Buck Mountain, which rises to the northeast of Sibbald Lake. From the Sibbald Forestry Exhibit, follow a trail between the lake and campground for one km (0.6 miles). The Ole Buck Loop Trail branches to the left at this point, crossing Bateman Creek from where the 2.4-km (1.5-mile) loop begins. Views from high points along the trail extend south to Moose Mountain.

© ANDREW HEMPSTEAD

Sibbald Lake

Deer Ridge Circuit

- Length: 6 km/3.7 miles (two hours) round-trip
- Elevation gain: 210 meters/690 feet
- Rating: easy/moderate
- Trailhead: Sibbald Lake day-use area

Take the trail south following the access road for 150 meters (0.1 miles), then skirt the south shore of Moose Pond to a trail junction. The left fork is the Eagle Hill Trail, while the trail to the right climbs steadily up Deer Ridge. A short spur from the ridge leads to a lookout with views south to Moose Mountain. Returning to the main trail, turn left, descending along the north face of the ridge and back to the trailhead.

PRACTICALITIES

Campgrounds

Sibbald Lake Campground lies within easy walking distance of Sibbald Lake and is signposted off Highway 68, 24 km (15 miles) west of the TransCanada Highway and 12 km (7.5 miles) east of Highway 40. It contains 134 sites spread along five loops (Loop E comes closest to the lake) winding through a mixed forest of aspen, spruce, and lodgepole pine. Amenities include pit toilets, picnic tables, fire rings, and drinkable well water; $17 per site. Equestrian campers can park and camp at **Dawson Equestrian Campground,** a short distance from Highway 68 along the Powderface Trail. This is a staging area for many horse trails; $17 per night. Both are open mid-May to mid-October.

The closest information center in Sibbald is **Barrier Lake Visitor Information Centre,** two km (1.2 miles) north of the Highway 68 and 40 junction, 403/673-3985; open daily 9 A.M.–6 P.M.

Elbow River Valley and Vicinity

The Elbow River has its source at Elbow Lake (see "Hiking" in the Peter Lougheed Provincial Park section of this chapter), among the high peaks of Elbow-Sheep Wildland Provincial Park. As it cuts east through the foothills, the Elbow River Valley gradually opens up, exiting Kananaskis Country near the picturesque hamlet of **Bragg Creek** and continuing its eastward flow, draining into the Bow River within Calgary city limits (the "elbow" for which the river was named by David Thompson in 1814 occurs at what is now Glenmore Reservoir, the source of Calgary's drinking water).

The main access is Elbow Falls Road (Hwy. 66) west from Bragg Creek. It enters Kananaskis Country after eight km (five miles), at the Elbow River Valley Visitor Centre. Close to the eastern boundary lie two good fishing spots: **McLean Pond** and **Allen Bill Pond.** Both are stocked with rainbow trout. Moose Mountain, home to a fire lookout since 1929, can be seen north of the highway. Continuing west is six-meter-high (20-foot-high) **Elbow Falls,** the highest road-accessible waterfall in Kananaskis Country. Just before the falls an unpaved road leads north to **Ing's Mine,** where a small coal mine operated from 1915 to 1920. Beyond the falls, the road first ascends through an area charred by a 1981 wildfire, then descends to its end at a camping spot and picnic areas, 42 km (26 miles) from Bragg Creek.

HIKING

Sulphur Springs

- Length: 2 km/1.2 miles (40 minutes) one-way
- Elevation gain: 200 meters/656 feet
- Rating: easy/moderate
- Trailhead: Sulphur Springs Creek, Highway 66

Park at Sulphur Springs Creek (just east of Paddy's Flat Campground) and follow the north bank of the small creek upstream, veering left at the cutline to reach the springs. Fed by sulphur-rich water, the springs were diverted through an iron casing in the 1930s.

Paddy's Flat

- Length: 2.2 km/1.2 miles (30 minutes) round-trip
- Elevation gain: minimal
- Rating: easy
- Trailhead: Loop B, Paddy's Flat Campground, 20 km (12.4 miles) west of Bragg Creek

This interpretive trail passes through a forest of lodgepole pine interspersed with white spruce, aspen and, along a spring-fed creek, poplar before looping back around and following the Elbow River downstream, back to the trailhead. Numbered posts correspond with a brochure available at the beginning of the trail.

Moose Mountain

- Length: 7 km/4.3 miles (2.5–3 hours) one-way
- Elevation gain: 670 meters/2,200 feet
- Rating: moderate/difficult
- Trailhead: seven km (4.3 miles) along an unmarked gravel road that spurs north of Hwy. 66 700 meters (0.4 miles) west of Paddy's Flat Campground

Rising to an elevation of 2,438 meters (8,000 feet), Moose Mountain is the dominant peak in the Elbow River Valley area. Its summit provides 360-degree views over the entire region. From 500 meters (0.3 miles) before a gate across the road, the trail follows an old fire-lookout road for four km (2.5 miles), climbing steadily just below the ridgeline. It then descends before climbing again into an open meadow. Here begins the relentless slog to the domelike lower summit, from where it's another 100 vertical meters (330 vertical feet), via switchbacks or a direct climb up a ridge, to the upper summit and fire lookout.

Little Elbow

- Length: 2.5 km/1.6 miles (50 minutes) one way
- Elevation gain: minimal
- Rating: easy
- Trailhead: Forget-me-not Pond, near the end of Highway 66

This interpretive trail explores a short stretch of the Little Elbow River, just before its confluence with the Elbow River. From Forget-me-not Pond, the trail passes between the road and the river, then it continues upstream, looping past interpretive boards that describe the river and the mammals that live along its length.

PRACTICALITIES

Campgrounds

Five campgrounds, with a combined total of 551 sites, lie along the Elbow River Valley. The most-developed of the five is **McLean Creek Campground,** 12 km (7.5 miles) west of Bragg Creek and just south of Highway 66, by McLean Creek. At the campground entrance is the Camper Centre with groceries, coin showers, and firewood ($6 per bundle). Like all campgrounds in Kananaskis Country, each of the 170 sites has a picnic table and firepit. Unpowered sites are $20 per night, powered sites $23. This is also the only campground along the Elbow Valley that takes reservations; call **Elbow Valley Campgrounds,** 403/949-3132, or book online at www.ev camp.com. The other campgrounds and their distances from Bragg Creek are **Gooseberry** (10 km/6.2 miles), **Paddy's Flat** (20 km/12.4 miles), **Beaver Flat** (30 km/18.6 miles), and, at the end of the road, **Little Elbow** (50 km/31 miles). The latter has facilities for campers with horses. Each of these campgrounds has only basic facilities—pit toilets and hand-pumped drinking water—but, still, sites are $17 per night. As at McLean Creek, firewood is available at $6 per bundle. McLean Creek is open year-round, while the other four campgrounds begin opening in mid-May and close between early September and the end of October.

Information

The **Elbow Valley Visitor Information Centre,** 403/949-4261, is at the entrance to Kananaskis Country, 10 km (6.2 miles) west of Bragg Creek on Highway 66. It's open May–September, 9 A.M.–5 P.M.

BRAGG CREEK

Bragg Creek is a rural hamlet nestled in the foothills of the Canadian Rockies, 40 km (25 miles) west of Calgary. It lies on the edge of Kananaskis Country, at the entrance to the Elbow River Valley. The town and its quiet, tree-lined streets are a far cry from the hustle and bustle of nearby Canmore and Banff, providing an ideal retreat to kick back and do some golfing, dining, and relaxing in one of the mountains' true gems.

The **Stoney Trail,** an Indian trading route that passed through the area, had been in use for generations when the first white people arrived in the early 1880s. The first settlers were farmers, followed by Calgarians who built weekenders in town. Today many of Bragg Creek's 1,000 residents commute daily to nearby Calgary. The ideal location and quiet lifestyle have attracted artists and artisans—the town claims to have more painters, potters, sculptors, and weavers than any similarly sized town in Alberta.

Sights and Recreation

Arriving along Highway 22 from either the north or south, you'll be greeted on arrival in Bragg Creek by a slightly confusing four-way stop intersection with a treed triangle of land in the middle. Take the option along the north (right) side of the distinctive polished log Bragg Creek Trading Post II to access the main shopping center, a Western-themed collection of basic town services interspersed with craft shops and cafés. White Avenue, also known as **Heritage Mile** and originally the main commercial strip, has more of the same and leads through an appealing residential area. This road continues southwest to 122-hectare (300-acre) **Bragg Creek Provincial Park,** a day-use area alongside the Elbow River. With a basket of goodies from one of Bragg Creek's many food outlets, leave the main parking lot behind to enjoy a picnic lunch on one of the many riverside picnic tables.

Wintergreen, 403/949-5100, www.skiwintergreen.com, is a four-season sporting facility located six km (3.7 miles) north of town

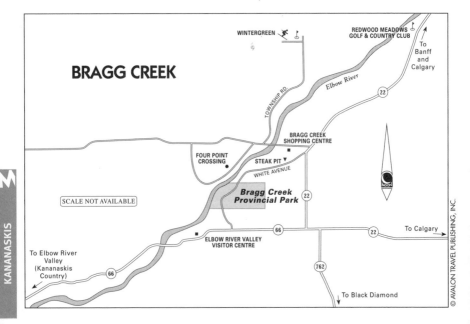

from the west side of the Elbow River. It's immaculately manicured golf course features water hazards on 14 of 18 holes, and four sets of tees designed to fit all levels of golfer (ranging 5,000–6,692 yards). Greens fees are $59 Fri.–Sun., $49 Mon.–Thur., which includes use of an excellent practice facility. Seniors enjoy a discounted rate Mon.–Thur. of $37. (The twilight rate of $37 is one of the better golfing deals in the Canadian Rockies.)

A huge log clubhouse that overlooks the course is the epicenter for a great variety of other activities, including swimming in the outdoor pool, mountain biking the adjacent ski slopes ($7 for an all-day trail pass; lifts operate in summer Thur.–Sun. 10:30 A.M.–8:30 P.M.), and horseback riding (one-hour ride $25). In winter a small ski area with five lifts and a vertical rise of 190 meters (620 feet) operates. Night skiing and boarding is offered on Thur.–Sat. until 9 P.M. Boarders are also catered for with a one-hectare (2.5-acre) terrain park and a halfpipe. Lift tickets are $32 adults, $20 seniors, $13 children.

Bragg Creek and its quiet, tree-lined streets are a far cry from the hustle and bustle of nearby Canmore and Banff, providing an ideal retreat to kick back and do some golfing, dining, and relaxing in one of the mountains' true gems.

Accommodations

Although lacking motels and campgrounds (closest camping is along the Elbow River Valley in Kananaskis Country), Bragg Creek is a popular overnight escape for folks from Calgary. The best of the bunch is **Four Point Crossing,** 11 Elton Ct., 403/949-2247, a large country-style house nestled among stands of trees, yet within walking distance of restaurants and shops. The home has two comfortable guest rooms—one Western-themed and one overlooking the garden—a spacious guest lounge with fireplace, and a library. A hearty breakfast is included in the rates of $100 s, $125 d.

Food

Bragg Creek Shopping Centre holds a wide variety of eateries as well as most services. At the east end, **Pies Plus,** 403/949-3450, specializes in meat and fruit pies at reasonable prices, but doesn't open until 10 A.M. and is closed Monday. Early risers should head to the opposite end of the parking lot to **Bragg Creek Coffee Company,** 403/949-3251, which opens weekdays at 6 A.M. and weekends at 8 A.M. Join locals for an early-morning coffee or head here for the daily $7 soup-and-sandwich lunch special.

Back beyond Pies Plus, **Red Sage Restaurant,** 403/949-7243, presents a contemporary ranch-style menu using lots of local game and produce. Choose from a three-bean chili topped with corn-crusted oysters ($13) or stifle those carnivorous cravings with the grilled buffalo rib eye ($22). It's open daily for lunch and dinner, with most lunches less than $10. At the same corner is the **Powderhorn Saloon,** 403/949-3946, which serves good pub food and has a few pool tables. Across the Elbow River and six km (3.7 miles) north, the **Wintergreen** clubhouse, 403/949-5100, has a lounge and dining room. It's busiest during Sunday brunch, which costs a reasonable $15 and is offered 10 A.M.–2 P.M.

The Steak Pit, 43 White Ave., 403/949-3633, is a fantastic restaurant. The décor is early Canadian, yet realistic and elegant. The dining room, decorated with hand-hewn cedar furniture, is only a small part of the restaurant, which also has a café, lounge, sports bar, and gift shop. Eating here isn't cheap but is comparable to Calgary restaurants. The menu features mostly Alberta beef (charbroiled steak is the specialty) but has enough choices to please everyone. Open daily for lunch and dinner from 11:30 a.m.; closing times vary with the season.

KANANASKIS

Sheep River Valley

The Sheep River Valley lies immediately south of the Elbow River Valley, in an area of rolling foothills between open ranchlands to the east and the high peaks bordering **Elbow-Sheep Wildland Provincial Park** to the west. Access is from the town of **Turner Valley** (take Sunset Blvd. west from downtown), along Highway 546. The Kananaskis Country boundary lies 25 km (15.5 miles) west of Turner Valley through rolling ranching land, from which point the highway follows the Sheep River for another 21 km (13 miles) to its confluence with Bluerock Creek.

A short distance west of the entrance to Kananaskis Country is Sandy McNabb Campground and various interpretive trails. Continuing along Highway 546, the road enters **Sheep River Provincial Park.** Originally set aside in 1973 as Sheep River Wildlife Sanctuary, the park protects the winter range of bighorn sheep. The sheep spend summer further up the valley, and for hundreds of years have migrated down to the open slopes alongside the Sheep River each fall.

Sheep are the most common large mammal in the valley; explorer David Thompson reported that the natives also named the valley for its sheep ("itou-kai-you" in their language). At Bighorn day-use area, a short trail leads to a viewpoint of open meadows that are critical winter habitat for approximately 200 sheep. **Sheep River Falls,** a short distance before the end of the road, is reached by a short walk.

HIKING
Price's Camp
- Length: 5 km/3.1 miles (1.5 hours) one-way
- Elevation gain: 50 meters/164 feet
- Rating: easy/moderate
- Trailhead: Sandy McNabb day-use area, Highway 546

Although the trail itself is easy, it requires fording the Sheep River, is reached through a maze of cutlines and old logging roads, and can be muddy

Sheep River Falls

after rainfall. If all that hasn't put you off, wade across the river upstream of Coal Creek to reach the trailhead. Head west (to the right), following a grassy bench along the river, from which the trail enters a forest of lodgepole pine. When the trail crosses March Creek, head 300 meters (0.2 miles) up the north bank of the creek to this abandoned logging camp, a pleasant destination for a picnic lunch.

Foran Grade Ridge

- Length: 2.5 km/1.6 miles (50 minutes) one-way
- Elevation gain: 190 meters/620 feet
- Rating: easy/moderate
- Trailhead: unmarked pullout 1.5 km (0.9 miles) west of the winter closure gate at Sandy McNabb day-use area

Climbing steadily from Highway 546, this trail traverses an open field and passes through an aspen forest before reaching the high point of the ridge. From here, views extend up the Sheep River Valley all the way to the Opal Range. The distance given is to this first vantage point. An alternative to returning along the same route is to continue along the ridge for another 2.5 km (1.6 miles), then descend the west side of the ridge to Windy Point Creek, which the trail follows downstream to Highway 40. Either walk back to the trailhead along the highway, or cross the road and link up with a trail running through the valley floor for a total trail length of 11 km (6.8 miles).

PRACTICALITIES

Campgrounds

Along Highway 546 are two campgrounds. **Sandy McNabb Campround** is the first you'll come to, a short walk from the river right by the entrance to Kananaskis Country. It's named for an Albertan oilman who made an annual pilgrimage to this spot with his family. Each of 98 sites has a picnic table and firepit (firewood is $6 per bundle). Other facilities are limited to pit toilets and hand-pumped water. Sites cost $17 per night and are open May to mid-October.

At the end of Highway 546, 21 km (13 miles) further west, is **Bluerock Campground,** where some of the 66 sites are set aside for equestrian campers. This campground has similar services to Sandy McNabb, and it's open mid-May to mid-October; $17 per night.

Both facilities are operated by High Country Camping, 403/558-2373 or 866/366-2267, www.campingalberta.com. All sites are filled on a first-come, first-served basis.

Highwood/Cataract Creek

The Highwood/Cataract Creek areas stretch from Peter Lougheed Provincial Park to the southern border of Kananaskis Country. This is the least-developed area in Kananaskis Country. The jagged peaks of the Highwood Mountains are its most dominant feature; high alpine meadows among the peaks are home to bighorn sheep, elk, and grizzlies. Lower down, spruce and lodgepole pine forests spread over most of the valley, giving way to grazing lands along the eastern flanks. Higher elevations, including along the Continental Divide, are protected by **Don Getty Wildland Provincial Park.**

The main access from the north is along Highway 40, which drops 600 vertical meters (1,970 feet) in the 35 km (22 miles) between **Highwood Pass** and **Highwood Junction.** From the east, Highway 541 west from Longview joins Highway 40 at Highwood Junction. A lesser-used access is Highway 532, which branches west from Highway 22 about 37 km (23 miles) south of Longview. This unpaved road passes Indian Graves Campground then begins a steep climb to **Plateau Mountain,** high above the treeline and with stunning views back across to the Porcupine Hills. The main summer activities in this area of Kananaskis Country are hiking, horseback riding, climbing, and fishing. Winter use is primarily by snowmobilers.

KANANASKIS

HIKING

Only a few formal hiking trails are signposted. The rest are traditional routes that aren't well traveled; many require river crossings.

Picklejar Lakes

- Length: 4.2 km/2.6 miles (90 minutes) one-way
- Elevation gain: 470 meters/1540 feet
- Rating: moderate
- Trailhead: Lantern Creek day-use area (not Picklejar day-use area), three km (1.9 miles) south of the Mist Creek day-use area, Highway 40

The name of these lakes was coined by early anglers, who claimed fishing them was as "easy as catching fish in a pickle jar." The name stuck, and it's still mostly anglers who are attracted to the four lakes. They lie at the southern end of Elbow-Sheep Wildland Provincial Park. To access the trail, cross the road from Lantern Creek day-use area and walk up the hill 100 meters (330 feet). The trail is unmarked but easy to follow as it passes through a lightly forested area and open meadows to a ridge above Picklejar Creek. Descend and cross the creek, following its north bank up a steep, open slope, or stay high and right across a scree slope to reach the pass at 2,180 meters (7,150 feet). The first lake is 300 meters (0.2 miles) beyond the pass. The trail continues past two more lakes before ending at the fourth, which is the largest and has incredibly clear water. A lightly marked trail encircles the fourth lake.

Zephyr Creek

- Length: 4.5 km/2.8 miles (90 minutes) one-way
- Elevation gain: 180 meters/590 feet
- Rating: moderate
- Trailhead: Sentinel day-use area, east of Highwood Junction along Highway 541

The walk itself along Zephyr Creek is easy enough, but the trail only commences after a difficult ford of the Highwood River from Highway 541. From the picnic area, descend and wade across the river to an old logging road. Turn right, then keep left, climbing slowly into the valley through which Zephyr Creek flows. The trail crosses the creek twice before reaching a small cairn marking the entrance into Painted Creek Valley. Where the valley walls close in, 800 meters (0.5 miles) from Zephyr Creek, pictographs can be found on the rocky canyon wall, one meter (three feet) up from the ground.

PRACTICALITIES

Campgrounds

All three campgrounds in the Highwood/Cataract Creek areas are south of Highwood Junction. Open May–November, **Etherington Creek** is seven km (4.3 miles) south of the junction while **Cataract Creek** is a further five km (3.1 miles) south and is open mid-May to early September. Both offer primitive facilities, including water, pit toilets, firewood, fire pits, and picnic tables; $17 per night. Continuing south, along Highway 532 up and over Plateau Mountain Ecological Reserve, is 16-site **Indian Graves Campground.** It's open mid-May to mid-September and costs $15 per night. Reservations are taken for camping at Etherington Creek only; to reserve a site or for general camping information, contact High Country Camping, 403/558-2373 or 866/366-2267, www.campingalberta.com.

Information and Services

Highwood House, at Highwood Junction, has gas and a grocery store. It's open May–June, Fri.–Sun. 9 A.M.–5 P.M.; July–Sept., daily 9 A.M.–8 P.M.; and Oct.–Apr., weekends only 9:15 A.M.–5 P.M. The **Highwood Ranger Station,** also at the junction, is open in summer only, Thur.–Mon. 10 A.M.–6 P.M.; 403/558-2151.

Kootenay National Park and Vicinity

Shaped like a lightning bolt, this narrow 140,600-hectare park lies on the British Columbia side of the Canadian Rockies. The park's northern section is bordered by Banff National Park and Assiniboine Provincial Park to the east and Yoho National Park to the north. Highway 93, extending for 94 km (58 miles) through the park, provides spectacular mountain vistas. Along the route you'll find many short and easy interpretive hikes, scenic viewpoints, hot springs, picnic areas, and roadside interpretive exhibits. The park isn't particularly noted for its day-hiking opportunities, but backpacker destinations such as Kaufmann Lake and the Rockwall rival almost any other area in the Canadian Rockies.

Kootenay has the fewest services of the four contiguous mountain national parks. Day-use areas, a gas station and lodge, and three campgrounds are the only roadside services inside the park. The small service town of Radium Hot Springs, at the junction of highways 93 and 95 near the park's west gate, has a population less than 600 but offers a range of accommodations, cafés and restaurants, gas stations, and grocery stores. Radium and its surroundings are covered in their own section at the end of this chapter. The park is open year-round, although you should check road conditions in winter, when avalanche-control work and snowstorms can close Highway 93 for short periods.

© ANDREW HEMPSTEAD

one of Kootenay's classic U-shaped glacial valleys

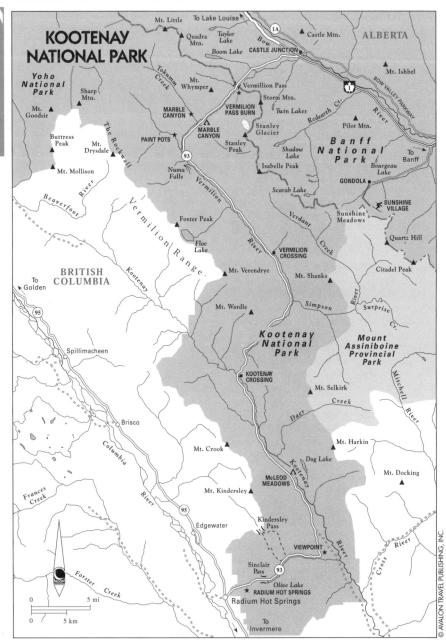

KOOTENAY
NATIONAL PARK

Yoho National Park

Kootenay National Park

Banff National Park

ALBERTA

BRITISH COLUMBIA

Mount Assiniboine Provincial Park

To Lake Louise

Mt. Little
Quadra Mtn.
Taylor Lake
Boom Lake
Castle Mtn.
CASTLE JUNCTION

Mt. Ishbel

Sharp Mtn.
Tokumm Creek
Mt. Whymper
Vermillion Pass
Storm Mtn.
VERMILION PASS BURN
BOW VALLEY PARKWAY
River

Mt. Goodsir
MARBLE CANYON
Twin Lakes
Redearth Cr.
Pilot Mtn.
To Banff

Buttress Peak
MARBLE CANYON
Stanley Glacier
Bourgeau Lake

Mt. Drysdale
PAINT POTS
Stanley Peak
Shadow Lake
GONDOLA

Mt. Mollison
Numa Falls
Isabelle Peak
SUNSHINE VILLAGE

Beaverfoot River
Scarab Lake
Verdant
Sunshine Meadows

The Rockwall
Foster Peak
Vermilion River
VERMILION CROSSING
Quartz Hill

To Golden
Floe Lake
Mt. Verendrye
Mt. Shanks
Citadel Peak

Vermilion Range
Kootenay
Mt. Wardle
Simpson
Surprise Cr.
River

Spillimacheen
Kootenay National Park
Mount Assiniboine Provincial Park
Mitchell River

Brisco
KOOTENAY CROSSING
Mt. Selkirk
Creek
Daer

Columbia River
Mt. Crook
Dog Lake
Mt. Harkin

Frances Creek
Mt. Kindersley
McLEOD MEADOWS
Kootenay
Mt. Docking

Edgewater
Kindersley Pass
VIEWPOINT
River

Sinclair Pass
Olive Lake
RADIUM HOT SPRINGS
Cross River

Radium Hot Springs

To Invermere

0   5 mi
0   5 km

© AVALON TRAVEL PUBLISHING, INC.

THE LAND

Kootenay National Park lies on the western side of the Continental Divide, straddling the Main and Western ranges of the Canadian Rockies. As elsewhere in the Canadian Rockies, the geology of the park is complex. Over the last 70 million years, these mountains have been pushed upward—folded and faulted along the way—by massive forces deep beneath the earth's surface. They've also been subject to erosion that entire time, particularly during the ice ages, when glaciers carved U-shaped valleys and high cirques into the landscape. These features, along with glacial lakes and the remnants of the glaciers themselves, are readily visible in the park today. The park protects the upper headwaters of the **Vermilion** and **Kootenay Rivers,** which drain into the Columbia River south of the park.

Flora

In the lowest areas of the park, in the Kootenay River Valley, **Douglas fir** and **lodgepole pine** find a home. Along the upper stretches of the Vermilion River Valley, where the elevation is higher, **Engelmann spruce** thrive, while immediately above lie forests of **subalpine fir.** The tree line in the park is at around 2,000 meters (6,560 feet) above sea level. This is the alpine, where low-growing species such as **willow** and

heather predominate. For a short period each summer, these elevations come alive with color as **forget-me-nots, avens,** and **avalanche lilies** flower. Of special interest is the Vermilion Pass Burn, where fire destroyed 2,400 hectares (5,930 acres) of forest in 1968. Lodgepole pine is the dominant species here.

Fauna

Large mammals tend to remain in the Kootenay and Vermilion river valleys. **White-tailed deer, mule deer, moose, black bears,** and **elk** live year-round at these lower elevations, as do **bighorn sheep,** which can be seen at mineral licks along Highway 93. The most common large mammal present in Kootenay is the **mountain goat,** but these flighty creatures stay at high elevations, feeding in alpine meadows throughout summer. **Grizzlies** number around 10 within the park; they range throughout the backcountry and occasionally are sighted in spring high on roadside avalanche slopes.

HISTORY

Although their traditional home was along the river valley to the south, the indigenous Kootenay people regularly came to this area to enjoy the hot springs—a meeting place for mountain and Plains bands. Natives called the springs Kootemik (Place of Hot Water). Early European visitors warped Kootemik into Kootenay and applied the name to the local residents. The natives traveled as far east as the Paint Pots area, to collect ocher for ceremonial painting purposes.

In 1905 Randolph Bruce, an Invermere businessman, persuaded the Canadian government and Canadian Pacific Railway (CPR) to build a road linking the Columbia River Valley to the prairie transportation hub of Calgary so that western produce could get out to eastern markets. Construction of the difficult **Banff-Windermere Road** began in 1911. But with three mountain ranges to negotiate and deep, fast-flowing rivers to cross, the money ran out after completion of only 22 km (13.6 miles). In order to get the highway project going again, the provincial government agreed to hand over an

---

PARK ENTRY

Permits are required for entry into Kootenay National Park. A National Parks Day Pass is $6 adults, $4.50 seniors, $3 children up to a maximum of $12 per family. It can also be used in Banff National Park and beyond, if that is your direction of travel, and is valid until 4 P.M. the day following its purchase. A National Parks of Canada Pass, good for entry into all Canadian national parks for one year from purchase, is $38 adults, $29 seniors up to a maximum of $75 per family. Both types of pass are available from the western park gate, park information centers, and campground kiosks. For more information, check the Parts Canada website, www.parkscanada.gc.ca.

eight-km-wide (five-mile-wide) section of land along both sides of the proposed highway to the federal government. In return, the federal government agreed to finance completion of the highway. Originally called the Highway Park, the land became known as Kootenay National Park in 1920. The highway was finally completed in 1922, and the official ribbon-cutting ceremony was held at Kootenay Crossing in 1923; a plaque marks the spot.

Sights and Recreation

ROAD-ACCESSIBLE SIGHTS

The eastern access to Kootenay National Park is Highway 93 (also known as the Banff-Windermere Highway), which branches west from the TransCanada Highway at **Castle Mountain Junction,** 29 km (18 miles) northwest of Banff and 27 km (16.8 miles) southeast of Lake Louise. From this point, Highway 93 climbs steadily for six km (3.7 miles) to the Continental Divide, crossing it at an elevation of 1,640 meters (5650 feet). The divide marks the border between Kootenay National Park to the west and Banff National Park to the east.

West from the Continental Divide

Immediately west of the divide is the **Vermilion Pass Burn.** Lightning started the fire that roared through this area in 1968, destroying thousands of hectares of trees. Lodgepole pine, which require the heat of a fire to release their seeds, was the first plant species to sprout up through the charred ground. More than 30 years later, effects of the devastating fire are still obvious. Along the short **Fireweed Trail** you'll see the growth of a new forest on the floor of the old. **Mt Storm** (3,161 m/10,370 ft) is the distinctive peak to the east.

Marble Canyon

Be sure to stop and take the enjoyable self-guided trail, one km (0.6 mile) each way, which leads along this ice-carved, marble-streaked canyon. The walk takes only about 30 minutes or so, yet as one of several interpretive plaques says, it takes you back more than 500 million years.

From the parking lot, the trail follows a fault in the limestone and marble bedrock through Marble Canyon, which has been eroded to depths of 37 meters (130 ft) by fast-flowing Tokumm Creek. As the canyon narrows, water roars down through it in a series of falls. The trail ends at a splendid viewpoint where a natural rock arch spans a gorge. Marble Canyon is also the trailhead for the Kaufmann Lake Trail (see "Hiking").

Paint Pots

A scenic one-km trail (20 minutes each way) leads over the Vermilion River to this unique natural wonder: three circular ponds stained red, orange, and mustard yellow by oxide-bearing springs. The natives, who believed that animal spirits resided in these springs, collected ocher from around the pools. They mixed it with animal fat or fish oil and then used it in ceremonial body and rock painting. The ocher had a spiritual association and was used in important rituals. Europeans, seeing an opportunity to "add to the growing economy of the nation," mined the ocher in the early 1900s and shipped it to paint manufacturers in Calgary.

Several much longer hiking trails lead off the Paint Pots trail, including one of many routes to the Rockwall (see "Hiking").

Along the Vermilion River

From the Paint Pots, the highway parallels the glacial-fed Vermilion River for 30 km (19 miles). The first worthwhile stop is **Numa Falls,** where the Vermilion River tumbles over exposed bedrock. Continuing downstream, extensive devastation along the southwestern flanks of Mount Shanks is the result of fire started by lightning strike. The fire destroyed more than 4,000 hectares (9,884 acres) of forest over a two-month period starting in July 2001.

Vermilion Crossing holds the only commercialism in the heart of the park, but compared to neighboring Banff, the development is miniscule. Here you'll find the **Kootenay Park Lodge** complex, which includes historic cabin accommodations, a restaurant, a general store, gas, and an official park information center (open mid-May to mid-Oct.). Across the road from the lodge is a riverside picnic area.

Continuing south, the highway passes two signposted mineral licks (watch for bighorn sheep, mountain goats, and moose), then climbs to a viewpoint for **Hector Gorge.** A pleasant picnic area along this stretch of highway is beside **Wardle Creek.**

Kootenay Valley

As you continue to climb from the Vermilion River and pass small, green Kootenay Pond, your eyes will revel in views of milky green rivers, lush grassy meadows, tree-covered hills, and craggy, snowcapped peaks; keep your eyes peeled for mountain goats. The highway then descends to cross the Kootenay River at **Kootenay Crossing.** This was where the official ribbon-cutting ceremony opening the Banff-Windermere Road took place in 1923. Today you'll find a roadside historical exhibit, hiking trails, and a warden's station. The following stretch of highway passes through an area of high wildlife concentration. Black bears, elk, deer, moose, coyotes, and in winter, wolves are all regular visitors to cleared areas along the highway.

After passing McLeod Meadows Campground and a riverside picnic area inhabited by a healthy population of chirpy Columbian ground squirrels, Highway 93 climbs to a pullout that affords panoramic views of the entire valley and across to the Mitchell and Vermilion ranges.

West from Sinclair Pass

Beyond the Kootenay Valley viewpoint, Highway 93 tops out at 1,486 meters (4,875 feet) atop **Sinclair Pass.** Just beyond the pass, tiny **Olive Lake** is worth a stop. With outlets that flow in opposite directions and into two different watersheds, the lake is geologically interest-

As you continue to climb from the Vermilion River and pass small, green Kootenay Pond, your eyes will revel in views of milky green rivers, lush grassy meadows, tree-covered hills, and craggy, snowcapped peaks; keep your eyes peeled for mountain goats.

ing, but for the younger set, spotting brook trout from the viewing platform will prove more attention grabbing.

From Olive Lake, it's a steep 12-km (7.5-mile) descent along Sinclair Creek to the park's western boundary and the town of Radium Hot Springs. Just after the halfway point is the only road tunnel in the Canadian Rockies. After emerging from the tunnel, a parking lot on the south side of the road provides the perfect viewing point for sheer red cliffs that form the highpoint of the Redwall Fault. Through this fracture in the Earth's crust, mineral springs have been bubbling to the surface for thousands of years, staining the surface with red-colored iron oxide.

Radium Hot Springs

This was a popular destination for the early Kootenay people, who, like today's visitors, came to enjoy the odorless mineral water that gushes out of the Redwall Fault at 44°C (111°F) three km (1.9 miles) northeast of the town of the same name. Englishman Roland Stuart purchased the springs for $160 in 1890 and built rough concrete pools to contain the water. Development continued when a visiting millionaire—impressed by the improvement in his paralysis after soaking in the springs—contributed more money to the project. Originally known as Sinclair Hot Springs, after an early settler, the name was changed to Radium in 1915 for the high level of radioactivity in the water. With the declaration of Kootenay National Park in 1922, ownership reverted to the government.

Today the water is diverted from its natural course into the commercial pools, including one that is Canada's largest. Steep cliffs tower directly above the hot pool, whose waters are colored a milky blue by dissolved salts, which include calcium bicarbonate and sulfates of calcium, magnesium, and sodium. The hot pool (39°C, 97°F) is particularly stimulating in winter, when it's

KOOTENAY

edged by snow and covered in steam—your head is almost cold in the chill air, but your submerged body melts into oblivion.

The entire complex saw multi-year renovations through the second half of the 1990s, which included relining the pools, upgrading surrounding facilities, and constructing an observation deck by the source of the springs.

The pools are open year-round. Summer hours are daily 9 A.M.–11 P.M., the rest of the year noon–9 P.M.; $6.25 adults (day pass $9.25), $5.25 seniors and children (day pass $8.25). Towel and locker rentals are available. Three short trails lead from the springs to Redstreak Campground. For information, call 250/347-9485.

Sinclair Canyon

From the hot springs, Highway 93 passes through narrow Sinclair Canyon, descending quickly to the town of Radium Hot Springs. The canyon was eroded by the fast-flowing waters of Sinclair Creek, but not enough for a two-lane highway. But that was nothing a stick of dynamite wouldn't fix. In addition to artificially widening the canyon, road builders constructed the highway over the top of the creek where it flows through the narrow gap. Small parking lots above and below the canyon provide an opportunity to pull over and walk through the canyon.

HIKING

Some 200 km (124 miles) of trails lace Kootenay National Park. Hiking opportunities range from short interpretive walks (see "Sights") to challenging treks through remote backcountry. All trails start from Highway 93 on the valley floor, so you'll be facing a strenuous climb to reach the park's high alpine areas, especially those in the south. For this reason, many hikes require an overnight stay in the backcountry. The following hikes are listed from east to west.

Stanley Glacier

- Length: 4.2 km/2.6 miles (90 minutes) one-way
- Elevation gain: 350 meters/1,150 feet
- Rating: moderate
- Trailhead: Highway 93, seven km (4.4 miles) west of the Continental Divide

Sinclair Canyon

© ANDREW HEMPSTEAD

Although this glacier is no more spectacular than those alongside the Icefields Parkway just a few minutes drive away, the sense of achievement of traveling on foot makes this trail well worth the effort. From Highway 93, the trail crosses the upper reaches of the Vermilion River, then begins a steady climb through an area burned by devastating fires in 1968. After two km (1.3 miles), the trail levels off and begins winding through a massive U-shaped glacial valley, crossing Stanley Creek at the 2.4-km (1.5-mile) mark. In open areas, fireweed, harebells, and yellow columbine carpet the ground. To the west, the sheer face of Mount Stanley rises 500 meters (1,640 feet) above the forest.

The trail officially ends atop the crest of a moraine after 4.2 km (2.6 miles), with distant views to Stanley Glacier. It's possible (and worthwhile) to continue 1.3 km (0.8 miles) to the tree-topped plateau visible higher up the valley. After reaching the top of the first moraine beyond the official trailend, take the left fork, which switchbacks up and over another crest before making a steady ascent through slopes of loose scree to the plateau. Surprisingly, once on the plateau, you'll find a gurgling stream, a healthy population of marmots, and incredible views west to Stanley Glacier and north back down the valley. Be especially careful on the return trip—it's extremely easy to lose your footing on the loose rock.

Although Stanley Glacier is no more spectacular than those alongside the Icefields Parkway just a few minutes drive away, the sense of achievement of traveling on foot makes this trail well worth the effort.

Kaufmann Lake

- Length: 15 km/9.3 miles (five hours) one-way
- Elevation gain: 570 meters
- Rating: moderate
- Trailhead: Highway 93, Marble Canyon parking lot

This is an overnight backpack trip to a beautiful lake in the extreme north end of the park. The trail follows Tokumm Creek the entire distance, passing through a forest of lodgepole pine before entering an open meadow and crossing many small waterways. Most elevation gain is made in the final two km (1.2 miles), as the trail switchbacks up to the glacial cirque holding Kaufmann Lake. The exquisite lake is surrounded by peaks jutting as high as 3,400 meters (11,150 feet). Two campgrounds lie at the end of the trail.

The Rockwall

- Length: 54 km/33.6 miles (three days) round-trip
- Elevation gain: 760 meters/2,490 feet
- Rating: moderate/difficult
- Trailhead: various points along Highway 93

This is one of the classic hikes in all of the Canadian Rockies. The Rockwall is a 30-km-long (18.6-mile) east-facing escarpment that rises more than 1,000 meters (3,280 feet) from an alpine environment. Four different routes provide access to the spectacular feature; each begins along Highway 93 and traverses a steep valley to the Rockwall's base.

The most popular trail starts at the Paint Pots and follows Helmet Creek 12 km (7.5 miles) to spectacular 365-meter (1,200-feet) Helmet Falls. A further 2.4 km (1.5 miles) takes you to the beginning of the Rockwall trail and a campground, the first of five along the route. The trail then follows the Rockwall in a southeasterly direction for 30 km (18.6 miles), passing magnificent glaciers, waterfalls, and lakes, before ending at Floe Lake (see following entry), 10.4 km (6.5 miles) from the highway.

The Tumbling Creek and Numa Creek drainages provide alternative access routes to the Rockwall and require similar elevation gains. The elevation gain noted here is for the initial climb from the highway; along the route ascents are made to four additional passes, with elevation gains ranging 280–830 meters (920–2,720 feet).

Hikers will need to make arrangements for shuttle transportation between the beginning and end of this route—about 13 km (eight miles) apart—or allow extra time to hike back. As else-where in the park, all hikers spending the night in the backcountry must register and pick up a per-mit ($6 per person per night) at either of the park information centers.

Floe Lake

- Length: 10.4 km/6.5 miles (3.5 hours) one-way
- Elevation gain: 730 meters/2,395 feet
- Rating: moderate/difficult
- Trailhead: Highway 93, eight km (five miles) north of Vermilion Crossing

Of all the lakes in Kootenay National Park, this would have to be the most beautiful. Unfortu-nately, reaching it requires a strenuous day-trip or an overnight expedition. From Highway 93, the trail crosses the Vermilion River then be-gins its long ascent of the Floe Creek water-shed, passing through a forest of lodgepole pine and making many long switchbacks before lev-eling off 400 meters (1,310 feet) before the lake. Nestled in a glacial cirque, the gemlike lake's aquamarine waters reflect the Rockwall, a sheer limestone wall rising 1,000 meters (3,280 feet) above the far shore. In fall, stands of stunt-ed larch around the lakeshore turn brilliant col-ors, adding to the incredible beauty.

Dog Lake

- Length: 2.6 km/1.6 miles (40 minutes) one-way
- Elevation gain: 80 meters (260 feet)
- Rating: easy
- Trailhead: McLeod Meadows Picnic Area, Highway 93

Dog Lake is no Mona Lisa, but it is a popular and easily reached destination, especially for those staying in McLeod Meadows Campground (if you're not camping, park at the picnic area 500 meters/0.3 miles to the south). The trail first crosses the wide Kootenay River by footbridge. Then it hops a low ridge over to the shallow lake, which is fringed by marshes at the north end.

Kindersley Summit

- Length: 10 km/6.2 miles (four hours) one-way
- Elevation gain: 1,050 meters/3,445 feet
- Rating: difficult
- Trailhead: Highway 93, two km (1.2 miles) west of Sinclair Pass

The elevation gain on this strenuous day-hike will be a deterrent for many, but views from the summit will make up for the pain endured along the way. From Highway 93, the trail climbs through a valley for about three km (1.9 miles), then switchbacks up across several avalanche paths and through more forest before emerging at an alpine meadow on Kindersley Pass. The final two-km (1.2-mile) slog gets you higher, to an elevation of 2,400 meters (7,870 feet) at Kinder-sley Summit, a saddle between two slightly high-er peaks. This is where the scenery makes the journey worthwhile. You'll enjoy views west to the Purcell Mountains, east to the Continental Di-vide, and, most spectacularly, north over the Kootenay River Valley. An alternate return route to the valley floor follows Sinclair Creek down from Kindersley Summit. This cuts two km (1.2 miles) off the return distance.

Juniper Trail

- Length: 3.2 km/2 miles (one hour) round-trip
- Elevation gain: 90 meters/295 feet
- Rating: easy
- Trailhead: Highway 93, uphill from the west park gate

Named for the abundance of juniper along one section, this trail traverses a variety of terrain in a relatively short distance. You'll pass Sinclair Creek, an avalanche slope, and a lookout offering views of Windermere Valley and the Purcell Moun-tains. Beginning on the north side of the road just inside the park boundary, this trail rejoins the highway 1.5 km (0.9 miles) farther into the park. There you can retrace your steps back to the start or return along the highway via Sinclair Canyon.

Practicalities

ACCOMMODATIONS

Accommodations within the park are limited, but the town of Radium Hot Springs (see following section) has a wide range of accommodations to suit all budgets.

$50–100

Kootenay Park Lodge, at Vermilion Crossing, 65 km (40 miles) from Radium Hot Springs, 403/762-9196, www.kootenayparklodge.com, is the only accommodation in the park. Although no railway passes through the park, the lodge was built by the CPR in 1923. It consists of a main lodge with restaurant, 10 cabins, a restaurant, and a gas station/grocery store. The most basic cabins ($85 s or d) have a bathroom, small fridge, and coffeemaker, with rates rising to $100–115 for a cabin with cooking facilities and a fireplace. The lodge is open mid-May to September.

Campgrounds

The park's largest camping area is **Redstreak Campground** on a narrow plateau in the extreme southwest (vehicle access from Highway 93/95 on the south side of Radium Hot Springs township), which holds 242 sites, showers, and kitchen shelters. In summer, free slideshows and talks are presented by park naturalists five nights a week and typically feature topics such as wolves, bears, the park's human history, or the effects of fire. Trails lead from the campground to the hot springs, town, and a couple of lookouts. Unserviced sites are $19, hookups $22–25. Fire permits cost $6 per site per night. This facility is open mid-May to mid-October.

The park's two other campgrounds lie to the north of Radium Hot Springs along Highway 93. Both offer fewer facilities (no hookups or showers). The larger of the two is **McLeod Meadows Campground,** beside the Kootenay River 27 km (16.8 miles) from Radium Hot Springs. Facilities include flush toilets, kitchen shelters, and a firepit and picnic table at each of the 98 sites. **Marble Canyon,** across the highway from the natural attraction of the same name, offers 61 sites and similar facilities. Both are open mid-May to early September, and all sites cost $14. No reservations are taken in national park campgrounds, but for information, contact the park headquarters at 250/347-9615.

Hikers planning overnight trips in the backcountry must register at either of the park information centers and pick up a Wilderness Pass ($6 per person per night).

INFORMATION

Kootenay Park Information Centre is outside the park in the town of Radium Hot Springs, at the base of the access road to Redstreak Campground in the town of Radium Hot Springs, 250/347-9615. Here you can collect a free map with hiking trail descriptions; find out about trail closures and campsite availability; get the weather forecast; browse through a gift shop; buy park passes and fishing licenses; and register for overnight backcountry trips. It's open in summer daily 9 A.M.–7 P.M., the rest of the year weekdays only 9 A.M.–5 P.M.

The other source of park information is at **Kootenay Park Lodge,** at Vermilion Crossing. It's open Apr.–May, Fri.–Sun. 11 A.M.–6 P.M.; June–Sept., daily 10 A.M.–7 P.M.; and the early part of Oct., Fri.–Sun. 11 A.M.–6 P.M. (It's worth noting that this is the only privately operated official information center in any Canadian national park—a reflection on the folks running this lodge).

For further park information, write the Superintendent, Kootenay National Park, P.O. Box 220, Radium Hot Springs, BC V0A 1M0, or call 250/347-9615; website: www.parkscanada.gc.ca/kootenay. For park road conditions, call 403/762-1450.

Radium Hot Springs

The small service center of Radium Hot Springs (pop. 800) sits at the southwest entrance to Kootenay National Park, 103 km (64 miles) southwest of Castle Mountain Junction (Banff National Park). Its setting is spectacular; most of town lies on benchlands above the Columbia River, from which the panoramic views take in the Canadian Rockies to the east and the Purcell Mountains to the west. As well as providing accommodations and other services for park visitors and highway travelers, Radium is a destination in itself for many travelers. The town is just three km (two miles) from the hot springs for which it is named and boasts a wildlife-rich wetland on its back doorstep, two excellent golf courses, and many other recreational opportunities.

SIGHTS AND RECREATION
Columbia River Wetland

Radium sits in the Rocky Mountain Trench, which has been carved over millions of years by the Columbia River. From its headwaters south of Radium, the Columbia flows northward through a 180-km-long (110-mile-long) wetland to Golden, continuing north for a similar distance before reversing course and flowing south into the United States. The wetland nearby Radium holds international significance, not only for its size (26,000 hectares/64,250 acres), but also for the sheer concentration of wildlife it supports. More than 100 species of birds live among the sedges, grasses, dogwoods, and black cottonwoods surrounding the convoluted banks of the Columbia. Of special interest are blue herons in large numbers and ospreys in one of the world's highest concentrations.

The wetland also lies along the Pacific Flyway, so particularly large numbers of ducks, Canada geese, and other migratory birds gather here in spring and autumn. The northbound spring migration is celebrated with the **Wings over the Rockies Bird Festival,** which is held in the first week of May in conjunction with In-

© ANDREW HEMPSTEAD

The closest thing Radium has to a museum is this home of a local woodcarver.

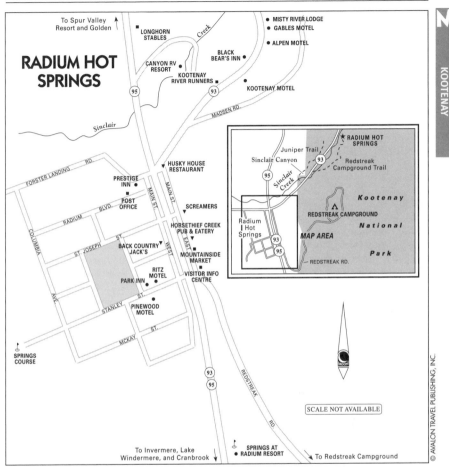

RADIUM HOT SPRINGS

To Spur Valley Resort and Golden

LONGHORN STABLES

CANYON RV RESORT

KOOTENAY RIVER RUNNERS

BLACK BEAR'S INN

MISTY RIVER LODGE
GABLES MOTEL
ALPEN MOTEL

KOOTENAY MOTEL

MADSEN RD.

Sinclair

FORSTER LANDING RD.

HUSKY HOUSE RESTAURANT

PRESTIGE INN

POST OFFICE

SCREAMERS

HORSETHIEF CREEK PUB & EATERY

RADIUM BLVD.

COLUMBIA AVE.

ST. JOSEPH ST.

BACK COUNTRY JACK'S

MAIN ST.

WEST

EAST

MOUNTAINSIDE MARKET

RITZ MOTEL

PARK INN

VISITOR INFO CENTRE

STANLEY ST.

PINEWOOD MOTEL

MCKAY ST.

SPRINGS COURSE

93 95

REDSTREAK RD.

SCALE NOT AVAILABLE

To Invermere, Lake Windermere, and Cranbrook

SPRINGS AT RADIUM RESORT

To Redstreak Campground

RADIUM HOT SPRINGS

Juniper Trail

Sinclair Canyon

Sinclair Creek

Redstreak Campground Trail

Kootenay

REDSTREAK CAMPGROUND

Radium Hot Springs

National

MAP AREA

Park

REDSTREAK RD.

© AVALON TRAVEL PUBLISHING, INC.

ternational Migratory Bird Day. The festival features a variety of ornithologist speakers, field trips on foot and by boat, workshops, and events tailored especially for children, all of which take place in Radium and throughout the valley. For details, call 888/933-3311.

Golfing

The Columbia River Valley supports many golf courses and is marketed around western Canada as a golfing destination. Aside from the excellent resort-style courses and stunning Canadian Rockies scenery, golfers here enjoy the area's mild climate. Warm temperatures allow golfing as early as March and as late as October—a longer season than is typical at other mountain courses.

The 36-hole **Springs at Radium Golf Resort** is a highlight of golfing the Canadian Rockies, comprising two very different courses. One of them, the 6,767-yard, par 72 Springs Course, is generally regarded as one of British Columbia's top 10 resort courses. It lies between the town and steep cliffs that descend to the Columbia River far below. Immaculately groomed fairways following the land's natural contours, near-perfect greens, and more than 70 bunkers filled with imported sand do little to take away from the surrounding mountainscape. Greens fees are $70 for 18 holes (discounted $5 after 2:30 P.M. and then to $50 after 4 P.M.). Call 250/347-6200 or 800/667-6444 for tee times. The resort's second course, the **Radium Course,** is much shorter (5,306 yards from the tips), but tighter and still challenging. It is nestled in the shadow of the Rockies to the south of Radium, circling the resort's other facilities, which include accommodations, tennis courts, and many other exercise facilities. Greens fees are $45, discounted to $30 after 4 P.M. For tee times, call 250/347-6266 or 800/667-6444. Both courses have club and cart rentals, with the Springs Course also home to a driving range and renowned academy.

Other Recreation

The town of Radium Hot Springs is a base of operations for recreation opportunities outside the park. In summer, locals and visitors enjoy fishing and boating on nearby Windermere Lake. White-water-rafting trips are offered by **Kootenay River Runners,** 250/347-9210 or 800/599-4399; from $68 for a half-day trip, $105 full-day. This company also offers a more relaxing evening float through the Columbia River Wetland in large and stable Voyageur canoes. Departing daily at 5 P.M., the cost is $49 adults, $35 children. Horse fanciers can rent a ride at **Longhorn Stables,** one km (0.6 miles) north of town, 250/347-9755.

ACCOMMODATIONS

Radium, with a population of just 800, has more than 30 motels, an indication of its importance as a highway stop for overnight travelers. Those that lie along the access road to Kootenay National Park come alive with color through summer as each tries to outdo the other with floral landscaping. When booking any of these accommodations, ask about free passes to the hot pools.

Less Than $50

At the top end of the motel strip, closest to the national park, **Misty River Lodge** (also known as Radium International Hostel), 250/347-9912, www.radiumhostel.bc.ca, provides dormitory-style accommodations, as well as two private rooms, a kitchen, a lounge stocked with reading material, and a bike workshop. An elevated deck provides the ideal location to watch the sun setting over the Purcell Mountains. Dorm beds are $21 pp, or pay $55 s or d for a private room.

$50–100

Kootenay Motel is along Highway 93, up the hill from the junction of Highway 95, 250/347-9490 or 877/908-2020. The rooms are basic (but air-conditioned) and rent from $48 s, $55 d, $5 extra for a kitchenette. Also on-site is a barbecue area and pleasant gazebo. Up the hill a little, across the road, and similarly priced, is **Black Bear's Inn,** 250/347-9565 or 800/688-6138, www.blackbearsinn.com, with a pleasant outdoor barbecue area; basic sleeping rooms are $69 s or d, or pay $99 for a room with a private balcony overlooking the valley.

Continuing toward the national park entrance is the **Gables Motel,** Hwy. 93, 250/347-9866 or 877/387-7007, www.gablesmotel.ca, where each of the smallish rooms has mountain views and is well-furnished; $69 s or d. Back down toward town is the **Alpen Motel,** 250/347-9823 or 888/788-3891, www.alpenmotel.com, which is probably the best-value accommodation in town (and arguably has the best and brightest flowers out front). The air-conditioned rooms are modern and the rates right; $69 s or d in spring and fall and $89 s, $99 d in summer. The Alpen is closed November–February.

Several older motels lie in the residential streets west of highways 93/95. Least expensive is the **Ritz Motel,** 4883 Stanley St., 250/347-9644 or 877/347-9644, which is an older motel but the 13 rooms are large, with separate sleeping areas. Some have kitchens and are air-conditioned. Summer rates range $70–90 s or d. Although it's undergone renovations, the **Pinewood Motel,** 4870 Stanley St., 250/347-9529 or 888/557-5567, www.pinewoodmotel.ca, still offers rooms starting at a reasonable $70 s or d; $85 with a kitchen. The best of the bunch on the west side of the highway is the **Park Inn,** 4873 Stanley St., 250/347-9582 or 800/858-1155, www.parkinn.bc.ca, which features an indoor pool and a covered barbecue area. Standard rooms are $70 s, $75 d, while those with kitchenettes are $80 s, $85 d.

More Than $100

Three km (1.9 miles) south of town, **Radium Resort,** 250/347-9311 or 800/667-6444, www.radiumresort.com, is surrounded by an 18-hole golf course and holds a wide variety of facilities, including a health club, indoor pool, restaurant, and lounge. Guest rooms overlook the golf course and are linked to the main lodge building by a covered walkway. Regular motel rooms range $160–190 s or d, while kitchen-equipped condos sleeping up to six people start at $240 per night. Check the website or call for specials (rooms are often sold for less than $100 even in the middle of summer). Additionally, golf, ski, and spa packages lower rates considerably, especially before and after summer's peak season.

Radium's newest accommodation, the **Prestige Inn,** opened for the 2001 summer season right at the town's main intersection, 7493 Main St. W, 250/347-2300 or 877/737-8443, www.prestigeinn.com. Facilities include a fitness room, indoor pool, gift shop, spa services, an Italian restaurant, and a smoky lounge bar. Summer rates are $170–220 s or d, but these rates are almost halved in winter.

Campgrounds

Within Kootenay National Park, but accessed from in town off highways 93/95, is **Redstreak Campground** (see "Campgrounds" in the section on the park). The closest commercial camping is at **Canyon RV Resort,** nestled in its own private valley immediately north of the Highway 93/95 junction, 250/347-9564, www.canyon-rv.com. Treed sites are spread along a pleasant creek and all facilities are provided; $20–25 per night. It's open April–October.

Spur Valley Resort, 18 km (11 miles) north of Radium along Highway 95, 250/347-9822,

www.spurvalley.com, has 100 sites set around a large grassy area. Part of the resort is a full-length nine-hole golf course (across the road) and tennis courts. Sites range $17–22, with firewood an extra $5 per bundle. Perfectly described by its name, **Dry Gulch Provincial Park** offers 26 sites four km (2.5 miles) south of town. Each site has a picnic table and firepit; $14 per night.

FOOD

The town of Radium Hot Springs holds several good choices for a food break. For breakfast, head to **Springs Course** restaurant, at the golf course on Stanley Street (on the west side of the highway), 250/347-9311. The view from the deck, overlooking the Columbia River and Purcell Mountains, is nothing short of stunning. The food is good and remarkably inexpensive; in the morning, for example, an omelet with three fillings, hash browns, and toast is just $9. Lunch and dinner are also well priced, with a massive Caesar salad for $7 and main meals $10–18.50, including pastas for $11. It's open throughout the golf season, daily 7 A.M.–9 P.M.

Back in town, **Back Country Jack's,** Main St. W., 250/347-0097, is decorated with real antiques and real hard bench seats in private booths. There's a wide variety of platters to share, including Cowboy Caviar (nachos and baked beans) for $7.50 and a surprisingly good barbecued chicken soup ($5). For a main, the half-chicken, half-ribs, and all the extras for two ($20) is a good deal. It's open daily 11 A.M.–11 P.M. Across the road, **Horsethief Creek Pub and Eatery,** Main St. E., 250/347-6400, serves up similar fare in more modern surroundings. Both places have a few outdoor tables.

As always, **Husky House Restaurant,** at the corner of highways 93 and 95, 250/347-9811, serves a good, solid menu of typical Canadian fare at reasonable prices. This one is open daily 7 A.M.—11 p.m. Just around the corner is **Screamer's,** the place to hang out with an ice cream on a hot summer's afternoon. The ice cream here has been researched

KOOTENAY

many times, most often when returning from camping trips in the Columbia Valley. Also along this strip is **Mountainside Market,** with an excellent choice of groceries and an in-house deli and butcher.

The restaurant at the **Radium Resort,** three km (1.9 miles) south of town, 250/347-9311, caters mostly to golfers throughout the day and resort guests in the evening, but everybody is welcome. Enjoy lunch on the outdoor patio for less than $10, or dine on sea bass smothered with a fruit-filled salsa for $24 in the evening. Buffets are offered on Wednesday and Friday night from 6 P.M. ($20 pp).

INFORMATION

On the east side of the highway, just south of the Highway 93/95 junction is the **Radium Hot Springs Visitor Info Centre,** 250/347-9331 or 800/347-9704, www.rhs.bc.ca. This building is also home to the national park information center. It's open weekdays year-round and in the busier summer months daily 9 A.M.–7 P.M.

NORTH FROM RADIUM ALONG HIGHWAY 95

From Radium, Highway 95 follows the Columbia River north for 105 km (65 miles) to Golden, from where the TransCanada Highway heads east, through Yoho National Park and across the Continental Divide to Banff National Park. Between Radium and Golden are several small, historic towns worthy of a stop. The first is **Edgewater,** where a farmer's market is held each Saturday. Continuing north is **Brisco,** gateway to the mountaineering mecca of **Bugaboo Provincial Park.** Named for a member of the 1859 Palliser expedition, Brisco was founded on the mining industry and later grew as a regional center for surrounding farmland. Brisco General Store is a throwback to those earlier times, selling just about everything. Nearby **Spillimacheen** ("whitewater" to the natives) sits at the confluence of the Spillimacheen River and Bugaboo Creek.

SOUTH ALONG HIGHWAY 93/95

The highway south from Radium takes you 140 km (87 miles) to the city of Cranbrook, which sits on Highway 3, a major transprovincial route across the southern portion of British Columbia. This highway accesses four provincial parks, **Whiteswan, Top of the World, Elk Lakes,** and **Height of the Rockies;** these are covered in the chapter "Lesser-Traveled Parks."

Invermere

The commercial center of the Columbia River Valley is Invermere (pop. 3,000), 15 km (nine miles) south of Radium. Off the Invermere access road, toward Wilmer, a small plaque marks the site of Kootenae House. Established by David Thompson in 1807, it was the first trading post on the Columbia River. The valley's first permanent settlement, known as Athalmer, was alongside the outlet of Lake Windermere, but continual flooding led to the town's expansion on higher ground. The old townsite is now a popular recreation area, where a pleasant grassy area dotted with picnic tables runs right down to a sandy beach and the warm, shallow waters of the lake. It's on the left as you travel along the Invermere access road. As you approach the town itself, consider a stop at **Windermere Valley Museum,** 622 3rd St., 250/342-9769, where the entire history of the valley is contained in seven separate buildings.

Invermere holds motels, eateries, grocery stores, gas stations, a Greyhound bus depot, and a laundry. The motels downtown are a bit overpriced; the best option is **Delphine Lodge,** 250/342-6851, two km (1.2 miles) north in the small village of Wilmer. Restored to its former glory, this 19th-century hotel has been converted to a boutique bed-and-breakfast. The six guest rooms share bathrooms but are comfortable, and guests have the use of a private garden, lounge, and library. Rates of $65–80 s, $75–90 d include breakfast. If you prefer motel-style lodging, **Best Western Invermere Inn,** 1310 7th Ave., 250/342-9246 or 800/661-8911, www.bestwestern.com, offers the best rooms in town, as well as a restaurant and bar; from $85 s, $95 d.

The usual array of fast-food joints line the access road into town, but Invermere is also home to **Strand's,** 818 12th Street (up the hill from 7th Ave.), 250/342-6344, one of the best restaurants in the Columbia Valley. It's contained in a restored 1912 heritage house set on landscaped gardens, with diners seated in small, intimate rooms and offered an immaculately presented seasonal menu that often includes delicacies such as trout, salmon, and venison that are served with a wide selection of vegetables. Dine before 6:15 P.M. to take advantage of a three-course special for $12. It opens daily at 5 P.M.

Along the main drag, on the corner of 5th Street and 7th Ave., is the **Invermere Visitor Info Centre,** 250/342-2844; open July–Aug., daily 9 A.M.–5 P.M. The website www.adventurevalley.com provides information about local recreational opportunities.

Panorama Resort

Recent years have seen a big push at promoting Panorama, in the Purcell Mountains immediately west of Invermere, as a year-round destination by its owners, Intrawest. The resort has a long way to go before becoming the "next Whistler," also owned by Intrawest, but Panorama Mountain Village, comprising a redeveloped base area, a residential subdivision, an open-air gondola to move visitors between the two main villages, a year-round waterpark, and a resort-style golf course, is just the first step in future plans. **Grey-wolf Golf Course,** which opened amid much fanfare in summer 1999, is a challenging 7,140 yards from the back tees, with water coming into

play on 14 of the 18 holes, including the signature sixth hole, "the Cliffhanger," which requires an accurate tee shot across a narrow canyon to green backed by towering cliffs. Greens fees are $110, dropping to $75 for twilight rates. Also during the warmer months, there's chairlift rides (noon–5 P.M.), white-water-rafting and inflatable kayak trips down Toby Creek, horseback riding, and in the village itself you'll find tennis, a climbing wall, and a swimming pool.

Skiing first put Panorama on the map, mainly because the resort boasts the third-highest vertical rise of all North American winter resorts (1,200 meters/3,940 feet), behind only Whistler/Blackcomb, also in British Columbia, and Big Sky, Montana. Despite the impressive relief, Panorama offers slopes suitable for all levels of expertise, including an additional 800 hectares (1,980 acres) that have opened since the 1995–1996 season. Lift tickets are $54 adults, $36 children. For snow reports call 250/345-6413.

The village is also home to **R.K. Heli-Ski,** 250/342-3889 or 800/661-6060, www.rkheliski.com, who operate out of their own "heli-plex," complete with a lounge and restaurant. The company is one of the few heli-ski operations that specializes in day trips. Their 135 named runs are spread throughout the Purcell Mountains.

Accommodations in Panorama Mountain Village are all relatively new and can be booked through the resort, as can all summer activities; call 250/342-6941 or 800/663-2929, www.panoramaresort.com. Outside of the resort's marketing department, summer is still thought of as the off-season, and there are some great summer deals to be had, such as two nights' accommodation and unlimited use of the chairlift for $99 pp.

Yoho National Park and Vicinity

Yoho, a Cree word of amazement, is a fitting name for this 131,300-hectare (324,450-acre) national park in British Columbia on the western slopes of the Canadian Rockies. The TransCanada Highway bisects the park on its run between Lake Louise (Alberta) and Golden (British Columbia). Banff National Park borders Yoho to the east, while Kootenay National Park lies immediately to the south.

Yoho is the smallest of the four contiguous Canadian Rockies national parks, but its wild and rugged landscape holds spectacular waterfalls, extensive icefields, a lake to rival those in Banff, and one of the world's most intriguing fossil beds. In addition, you'll find some of the finest hiking in all of Canada on the park's 300-km (186-mile) trail system.

Within the park are four lodges, four campgrounds, and the small railway town of **Field,** where you'll find basic services. The park is open year-round, although road conditions in winter can be

Emerald Lake

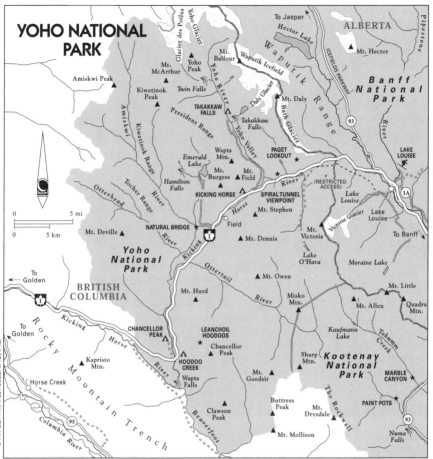

YOHO NATIONAL PARK

treacherous, and occasional closures occur on Kicking Horse Pass. The road out to Takakkaw Falls is closed through winter, and it often doesn't reopen until mid-June.

THE LAND

The park extends west from the Continental Divide to the western main ranges of the Rocky Mountains. The jagged peaks along this section of the Continental Divide—including famous Mount Victoria, which forms the backdrop for Lake Louise—are some of the park's highest. But

the award for Yoho's loftiest summit goes to 3,562-meter (11,686-foot) **Mount Goodsir,** west of the Continental Divide in the Ottertail Range.

The park's only watershed is that of the **Kicking Horse River,** which is fed by the Wapta and Waputik icefields. The Kicking Horse, wide and braided for much of its course through the park, flows westward, joining the mighty Columbia River at Golden. The park's many individual geological features of interest—such as Takakkaw and Twin Falls, Natural Bridge, Leanchoil Hoodoos, Emerald Lake, and Lake O'Hara—are covered under "Sights and Recreation."

Flora

Elevations within the park cover a range of more than 2,500 meters (8,200 feet), making for distinct vegetation changes, and more than 600 recorded species of plants. **Douglas fir** is the climax species at lower elevations, but **lodgepole pine** dominates areas affected by fire. **Western red cedar, hemlock,** and the delightful **calypso orchid** can be found in the damp eastern shoreline of Emerald Lake. At higher elevations, where temperatures are lower and precipitation is higher, the familiar subalpine forests of **Engelmann spruce** and **subalpine fir** thrive. The northernmost extent of **larch** exists around Lake O'Hara. Larch is a conifer (evergreen), but its needles turn a stunning orange in fall—a photographer's delight. Above the treeline, where wind and rain have deposited soil, wildflowers such as **heather, Indian paintbrush,** and **arnica** create a carpet of color for a few short weeks midsummer.

Fauna

The animals for which Yoho is best known are fossilized in beds of shale and have been dead for more than 500 million years. But they still create great interest for the role their remains have played in our understanding of life on earth in prehistoric times. (See the special topic, "Burgess Shale.")

Large mammals are not as common in Yoho as in the other parks of the Canadian Rockies, simply because the terrain is so rugged. Valleys are inhabited by **mule deer, elk, moose,** and **black bears,** as well as a wide variety of smaller mammals. **Porcupines** are common along Yoho Valley Road. The park has a healthy population of **grizzly bears,** but sightings are relatively rare because the grizzly tends to remain in remote valleys far from the busy TransCanada Highway corridor. Much of the park is above the treeline; here noisy **marmots** and **pikas** find a home, along with an estimated 400 **mountain goats.** More than 200 bird species have been recorded within the park.

HISTORY

The Kootenay and Shuswap tribes of British Columbia were the first humans to travel through

PARK ENTRY

Unless you're traveling straight through and not stopping, a permit is required for entry into Yoho National Park. A National Parks Day Pass is $6 adults, $4.50 seniors, $3 children up to a maximum of $12 per vehicle. It can be used in the other national parks, and is valid until 4 P.M. the day following its purchase. An annual National Parks of Canada Pass, good for entry into all 27 of Canada's national parks, is $38 adults, $29 seniors, $75 families. Both types of pass are available from the Field Visitor Centre and campground kiosks. For more information on passes, go to the Parks Canada website, www.parkscanada.gc.ca.

the rugged area that is now the national park. It's believed the men hid their families in the mountains before crossing over to the prairies to hunt buffalo and to trade with other tribes. On their return they set up seasonal camps along the Kicking Horse River to dry the buffalo meat and hides. They used a more northern route than that taken by travelers today, crossing the divide at Howse Pass and descending to the Kootenay Plains beyond the present-day junction of highways 93 and 11.

The first Europeans to explore the valley of the Kicking Horse River were members of the 1858 Palliser Expedition, which set out to survey the west and report back to the British government on its suitability for settlement. The party approached from the south, climbing the Kootenay and Vermilion watersheds of present-day Kootenay National Park before descending to Wapta Falls. It was here that the unfortunate expedition geologist, Dr. James Hector, inadvertently gave the Kicking Horse River its name. While walking his horse over rough ground, he was kicked unconscious and took two hours to come to, by which time, so the story goes, other members of his party had begun digging his grave.

Guided by outfitter Tom Wilson, Major A.B. Rogers (for whom Rogers Pass to the west is named) surveyed Kicking Horse Pass in 1881. His favorable report to the Canadian Pacific

BURGESS SHALE

High on the rocky slopes above Mount Field is a layer of sedimentary rock known as the Burgess Shale, which contains what are considered to be the world's finest fossils from the Cambrian Period. The site is famous worldwide because it has unraveled the mysteries of a major stage of evolution.

In 1909, Smithsonian Institute paleontologist Charles Walcott was leading a pack train along the west slope of Mount Field, on the opposite side of the valley from the newly completed Spiral Tunnel, when he stumbled across these fossil beds. Encased in the shale, the fossils here are of marine invertebrates about 530 million years old. Generally, fossils are the remains of vertebrates, but at this site some freak event—probably a mud slide—suddenly buried thousands of soft-bodied animals (invertebrates), preserving them by keeping out the oxygen that would have decayed their delicate bodies. Walcott excavated an estimated 65,000 specimens from the site. Today paleontologists continue to uncover perfectly preserved fossils here—albeit in far fewer numbers than in Walcott's day. They've also uncovered additional fossil beds, similar in

makeup and age, across the valley, on the north face of Mount Stephen.

Protected by UNESCO as a World Heritage Site, the two research areas are open only to those accompanied by a licensed guide. The Yoho-Burgess Shale Foundation guides trips to both sites between July and September. The access to Walcott's Quarry is along a strenuous 10-km (6.2-mile) trail that gains 760 meters (2,493 feet) in elevation. Trips leave Friday–Monday at 8 A.M. from the trading post at the Field intersection, returning around 6:30 P.M.; $55 per person. Trips to the more easily reached Mount Stephen Fossil Beds depart Saturday and Sunday at 10 A.M., returning at around 4:30 P.M.; $35 per person. The trail to the Mount Stephen beds gains 520 meters (1,706 feet) of elevation in three km (1.9 miles). The trails to both sites are unrelenting in their elevation gain—you must be fit to hike them.

Reservations are a must; call 800/343-3006 Monday–Friday between 10 A.M.–3:30 P.M. For further information, contact Yoho-Burgess Shale Foundation, P.O. Box 148, Field, BC V0A 1G0, 250/343-6006, www.burgess-shale.bc.ca.

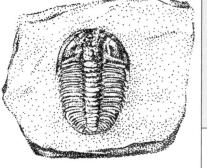

Bathyuriscus fossil

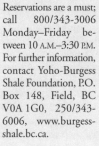

Railway (CPR) led to this route being chosen for the much-awaited transcontinental railway. The railbed was laid in 1884 and its grade was terribly steep; the first train to attempt the run suffered a brake failure and derailed, killing three workers. In 1909, after dozens more wrecks and derailments, the CPR rerouted the steepest section of the line through the Spiral Tunnels. The highway now follows the original rail grade.

The small township of Field started as a railway maintenance depot at the bottom of treacherous Big Hill. In 1886 the CPR opened Mount

Stephen House in Field, both to encourage visitors to this side of the mountains and as a dining stop for customers of the railway. The CPR then built lodges at several natural attractions in the area, including **Emerald Lake Lodge** in 1902, **Lake O'Hara Lodge** in 1913, and **Wapta Lodge Bungalow Camp** in 1921.

Like adjacent Banff, the coming of the railway was a prime catalyst in the formation of Yoho National Park. Upon opening the railway line in 1886, 2,600 hectares (6425 acres) of land around the base of Mount Stephen were set aside as Mount Stephen Park Reserve,

BOB RACE

Canada's second national park. In 1901 the reserve was expanded, and after three further boundary changes, the park of today came into being in 1930. Mining of lead, zinc, and silver continued until 1952, and today remnants of the Monarch and Kicking Horse mines can still be seen on the faces of Mount Stephen and Mount Field, respectively.

Sights and Recreation

ROAD-ACCESSIBLE SIGHTS

As with all other parks of the Canadian Rockies, you don't need to travel deep into the backcountry to view the most spectacular features—many are visible from the roadside. The following sights are listed from east to west, starting at the park boundary (the Continental Divide).

Spiral Tunnel Viewpoint

The joy CPR president William Van Horne felt upon completion of his transcontinental rail line in 1886 was tempered by massive problems along a stretch of line west of Kicking Horse Pass. Big Hill was less than five km (3.1 miles) long, but its gradient was so steep that runaway trains, crashes, and other disasters were common. A trail from Kicking Horse Campground takes you past the remains of one of those doomed trains.

Nearly 25 years after the line opened, railway engineers and builders finally solved the problem. By building two spiral tunnels down through two km (1.2 miles) of solid rock to the valley floor, they lessened the grade dramatically and the terrors came to an end. Today the TransCanada Highway follows the original railbed. Along the way is a viewpoint with interpretive displays telling the fascinating story of Big Hill.

Yoho Valley

Fed by the Wapta Icefield in the far north of the park, the **Yoho River** flows through this spectacularly narrow valley, dropping more than 200 me-

Meaning "wonderful" in the language of the Cree, Takakkaw tumbles over a sheer rock wall at the lip of the Yoho Valley, creating a spray bedecked by rainbows. It's well worth the easy 10-minute stroll over the Yoho River to appreciate the sight in all its glory.

ters (660 feet) in the last kilometer (0.6 mile) before its confluence with the Kicking Horse River. The road leading up the valley passes the park's main campground, climbs a *very* tight series of switchbacks (watch for buses reversing through the middle section), and emerges at **Upper Spiral Tunnel Viewpoint,** which offers a different perspective on the aforementioned tunnel. A further 400 meters (0.2 miles) along the road is a pullout for viewing the confluence of the Yoho and Kicking Horse Rivers—a particularly impressive sight as the former is glacier-fed and therefore silty, while the latter is lake-fed and clear.

Yoho Valley Road ends 14 km (8.7 miles) from the main highway at **Takakkaw Falls,** the most impressive waterfall in the Canadian Rockies. The falls are fed by the Daly and Des Poilus Glaciers of the Waputik Icefield, which straddles the Continental Divide. Meaning "wonderful" in the language of the Cree, Takakkaw tumbles 254 meters (830 feet) over a sheer rock wall at the lip of the Yoho Valley, creating a spray bedecked by rainbows. It can be seen from the parking lot, but it's well worth the easy 10-minute stroll over the Yoho River to appreciate the sight in all its glory.

Natural Bridge

Three km (1.9 miles) west of Field is the turnoff to famous Emerald Lake. On your way out to the lake, you'll first pass another intriguing sight. At Natural Bridge, two km (1.2 miles) down the road, the Kicking Horse River has worn a

© ANDREW HEMPSTEAD

Natural Bridge

narrow hole through a limestone wall, creating a bridge. Over time, the bridge will collapse and, well, it won't be such an intriguing sight anymore. A trail leads to several viewpoints—try to avoid the urge to join the idiots clambering over the top of the bridge.

Emerald Lake

Outfitter Tom Wilson stumbled on stunning Emerald Lake while guiding Major A.B. Rogers through the Kicking Horse River Valley in 1881. He was led to the lake by his horse, which had been purchased from natives. He later surmised that the horse had been accustomed to traveling up to the lake, meaning that the horse's former owners must have known about the lake before the white man arrived.

One of the jewels of the Canadian Rockies, the beautiful lake is surrounded by a forest of Engelmann spruce, as well as many peaks more than 3,000 meters (9,840 feet). It is covered in ice most of the year, but comes alive with activity for a few short months in summer when hikers, canoeists,

and horseback riders take advantage of the magnificent surroundings. **Emerald Lake Lodge** is the grandest of Yoho's accommodations, offering a restaurant, café, lounge, and recreation facilities for both guests and nonguests (see "Other Recreation" and "Accommodations and Camping").

LAKE O'HARA HIKING

Nestled in a high bowl of lush alpine meadows, Lake O'Hara, 11 km (6.8 miles) from the nearest road, is surrounded by dozens of smaller alpine lakes and framed by spectacular peaks permanently mantled in snow. As if that weren't enough, the entire area is webbed by a network of hiking trails established over the last 90 years by luminaries such as Lawrence Grassi. Trails radiate from the lake in all directions; the longest is just 7.5 km (4.7 miles), making Lake O'Hara an especially fine hub for day hiking. What makes this destination all the more special is that a quota system limits the number of visitors.

Book the Bus

It's possible to walk to Lake O'Hara, but most visitors take the shuttle bus. The departure point is a signed parking lot 15 km (9.3 miles) east of Field and three km (1.9 miles) west of the Continental Divide. Buses for day visitors depart between mid-June and early October at 8:30 A.M. and 10:30 A.M. returning at 3:30 P.M. and 6:30 P.M. To book a seat, call the dedicated reservations line (250/343-6433) up to three months in advance. Lines are open mid-March to April, Mon.–Thurs. 8 A.M.–4 P.M.; May, Mon.–Fri. 8 A.M.–4 P.M.; June to mid-Sept., daily 8 A.M.–4 P.M.; and mid-Sept. to early October, Mon.–Thurs. 8 A.M.–4 P.M. The reservation fee is $10 per booking and the fare is $12 per person round-trip. Make reservations as far in advance as possible.

Six places are allotted for the following day on a first-come, first-served basis. Show up at the **Field Visitor Centre** the day *before* you want to go. Although the center officially opens at 9 A.M., staff come to the locked front door and take names at 8 A.M. Plan to arrive before 8 A.M. as there's usually a line for these last-minute seats.

YOHO

Cancellations are filled on a standby basis by folks waiting around at the parking lot on the day of departure (generally, arrive around 7:30 A.M., head to the covered shelter, and you'll be the first in line). You have the best chance of snagging a seat on the 8:30 A.M. bus, especially if the weather is bad.

Other Considerations

After the 20-minute bus trip to the lake, day hikers are dropped off at **Le Relais**, a homely log shelter where books and maps are sold, including the recommended Gem Trek Lake Louise and Yoho map. Hot drinks and light snacks are served—something to look forward to at the end of the day, as this is also the afternoon meeting place for the return trip (no reservations necessary).

Several overnight options are available at the lake—including a lodge, a campground, and a rustic hut—but each should be booked well in advance (see "Accommodations and Camping").

Lake O'Hara Shoreline

- Length: 2.8 km/1.7 miles (40 minutes) one-way
- Elevation gain: minimal
- Rating: easy
- Trailhead: warden's cabin, across from Le Relais

Most people use sections of this easy loop around Lake O'Hara to access the trails, but it is an enjoyable walk in its own right, especially in the evening. Across from Le Relais, behind the warden's cabin, interpretive boards lay out the various options throughout the valley and explain local history. Heading in a clockwise direction from this point, the trail crosses Cataract Creek, the lake's outlet, then passes along the north shoreline, crossing gullies then reaching Seven Veil Falls at the 1.2-km (0.7-mile) mark. Traversing the cool, damp, southern shoreline, the trail passes branches to the Opabin Plateau and a short detour to Mary Lake. Lake O'Hara Lodge is passed at the 2.4-km (1.5-mile) mark,

from where it's a short stroll back along the road to Le Relais.

Lake Oesa

- Length: 3 km/1.9 miles (one hour) one-way
- Elevation gain: 240 meters/790 feet
- Rating: easy/moderate
- Trailhead: Shoreline Trail, 800 meters (0.5 miles) beyond Cataract Creek

With the Continental Divide peaks of Mount Victoria (3,464 meters/11,365 feet) and Mount Lefroy (3,423 meters/11,230 feet) as a backdrop, this small aqua-colored lake surrounded by talus slopes is one of the area's gems. All the elevation gain is made in the first 2.4 km (1.6 miles), as the trail switchbacks to a ledge overlooking Lake O'Hara. The trail then levels out, passing three small bodies of water before climbing over a low rise and entering the cirque in which Lake Oesa lies.

High above the tree-line and dotted with small lakes, Opabin Plateau is one of the most picturesque destinations in the Canadian Rockies. It's easy to spend an entire day exploring the alpine plateau and scrambling around the surrounding slopes.

Opabin Plateau Circuit

- Length: 5.9 km/3.7 miles (two hours) round-trip
- Elevation gain: 250 meters/820 feet
- Rating: easy/moderate
- Trailhead: Shoreline Trail

Separated from Lake Oesa by 2,848-meter (9,344-foot) Mount Yukness, this plateau high above the treeline dotted with small lakes is one of the most picturesque destinations in the Canadian Rockies. The time quoted is an absolute minimum because it's easy to spend an entire day exploring the alpine plateau and scrambling around the surrounding slopes. Two trails lead up to the plateau, which itself is laced with trails. The most direct route is the Opabin Plateau West Circuit, which branches right from the Shoreline Trail 300 meters (0.2 miles) beyond Lake O'Hara Lodge. It then passes Mary Lake, climbs steeply, and reaches the plateau in a little less than two km (1.2 miles). Opabin Prospect is an excellent lookout along the edge of the plateau.

From this point, take the right forks to continue to the head of the Cirque and Opabin Lake. This section of trail passes through a lightly forested area of larch that comes alive with color the second week of September. From Opabin Lake, the East Circuit traverses the lower slopes of Yukness Mountain, passing Hungabee Lake then descending steeply to Lake O'Hara and ending back along the Shoreline Trail 600 meters (0.4 miles) east of Lake O'Hara Lodge.

Lake McArthur

- Length: 3.5 km/2.2 miles (80 minutes) one-way
- Elevation gain: 300 meters (980 feet)
- Rating: easy/moderate
- Trailhead: Le Relais

A personal favorite, this trail leads to the largest and (in my opinion) most stunning body of water in the Lake O'Hara area. Beginning from behind Le Relais, the trail passes through an open meadow and the Elizabeth Parker Hut; stay left to reach Schäffer Lake after 1.6 km (one mile). At a junction beyond that lake, the left fork leads to Lake McArthur and the right fork to McArthur Pass. The lake option climbs steeply for 800 meters (0.5 miles) then levels out and traverses a narrow ledge before entering the Lake McArthur Cirque. (Stay high, even if trails descending into the McArthur Valley look like they offer an easier approach). After leveling off, the trail enters the alpine and quickly reaches its maximum elevation and the first views of Lake McArthur. Backed by Mount Biddle and the Biddle Glacier, the deep-blue lake and colorful alpine meadows are an unforgettable panorama.

Odaray Highline

- Length: 2.6 km/1.6 miles (one hour) one-way
- Elevation gain: 280 meters/920 feet
- Rating: easy/moderate
- Trailhead: Le Relais

For a panoramic overview of the Lake O'Hara area with a minimum of energy output, it's hard to beat this trail, which ends atop the Odaray Plateau west of lake. This trail passes through an important wildlife corridor and a voluntary program to limit use—and therefore human interference—is in place. Check with park staff for the latest access restrictions. From Le Relais, follow the Lake McArthur Trail to Schäffer Lake as detailed previously, then take the right fork, which climbs gently toward to McArthur Pass. Just before the pass, take the right fork. From this point, it's a steep one km (0.6 miles) up to the lofty perch below Odaray Mountain.

Cathedral Basin

- Length: 7.5 km/4.7 miles (2.5 hours) one-way
- Elevation gain: 300 meters/980 feet
- Rating: moderate
- Trailhead: Lake O'Hara Campground

The trail out to Cathedral Basin is the longest in the Lake O'Hara area, yet it's still an easy day trip for most people. Reach the trailhead from Le Relais by walking the short distance back down the access road or by following Cataract Creek downstream from behind the warden's cabin. From the campground the trail heads northwest, crossing Morning Glory Creek at the 2.4-km (1.5-mile) mark then passing Linda Lake. The final ascent to Cathedral Basin makes a wide loop through an area of ancient rock slides. From this point, the magnificent panorama of the Lake O'Hara area and the backdrop of the Continental Divide are laid out to the southeast.

EMERALD LAKE HIKING

Emerald Lake Loop

- Length: 5.2 km/3.2 miles (1.5 hours) round-trip
- Elevation gain: minimal
- Rating: easy
- Trailhead: Emerald Lake Parking Lot, nine km (5.6 miles) from Highway 1

One of the easiest yet most enjoyable walks in Yoho is around the park's most famous lake. The trail encircles the lake and can be hiked in either direction. The best views are from the western shoreline, where a massive avalanche has cleared away the forest of Engelmann spruce. Across the lake from this point, Mount Burgess can be seen rising an impressive 2,599 meters

(8,530 feet). Traveling in a clockwise direction, beyond the avalanche slope, the trail to Emerald Basin veers off to the left, and at the 2.2-km (1.4-mile) mark, a small bridge is crossed. Views from this point extend back across the lodge to the Ottertail Range. Beyond the lake's inlet, the vegetation changes dramatically. A lush forest of towering western red cedar creates a canopy, protecting moss-covered fallen trees, thimbleberry, and bunchberry extending to the water's edge. Just over one km (0.6 miles) from the bridge, the trail divides: the left fork leads back to the parking lot via a small forest-encircled pond, or continue straight ahead through the grounds of Emerald Lake Lodge. Park staff lead a guided hike around the lake every Saturday morning, departing at 10 A.M. from the parking lot trailhead.

Hamilton Falls

- Length: 800 meters/0.5 miles (40 minutes) one-way
- Elevation gain: 60 meters/200 feet
- Rating: easy
- Trailhead: Information Kiosk, Emerald Lake Parking Lot

The trail to these falls begins from the Emerald Lake parking lot, down the hill from the bridge to the lodge. It's an easy walk through a forest of Engelmann spruce and subalpine fir to a viewpoint at the base of the falls. A little farther along, the trail begins switchbacking steeply and offers even better views of the cascade.

The trail continues beyond the waterfall to **Hamilton Lake,** which lies in a small glacial cirque a steep 880 vertical meters (2,890 feet) above Emerald Lake. Total distance from Emerald Lake to Hamilton Lake is 5.5 km/3.4 miles (2.5 hours) one-way.

Emerald Basin

- Length: 4.5 km/2.8 miles (1.5–2 hours) one-way
- Elevation gain: 280 meters/920 feet
- Rating: easy/moderate
- Trailhead: Emerald Lake Loop, 1.5 km (0.9 miles) from the parking lot

The trail to the delightful Emerald Basin begins from the west shore of Emerald Lake, from where it's a steady three-km (1.9-mile) climb through a subalpine forest to the basin, which, chances are, you'll have to yourself. The most impressive sight awaiting you there is the south wall of the President Range, towering 800 vertical meters (2,625 feet) above.

YOHO VALLEY HIKING

The valley for which the park is named lies north of the TransCanada Highway. As well as the sights discussed previously, it provides many fine opportunities for serious day-hikers to get off the beaten track. The following day hikes begin from different trailheads near the end of the road up Yoho Valley. In each case, leave your vehicle in the Takakkaw Falls parking lot.

Twin Falls

- Length: 8 km/5 miles (2.5 hours) one-way
- Elevation gain: 300 meters/980 feet
- Rating: moderate
- Trailhead: Takakkaw Falls parking lot, 14 km (8.7 miles) from Hwy. 1

This trail takes over where the road through the Yoho Valley ends, continuing in a northerly direction up the Yoho River to Twin Falls, passing many other waterfalls along the way. At spectacular Twin Falls, water from the Wapta Icefield divides in two before plunging off an 80-meter-high (262-foot-high) cliff. Mother Nature may work in amazing ways, but sometimes she needs a helping hand—or so the CPR thought. In the 1920s, the company dynamited one of the channels to make the falls more symmetrical. **Twin Falls Chalet** was built below the falls by the CPR in 1923 and today offers hikers light snacks through the middle of the day.

Iceline

- Length: 6.4 km/4 miles (2.5 hours) one-way
- Elevation gain: 690 meters/2,260 feet
- Rating: moderate/difficult
- Trailhead: Whiskey Jack Hostel

TAKAKKAW FALLS

Much discussion is made of which is Canada's highest waterfall. Della Falls, on Vancouver Island, also in British Columbia, is 440 meters high, but this drop is broken by a ledge. Takakkaw Falls is considerably lower, at 254 meters, but the drop is unbroken, which, officially, makes it Canada's highest. There is one thing of which there is no doubt: Takakkaw Falls will leave you breathless, much as it did famous alpinist Sir James Outram and everyone who has viewed the spectacle since.

The torrent, issuing from an icy cavern, rushes tempestuously down a deep, winding chasm till it gains the verge of the unbroken cliff, leaps forth in sudden wildness for a hundred and fifty feet, and then in a stupendous column of pure white sparkling water, broken by giant jets descending rocketlike and wreathed in volumed spray, dashes upon the rocks almost a thousand feet below, and, breaking into a milky series of cascading rushes for five hundred feet more, swirls into the swift current of the Yoho River.

—Sir James Outram,
In the Heart of the Canadian Rockies

© ANDREW HEMPSTEAD

YOHO

Constructed in 1987, this is one of the most spectacular day hikes in the Canadian Rockies. The length given is from Whiskey Jack Hostel to the highest point along the trail (2,250 meters/7,380 feet). (Day-hikers are asked to leave their vehicles across the road from the hostel, in the Takakkaw Falls parking lot.) From the hostel, the trail begins a steep and steady one-km (0.6-mile) climb to a point where three options present themselves: the Iceline Trail is to the right, Yoho Pass is straight ahead, and Hidden Lakes is a 300-meter (0.2-mile) detour to the left. The Iceline Trail option now enters its highlight—a four-km (2.5-mile) traverse of a moraine below Emerald Glacier. Views across the valley improve as the trail climbs to its 2,220-meter (7,283-foot) crest. Many day-hikers return from this point, although officially the trail continues into

Little Yoho River Valley. Another option is to continue beyond Celeste Lake and loop back to Takakkaw Falls and the original trailhead, a total distance of 18 km (11.2 miles).

Yoho Pass

- Length: 4.7 km/2.9 miles (two hours) one-way
- Elevation gain: 530 meters/1,740 feet
- Rating: moderate
- Trailhead: Whiskey Jack Hostel

The trail to Yoho Pass, which can be combined with the Iceline Trail, officially begins on the west side of Whiskey Jack Hostel, but hikers are asked to leave their vehicles across the road in the Takakkaw Falls parking lot. It leads 3.7 km (2.3 miles) to picturesque, spruce-encircled Yoho Lake, then continues another easy one km (0.6 miles) to the pass. The pass is below the treeline, so views are limited, but from this point it's 5.5 km (3.4 miles) and an elevation loss of 530 meters (1,740 feet) down to Emerald Lake; six km (3.7 miles) and an elevation gain of 300 meters (985 feet) to spectacular Burgess Pass; or 2.4 km (1.5 miles) north, with little elevation gain or loss, to an intersection with the Iceline Trail.

HIKES IN OTHER AREAS OF THE PARK

The hikes detailed as follows are along the Trans-Canada Highway. The hike to the world-famous Burgess Shale is detailed in the corresponding special topic, **Burgess Shale.**

Paget Lookout

- Length: 3.5 km/2.2 miles (90 minutes) one-way
- Elevation gain: 520 meters/1,700 feet
- Rating: moderate
- Trailhead: Wapta Lake picnic area five km (3.1 miles) west of the Continental Divide

The trail to this viewpoint is moderately strenuous but worthwhile for the panorama of the Kicking Horse River Valley. The first section of trail traverses a forest of Engelmann spruce. Then the trail breaks out above the treeline just below the lookout, the site of an abandoned fire tower. As an alternative, branch right 1.4 km (0.9 miles) along the trail and continue two km (1.2 miles) to **Sherbrooke Lake,** which is fed by the Waputik Icefield.

Hoodoo Trail

- Length: 3 km/1.9 miles (60–90 minutes) one-way
- Elevation gain: 460 meters/1,510 feet
- Rating: moderate
- Trailhead: Hoodoo Creek Campground, 23 km (14.3 miles) southwest of Field

Hoodoos are found in varying forms throughout the Canadian Rockies, but this outcrop, officially known as the Leanchoil Hoodoos, is among the most impressive. Hoodoos are formed by the erosion of relatively soft rock from beneath a cap of harder, more weather-resistant rock. Although these examples require some effort to reach, their intriguing appearance makes the trip worthwhile. The first half of the trail is relatively flat, leaving all the elevation gain to be made in the last, painful 1.5 km (0.9 miles).

Wapta Falls

- Length: 2.4 km/1.5 miles (45 minutes) one-way
- Elevation loss: minimal
- Rating: easy
- Trailhead: unmarked parking lot beside Hwy. 1 25 km (15.5 miles) west of Field and five km (3.1 miles) east of park boundary

In the park's extreme southwestern corner, this trail follows an old fire road for three km (1.9 miles), then narrows for an easy stroll through thick forest to a viewpoint above these 30-meter high (100-feet-high) falls on the Kicking Horse River. A steep, switch backing descent leads 500 meters (0.3 miles) to a viewpoint at the base of the falls.

OTHER RECREATION

Boating and Fishing

No river or stream is particularly well known for fishing, mainly because most of the water is glacially derived and therefore heavily silt-laden. Species present in the park's lakes and rivers include Dolly Varden and rainbow, lake, and cutthroat trout. A national park **fishing permit** costs $6 for seven days or $13 annually. **Emerald Lake Canoe Rentals,** in a small boatshed on the shore of Emerald Lake, 250/343-6000, rents canoes and small boats for $20 per hour, $35 for two hours, or $60 all day. Rentals are available June–Sept. 9 A.M.–8 P.M. Fishing in Emerald Lake isn't world-class, but there are some trout in the waters, and Emerald Lake Canoe Rentals offers a range of fishing tackle for rent or sale.

Horseback Riding

Emerald Lake Stables, at the lake of the same name, 250/344-8982, rents horses. A one-hour trip along the west shore of Emerald Lake costs $35. Two-hour rides are $70, three-hour rides $100, four-hour rides $130, and all-day rides with lunch go for $175.

Wintertime

The TransCanada Highway through the park is open year-round, but facilities are only open June through mid-September. Some of the trails at higher elevations are impassable until July. Wintertime attracts cross-country skiers who happily slide along the Yoho Valley to frozen Takakkaw Falls or follow the Lake O'Hara trails.

Practicalities

ACCOMMODATIONS

Less Than $50

Hostelling International operates **Hostelling International–Whiskey Jack Wilderness Hostel** in a meadow opposite Takakkaw Falls. Formerly cabins used by the CPR, then staff quarters for a privately run lodge that was destroyed by an avalanche, the hostel provides basic dormitory accommodations for up to 27 guests, who have use of a communal kitchen and showers. Members of Hostelling International pay $15 per night, nonmembers $19. Book at 403/760-7580 or 866/762-4122, www.hihostels.ca. Check-in is 5–11 P.M. This hostel is only open mid-June to September.

$100–150

The streets of Field are lined with private homes offering reasonably priced overnight accommodations in rooms of varying privacy and standard. One of the better choices is the **Alpine Guesthouse,** 313 2nd Ave., 250/343-6878, www.alpineguesthouse.ca, with a two-bedroom suite—complete with a kitchen, cable TV, outdoor patio, and private entrance for $110 per night.

Also in Field is simple yet elegant **Kicking Horse Lodge,** 100 Centre St., 250/343-6303 or 800/659-4944, www.kickinghorselodge.net, which offers 14 well-furnished rooms, a large comfortable lounge, and a restaurant (open in summer only). In July and August, rates are $124 s or d, $138 with a kitchenette. The rest of the year, these same rooms are discounted to just $60 and $68, respectively—a great alternative to higher priced Lake Louise for winter visitors.

Comprising 20 cabins set around a main lodge alongside the Kicking Horse River, the **Cathedral Mountain Lodge and Chalets** complex lies one km (0.6 miles) along Yoho Valley Road from the TransCanada Highway. The original cabins cost $135 s or d and have basic cooking facilities. Newer log cabins dating to 1996 are larger and more comfortable; each has a stone fireplace, full bath, fridge, and private deck; $169–189 s or d. A restaurant and grocery store are on the premises. Cathedral Mountain is open mid-May to 1 October. For bookings, call 250/343-6442. In the off-season, call 403/762-0514. The lodge's website is www.cathedralmountain.com.

More Than $150

Emerald Lake Lodge is a grand, luxury-class accommodation along the southern shore of one of the Canadian Rockies' most magnificent lakes. The original lodge was built in 1902 in the same tradition as the Fairmont Chateau Lake Louise and Fairmont Banff Springs—as a playground for wealthy railway travelers. No original buildings remain (although the original framework is used in the main building). In 1986 the lodge underwent considerable renovation and expansion. It now boasts 85 units, as well as a hot tub and sauna, swimming pool, restaurant, lounge, and café. Guests can also go horseback riding, or go boating and fishing on Emerald Lake. The rooms are large, and many of the more expensive ones are on the lakefront in cabin-style buildings. Rates range $335–700 s or d per night, with sharp discounts in the off-season (rates as low as $150 in November). For bookings, call 403/609-6150 or 800/663-6336, or visit website: www.crmr.com.

© ANDREW HEMPSTEAD

Overnighting in a waterfront cabin at Lake O'Hara allows visitors to enjoy the backcountry without sacrificing modern comforts.

Spending a night at **Lake O'Hara Lodge** is a special experience, and one that draws familiar faces year and after year. On a practical level, it allows hikers not equipped for overnight camping the opportunity to explore one of the finest hiking destinations in all of the Canadian Rockies at their leisure. The 15 cabins, each with a private bathroom, are spread around the lakeshore, while within the main lodge are eight rooms, most of which are twins and share bathrooms. Rates of $395 d for a room in the main lodge (shared bathrooms) and $525–585 d for a lakeside cabin include all meals, taxes, gratuities, and transportation mid-June to September. Located 13 km (eight miles) from Highway 1, guests are transported by shuttle bus to and from a parking lot three km (1.9 miles) west of the Continental Divide and 15 km (nine miles) east of Field. Between February and April, the eight rooms in the main lodge are available for cross-country skiers for $225 pp, inclusive of meals and ski tours. The lodge books up well in advance; for reservations, call 250/343-6418 (call 403/678-4110 in the off-season), or visit website: www.lakeohara.com.

Campgrounds

As in other national parks, no reservations are taken for camping in Yoho's vehicle-accessible campgrounds. All sites have a picnic table and fire ring, with a fire permit costing $6 (includes firewood). When all campgrounds are filled, campers will be directed to overflow areas.

The park's main camping area is **Kicking Horse Campground,** five km (three miles) northeast of Field along the road to Takakkaw Falls. Facilities include coin showers ($1), flush toilets, and kitchen shelters. Unserviced sites are $19. The campground is open mid-May to mid-October. Back toward the TransCanada Highway, **Monarch Campground** offers more limited facilities and less private sites; $15. **Hoodoo Creek Campground,** along the TransCanada Highway 23 km (14 miles) southwest of Field, provides 106 private sites among the trees for $15 per vehicle. Facilities include flush toilets, hot water, kitchen shelters, and an interpretive program.

At the end of the road up the Yoho Valley, **Takakkaw Falls Campground** is designed for tent campers only. Park at the end of the road and load up the carts with your gear for a pleasant

400-meter (0.2-mile) walk along the valley floor. No showers are provided, and the only facilities are pit toilets and picnic tables; $14 per site. It's open July to mid-September.

Just below **Lake O'Hara,** alongside the access road, is a delightful little campground surrounded by some of the region's finest hiking. Each of 30 sites has a tent pad, fire pit, and picnic table, while other facilities include pit toilets, two kitchen shelters with woodstoves, and bearproof food caches. Reservations for sites are made in conjunction with the bus trip along the restricted access road from Highway 1 to Lake O'Hara. Buses for campers depart mid-June to October, daily at 4:30 P.M. and 7:30 P.M. Even though access is aboard a bus, you should treat the trip as one into the backcountry; passengers are limited to one large or two small bags, and no coolers or fold-up chairs are permitted onboard the shuttle. To book a seat and site, call 250/343-6433 up to three months in advance. Lines are open mid-March to April, Mon.–Thurs. 8 A.M.–4 P.M.; May, Mon.–Fri. 8 A.M.–4 P.M.; June to mid-Sept., daily 8 A.M.–4 P.M.; and mid-Sept. to early October, Mon.–Thurs. 8 A.M.–4 P.M. Camping is $6 per person per night, the bus costs $12 per person round-trip, and the reservation fee is $10 per booking. Make reservations as far in advance as possible. A limited number of sites can be reserved in person at the Field Visitor Centre (from 8 A.M.) the day before you want to go in. Get there early because these first-come, first-served spots fill up fast.

FOOD

Field

Truffle Pigs Café, in downtown Field at 318 Stephen St., 250/343-6462, is one of those unexpected finds that makes traveling such a joy. It's contained at the back of a general store, beyond racks of food basics and rental movies, with seating in a section off to the side or outside on a small patio. The best of the breakfast and lunch dishes are described on a massive blackboard, with freshly baked cookies and locally brewed coffee complementing sandwiches made to order from the glass-fronted deli. In the evening this place really

shines, with dishes as adventurous as the Spinach Maple Pecan Salad ($11) and as simple as an Albertan-raised buffalo ribeye steak served with a port-based au jus and a baked potato ($25). It's open in summer, daily 7:30 A.M.–10 P.M., the rest of the year it's also open daily, but dinner is only served Friday and Saturday.

Across the road, the **Kicking Horse Lodge,** 250/343-6303, has a small restaurant that has views over the valley floor. It offers a short but varied dinner menu featuring dishes of wide-ranging appeal (including a delicious herb-crusted pork tenderloin smothered in a mango apple chutney) as well as a daily special and a soup of the day, both of which actually are *special.* It's open daily for breakfast 8 A.M.–11 A.M., for lunch noon–2:30 P.M., and for dinner 5–9 P.M.

Other Dining Options

Overlooking Emerald Lake, **Cilantro on the Lake** is a casual café featuring magnificent views from tables inside an open-fronted, log chalet-style building or out on the lakefront deck. The menu is varied—you can sit and sip a coffee or have a full lunch or dinner. Starters—such as thick and creamy corn and potato chowder—are all less than $10, while mains range from $22–33 for an extravagantly rich beef tenderloin served with a lobster and mushroom cream sauce. Within the main lodge you'll find a more formal dining room and a bar.

The final option for park dining is the restaurant at **Cathedral Mountain Chalets,** 250/343-6442, a casual, inexpensive restaurant open daily through summer 7 A.M.–10 P.M. Breakfast comprises healthy choices such as fresh fruit, croissants, and home-baked bread, then it's soup and sandwiches through to the evening, when a basic menu of chicken, beef, and seafood is offered.

TRANSPORTATION

Transportation to and around the park is limited. **Greyhound,** 403/762-6767 or 800/661-8747, stops in Field daily on its route between Banff and Golden, from where it continues west to Vancouver. **Brewster,** 403/762-6767, offers a 3.5-hour

YOHO

tour of the park, departing Lake Louise daily at 12:30 P.M. (summer only). This tour takes in both the Yoho Valley and Emerald Lake. The cost is $51 adults, $23 children. Brewster's Mountain Lakes and Waterfalls Tour is an extended version of the previous tour, combining the best of Banff National Park with a trip over the divide into Yoho. It departs the Banff depot mid-June to early-October daily at 8:10 A.M. through summer. The tour takes nine hours and costs $72 per person.

INFORMATION

The main source of information about the park is the Field Visitor Centre on the TransCanada Highway at Field, 250/343-6783. Inside you'll find helpful staff, information boards, and interpretive panels. This is also the place to try and make a last-minute reservation for the Lake O'Hara bus, pick up backcountry camping permits, buy topographical maps, and find out schedules for the interpretive programs. The center is open in peak summer season, daily 9 a.m.–7 p.m.; the rest of year, daily 9 a.m.–4 p.m. For more information, write Yoho National Park, P.O. Box 99, Field, BC V0A 1G0; or surf the Internet to the park's website, www.parkscanada.gc.ca/yoho. For park road conditions, call 403/762-1450; for avalanche reports, call 403/762-1460.

Golden

From the western boundary of Yoho National Park, the TransCanada Highway meanders down the beautiful Kicking Horse River Valley to the town of Golden (pop. 5,300), at the confluence of the Kicking Horse and Columbia Rivers. As well as being a destination in itself, Golden makes a good central base for exploring the region or as an overnight stop on a tour through the Canadian Rockies that takes in the national parks on the western side of the Continental Divide.

Although Golden is an industrial town through and through—with local mines and huge logging operations that include a lumber mill that opened in 1999—it's also gaining a reputation for local outdoor-recreation opportunities, most notably for its new four-season resort and white-water-rafting trips down the Kicking Horse River.

SIGHTS AND RECREATION

Take Highway 95 off the TransCanada Highway and you'll find yourself in the old section of town, a world away from the commercial strip along the main highway. There's not really much to see in town, although you may want to check out the small museum on 14th Street. The 8.8-km (5.5-mile) **Rotary Loop** is a paved walking and biking trail that leads across the river from downtown via an impressive timber-frame pedestrian bridge then upstream across Highway 95 (10th Ave. S) to the campground.

The **Columbia River Wetlands** (see "Sights and Recreation" under "Radium Hot Springs" in the Kootenay National Park and Vicinity chapter) extend as far north as Golden. One easily accessible point of the wetlands is **Reflection Lake,** on the southern outskirts of Golden. Here you'll find a small shelter with a telescope for viewing the abundant bird life.

Kicking Horse Mountain Resort

What was formerly locally owned Whitetooth Ski Area, spread across the lower slopes of the Purcell Mountains (the runs are easily spotted across the valley as you enter town from the east) is currently undergoing a massive redevelopment program slated for completion in 2007. As well as a new name, Kicking Horse Mountain Resort is basically being rebuilt from scratch, with $75 million invested in new lifts, luxurious ski-in, ski-out hotels, condominiums, restaurants, and other facilities that will make the resort a year-round destination.

The eight-person detachable Golden Eagle Express transports visitors high into the alpine late June through early September in just 12 minutes. The 360-degree panorama at the summit is

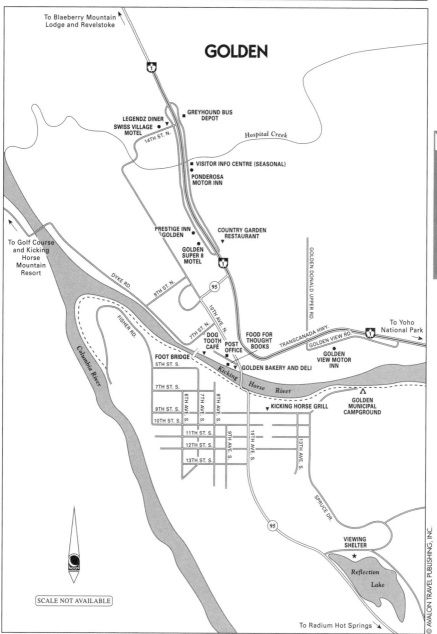

GOLDEN

To Blaeberry Mountain Lodge and Revelstoke

GREYHOUND BUS DEPOT

LEGENDZ DINER

SWISS VILLAGE MOTEL

14TH ST. N.

Hospital Creek

VISITOR INFO CENTRE (SEASONAL)

PONDEROSA MOTOR INN

PRESTIGE INN GOLDEN

COUNTRY GARDEN RESTAURANT

GOLDEN SUPER 8 MOTEL

To Golf Course and Kicking Horse Mountain Resort

DYKE RD.

9TH ST. N.

GOLDEN DONALD UPPER RD.

95

10TH AVE. N.

7TH ST. N.

FISHER RD.

DOG TOOTH CAFÉ

POST OFFICE

FOOD FOR THOUGHT BOOKS

TRANSCANADA HWY.

To Yoho National Park

GOLDEN VIEW RD.

GOLDEN VIEW MOTOR INN

FOOT BRIDGE

5TH ST. S.

Kicking Horse River

GOLDEN BAKERY AND DELI

Columbia River

7TH ST. S.

9TH ST. S.

10TH ST. S.

6TH AVE. S.

7TH AVE. S.

8TH AVE. S.

KICKING HORSE GRILL

GOLDEN MUNICIPAL CAMPGROUND

11TH ST. S.

9TH AVE. S.

10TH AVE. S.

12TH ST. S.

13TH ST. S.

13TH AVE. S.

SPRUCE DR.

95

VIEWING SHELTER

Reflection Lake

SCALE NOT AVAILABLE

To Radium Hot Springs

YOHO

equal to any other accessible point in the Canadian Rockies, with the Purcell Mountains immediately to the west and the Columbia Valley laid out below. Graded hiking trails lead from the upper terminal through a fragile, treeless environment, while mountain bikers revel in a challenging descent in excess of 1,000 meters (3,280 feet). A single gondola ride is $16 adults, $13 seniors, $8 children (ask about excellent breakfast and lunch deals at the Eagle's Eye Restaurant that basically equate to a free ride). Mountain bikers pay $17.75 for a single ride or $25 to ride all day. A rent-and-ride package costs $63 for the full day, including a full-suspension bike. The gondola operates through summer, daily 8 A.M.–8 P.M. (from noon for mountain bikers). For dining details, see "Food" section.

With a vertical rise of 1,260 meters (4,130 feet), 50 percent of terrain designated for experts, lots of dry powder snow, and minimal crowds, Kicking Horse has developed a big reputation since opening for the 2000–2001 winter season. In addition to the 3.5-km (2.2-mile)-long gondola, other chairlifts transport skiers and boarders to hidden bowls and, as of the 2002–2003 season, to a high point of 2,450 meters (8,040 feet), giving the resort North America's second-highest vertical rise (1,260 meters/4,135 feet). Lifts operate mid-December to early April and tickets are $52 adults, $40 seniors and students, $22 children. Facilities in the base lodge include rentals, a cafeteria, and a ski school, while the summit restaurant is also open daily for lunch and Friday and Saturday for dinner.

To get to Kicking Horse, follow the signs from Highway 1 into town and take 7th St. N west from 10th Ave. N.; it's over the Columbia River and 13 km (eight miles) uphill from this intersection. Contact the resort at 250/439-5400 or 866/754-5425, www.kickinghorseresort.com.

White-Water Rafting

Anyone looking for white-water-rafting action will want to run the Kicking Horse River. The rafting season runs late May to mid-September, with river levels at their highest in late June. The Lower Canyon, immediately upstream of Golden, offers the biggest thrills, including a three-km

© ANDREW HEMPSTEAD

Take a gondola to the top of Kicking Horse Mountain Resort to enjoy the sublime view.

(1.9-mile) stretch of continuous rapids. Upstream of here the river is tamer but still makes for an exciting trip, while even farther upstream, near the western boundary of Yoho National Park, it's more of a float—a good adventure for the more timid visitor. The river is run by several companies, most of which offer the option of half-day ($60–80) or full-day ($90–105) trips. The cost varies with inclusions such as transportation from Banff and lunch.

Whitewater Voyageurs, 250/344-7335 or 800/667-7238, is one of the original operators. They offer half- and full-day trips as well as transportation from Lake Louise. **Alpine Rafting**, 250/344-6778 or 888/599-5299, offer a wide variety of trips, including an easy float and a trip down the Lower Canyon. Transportation from Banff, Lake Louise, and Canmore is an extra charge. Also based in Golden is **Wet 'n' Wild Adventures**, 250/344-6546 or 800/668-9119. This company offers transportation from Banff, but at an extra charge and only for their full-day trips. **Rocky Mountain Rafting Company**, 250/344-6979 or 888/518-7238, offers a variety of combinations, as well as providing transportation from as far away as Canmore. From Lake Louise, **Wild Water Adventures,** 403/522-2211 or 888/647-6444, leads half-day trips down the river for $64, including a narrated bus trip to their purpose-built Day Base put-in point 27 km (17 miles) east of Golden. Departures are from Lake Louise at 8:30 a.m. and 1:30 p.m. Their full-day trip ($89) is broken up by a riverside lunch.

Other Summertime Recreation

Golden Golf and Country Club is a challenging 18-hole course set in a forested section of the valley through town and to the north. This course is generally in excellent condition, with water coming into play on many holes—including the signature 11th and 12th holes along Holt Creek—and numerous streams and lakes to catch wayward shots. Greens fees are $55, or there's a $42 twilight rate. For tee times, call 250/344-2700 or 866/727-7222.

Check out the website of **Golden Mountain Adventures,** www.adventurerockies.com, for the full range of activities available. This company can also book packages using local operators and accommodations.

Adventurous souls are drawn to Golden for its thermals, perfect for hang-gliding and paragliding, and to the steep face of Jubilee Mountain, a renowned sport-climbing destination. A different type of Canadian, cowboys, descend on town the first weekend of August for **Golden Rodeo Days.**

ACCOMMODATIONS

It's easy to find a place to stay in Golden because the town holds more than 20 motels, most of which lie right along the TransCanada Highway.

$50–100

At the western entrance to town is the budget-priced **Swiss Village Motel,** 250/344-2276; $56 s, $62 d, with kitchenettes an additional $8.

The distinctive two-story, lime-green **Ponderosa Motor Inn,** on the TransCanada by 12th Ave., 250/344-2205 or 800/881-4233, www.ponderosamotorinn.bc.ca, has 85 older rooms, but offers impressive mountain views, a hot tub, a picnic area and gazebo, and a playground, making it a good value at just $78 s, $88 d ($52 s, $60 d outside of summer).

Blaeberry Mountain Lodge, nine km (5.6 miles) north of Golden along Highway 1 then seven km (4.3 miles) farther north along Moberly School Road, 250/344-5296, www.blaeberrymountainlodge.bc.ca, is set on a 62-hectare (150-acre) property among total wilderness. Rooms are in the main lodge or self-contained cabins, with plenty of activities available to guests. Standard rooms with shared bathroom are $65, and the large cabins, which feature a separate bedroom and full kitchen, are $125. Breakfast and dinner are offered for $10 and $20, respectively.

$100–150

The **Golden Super 8 Motel,** 1047 TransCanada Hwy., 250/344-0888 or 800/800-8000, www.super8.com, is a modern air-conditioned facility where breakfast is included in the rates of $100 s, $105 d.

Next door to the Super 8 is the **Prestige Inn Golden,** 1049 TransCanada Hwy., 250/344-7902 or 877/737-8443, www.prestigeinn.com, where you'll find the town's highest-standard rooms, along with views that extend well down the Columbia Valley. Amenities include an indoor pool, hot tub, fitness center, lounge, and restaurant. Rates range $110–150 s or d.

Along Highway 1 back toward Yoho National Park, **Kicking Horse River Chalets,** 2924 Kicking Horse Rd., 866/502-5171, www.kickinghorseriverchalets.com, comprises luxurious peeled-log cabins, each with full kitchen and dishwasher, wood-burning fireplace, balcony, and loft. The rate is $200 per night for up to four people.

Campgrounds

Continue south through the old part of town over the Kicking Horse River and take 9th Street South east at the traffic lights to reach **Golden Municipal Campground,** 250/344-5412. It's a quiet place, strung out along the river and two km (1.2 miles) from downtown along a river-

YOHO

front walkway. Facilities include picnic shelters, hot coin-operated showers, and 70 sites with fire pits. Adjacent is a recreation center with a swimming pool and fitness facility. Unpowered sites are $14, powered sites $16. It's open mid-May to mid-October.

Golfers can stay out at the golf course in a specially developed area for $14 per night.

FOOD

Eagle's Eye Restaurant

At an elevation of 2,347 meters (7,700 feet), the Eagle's Eye is the crowning glory of Kicking Horse Mountain Resort and is Canada's highest restaurant. Access is by gondola from the resort's base village, 13 km (eight miles) west of downtown Golden, 250/439-5400 or 866/754-5425 (reservations are only required for dinner). As you'd expect, the views are stunning and are set off by a stylish timber and stonework interior, including a floor-to-ceiling fireplace and a wide wraparound deck protected from the wind by glass paneling. It's open daily at 8 A.M. for a simple cold and cooked breakfast buffet costing $17 adults, $10 children, which includes the gondola ride (tables behind the fireplace catch the morning sun in all its glory).

"Sky Lunch," served noon–4 P.M., includes the ride up and a choice from the menu—such as cedar plank salmon or seafood linguine—for $20. Between 7 and 10 P.M. the setting becomes more romantic and the food more adventurous but remains distinctly Canadian. Dinner mains range $25–40 and include such delights as salmon baked in a saffron-vanilla cream and served with strawberry salsa ($28). All evening diners enjoy a complimentary gondola ride.

Downtown

Start your day with the locals at the **Golden Bakery & Deli,** 419 9th Ave., 250/344-2928, where the coffee is always fresh and the faces friendly. Baked goodies include breads, pastries, cakes, and meat pies, with inexpensive daily specials displayed on a blackboard in a seated section off to the side of the main counter. It's open Mon.–Sat. 6:30 A.M.–6 P.M.

Tucked behind the row of shops along 9th Avenue is the funky little **Dog Tooth Café,** 1007 11th Ave. S, 250/344-3660. Seating is indoors below the main service area or out back in an adobe-style terrace facing the pedestrian bridge over the Kicking Horse River. The menu includes basic café fare and specialties

Enjoy the view from Canada's highest restaurant, the aptly named Eagle's Eye.

© ANDREW HEMPSTEAD

such as a huge serving of Thai noodle salad for just $7. It's open Mon.–Sat. 7 A.M.–8 P.M., Sun. 9 A.M.–6 P.M.

Constructed of rough-cut logs complete with bulging burls, the **Kicking Horse Grill,** 1105 9th St. S, 250/344-2330, is one of Golden's finest restaurants. The menu changes with the seasons but always offers distinctly international dishes ranging from paella to sushi. All but the beef dishes are less than $20, with generously portioned starter salads ranging $6.50–8.50. It's open daily for dinner only.

Out on the Highway

All the usual fast-food places line the Trans-Canada Highway, as well as **Legendz Diner,** on the west side of the highway, 250/344-5059. As the name suggests, it's a 1950s-style diner, complete with attentive staff and filling meals from $9. Across the road, the **Country Garden Restaurant,** 1002 TransCanada Hwy., 250/344-5971, is a large, casual family-style restaurant with an excellent range of buffets throughout the day, including dinner for $18.

INFORMATION AND SERVICES

While accommodations, fast-food restaurants, and gas stations line the TransCanada Highway, downtown Golden holds other basic services, including the **post office** at 502 9th Avenue. Ninth Avenue also has a variety of outdoor equipment shops and **Food for Thought Books** at 407 9th Ave., 250/344-5600. Open Mon.–Sat. 9:30 A.M.–6 P.M., it offers a wide selection of new and used books, with plenty of local reading and detailed maps of the Columbia Valley. Next door, at 409 9th Ave., **Images Plus,** 250/344-5414, offers one-hour developing and basic photography supplies.

Transportation

Greyhound buses stop four times daily in Golden, utilizing an ATCO trailer tucked away beside the ESSO gas station as a depot, 250/344-6172. **National,** 250/344-9899, is the only car rental agency in town. For a cab, call **Mount Seven Taxi,** 250/344-5237.

Information

The year-round **Golden Visitor Info Centre** is in the old railway station building at 500 10th Avenue, 250/344-7125 or 800/622-4653. It's open weekdays 8:30 a.m.–4:30 p.m. Back out on the highway is a seasonal information center, in a converted gas station beside the Ponderosa Motor Inn. In addition to all the regular brochure racks, it has public Internet access and a handy map of local bike trails; open in summer, daily 9 a.m.–5 p.m. The website of the Golden Tourism Association is www.go2rockies.com.

YOHO

Jasper National Park

Note: Please see color map of
Jasper National Park *on pages vi-vii.*

Snowcapped peaks, vast icefields, beautiful glacial lakes, soothing hot springs, thundering rivers, and the most extensive backcountry trail system of any Canadian national park make Jasper a stunning counterpart to its sister park, Banff. Lying on the Albertan side of the Canadian Rockies, Jasper protects the entire upper watershed of the Athabasca River, extending to the Columbia Icefield (and Banff National Park) in the south. To the east are the foothills, to the west the Continental Divide (which marks the Alberta–British Columbia border) and Mount Robson Provincial Park. Encompassing 10,900 square km (4,208 square miles), Jasper is a haven for wildlife; much of its wilderness is traveled only by wolves and grizzlies.

The park's most spectacular natural landmarks can be admired from two major roads. The **Yellowhead Highway** runs east-west from Edmonton to British Columbia through the park. The **Icefields Parkway,** regarded as one of the world's great mountain drives, runs north-south, connecting Jasper

Athabasca Glacier, Columbia Icefield

© ANDREW HEMPSTEAD

to Banff. At the junction of these two highways is the park's main service center—the town of **Jasper.** With half the population of Banff, its setting—at the confluence of the Athabasca and Miette Rivers, surrounded by rugged, snowcapped peaks—is a little less dramatic, though still beautiful. But the town is also less commercialized than Banff and its streets a little quieter—a major plus for those looking to get away from it all.

Many of the park's campgrounds are accessible by road, while others dot the backcountry. Hiking is the number one attraction, but fishing, boating, downhill skiing and snowboarding, golfing, horseback riding, and white-water rafting are also popular. The park is open year-round, although road closures do occur on the Icefields Parkway during winter months due to avalanche-control work and snowstorms.

THE LAND

Although the peaks of Jasper National Park are not particularly high, they are among the most spectacular along the range's entire length. About 100 million years ago, layers of sedimentary rock—laid down here up to a billion years ago—were forced upward, folded, and twisted under tremendous pressure into the mountains seen today. The land's contours were further altered during four ice ages that began around one million years ago. The last Ice Age ended about 10,000 years ago, and the vast glaciers began to retreat. A remnant of this final sheet of ice is the huge Columbia Icefield; covering approximately 325 square km (125 square miles) and up to 400 meters (1,300 feet) deep, it's the most extensive icefield in the Rocky Mountains. As the glaciers retreated, piles of rock melted out and were left behind. Meltwater from the glaciers flowed down the valleys and was dammed up behind the moraines. **Maligne Lake,** like many other lakes in the park, was created by this process. The glacial silt suspended in the lake's waters produces amazing emerald, turquoise, and amethyst colors; early artists who painted these lakes had trouble convincing people that their images were real.

PARK ENTRY

Permits are required for entry into the park. A **National Parks Day Pass** is $6 adults, $4.50 seniors, $3 children up to a maximum of $12 per vehicle ($9 for seniors). It can also be used in neighboring Banff National Park if you're traveling down the Icefields Parkway, and is valid until 4 P.M. the day following its purchase. An annual **National Parks of Canada Pass**—good for entry into all 27 of Canada's national parks—is $38 adults and $29 seniors up to a maximum of $75 per vehicle ($58 for seniors).

Both types of pass can be purchased at the park information center, at the booth along the Icefields Parkway a few kilometers south of Jasper townsite, and at campground kiosks. If you're traveling north along the Icefields Parkway, you'll be required to stop and purchase a park pass just beyond Lake Louise. The Parks Canada website, www.parkscanada.gc.ca, has detailed pass information.

In addition to creating the park's gemlike lakes, the retreating glaciers carved out the valleys that they ever-so-slowly flowed through. The Athabasca River Valley is the park's largest watershed, a typical example of a U-shaped, glacier-carved valley. The Athabasca River flows north through the valley into the Mackenzie River System and ultimately into the Arctic Ocean. The glacial silt that paints the park's lakes is also carried down streams into the Athabasca, giving the river a pale-green milky look. Another beautiful aspect of the park's scenery is its abundance of waterfalls. They vary from the sparkling tumble of Punchbowl Falls, where Mountain Creek cascades down a limestone cliff into a picturesque pool, to the roar of Athabasca Falls, where the Athabasca River is forced through a narrow gorge.

FLORA

Elevations in the park range from 980 meters (3,215 feet) to more than 3,700 meters (12,140 feet). That makes for a wide range of resident plant life. Only a small part of the park lies in the montane zone. It is characterized by stands of

JASPER

Douglas fir (at its northern limit) and **lodge-pole pine, while balsam poplar, white birch,** and **spruce** also occur. Savanna-like grasslands occur on drier sites in valley bottoms. Well-developed stretches of montane can be found along the floors of the Athabasca and Miette River Valley, providing winter habitat for larger mammals such as elk.

The subalpine zone, heavily forested with evergreens, extends from the lower valley slopes up to the treeline at an elevation of around 2,200 meters (7,220 feet). The subalpine occupies 40 percent of the park's area. The dominant species in this zone is lodgepole pine, although **Engelmann spruce, subalpine fir, poplar,** and **aspen** also grow here. The park's extensive stands of lodgepole pine are inhabited by few large mammals because the understory is minimal. Wildflowers are common in this zone and can be found by the roadside, in clearings, or on riverbanks.

Timberline here lies at an elevation of 2,050–2,400 meters (6,275–7,870 feet) above sea level. Above this elevation is the alpine zone, where the climate is severe (the average yearly temperature is below freezing), summer is brief, and only a few stunted trees survive. The zone's plant species grow low to the ground, with extensive root systems to protect them during high winds and through the deep snow cover of winter. During the short summer, these open slopes and meadows are carpeted with a profusion of flowers such as **golden arnicas, bluebells, pale columbines,** and red and yellow **paintbrush**. Higher still are brightly colored **heathers, buttercups,** and **alpine forget-me-nots.**

FAUNA

Wildlife is abundant in the park and can be seen throughout the year. During winter many larger mammals move to lower elevations where food is accessible. February and March are particularly good for looking for animal tracks in the snow. By June, most of the snow cover at lower elevations has melted, the crowds haven't arrived, and animals can be seen feeding along the valley floor. In fall, tourists move to warmer climates, the rutting season begins, bears go into hibernation, and a herd of **elk** moves into downtown Jasper for the winter.

While the park provides ample opportunities for seeing numerous animals in their natural habitat, it also leads to human–animal encounters that are not always positive. For example, less than 10 percent of the park is made up of well-vegetated valleys. These lower areas are essential to the larger mammals for food and shelter but are also the most heavily traveled by visitors. Game trails used for thousands of years are often bisected by roads, and hundreds of animals are killed each year by speeding motorists. Please drive slowly in the park.

Campground Critters

Several species of small mammals thrive around campgrounds, thanks to an abundance of humans who are careless with their food. **Columbian ground squirrels** are bold and will demand scraps of your lunch. **Golden-mantled ground squirrels** and **red squirrels** are also common. The **least chipmunk** (often confused with the golden-mantled ground squirrel thanks to similar stripes) can also be seen in campgrounds; they'll often scamper across your hiking trail then sit boldly on a rock waiting for you to pass.

Aquatic Species

Beaver dams are common between the town of Jasper and the park's east gate. Dawn and dusk are the best times to watch these intriguing creatures at work. Wabasso Lake, a 2.6-km (1.6-mile) hike from the Icefields Parkway, was created by beavers; their impressive dam has completely blocked the flow of Wabasso Creek. Also common in the park's wetlands are **mink** and **muskrat;** search out these creatures around the lakes on the benchland north of the town of Jasper.

Ungulates

Five species of deer inhabit the park. The large-eared **mule deer** is commonly seen around the edge of the town or grazing along the north end of the Icefields Parkway. **White-tailed deer** can be seen throughout the park. A small herd of **woodland caribou** roams throughout the park;

they are most commonly seen during late spring, feeding in river deltas. The town of Jasper is in the home range of about 500 **elk,** which can be seen most of the year around town or along the highway northeast and south of town. **Moose,** although numbering fewer than 100 in all of Jasper, can occasionally be seen feeding on aquatic plants along the major drainage systems.

In summer, **mountain goats** browse in alpine meadows. A good place for goat watching is Goat Lookout on the Icefields Parkway. Unlike most of the park's large mammals, these surefooted creatures don't migrate to lower elevations in winter, but stay sheltered on rocky crags where wind and sun keep the vegetation snow free. Often confused with the goat is the darker **bighorn sheep.** The horns on the males of this species are thick and often curl 360 degrees. Bighorns are common in the east of the park at Disaster Point and will often approach cars. An estimated 2,500 bighorn reside in the park.

Bears

Numbering around 80 within Jasper National Park, **black bears** are widespread and occasionally wander into campgrounds looking for food. They are most commonly seen along the Icefields Parkway in spring, when they first come out of hibernation. **Grizzly bears** are occasionally seen crossing the Icefields Parkway at higher elevations early in summer. For the most part they remain in remote mountain valleys, and if they do see, smell, or hear you, they'll generally move away. Read *Keep the Wild in Wildlife* before setting out into the woods; the pamphlet is available at information centers throughout the park.

Reclusive Residents

Several of the park's resident species keep a low profile, usually out of sight of humans. Populations of the shy and elusive **lynx** fluctuate with that of their primary food source, the snowshoe hare. The largest of the big cats in the park is the **cougar** (also called the mountain lion), a solitary carnivore that inhabits remote valleys. Jasper's **wolves** are one of the park's success stories. After being driven to near extinction, the species has rebounded. Five packs now roam the park,

but they keep to the deep wilderness rarely traveled by people. While not common in the park, **coyotes** can be seen in cleared areas alongside the roads; usually at dawn and dusk.

Other Mammals

The **pine marten** is common but shy; look for them in subalpine forests. The **short-tailed weasel**—a relative of the marten—is also common, while the **long-tailed weasel** is rare. At higher elevations look for **pikas** in piles of fallen rock. **Hoary marmots** live near the upper limits of vegetation growth, where their shrill warning whistles carry across the open meadows; The Whistlers area, accessed by tramway, supports a healthy population of these noisy creatures.

Birds

The extensive tree cover in the lower valleys hides many species of birds, making them seem less abundant than they are. A total of 248 species have been recorded. The two you're most likely to see are the **gray jay** and **Clark's nutcracker,** which regularly joins picnickers for lunch. Also common are black-and-white **magpies,** raucous **ravens,** and several species of

White-tailed ptarmigans inhabit alpine meadows throughout Jasper National Park.

ducks, which can be seen around lakes in the Athabasca River Valley. Harlequin ducks nest in the park during early summer. A stretch of the Maligne River is closed during this season to prevent human interference.

The colony of **black swifts** in Maligne Canyon is one of only two in Alberta. Their poorly developed legs make it difficult for them to take off from their nests in the canyon walls—they literally fall before becoming airborne. High alpine slopes are home to **white-tailed ptarmigans,** a type of grouse that turns white in winter. Also at this elevation are flocks of **rosy finches** that live under overhanging cliffs. In subalpine forests the songs of **thrushes** and the tapping of **woodpeckers** can be heard.

At dusk, **great horned owls** swoop silently through the trees, their eerie call echoing through the forest. **Golden eagles** and **bald eagles** can be seen soaring high above the forests, and 15 pairs of **ospreys** are known to nest in the park, many along the Athabasca River between town and the east park gate.

HISTORY

In the summer of 1810, David Thompson, one of Canada's greatest explorers, became the first white man to enter the Athabasca River Valley. The following winter, when Thompson was making the first successful crossing of the Continental Divide, some of his party remained in the Athabasca River Valley and constructed a small supply depot east of the present town. The depot grew into a small trading post named Henry House and was used for many years by the North West Company. Other trading posts were built along the Athabasca River, including one that became known as Jasper's House, for the clerk Jasper Hawse. This particular post was first established in 1813, then moved to the outlet of Jasper Lake in 1829.

By 1865, with the fur trade over and the Cariboo goldfields emptying along routes easier than over Yellowhead Pass, the Athabasca River Valley had no permanent residents. One prospector who did return over Yellowhead Pass was Lewis Swift, who in 1892 made his home in the abandoned buildings of Jasper's House, farming a small plot of land beside the Athabasca River. "Old Swift" became known to everyone, providing fresh food and accommodations for travelers and generating many legendary tales, such as the day he held the Grand Trunk Pacific Railway at gunpoint until they agreed to reroute the line away from his property.

In 1907, aware that the coming of the railway would mean an influx of settlers, the federal government set aside 5,000 square miles as Jasper Forest Park, buying all the land, save for the parcel owned by Lewis Swift. A handful of homesteaders continued to live in the valley, but the land on which they lived was leased. The threat of oversettlement of the valley had been abated, but as a designated forest park, mining and logging were still allowed.

In 1908, Jasper Park Collieries staked claims in the park. By the time the railway came through in 1911, mining activity was centered at Pocahontas (near the park's east gate), where a township was established and thrived. During an extended miners' strike, the men spent their spare time constructing log pools at Miette Hot Springs, which were heavily promoted to early park visitors. The mine closed in 1921 and many families relocated to Jasper, which had grown from a railway camp into a popular tourist destination. By this time the park boundaries had changed dramatically. In 1911, the park had been reduced to two-thirds its original size, then in 1914 enlarged to include Maligne Lake and Columbia Icefield, then enlarged yet again in 1928 to take in Sunwapta Pass. Today's borders were set in 1930, when Jasper was officially designated a national park.

And what of Old Swift? Well, after working as the park's first game warden for four years, he hung onto his land until 1935. The government of the day made various offers, but Swift ended up selling to a wealthy Englishman who operated a dude ranch on the site until finally selling the land to the government in 1962.

Town of Jasper

In 1911, a construction camp was established for the Grand Trunk Pacific Railway near the present site of downtown Jasper. When the northern line was completed, visitors flocked into the remote mountain settlement, and its future was assured. The first accommodation for tourists was 10 tents on the shore of Lac Beauvert that became known as Jasper Park Camp. In 1921, the tents were replaced and the original Jasper Park Lodge was constructed. By the summer of 1928, a road was completed from Edmonton and a golf course was built. As the number of tourists to the park continued to increase, existing facilities were expanded. In 1940 the Icefields Parkway opened, linking Jasper to Banff and making the park more accessible.

The modern infrastructure of Jasper began developing in the 1960s, but until 2002 the townsite was run from Ottawa by Parks Canada. Jasper is now officially incorporated as a "town," with locally elected residents serving as mayor and council members. Decisions made by the council must still balance the needs of living in a national park, but also represent locals who call the park home. On the surface, obvious visible changes of this autonomy are a new emergency services building, a new wastewater treatment plant, and improvements to an ever-increasing downtown parking problem. One thing hasn't changed, and that's the basic premise of the town's existence: more than 50 percent of Jasper's 5,200 residents work in the hospitality industry, serving the needs of two million visitors annually.

Sights and Drives

COLUMBIA ICEFIELD

The largest and most accessible of 17 glacial areas along the Icefields Parkway is 325-square-km (125-square-mile) Columbia Icefield, beside the Icefields Parkway at the south end of the park, 105 km (65 miles) south from Jasper and 132 km (82 miles) north from Lake Louise. It's a remnant of the last major glaciation that covered most of Canada 20,000 years ago, and it has survived because of its elevation at 1,900–2,800 meters (6,230–9,190 feet) above sea level, cold temperatures, and heavy snowfalls. From the main body of the ice cap, which sits astride the Continental Divide, six glaciers creep down three main valleys. Of these, **Athabasca Glacier** is the most accessible and can be seen from the Icefields Parkway; it is one of the world's few glaciers that you can drive right up to. It is an impressive 600 hectares (1,480 acres) in area and up to 100 meters (330 feet) deep. The speed at which glaciers advance and retreat varies with the long-term climate. Athabasca Glacier has retreated to its current position from across the highway, a distance of more than 1.6 km (one mile) in a little more than 100 years. Currently it retreats up to two meters (six feet) per year. The rubble between the toe of Athabasca Glacier and the highway is a mixture of rock, sand, and gravel known as *till,* deposited by the glacier as it retreats.

The icefield is made more spectacular by the impressive peaks that surround it. **Mount Athabasca** (3,491 meters/11,450 feet) dominates the skyline, and three glaciers cling to its flanks. **Dome Glacier** is also visible from the highway; although part of Columbia Icefield, it is not actually connected. Instead it is made of ice that breaks off the icefield 300 meters (980 feet) above, supplemented by large quantities of snow each winter.

Exploring the Icefield

From the Icefields Parkway, an unpaved road leads down through piles of till left by the retreating Athabasca Glacier to a parking area beside Sunwapta Lake. An interesting alternative is to leave your vehicle beside the highway and take the 1.6-km (one-mile) hiking trail through the lunarlike landscape to the parking area described previously. From this point, a short path leads up to the toe of the glacier. (Along the access road, look for the small markers showing how far the toe of the glacier reached in years gone by; the farthest marker is across the highway beside the stairs leading up to the Icefield Centre.)

The icefield can be dangerous for unprepared visitors. Like all glaciers, the broken surface of the Athabasca is especially hazardous because snow

JASPER

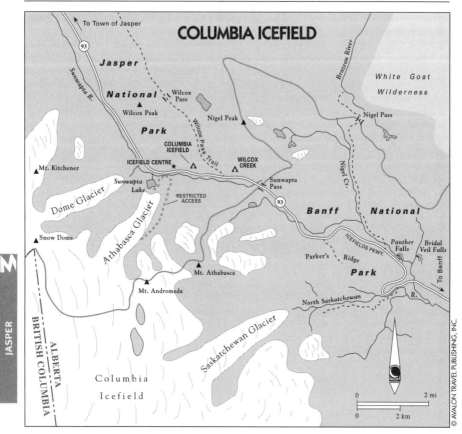

COLUMBIA ICEFIELD

bridges can hide its deep crevasses. The crevasses are uncovered as the winter snows melt. The safest way to experience the glacier firsthand is on specially developed vehicles with balloon tires that can travel over the crevassed surface. These Snocoaches are operated by **Brewster,** 780/852-3332, www.brewster.ca. The 90-minute tour of Athabasca Glacier includes time spent walking on the surface of the glacier. The tour, which begins with a bus ride from the Icefield Centre, costs $28 adults, $14 children, and operates from mid-April to mid October 9 A.M.–5 P.M. (try to plan your tour for after 3 P.M., after the tour buses have departed for the day). The ticketing office is on the main floor of the Icefield Centre (no reservations are taken), with the surrounding

area resembling an airport departure lounge—check the television screens for departure times and ensure you make your way to the correct gate. Early in the season the glacier is still covered in a layer of snow and is therefore not as spectacular as during the summer. If you're in Banff without transportation, consider Brewster's day trip to the Columbia Icefield, which lasts 10 hours and costs $95 per person, excluding Snocoach (eight hours and $85 from Lake Louise).

Icefield Centre

The magnificent Icefield Centre, which opened in summer 1996, is nestled at the base of Mount Wilcox, overlooking the Athabasca Glacier. Costing more than $16 million, the building is as environmentally friendly as possible: lights work on motion sensors to reduce electricity, some water is reused, suppliers must take their packaging with them after deliveries, and the entire building freezes in winter.

The center is the staging point for Snocoach tours, but before heading out onto the icefield, don't miss the **Glacier Gallery** on the lower floor. This large display area details all aspects of the frozen world, including the story of glacier formation and movement. The centerpiece is a scaled-down fiberglass model of the Athabasca Glacier, which is surrounded by hands-on displays and audiovisual presentations.

Back on the main floor of the center you'll find a Parks Canada desk (780/852-6288)—a good source of information for northbound visitors—Snocoach ticketing desk, restrooms, and the obligatory gift shop.

Upstairs you'll find the cavernous **Columbia Café,** with snacks and hot drinks to go on the right and an overpriced cafeteria-style restaurant to the left. Both are open daily 9 A.M.–6 P.M. Across the hallway is the **Glacier Dining Room,** open daily 7–10 A.M. for a breakfast buffet, reopening 6–9:30 P.M. for ordinary Chinese-Canadian fare (mains range $17–30). The only redeeming feature of these dining options has nothing to do with the food—the view from both inside and out on the massive deck is stupendous. (For northbound travelers, my advice is to pick up lunch at Laggan's Mountain Bakery in Lake Louise.)

The Icefield Centre also holds a limited number of hotel rooms. Check-in is on the main level, and details can be found in the Accommodations section of this chapter.

The entire Icefield Centre closes down for the winter in mid-October, reopening the following year in mid-April. During summer, the complex (including display area) is open daily 9 a.m.–11 p.m. with reduced hours outside of July and August.

ICEFIELDS PARKWAY

Sunwapta Pass (2,040 meters/6,690 feet), four km (2.5 miles) south of the Columbia Icefield,

marks the boundary between Banff and Jasper National Parks.

The following sights along the Icefields Parkway are detailed from south to north, from the Icefield Centre to the town of Jasper, a distance of 105 km (65 miles). The scenery along this stretch of road is no less spectacular than the other half through Banff National Park, and it's easy to spend at least a full day en route.

For details of accommodations along this stretch of highway, see Accommodations. No gas is available along this stretch of the Icefields Parkway. The nearest gas stations are at Saskatchewan River Crossing (Banff National Park) and in the town of Jasper, a total distance of 150 km (93 miles), so keep your tank topped up to be safe.

Between the Columbia Icefield and Sunwapta Falls

Sunwapta Lake, at the toe of the Athabasca Glacier, is the source of the **Sunwapta River,** which the Icefields Parkway follows for 48 km (30 miles) to Sunwapta Falls.

Immediately north of Icefield Centre is an unheralded pullout that few travelers stop at, but that allows for an excellent panorama of the area away from the crowds. Across the glacial-green Sunwapta River is a wasteland of till and a distinctive terminal moraine left behind by the retreating **Dome Glacier.** Between the Dome and Athabasca glaciers is 3,459-meter (11,350-foot) **Snow Dome.**

Eight km (five miles) north from the Icefield Centre, the road descends to a viewpoint for **Stutfield Glacier.** Most of the glacier is hidden from view by a densely wooded ridge, but the valley floor below its toe is littered with till left by the glacier's retreat. The main body of the Columbia Icefield can be seen along the clifftop high above, and south of the glacier you can see Mount Kitchener.

Six km (3.7 miles) farther down the road is **Tangle Ridge,** a grayish-brown wall of limestone over which Beauty Creek cascades. At this point the Icefields Parkway runs alongside the Sunwapta River, following its braided course through the **Endless Range,** the eastern wall of a classic glacier-carved valley.

A further 41 km (25 miles) along the road a 500-meter (0.3-mile) spur at Sunwapta Falls Resort leads to **Sunwapta Falls.** Here the Sunwapta River changes direction sharply and drops into a deep canyon. The best viewpoint is from the bridge across the river, but it's also worth following the path on the parking lot side of the river downstream along the rim of the canyon. Two km (1.2 miles) further downstream the river flows into the much-wider Athabasca Valley.

Goat Lookout

After following the Athabasca River for 17 km (11 miles), the road ascends to a lookout with picnic tables offering panoramic riverviews. Below the lookout is a steep bank of exposed glacially ground material containing natural deposits of salt. The local mountain goats spend most of their time on the steep slopes of Mount Kerkeslin, to the northeast, but occasionally cross the road and can be seen searching for the salt licks along the riverbank, trying to replenish lost nutrients.

Athabasca Falls

Nine kilometers (5.6 miles) beyond Goat Lookout and 32 km (20 miles) south of Jasper, the Icefields Parkway divides when an old stretch of highway (Hwy. 93A) crosses the Athabasca River and continues along its west side for 25 km (15.5 miles) before rejoining the Parkway seven km (4.3 miles) south of the town. At the southern end of this loop, the Athabasca River is forced through a narrow gorge and over a cliff into a cauldron of roaring water below. As the river slowly erodes the center of the riverbed, the falls will move upstream. Trails lead from a day-use area to various viewpoints above and below the falls. The trail branching under Highway 93A follows an abandoned river channel before emerging at the bottom of the canyon. Facilities at the Athabasca Falls include picnic tables and toilets.

Continuing North to Jasper

Take Highway 93A beyond Athabasca Falls to reach Mount Edith Cavell, or continue north along the Icefields Parkway to access the following sights. The first worthwhile stop along this route is **Horseshoe Lake,** reached along a 350-meter

Tangle Ridge

© ANDREW HEMPSTEAD

(0.2-mile) trail from a parking lot three km (1.9 miles) north of Athabasca Falls. The southern end of this delightful little body of water is ringed by a band of cliffs (popular with locals in summer as a cliff-diving spot), but many private (unofficial) picnic spots line its western shoreline.

Two km (1.2 miles) north of the Horseshoe Lake parking lot are a couple of lookouts with spectacular views across the Athabasca River to **Athabasca Pass,** used by David Thompson on his historic expedition across the continent. To the north of the pass lies Mount Edith Cavell. From this lookout it is 26 km (16 miles) to the town of Jasper.

MOUNT EDITH CAVELL

This 3,363-meter (11,033-foot) peak is the most distinctive and impressive in the park. Known to Indians as the "White Ghost" for its snowcapped summit, the mountain was given its official name in honor of a British nurse who was executed for helping prisoners of

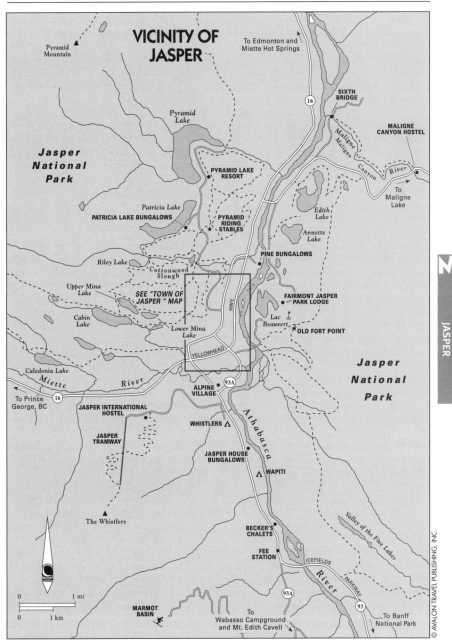

VICINITY OF JASPER

Pyramid
Mountain

To Edmonton and
Miette Hot Springs

SIXTH
BRIDGE

16

MALIGNE
CANYON HOSTEL

Pyramid
Lake

*Jasper
National
Park*

PYRAMID LAKE
RESORT

Maligne

Canyon

River

To
Maligne
Lake

Patricia Lake

PATRICIA LAKE BUNGALOWS

PYRAMID
RIDING
STABLES

*Edith
Lake*

*Annette
Lake*

Riley Lake

PINE BUNGALOWS

*Cottonwood
Slough*

*SEE "TOWN OF
JASPER" MAP*

FAIRMONT JASPER
PARK LODGE

Upper Mina
Lake

HWY

Cabin
Lake

*Lac
Beauvert*

OLD FORT POINT

*Lower Mina
Lake*

*Jasper
National
Park*

YELLOWHEAD

Caledonia Lake

Miette

River

To Prince
George, BC

16

93A

ALPINE
VILLAGE

JASPER INTERNATIONAL
HOSTEL

WHISTLERS

Athabasca

JASPER
TRAMWAY

JASPER HOUSE
BUNGALOWS

WAPITI

The Whistlers

Valley of the Five Lakes

BECKER'S
CHALETS

FEE
STATION

ICEFIELDS

0   1 mi

0   1 km

MARMOT
BASIN

To
Wabasso Campground
and Mt. Edith Cavell

93A

River

93

To Banff
National Park

N

JASPER

PARKWAY

war escape German-occupied Belgium during World War I. The peak was first climbed that same year; today the most popular route to the summit is up the east ridge (to the left of the summit). The imposing north face (facing the parking lot) has been climbed but is rated as an extremely difficult climb.

For those less adventurous, several vantage points, including downtown Jasper and the golf course, provide good views of the peak. But the most impressive place to marvel at the mountain is from directly below the north face. A 14.5-km (nine-mile) road winds up the Astoria River Valley from Highway 93A, ending right below the face. This steep, narrow road has many switchbacks. Trailers must be left in the designated area at the bottom. Highway 93A was the original Icefields Parkway, following the southeast bank of the Athabasca River. The route has now been bypassed by the more direct one on the other side of the river.

From the parking lot at the end of the road, you must strain your neck to take in the magnificent sight of the mountain's 1,500-meter (4,920-foot) north face and **Angel Glacier,** which lies in a saddle on the mountain's lower slopes. On warm days, those who are patient may be lucky enough to witness an avalanche tumbling from the glacier, creating a roar that echoes across the valley. From the parking area, the **Path of the Glacier Trail** (one hour round-trip) traverses barren moraines deposited by the receding Angel Glacier and leads to some great viewpoints. For other hiking opportunities in the vicinity of Mount Edith Cavell, see "Hikes near Mount Edith Cavell."

SIGHTS IN AND AROUND THE TOWN OF JASPER

With all the things to do and see in the park it's amazing how many people hang out in town. July and August are especially busy; much-needed improvements to the parking situation have had little impact on the traffic—try for a parking spot in the lot along the railway line. The best way to avoid the problem is to avoid town during the middle of the day. The Park Information Centre, on Connaught Drive, is the only real reason to

be in town. The shaded park in front of the center is a good place for people-watching, but you may get clobbered by a wayward hacky sack. Connaught Drive, the town's main street, parallels the rail line as it curves through town. In addition to the Park Information Centre, along this road you'll find the bus depot, rail terminal, restaurants, motels, and a parking lot. Behind Connaught Drive is Patricia Street (one-way eastbound), which has more restaurants and services and leads to more hotels and motels on Geikie Street. Behind this main core are rows of neat houses—much less pretentious than those in Banff—and all the facilities of a regular town, including a library, school, post office, museum, swimming pool, and hospital.

Downtown

At the back of town is the excellent **Jasper-Yellowhead Museum and Archives,** 400 Pyramid Lake Rd., 780/852-3013, as unstuffy as any museum could possibly be and well worth a visit even for nonmuseum types. The main gallery features colorful, modern picture boards featuring exhibits that take visitors along a timeline of Jasper's human history through the fur trade, the coming of the railway, and the creation of the park. Documentaries are shown on demand in a small television room. The museum also features extensive archives, including hundreds of historical photos, manuscripts, documents, maps, and videos. Admission is $3.50 adults, $2 children. It's open mid-June to September, daily 10 A.M.–9 P.M., the rest of the year Thur.–Sun. 10 A.M.–5 P.M.

The **Wildlife Museum,** in the darkened bowels of the Whistlers Inn at the corner of Connaught Dr. and Miette Ave., 780/852-3361, is a throwback to a bygone era, when displays of stuffed animals were considered the best way to extol the wonders of nature. "See animals in their natural setting" cries museum advertising, but the shrubbery looks suspiciously like fake Christmas trees and the bull elk seems to be screaming "Get me out of here!" Yep, they even charge you for it—exchange $3 for a token at the Whistlers' reception. It's open year-round, daily 9 A.M.–10 P.M.

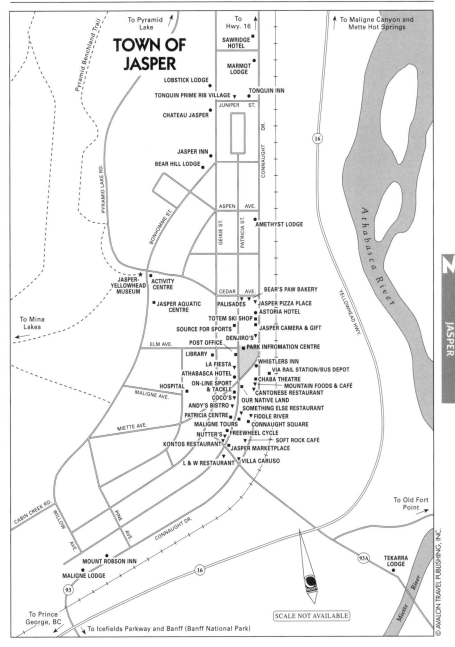

TOWN OF JASPER

To Pyramid Lake

To Hwy. 16

To Maligne Canyon and Mette Hot Springs

Pyramid Benchland Trail

SAWRIDGE HOTEL

MARMOT LODGE

LOBSTICK LODGE

TONQUIN PRIME RIB VILLAGE

TONQUIN INN

JUNIPER ST.

CHATEAU JASPER

CONNAUGHT DR.

JASPER INN

BEAR HILL LODGE

PYRAMID LAKE RD.

BONHOMME ST.

ASPEN AVE.

GEIKIE ST.

PATRICIA ST.

AMETHYST LODGE

16

Athabasca River

To Mina Lakes

JASPER-YELLOWHEAD MUSEUM

ACTIVITY CENTRE

CEDAR AVE.

BEAR'S PAW BAKERY

JASPER AQUATIC CENTRE

PALISADES

JASPER PIZZA PLACE

ASTORIA HOTEL

TOTEM SKI SHOP

SOURCE FOR SPORTS

JASPER CAMERA & GIFT

ELM AVE.

POST OFFICE

DENJIRO'S

PARK INFROMATION CENTRE

LIBRARY

WHISTLERS INN

LA FIESTA

VIA RAIL STATION/BUS DEPOT

ATHABASCA HOTEL

CHABA THEATRE

HOSPITAL

ON-LINE SPORT & TACKLE

MOUNTAIN FOODS & CAFÉ

MALIGNE AVE.

COCO'S

CANTONESE RESTAURANT

OUR NATIVE LAND

ANDY'S BISTRO

SOMETHING ELSE RESTAURANT

PATRICIA CENTRE

FIDDLE RIVER

MIETTE AVE.

MALIGNE TOURS

CONNAUGHT SQUARE

NUTTER'S

FREEWHEEL CYCLE

KONTOS RESTAURANT

SOFT ROCK CAFÉ

JASPER MARKETPLACE

L & W RESTAURANT

VILLA CARUSO

YELLOWHEAD HWY.

JASPER

To Old Fort Point

CABIN CREEK RD.

WILLOW AVE.

PINE AVE.

CONNAUGHT DR.

93A

TEKARRA LODGE

MOUNT ROBSON INN

MALIGNE LODGE

16

93

Miette River

To Prince George, BC

To Icefields Parkway and Banff (Banff National Park)

SCALE NOT AVAILABLE

© AVALON TRAVEL PUBLISHING, INC.

Patricia and Pyramid Lakes

A winding road heads through the hills at the back of town to these two picturesque lakes, formed when glacial moraines dammed shallow valleys. The first, to the left, is Patricia; the second, farther along the road, is Pyramid, backed by **Pyramid Mountain** (2,765 meters/9,072 feet). Both lakes are popular spots for picnicking, fishing, and boating. Boat rentals are available at **Pyramid Lake Boat Rentals,** across the road from the resort of the same name, 780/852-4900. Canoes, rowboats, paddleboats, and kayaks are $25 for the first hour and $15 for each additional hour. The resort also rents motorboats for $35 per hour. From the resort, the road continues around the lake to a bridge, which leads to an island popular with picnickers. The road ends at the quieter end of the lake.

Jasper Tramway

This tramway climbs more than 1,000 vertical meters (3,280 feet) up the steep north face of **The Whistlers,** named for the hoary marmots that live on the summit. The tramway operates two 30-passenger cars that take seven minutes to reach the upper terminal, during which time the conductor gives a lecture about the mountain and its environment. From the upper terminal, a 1.4-km (0.9-mile) trail leads to the 2,470-meter (8,104-foot) true summit. The view is breathtaking; to the south is the Columbia Icefield, and on a clear day you can see Mount Robson (3,954 meters/12,970 feet)—the highest peak in the Canadian Rockies—to the northwest. Free two-hour guided hikes leave the upper terminal for the true summit daily at 10 A.M., 11 A.M., 2 P.M., and 3 P.M. Round-trip fare is $18 adults, $9 children (younger than five free); allow two hours on top and, on a clear summer's day, two more hours in line at the bottom. The tramway is three km (1.9 miles) south of town on Highway 93 (Icefields Parkway) and then a similar distance up Whistlers Road. It operates in

Accommodations are not usually considered sights, but then this is the Rockies, where grand railway hotels attract as many visitors as the more legitimate natural attractions. Jasper Park Lodge has been the premier accommodation in the park since it opened in 1921.

summer daily 8:30 A.M.–10 P.M.; shorter hours Apr.–June and Sept.–Oct.; closed the rest of the year. For more information, call 780/852-3093.

Edith and Annette Lakes

These two lakes along the road to Jasper Park Lodge—across the Athabasca River from town—are perfect for a picnic, swim, or pleasant walk. They are remnants of a much larger lake that once covered the entire valley floor. The lakes are relatively shallow; therefore, the sun warms the water to a bearable temperature for swimming. In fact, they have the warmest waters of any lakes in the park. The 2.5-km (1.6-mile) **Lee Foundation Trail** encircles Lake Annette and is wheelchair accessible. Both lakes have day-use areas with beaches and picnic areas.

Jasper Park Lodge

Accommodations are not usually considered sights, but then this is the Rockies, where grand railway hotels attract as many visitors as the more legitimate natural attractions. Jasper Park Lodge has been the premier accommodation in the park since it opened in 1921. Back then it was a single-story structure, reputed to be the largest log building in the world. It burned to the ground in 1952 but was rebuilt. Additional bungalows were erected along Lac Beauvert, forming a basis for today's lodge. Rows of cabins radiate from the main lodge, which contains restaurants, lounges, and the town's only covered shopping arcade. Today up to 900 guests can be accommodated in 446 rooms. A large parking area for nonguests is located on Lodge Road, behind the golf clubhouse; you're welcome to walk around the resort, play golf, dine in the restaurants, and of course, browse through the shopping promenade—even if you're not a registered guest. On the lakeshore in front of the lodge is a boat rental concession; canoes and kayaks can be rented for $18 per 30 minutes.

From the main lodge, a hiking trail follows the shoreline of Lac Beauvert through the golf course, linking up with other trails at Old Fort Point. To walk from town will take one hour.

MALIGNE LAKE AND VICINITY

Maligne Lake, one of the world's most photographed lakes, lies 48 km (30 miles) southeast of Jasper. It's the source of the **Maligne River,** which flows northward to Medicine Lake and then disappears underground, eventually emerging downstream of Maligne Canyon. The river was known to the natives as *Chaba Imne* (River of the Great Beaver), but the name by which we know it today was coined by a missionary. After his horses were swept away by its swift-flowing waters in 1846, he described the river as being "la traverse maligne." Driving up the Maligne River Valley to the lake is a 600-million-year-old lesson in geology that can be appreciated by anyone.

Maligne Canyon

As the Maligne River drops into the Athabasca River Valley, its gradient is particularly steep. The fast-flowing water has eroded a deep canyon out of the easily dissolved limestone bedrock. The canyon is up to 50 meters (165 feet) deep, yet so narrow that squirrels often jump across. At the top of the canyon, opposite the teahouse, you'll see large potholes in the riverbed. These potholes are created when rocks and pebbles become trapped in what begins as a shallow depression; under the force of the rushing water, they carve jug-shaped hollows into the soft bedrock.

An interpretive trail winds down from the parking lot, crossing the canyon six times. The most spectacular sections of the canyon can be seen from the first two bridges, at the upper end of the trail. In summer a teahouse operates at the top of the canyon. To avoid the crowds at the upper end of the canyon, an alternative would be to park at Sixth Bridge, near the confluence of the Maligne and Athabasca Rivers, and walk *up* the canyon (see "Hiking in the Maligne Lake Area"). The **Maligne Lake Shuttle** stops at the canyon eight times daily along its run between 627 Patricia Street in downtown Jasper and Maligne Lake. For reservations, call 780/852-3370; fare is $9 one-way from town. In winter, guided tours of the frozen canyon are an experience you'll never forget (see "Wintertime").

Oft-photographed Spirit Island is the turn-around point for tour boats on Maligne Lake.

© ANDREW HEMPSTEAD

JASPER

Medicine Lake

From the canyon, Maligne Lake Road climbs to Medicine Lake, which does a disappearing act each year. The water level fluctuates due to a network of underground passages that emerge downstream in Maligne Canyon. At the northwest end of the lake, beyond where the outlet should be, the riverbed is often dry. In fall, when runoff from the mountains is minimal, the water level drops and, by November, the lake comprises a few shallow pools. Natives believed that spirits were responsible for the phenomenon, hence the name.

Maligne Lake

At the end of the road, 48 km (30 miles) from town, is Maligne Lake, the largest glacier-fed lake in the Canadian Rockies and second largest in the world. The first paying visitors were brought to the lake in 1929, and it has been a mecca for camera-toting tourists from around the world ever since. Once at the lake, activities are plentiful. But other than taking in the spectacular vistas, the only thing you won't need your wallet for is hiking one of the numerous trails in the area.

The most popular tourist activity at the lake is a 90-minute narrated cruise on a glass-enclosed boat up the lake to oft-photographed **Spirit Island.** Cruises leave in summer, every hour on the hour 10 A.M.–5 P.M., with fewer sailings in May and September; $32 adults, $15.50 children. Many time slots are booked in blocks by tour companies; therefore, reservations are suggested. Rowboats and canoes can be rented at the Boat House, a provincial historic site dating to 1929, for $15 per hour or $60 per day. Double sea kayaks go for $20 per hour and $85 per day. The lake also has excellent trout fishing (Alberta's record rainbow trout was caught here), horseback riding, and white-water rafting on the Maligne River. (For details, see "Other Recreation.")

All commercial operations to and around the lake are operated by **Maligne Tours,** based in downtown Jasper at 627 Patricia St., 780/852-3370, www.malignelake.com. At the lake itself, in addition to the cruises and boat rentals, Maligne Tours operates a souvenir shop and large café with a huge area of tiered outdoor seating overlooking the lake.

The **Maligne Lake Shuttle** runs from the Maligne Tours office at 627 Patricia St., 780/852-3370, and from various hotels out to the lake eight times daily through summer (four times daily in spring and fall). The first shuttle leaves for the lake each morning at 8:30 A.M.

CONTINUING EAST ALONG HIGHWAY 16

From Jasper, it's 50 km (31 miles) to the park's eastern boundary along Highway 16, following the Athabasca River the entire way. Beyond the turn-off to Maligne Lake, Highway 16 enters a wide valley flanked to the west by The Palisade and to the east by the Colin Range. The valley is a classic montane environment, with open meadows and forests of Douglas fir and lodgepole pine. After crossing the Athabasca River, 20 km (12 miles) from Jasper, the highway parallels **Jasper Lake,** left as the last Ice Age ended. Along the lake are several viewpoints and picnic areas. At the lake's northern outlet, a plaque marks the site of **Jasper House** (the actual site is across the river from the highway). The next worthwhile spot is **Disaster Point,** four km (2.5 miles) farther north. This is a great spot for viewing bighorn sheep, which gather at a mineral lick, an area of exposed mineral salts. Disaster Point is on the lower slopes of Roche Miette, a distinctive 2,316-meter-high (7,600-foot-high) peak that juts out into the Athabasca River Valley. Across the highway the braided Athabasca River is flanked by wetlands alive with migrating birds spring and fall.

Miette Hot Springs Road branches south from the highway 43 km (27 miles) east of Jasper. This junction marks the site of **Pocahontas,** a coal mining town in existence between 1910 and 1921. The mine itself was high above the township, with coal transported to the valley floor by cable car. All buildings have long since been removed, but a short interpretive walk leads through the remaining foundations. One km (0.6 miles) along Miette Hot Springs Road, a short trail leads to photogenic **Punchbowl Falls.** Here Mountain Creek cascades through a narrow crevice in a cliff to a pool of turbulent water.

Miette Hot Springs

After curving, swerving, rising, and falling many times, Miette Hot Springs Road ends 18 km (11 miles) from Highway 16 at the warmest springs in the Canadian Rockies. In the early 1900s, these springs were one of the park's biggest attractions. In 1910, a packhorse trail was built up the valley and the government constructed a bathhouse. The original hand-hewn log structure was replaced in the 1930s with pools that remained in use until new facilities were built in 1985. Water that flows into the pools is artificially cooled from 54°C (128°F) to a soothing 39°C (100°F). A newer addition to the complex is a cool plunge pool. Admission is $6 for a single swim or $8.25 for the day (discounted for seniors to $5 and $7.25, respectively). It's open mid-May to mid-October, 10:30 A.M.–9 P.M., with extended hours of 8:30 A.M.–10:30 P.M. in summer. For more information, call 780/866-3939.

Many hiking trails begin from the hot springs complex; the shortest is from the picnic area to the source of the springs (allow five minutes each way). The springs is also home to a café, while adjacent are a restaurant and lodging.

Hiking

The 1,200 km (745 miles) of hiking trails in Jasper are significantly different from those in the other mountain national parks. The park has an extensive system of interconnecting backcountry trails that, for experienced hikers, can provide a wilderness adventure rivaled by few areas on the face of the earth. For casual day-hikers, on the other hand, opportunities are more limited. Most trails in the immediate vicinity of the town have little elevation gain and lead through montane forest to lakes. The trails around Maligne Lake, at the base of Mount Edith Cavell, and along the Icefields Parkway have more rewarding objectives and are more challenging.

The most popular trails for extended backcountry trips are the **Skyline Trail,** between Maligne Lake Road and Maligne Lake (44.5 km/27.6 miles, three days each way); the trails to **Amethyst Lakes** in the Tonquin Valley (19 km/11.8 miles, one day each way) and **Athabasca Pass** (50 km/31 miles, three days each way), which was used by fur traders for 40 years as the main route across the Canadian Rockies; and the **South Boundary Trail,** which traverses a remote section of the front ranges into Banff National Park (160 km/100 miles, 10 days each way).

Before setting off on any hikes, whatever the length, go to the **Park Information Centre** in downtown Jasper or the Parks Canada desk in the Icefield Centre along the Icefields Parkway for trail maps, trail conditions, and trail closures. To prevent overuse on trails that require an overnight stay in the backcountry, you *must* pick up a Wilderness Pass before heading out; $6 per person per night.

HIKES AROUND THE TOWN OF JASPER

Pyramid Benchland

- Length: 7 km/4.3 miles (five hours) round-trip
- Elevation gain: 120 meters/400 feet
- Rating: easy
- Trailhead: Jasper-Yellowhead Museum, Pyramid Lake Road

Numerous official and unofficial hiking trails weave across the benchland immediately west of the town of Jasper. From the far corner of the parking lot beside the museum, a well-marked trail climbs onto the benchland. Keep right, crossing Pyramid Lake Road, and you'll emerge on a bluff overlooking the Athabasca River Valley. Bighorn sheep can often be seen grazing here. If you return to the trailhead from here, you will have hiked seven km (4.3 miles). The trail continues north, disappearing into the montane forest until arriving at Pyramid Lake. Various trails can be taken to return to town; get a map at the Park Information Centre before setting out.

JASPER

Mina Lakes

- Length: 2.5 km/1.5 miles (50 minutes) one-way
- Elevation gain: 70 meters/230 feet
- Rating: easy
- Trailhead: Jasper-Yellowhead Museum, Pyramid Lake Road

Lower and Upper Mina Lakes lie on the benchland described previously. The trailhead is the same as the Pyramid Lake Loop, except instead of keeping right, you'll need to take the first left fork (signposted as Route 8 to Cabin Creek West), which climbs up onto the bench, then crosses a treeless 100-meter-wide (328-foot-wide) corridor, cleared to act as a firebreak for the town. Cabin Lake Road passes along the firebreak, leading west (left) to manmade Cabin Lake and east (right) to Pyramid Lake Road. Continuing straight ahead, the trail climbs gradually through a typical montane forest of lodgepole pine, Douglas fir, and poplar before emerging at Lower Mina Lake. After a further 500 meters (0.3 miles) and just beyond the end of Lower Mina Lake, the upper lake and a pebbly stretch of beach are reached. The distance given above is to this point, but with a map in hand, it's possible to continue along the shore of the upper lake; two km (1.2 miles) beyond the end of the lake the trail forks—looping back along Cabin Lake Road via Cabin Lake to the left and to Riley Lake to the right.

Patricia Lake Circle

- Length: 5-km/3.1-mile loop (90 minutes round-trip)
- Elevation gain: minimal
- Rating: easy
- Trailhead: two km (1.2 miles) along Pyramid Lake Road

This trail begins across the road from the riding stables on Pyramid Lake Road. It traverses a mixed forest of aspen and lodgepole pine—prime habitat for a variety of larger mammals such as elk, deer, and moose. The second half of the trail skirts Cottonwood Slough, where you'll see several beaver ponds. Unlike the name suggests, this trail doesn't encircle Patricia Lake, but instead just passes along a portion of its southern shoreline.

The Palisade

- Length: 11 km/6.8 miles (four hours) one-way
- Elevation gain: 850 meters/2,790 feet
- Rating: difficult
- Trailhead: the end of Pyramid Lake Road, eight km (five miles) from town

The destination of this strenuous hike is the site of an old fire lookout tower atop a high ridge between the Athabasca River Valley and Pyramid Mountain. From the locked gate at the end of Pyramid Lake Road, the trail crosses Pyramid Creek after one km (0.6 miles) then climbs steadily for the entire distance along a forest-enclosed fire road (take the right fork at the 7.5-km/4.7-mile mark). Once at the end of the trail, it's easy to see why this site was chosen for the lookout; the panorama extends down the valley and across Jasper Lake to Roche Miette (2,316 meters/7,600 feet).

Old Fort Point

- Length: 6.5 km/4 miles loop (two hours round-trip)
- Elevation gain: 60 meters/200 feet
- Rating: easy
- Trailhead: take Hwy. 93A south from downtown, follow the first left after crossing Hwy. 16, and park beside the Athabasca River.

Old Fort Point is a distinctive knoll above the Athabasca River, to the east of town. Although it is not likely that a fort was ever located here, the first fur-trading post in the Rockies, Henry House, was located just downstream. It's easy to imagine fur traders and early explorers climbing to this summit for 360-degree views of the Athabasca and Miette Rivers. From the parking lot beyond the single-lane vehicle bridge over the Athabasca River, climb the wooden stairs, take the left trail to the top of the knoll, and then continue back to the parking lot along the north flank of the hill.

The Whistlers

- Length: 8 km/5 miles (three hours) one-way
- Elevation gain: 1,220 meters/4,000 feet
- Rating: difficult

• Trailhead: three km (1.9 miles) along Whistlers Road from Hwy. 93

This steep ascent, the park's most arduous day hike, is unique in that it passes through three distinct vegetation zones in a relatively short distance. (For the less adventurous, Jasper Tramway traverses the same route described here; see "Jasper Tramway" under "Sights in and around the Town of Jasper.") From the trailhead on Whistlers Road, immediately below the hostel, the trail begins climbing and doesn't let up until you merge with the crowds getting off the tramway at the top. The trail begins in a montane forest of aspen and white birch, climbs through a subalpine forest of Engelmann spruce and alpine fir, then emerges onto the open, treeless tundra, which is inhabited by pikas, hoary marmots, and a few hardy plants. Carry water with you because none is available before the upper tramway terminal. If you've taken the tramway, free guided hikes are offered around the summit area.

HIKING IN THE MALIGNE LAKE AREA

Maligne Lake, 48 km (30 miles) from the town of Jasper, provides more easy hiking with many opportunities to view the lake and explore its environs. To get there, take Highway 16 east for four km (2.5 miles) from town and turn south on Maligne Lake Road. The first three hikes detailed are along the access road to the lake; the others leave from various parking lots at the northwest end of the lake.

Maligne Tours, 627 Patricia St., 780/852-3370, organizes hikes led by knowledgeable guides along the Lake Trail (one hour; $10 per person) and into the Bald and Opal Hills (four hours; $40 per person). This same company provides transportation to the lake. The **Maligne Lake Shuttle** runs from downtown and some hotels out to the lake four to six times daily; $14 one-way.

Maligne Canyon
• Length: 3.7 km/2.3 miles (90 minutes) one-way
• Elevation gain: 125 meters/410 feet

• Rating: moderate
• Trailhead: turn off to Sixth Bridge 2.5 km (1.6 miles) along Maligne Lake Rd. from Hwy. 16

Maligne Canyon is one of the busiest places in the park, yet few visitors hike the entire length of the canyon trail. By beginning from the lower end of the canyon, at the confluence of the Maligne and Athabasca Rivers, you'll avoid starting your hike alongside the masses and you'll get to hike downhill on your return (when you're tired). To access the lower end of the canyon, follow the one-km (0.6-mile) spur off Maligne Lake Road to Sixth Bridge. Crowds will be minimal for the first three km (1.9 miles) to Fourth Bridge, where the trail starts climbing. By the time you get to Third Bridge, you start encountering adventurous hikers coming down the canyon, and soon thereafter you'll meet the real crowds—high heels, bear-bells, and all. Upstream of here the canyon is deepest and most spectacular. (See "Maligne Canyon" under "Maligne Lake and Vicinity" for details of the walk starting from the *top* of the canyon.)

Watchtower Basin
• Length: 10 km/6.2 miles (3.5 hours) one-way
• Elevation gain: 630 meters/2,070 feet
• Rating: moderate/difficult
• Trailhead: Maligne Lake Road, 24 km (15 miles) from Hwy. 16

Watchtower is a wide, open basin high above the crowds of Maligne Lake Road. All the elevation gain is made during the first six km (3.7 miles) from Maligne Lake Road, through a dense forest of lodgepole pine and white spruce. As the trail levels off and enters the basin, it continues to follow the west bank of a stream, crossing it at km 10 (mile 6.2) and officially ending at a campground. To the west and south the **Maligne Range** rises to a crest three km (1.9 miles) beyond the campground. From the top of this ridge, at the intersection with the Skyline Trail, it is 17.5 km (11 miles) northwest to Maligne Canyon, or 27 km (17 miles) southeast to Maligne Lake. By camping at Watchtower Campground, day trips can be made to a small lake in

MARY SCHÄFFER

In the early 1900s, exploration of mountain wilderness areas was considered a man's pursuit; however, one spirited and tenacious woman entered that domain and went on to explore areas of the Canadian Rockies that no white man ever had.

Mary Sharples was born in 1861 in Pennsylvania and raised in a strict Quaker family. She was introduced to Dr. Charles Schäffer on a trip to the Rockies, and in 1889 they were married. His interest in botany drew them back to the Rockies, where Charles collected, documented, and photographed specimens until his death in 1903. Mary also became apt at these skills. After hearing Sir James Hector (the geologist on the Palliser Expedition) reciting tales of the mountains, her

zest to explore the wilderness returned. In 1908, Mary, guide Billy Warren, and a small party set out for a lake that no white man had ever seen but that the Stoney Indians knew as *Chaba Imne* (Beaver Lake). After initial difficulties, they succeeded in finding the elusive body of water now known as Maligne Lake. In Mary's words, "There burst upon us . . . the finest view any of us have ever beheld in the Rockies." In 1915 Mary married Billy Warren, continuing to explore the mountains until her death in 1939. Her success as a photographer, artist, and writer were equal to any of her male counterparts, but she is best remembered for her unwavering love of the Canadian Rockies—her "heaven of the hills."

the basin or to highlights of the Skyline Trail such as the Snowbowl, Curator Lake, and Shovel Pass.

Jacques Lake

- Length: 12 km/7.5 miles (3–3.5 hours) one-way
- Elevation gain: 100 meters/330 feet
- Rating: moderate
- Trailhead: Beaver Lake Picnic Area, 28 km (17.4 miles) from Hwy. 16 along Maligne Lake Road

The appeal of this trail, which begins from the southeast end of Medicine Lake, is its lack of elevation gain and the numerous small lakes it skirts as it travels through a narrow valley. On either side, the severely faulted mountains of the Queen Elizabeth Ranges rise steeply above the valley floor, their strata tilted nearly vertical.

Lake Trail (Mary Schäffer Loop)

- Length: 3.2-km/2-mile loop (one hour round-trip)
- Elevation gain: minimal
- Rating: easy
- Trailhead: Boat House, Maligne Lake

This easy, pleasant walk begins from beside the Boat House, following the eastern shore of Maligne Lake through an open area of lakeside pic-

nic tables to a point known as **Schäffer Viewpoint,** named for the first white person to see the valley. Across the lake are the aptly named Bald Hills, the Maligne Range, and to the southwest, the distinctive twin peaks of Mount Unwin (3,268 meters/10,720 feet) and Mount Charlton (3,217 meters/10,550 feet). After dragging yourself away from the spectacular panorama, continue along a shallow bay before following the trail into a forest of spruce and subalpine fir, then looping back to the middle parking lot.

Opal Hills

- Length: 8.2-km/5.1-mile loop (three hours round-trip)
- Elevation gain: 455 meters/1,500 feet
- Rating: moderate
- Trailhead: north corner, upper parking lot, Maligne Lake

This trail begins from behind the information board in the corner of the parking lot, climbing steeply for 1.5 km (0.9 miles) to a point where it divides. Both options end in the high alpine meadows of the Opal Hills; the trail to the right is shorter and steeper. Once in the meadow, the entire Maligne Valley can be seen below.

Bald Hills

- Length: 5.2 km/3.2 miles (two hours) one-way
- Elevation gain: 495 meters/1,620 feet

- Rating: moderate
- Trailhead: picnic area at the end of Maligne Lake Road

This trail follows an old fire road for its entire distance, entering an open meadow near the end. This was once the site of a fire lookout. The 360-degree view takes in the jade-green waters of Maligne Lake, the Queen Elizabeth Ranges, and the twin peaks of Mount Unwin and Mount Charlton. The Bald Hills extend for seven km (4.3 miles), their highest summit not exceeding 2,600 meters (8,530 feet). A herd of caribou summers in the hills.

Moose Lake
- Length: 1.4 km/0.9 miles (30 minutes) one-way
- Elevation gain: minimal
- Rating: easy
- Trailhead: picnic area at the end of Maligne Lake Road

This trail begins 200 meters (0.1 miles) along the Bald Hills trail, spurring left along the Maligne Pass Trail (signposted). One km (0.6 miles) along this trail, a rough track branches left, leading to Moose Lake—a quiet body of water where moose are sometimes seen. To return, continue along the trail as it descends to the shore of Maligne Lake, a short stroll from the picnic area.

HIKES NEAR MOUNT EDITH CAVELL

Cavell Road begins from Highway 93A at 13 km (eight miles) south from the town of Jasper and winds through a subalpine forest, ascending 300 meters (980 feet) in 14.5 km (nine miles). Trailheads are located at the end of the road (Cavell Meadows Trail and a short interpretive trail) and across from the hostel two km (1.2 miles) from the end (Astoria River Trail). A third trailhead is on Marmot Basin Road where it crosses Portal Creek (Maccarib Pass Trail).

Cavell Meadows
- Length: 4 km/2.5 miles (1.5 hours) one-way
- Elevation gain: 380 meters/1,250 feet
- Rating: moderate

Jasper's backcountry holds a healthy population of grizzlies, but they are rarely encountered by hikers.

- Trailhead: parking lot at the end of Cavell Road, 27.5 km (17 miles) south of town

This trail, beginning from the parking lot beneath Mount Edith Cavell, provides access to an alpine meadow and panoramic views of Angel Glacier. The trail begins by following the paved Path of the Glacier Loop, then branches left, climbing steadily through a subalpine forest of Engelmann spruce and then stunted subalpine fir to emerge facing the northeast face of Mount Edith Cavell and Angel Glacier. The view of the glacier from this point is nothing less than awesome, as the ice spills out of a cirque, clinging to a 300-meter-high (984-foot-high) cliff face. The trail continues to higher viewpoints and an alpine meadow that, by mid-July, is filled with wildflowers.

Astoria River

- Length: 19 km/11.8 miles (6–7 hours) one-way
- Elevation gain: 450 meters/1,480 feet
- Rating: moderate
- Trailhead: opposite the hostel on Cavell Road

From Cavell Road, this trail descends through a forest on the north side of Mount Edith Cavell for five km (3.1 miles), then crosses the Astoria River and begins a long ascent into spectacular Tonquin Valley. Amethyst Lakes and the 1,000-meter (3,280-foot) cliffs of the Ramparts first come into view after 13 km (eight miles). At the 17-km (10.5-mile) mark the trail divides. To the left it climbs into Eremite Valley where there is a campground. The right fork continues, following Astoria River to Tonquin Valley, Amethyst Lakes, and a choice of four campgrounds.

Maccarib Pass

- Length: 21 km/13 miles (7–8 hours) one-way
- Elevation gain: 730 meters/2,400 feet
- Rating: moderate/difficult
- Trailhead: 6.5 km (four miles) up Marmot Basin Road

This trail is slightly longer and gains more elevation than the trail along Astoria River but is more spectacular. It strikes out to the southwest, following Portal Creek for a short distance, then passes under Peveril Peak before making a steep approach to Maccarib Pass, 12.5 km (7.8 miles) from the trailhead. The full panorama of the Tonquin Valley can be appreciated as the path gradually descends from the pass. At Amethyst Lakes it links up with the Astoria River Trail, and many options for day hikes head out from campgrounds at the lakes.

HIKES ALONG ICEFIELDS PARKWAY

Valley of the Five Lakes

- Length: 2.3 km/1.4 miles (40 minutes) one-way
- Elevation gain: 60 meters/200 feet
- Rating: easy
- Trailhead: Icefields Parkway, 10 km (6.2 miles) south of the town of Jasper

These lakes, nestled in an open valley, are small but make a worthwhile destination. From the trailhead, 10 km (6.2 miles) south of town along the Icefields Parkway, the trail passes through a forest of lodgepole pine, crosses a stream, and climbs a ridge from where you'll have a panoramic view of surrounding peaks. As the trail descends to the lakes, turn left at the first intersection to a point between two of the lakes. These lakes are linked to Old Fort Point by a tedious 10-km (6.2-mile) trail through montane forest.

Geraldine Lakes

- Length: 5 km/3.1 miles (two hours) one-way
- Elevation gain: 410 meters/1,350 feet
- Rating: moderate
- Trailhead: Geraldine Fire Road, off Hwy. 93A one km (0.6 miles) from Athabasca Falls

The first of the four Geraldine Lakes is an easy two-km (1.2-mile) hike from the end of the 5.5-km (3.4-mile) Geraldine Fire Road. The forest-encircled lake reflects the north face of Mount Fryatt (3,361 meters/11,030 feet). The trail continues along the northwest shore, climbs steeply past a scenic 100-meter-high (330-foot-high) waterfall, and traverses some rough terrain where the trail becomes indistinct; follow the cairns. At the end of the valley is another waterfall. The trail climbs east of the waterfall to a ridge above the second of the lakes, five km (3.1 miles) from the trailhead. Although the trail officially ends here, it does continue to a campground at the south end of the lake. Two other lakes, accessible only by bush bashing, are located farther up the valley.

Fortress Lake

- Length: 24 km/15 miles (7–8 hours) one-way
- Elevation gain: minimal
- Rating: moderate
- Trailhead: Sunwapta Falls, 58 km (36 miles) south of the town of Jasper

The trail to this seldom-visited lake straddling the Continental Divide gains little elevation, making it popular with mountain-bike riders experienced in backcountry travel. After crossing the canyon below Sunwapta Falls, the trail meanders along the east bank of the Athabasca River for 15 km (9.3 miles), then crosses it. Beyond the main bridge you'll need to ford the braided Chaba River, then continue southwest along the river flats for six km (3.7 miles) to the east end of Fortress Lake. The lake lies within British Columbia in **Hamber Provincial Park.** Its shores are difficult to traverse because they lack established trails. At the end of the trail, Fortress Lake Wilderness Retreat, 250/344-2639, www.fortress-lake.com, provides cabin accommodation, most-ly for anglers who fly in by helicopter from Golden, but hikers are also welcomed.

Wilcox Pass

- Length: 4 km/2.5 miles (90 minutes) one-way
- Elevation gain: 340 meters/1,115 feet
- Rating: moderate
- Trailhead: Wilcox Creek Campground, three km (1.9 miles) south of the Icefield Centre

Views of the Columbia Icefield from the Icefields Parkway pale in comparison with those achieved along this trail on the same side of the valley as the Columbia Icefield Centre. This trail was once used by northbound outfitters because, 100 years ago, Athabasca Glacier covered the valley floor and had to be bypassed. Beginning from the north side of Wilcox Creek Campground, the trail climbs through a stunted forest of Engelmann spruce and subalpine fir to a ridge with panoramic views of the valley, Columbia Icefield, and surrounding peaks. Ascending gradually from there, the trail enters a fragile environment of alpine meadows. From the pass, most hikers return along the same trail (the distance quoted), although it is possible to continue north, descending to the Icefields Parkway at Tangle Ridge, 11.5 km (7.1 miles) along the road from the trailhead.

Other Recreation

FAIR WEATHER

Several booking agents represent the many recreation-tour operators in Jasper. **Jasper Adventure Centre,** in the lobby of the Chaba Theatre at 604 Connaught Dr., 780/852-5595, takes bookings for all of the following activities, as well as for accommodations and for transportation to various points in the park and beyond. **Maligne Tours,** 627 Patricia St., 780/852-3370, operates all activities in the Maligne Lake area, including the famous lake cruise.

Mountain Biking

Bicycling in the park continues to grow in popularity: the ride between Banff and Jasper, along the Icefields Parkway, attracts riders from around the world. In addition to the paved roads, many designated unpaved bicycle trails radiate from the town. One of the most popular is the Athabasca River Trail, which begins at Old Fort Point and follows the river to a point below Maligne Canyon. Cyclists are particularly prone to sudden bear encounters; make noises when passing through heavily wooded areas. The brochure

Mountain Biking Trail Guide lists designated trails and is available from the information center and all local sport shops. Rental outlets include **On-line Sport & Tackle,** 600 Patricia St., 780/852-3630; **Source for Sports,** 406 Patricia St., 780/852-3654; **Freewheel Cycle,** 618 Patricia St., 780/852-3898; **Vicious Cycle,** 630 Connaught Dr., 780/852-1111; and the **Activity Centre** at Jasper Park Lodge, 780/852-5708. Expect to pay $5–8 per hour or $22–35 for any 24-hour period. Freewheel Cycle leads a five-hour bike tour along Maligne Lake Road, but most of the hard work is done for you, as transportation is provided to the lake, allowing a two-hour downhill run on the bikes; $95 per person.

Horseback Riding

On the benchlands immediately behind the town of Jasper is **Pyramid Riding Stables,** Pyramid Lake Road, 780/852-7433. The stables offer one-, two-, and three-hour guided rides for $28, $48, and $70, respectively. The one-hour trip follows a ridge high above town, providing excellent views of the Athabasca River Valley. **Skyline Trail Rides,** at the Jasper Park Lodge, 780/852-4215, offers a one-hour guided ride around Lake Annette ($25 per person) and a 4.5-hour ride to Maligne Canyon ($70 per person).

Overnight pack trips consist of 4–6 hours of riding per day, with a few nights spent at a remote mountain lodge where you can hike, boat, fish, or ride. Rates start at $150 per person per day. For details, contact **Skyline Trail Rides,** 780/852-4215 or 888/852-7787, www.skylinetrail.com; or **Tonquin Valley Adventures,** 780/852-1188, www.tonquinadventures.com.

White-Water Rafting

The Athabasca, Maligne, and Sunwapta Rivers are run by a half-dozen outfitters. On the Athabasca River, the Mile 5 Run is an easy two-hour float that appeals to all ages. Farther upstream, some operators offer a trip that begins from below Athabasca Falls, on a stretch of the river that passes through a narrow canyon; this run takes three hours. The boulder-strewn rapids of the Sunwapta and Maligne rivers offer more thrills and spills—these trips are for the more adventurous and last around three hours. Most companies offer a choice of rivers and provide transportation to and from downtown hotels. Expect to pay $40–55 for trips on the Athabasca and $55 for the Sunwapta and Maligne. The following companies run at least two of three rivers: **Maligne Rafting Adventures,** 780/852-3370; **Raven Adventures,** 780/852-4292; **Rocky Mountain River Guides,** 780/852-3777; and **White Water Rafting,** 780/852-7238 or 800/557-7238. **Jasper Raft Tours,** 780/852-2665, floats a 16-km (10-mile) stretch of the Athabasca River in large, stable inflatable rafts; $46 adults, $16 children.

Fishing

Fishing in the many alpine lakes—for rainbow, brook, Dolly Varden, cutthroat, and lake trout, as well as pike and whitefish—is excellent. Many outfitters offer guided fishing trips. Whether you fish with a guide or by yourself, you'll need a national park fishing license ($6 per week, $13 per year), available from the Park Information Centre or On-line Sport & Tackle at 600 Patricia Street. Maligne Lake is the most popular fishing hole; in 1980, a 10-kg (22-pound) rainbow trout was caught in its deep waters, setting an Albertan provincial record.

Stable 5.5-meter (18-foot) Freighter canoes with a small electric motor are the preferred fishing boat on Maligne Lake. They are available at the lakeside **Boat House,** 780/852-3370, for $90 per day, with rod and reel rentals extra. Guided fishing trips on the lake are offered from the Boat House by **Maligne Tours,** 780/852-3370; half-day $125 per person for two people, full-day $170 per person for two. The Boat House is open through summer, daily 8:30 A.M.–6:30 P.M.

Currie's Guiding, 780/852-5650, offers trips to Maligne Lake (full-day $190 per person) and to lakes requiring a 30- to 60-minute hike to access (from $150 per person for a half-day). These rates include equipment and instruction. **Source for Sports,** 406 Patricia St., 780/852-3654, and **On-line Sport & Tackle,** 600 Patricia St., 780/852-3630, sell and rent fishing tackle and also have canoe and boat rentals.

FLOAT BACK IN TIME

If white-water rafting sounds a little too adventurous for your liking, consider an easy float down the Athabasca River in a historic 10-meter (33-foot) **voyageur canoe.** These large, stable craft were developed more than 200 years ago specifically for travel along Canadian waterways. In those days, when the rivers and lakes were used as highways, voyageur canoes were the vessel of choice for everyone from fur traders to noted explorers such as David Thompson and Alexander Mackenzie.

The voyageur canoes used by Jasper's **Rocky Mountain Voyageur** company, 780/852-3343, www.jaspercanoes.com, are an exact replica in size and shape of the original design, but instead of birchbark, fiberglass and Kevlar are used in their construction, and they are sectional, allowing for easy transportation. Costumed guides—complete with plaid shirts and sashes—point out prominent natural features and relate historic tales as these canoes and up to 12 passengers float gently down the Athabasca River for about one hour from Old Fort Point. No rapids are encountered, and unless it's raining, you won't get wet. The cost is $45 adults, $26 children, which includes round-trip transfers from downtown Jasper. Departure times are daily at 9 A.M. and 2 P.M.

© ANDREW HEMPSTEAD

Golfing

The world-famous **Jasper Park Lodge Golf Course** was designed by renowned golf-course architect Stanley Thompson. The course opened in 1925, after 200 men had spent an entire year clearing trees and laying out the holes to Thompson's design. Renovations were made in 1994, but the course plays as it did when it first opened. It is consistently ranked as one of the top 10 courses in Canada. The 18-hole, 6,670-yard course takes in the contours of the Athabasca River Valley as it hugs the banks of turquoise-colored Lac Beauvert. It is a true test of accuracy, and with holes named The Maze, The Bad Baby, and The Bay, you'll need lots of balls. Greens fees for 18 holes vary with the season: $125 mid-June to Sept, less than $100 mid-May to mid-June, and less than $80 in early May and from October 1 through closing (usually mid-October). An electric cart is $32 per round. Golfing after 5 P.M. is $79 with a cart—a great deal during the long days of June and July. Other facilities include a driving range, club rentals ($28–42), a restaurant, and a lounge. Tee times can be reserved by calling 780/852-6090.

Indoor Recreation

The **Jasper Aquatic Centre,** 401 Pyramid Lake Road, 780/852-3663, has an Olympic-size swimming pool; admission $4.75. The **Jasper Activity Centre,** next door, 780/852-3381, has squash courts, indoor and outdoor tennis courts, a climbing wall, a weight room, and an indoor skate park; admission $6.

WINTERTIME

Winter is certainly a quiet time in the park, but that doesn't mean there's a lack of things to do. Marmot Basin offers world-class alpine skiing;

many snow-covered hiking trails are groomed for cross-country skiing; portions of Lac Beauvert and Pyramid Lake are cleared for ice-skating; horse-drawn sleighs travel around town; and Maligne Canyon is transformed into a magical, frozen world. Hotels reduce rates by 40–70 percent through winter, and many offer lodging and lift tickets for less than $70 per person.

Marmot Basin

The skiing at Marmot Basin is highly underrated. A huge injection of cash in recent years has meant even better facilities are offered, and new lifts have opened up additional terrain. Lifts now take skiers and boarders into Charlie's Basin, a massive powder-filled bowl, and to the summit of Eagle Ridge, which accesses open bowls and lightly treed glades of two other mountain faces. Local Joe Weiss saw the potential for skiing in the basin in the 1920s and began bringing skiers up from the valley. A road was constructed from the highway in the early 1950s, and the first paying skiers were transported up to the slopes in a Sno-Cat. The first lift, a 700-meter (2,300-foot) rope tow, was installed on the Paradise face in 1961, and the area has continued to expand ever since. Marmot Basin now has seven lifts servicing 600 hectares (1,500 acres) of terrain and a vertical rise of 900 meters (2,940 feet). The longest run is 5.6 km (3.5 miles). Marmot doesn't get the crowds of the three resorts in Banff National Park, so lift lines are uncommon. The season runs from early December to late April. Lift tickets are $52 adults, $37 seniors, $20 children. (Throughout Jasper in January celebrations, tickets are just $35.) Rentals are available at the resort or in town at **Totem Ski Shop,** 408 Connaught Dr., 780/852-3078. For more information on the resort, contact Marmot Basin Ski-lifts, 780/852-3816 or 800/363-3078, www.skimarmot.com.

Buses depart three times daily for Marmot Basin from most Jasper hotels; $8 one-way, $14 round-trip. The first departure is 8–8:30 A.M.

Cross-Country Skiing

For many people, traveling Jasper's hiking trails on skis is just as exhilarating as on foot. An extensive network of 300 km (185 miles) of summer hiking trails is designated for skiers, with around 100 km (62 miles) groomed. The four main areas of trails are along Pyramid Lake Road, around Maligne Lake, in the Athabasca Falls area, and at Whistlers Campground. A booklet available at the Park Information Centre details each trail and its difficulty. Weather forecasts and avalanche-hazard reports are also posted here.

Rental packages are available from **Source for Sports,** 406 Patricia St., 780/852-3654; the rental shop at **Jasper Park Lodge,** 780/852-3433; and **Totem Ski Shop,** offering rentals, repairs, and sales at 408 Connaught Drive, 780/852-3078.

Maligne Canyon

By late December, the torrent that is the Maligne River has frozen solid. Where it cascades down through Maligne Canyon, the river is temporarily stalled for the winter, creating remarkable formations through the deep limestone canyon. **Maligne Tours,** 627 Patricia St., 780/852-3370, offers exciting three-hour guided tours into the depths of the canyon throughout winter, daily at 9 A.M., 1 P.M., and 6 P.M.; $24 adults, $12.50 children.

ARTS AND ENTERTAINMENT
Theater and Cinemas

A local theater company, Jasper Heritage Theatre, 780/852-4204, puts on three productions of historical interest throughout summer. The brave exploits of nurse Edith Cavell, for whom the park's best-known peak is named, come alive in a theater performance of *Edith Cavell Returns* each Monday and Thursday. Captured by German soldiers while assisting Allied troops in German-occupied Belgium during World War I, Edith Cavell was executed in 1915. The *David Thompson Story* tells the tale of one of North America's great geographers and his links to the Canadian Rockies. This show runs each Sunday, Tuesday, and Friday. Finally, *Jasper in Song* is a lighthearted historic retrospective of the people and events that have made Jasper the popular destination it is today; it runs Wednesday and Saturday. Call for the latest venues (usually Jasper Park Lodge or the Jasper

© ANDREW HEMPSTEAD

Marmots inhabit boulder-strewn slopes throughout alpine areas of the Canadian Rockies. The summit of the Whistlers has a particularly high population.

JASPER

Inn). The plays cost $15 adults, $7.50 children and are performed June–Sept. at 8:30 P.M.

The **Chaba Theatre,** 604 Connaught Drive, 780/852-4749, shows first-run movies in its two theaters.

Bars and Nightclubs

The most popular nightspot in town is the **Atha-b,** in the Athabasca Hotel, 510 Patricia St., 780/852-3386, where bands play some nights. It gets pretty rowdy with all the seasonal workers, but it's still enjoyable; minimal cover charge. This hotel also has a large lounge and a bar with a pool table and a popular 5–7 P.M. happy hour. **Pete's,** upstairs at 614 Patricia St., 780/852-6262, has a jam on Tuesday night and bands playing Friday–Sunday. The music varies—it could be blues, rock, or Celtic. The **De'd Dog Bar and Grill,** in the Astoria Hotel at 404 Connaught Dr., 780/852-3351, is a large, dimly lit sports bar with pool tables and plenty of locals drinking copious amounts of beer, especially during the 5–7 P.M. happy hour. Right downtown, the **Whistle Stop Pub,** in the Whistlers Inn, 105 Miette Ave., 780/852-3361, has a great atmosphere with a classic wooden bar and memorabilia everywhere.

Escape the smoky bar scenes at the **Downstream Bar,** 620 Connaught Dr., 780/852-9449, a nonsmoking place that opens at 4 P.M. and has live music Friday and Saturday. You don't need to be a guest of Jasper's finest hotel, the **Jasper Park Lodge,** 780/852-3301, to enjoy the ambience of its three lounges: the **Emerald Lounge** has comfortable indoor seating and long outdoor terrace overlooking Lac Beauvert; **Tent City** is a sports-style bar with a relaxed atmosphere and two pool tables; while **Palisade's** is a winter-only bar attracting the après theater crowd each evening. Most of Jasper's other large hotels, including the Amethyst Lodge, Jasper Inn, and Marmot Lodge, also have cocktail lounges.

Shopping

Jasper certainly doesn't provide the shopping experience found in Banff, but several interesting shops beckon on rainy days. **Our Native Land,** 601 Patricia St., 780/852-5592, is a large shop chock-full of authentic arts and crafts produced by artisans from throughout western Canada. Search out everything from moosehide moccasins to masks (check out the musk ox head near the back of the store). They also stock Inuit soapstone carvings from the Canadian Arctic. **Bearberry,** 612 Connaught Dr., 780/852-1112, features a good cross-section of Canadiana. Beyond the information center, **Pine Cones & Pussy Willow,** 308 Connaught Dr., 780/852-5310, is a little less tacky than your average souvenir shop, with furry toys and plastic rulers complemented by the works of local artists.

Within 100 meters (330 feet) of the information center is **Source for Sports,** 406 Patricia St., 780/852-3654, and the **Totem Ski Shop,** 408 Connaught Dr., 780/852-3078, both with a good stock of camping gear and other outdoor equipment. Before getting carried away at these specialty stores, check out **Home Hardware,** at 625 Patricia St., 780/852-5555, for basic camping supplies.

Festivals and Events

Summer is prime time on the park's events calendar. **Canada Day** (1 July) celebrations begin with a pancake breakfast and progress to a flag-raising ceremony (in front of the information center) and a parade along Connaught Drive. Live entertainment and a fireworks display end the day. The **Jasper Lions Pro Indoor Rodeo,** on the second weekend of August, dates from 1933 and attracts pro cowboys from across Canada. Apart from the traditional rodeo events, the fun includes a mechanical bull, a children's rodeo, a casino, pancake breakfasts, the ever-popular stick-pony parade, and the crowning of Miss Jasper. Most of the action takes place in the arena at the Jasper Activity Centre, behind town on Pyramid Lake Road, 780/852-4622.

On the other side of the calendar, winter is not totally partyless—**Jasper in January** is a two-week celebration that includes fireworks, special evenings at local restaurants, a chili cook-off, discounted lift tickets at Marmot Basin, and all the activities associated with winter.

Park Interpretive Program

Parks Canada offers a wide range of interpretive talks and hikes throughout summer. Each summer night in the **Whistlers Campground Theatre** a different slideshow and movie program is shown. The theater is near the shower block. The **Wabasso Campfire Circle** takes place each Saturday night just before dusk; hot tea is supplied while various speakers talk about wildlife in the park.

Many different guided hikes are offered (all free) throughout summer; check bulletin boards at the Park Information Centre and campgrounds, or call 780/852-6176.

Accommodations and Camping

In summer, motel and hotel rooms here are expensive. Most of the motels and lodges are within walking distance of town and have indoor pools and restaurants. Luckily, alternatives to staying in $200-plus hotel rooms do exist. The best alternatives are the lodges scattered around the edge of town. Open in summer only, each offers a rustic yet distinct style of accommodation in keeping with the theme of staying in a national park. Additionally, many private residences have rooms for rent in summer; three hostels are close to town; and there's always camping in the good ol' outdoors. The park has nearly 2,000 campsites, and camping is virtually unlimited in the backcountry.

IN AND AROUND THE TOWN OF JASPER

Unless otherwise noted, accommodations discussed here are within walking distance of downtown Jasper. Rates quoted are for a standard room in summer. Outside the busy June–September period most lodgings reduce rates drastically (ask also about ski packages during winter).

Less Than $50

No accommodations other than hostels come close to falling into this price category. Hostelling International–Canada, www.hi-

"SUMMER ONLY" LODGING

The earliest tourists to Jasper came by train, but as the automobile gained popularity in the 1920s, accommodations were built specifically to cater to visitors who arrived by vehicle. Typically, these "bungalow camps" consisted of a cluster of cabins set around a central lodge where meals were served and—with no need for the railway—were spread throughout the park. This type of accommodation remains in various forms today, a popular alternative for those who don't need the luxuries associated with hotels and the services of downtown Jasper. They are generally only open May to early October.

hostels.ca, operates five hostels in Jasper National Park, but none right in downtown Jasper. Reservations are highly recommended at all hostels during July and August. Make these by calling Jasper International Hostel at 780/852-3215 or through other major hostels such as those in Lake Louise, Banff, Calgary, or Edmonton.

On the road to the Jasper Tramway, seven km (4.3 miles) south from town off the Icefields Parkway, is **Jasper International Hostel,** 780/852-3215, which has 80 beds in men's and women's dorms, a large kitchen, a common room, showers, public Internet access, an outdoor barbecue area, and mountain-bike rentals. Members of Hostelling International pay $18, nonmembers $23. In the summer months this hostel fills up every night. The front desk is open daily noon–midnight. Cab fare between downtown Jasper and the hostel is $18.

Maligne Canyon Hostel is on Maligne Lake Road, beside the Maligne River and a short walk from the canyon. Although rustic, it lies in a beautiful setting. The 24 beds are in two cabins; other amenities include electricity, a kitchen, and a dining area. Rates are $13 for members, $18 for nonmembers. For reservations, call 780/852-3215. Check-in is between 5 P.M. and 11 P.M. The hostel is closed on Wednesday during the months of October–April.

Mount Edith Cavell Hostel offers a million-dollar view for the price of a dorm bed. It's 13 km (eight miles) up Cavell Road off Highway 93A, and because of the location there's usually a spare bed. Opposite the hostel are trailheads for hiking in the Tonquin Valley, and it's just a short walk to the base of Mount Edith Cavell. The hostel is rustic but has a kitchen, dining area, and outdoor wood sauna. Members pay $13 per night, nonmembers pay $18. It's open mid-June to October, and check-in is 5–11 P.M. For reservations, call 780/852-3215.

$50–100

Jasper's least expensive hotel rooms can be found right downtown in the **Athabasca Hotel,** 510 Patricia St., 780/852-3386 or 877/542-8422, www.athabascahotel.com. This historic three-story brick building dates to 1928, replacing the original structure of the same name, which was the town's first hotel. The cheapest of its 61 rooms share bathrooms and are above a noisy bar, but the price is right—$75–89 s or d. This hotel also has more expensive rooms, each with a private bathroom; $118–154 s or d.

The cheapest motel-style units at **Patricia Lake Bungalows,** 780/852-3560, www.patricialakebungalows.com, beside the lake of the same name, a five-minute drive north from Jasper along Pyramid Lake Road, fall into this price range (from $85 per night), but it is worth paying extra for a freestanding unit. Comfortable but older cottages with kitchens and TV start at $135 s or d, rising to $155 for those with either a lake view or fireplace. Suites ($190–250) are a good value in relation to similar-sized rooms elsewhere in town. Other facilities include a barbecue area and an outdoor hot tub.

Typifying a bungalow camp of the 1950s, **Pine Bungalows,** 780/852-3491, lies on a secluded section of the Athabasca River opposite the northern entrance to town. Sparse but comfortable motel-style units with kitchenettes are $90 s or d, individual wooden cabins with kitchens and fireplaces begin at $120 (most cabins face the river but numbers 1 and 3 enjoy the best views). More modern two-bedroom log cabins are $155. Pine Bungalows is open May to mid-October.

JASPER

PRIVATE HOME ACCOMMODATIONS

At last count, Jasper had more than 100 residential homes offering accommodations. They often supply nothing more than a room with a bed, but the price is right at $50–100 single or double. Use of a bathroom is usually shared with other guests or the family; few have kitchens and only a few supply light breakfast. In most cases, don't expect too much with the lower-priced choices. The positive side, apart from the price, is that your hosts are usually knowledgeable locals, and downtown is only a short walk away. For a full listing that includes the facilities at each approved property, write Jasper Home Accommodation Association, P.O. Box 758, Jasper, AB T0E-1E0, or check out website: www.stayinjasper.com. The Park Information Centre has a board listing private home accommodations with rooms available for the upcoming night. Most have signs out front, so you could cruise the residential streets (try Connaught, Patricia, and Geikie) looking for a Vacancy sign, but checking at the information center is easier.

$100–150

No hotels fall into this price range, but the three accommodations detailed as follows all offer excellent value for money. **Bear Hill Lodge,** 100 Bonhomme St., 780/852-3209, www.bearhilllodge.com, is the only summer-only cabin accommodation right in the town of Jasper. The original cabins are basic, but each has a TV, bathroom, gas fireplace, and coffee-making facilities ($135 s or d; $155 with a kitchenette). Chalet Rooms are larger and more modern, and each has a wood-burning fireplace, but no kitchen ($155). Colin Rooms are more spacious still; each has a jetted tub, gas fireplace, and limited cooking facilities ($175). Bear Hill is open mid-April to mid October, with all units discounted 40 percent during the first and last month of operation.

One of the least expensive of a string of lodges immediately south of downtown is family-run **Jasper House Bungalows,** four km (2.5 miles) south along the Icefields Parkway, 780/852-4535, www.jasperhouse.com. It offers 56 cedar log cabins, each with a TV and coffeemaker, ranging $140–195 s or d (those at the upper end of this price range are fully self-contained and overlook the river). Basic motel-style units are $140 s or d, $160 with a kitchenette. It's open May to mid-October.

Continuing south along the Icefields Parkway, **Becker's Chalets,** 780/852-3779, www. beckerschalets.com, is spread along a picturesque bend on the Athabasca River six km (3.7 miles) south of town. This historic lodging took its first guests more than 50 years ago and continues to be a park favorite, with many guests coming back year after year. The original cabins still stand. Moderately priced chalets each with kitchenette, gas fireplace, and double bed ($125, or $155 for those on the riverfront) are an excellent deal. Premium log duplexes featuring all the modern conveniences, including color TV, range $170–220. Also available are a limited number of one-bed sleeping rooms ($85). Becker's also boasts one of the park's finest restaurants.

$150–200

Appealing **Tekarra Lodge,** Hwy. 93A, 780/852-3058 or 888/404-4540, www.tekarralodge.com, is on a plateau above the confluence of the Miette and Athabasca Rivers, 1.5 km (0.9 miles) south of downtown Jasper. Ensuite rooms in the main lodge are $154 s or d, but Tekarra's historic self-contained cabins really shine. Each has been totally modernized yet retains a cozy charm, with comfortable beds, fully equipped kitchenettes, wood-burning fireplaces, and smallish but adequate bathrooms. Also on site is a restaurant open for breakfast (7:30–11 A.M.) and dinner (5–11 P.M.), bike rentals, and a laundry room. From the lodge, hiking trails lead along the Athabasca River in both directions as well as over the river to the golf course and Jasper Park Lodge. Tekarra is open May to early October.

Continuing a short distance south along Highway 93A from Tekarra Lodge, at the junction of the Icefields Parkway three km (1.9

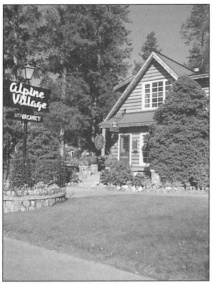

Alpine Village is one of many accommodations offering peaceful settings away from downtown.

miles) south of town, is **Alpine Village,** 780/852-3285, www.alpinevillagejasper.com. This resort is laid out across well-manicured lawns, and all buildings are surrounded by colorful gardens of geraniums and petunias. Across the road is the Athabasca River. The older sleeping cabins have been renovated ($150 s or d, $170 with a kitchen and fireplace), while the newer deluxe one-bedroom log cabins feature stone fireplaces and modern furnishings ($190). Alpine Village is open late April to mid-October.

This is the price range that most downtown Jasper hotel rooms fall within. One of the best values of these is the **Tonquin Inn,** at the northern edge of town on Juniper Street, 780/852-4987 or 800/661-1315, www.tonquininn.com. Guests enjoy luxurious rooms, a beautiful indoor pool, an outdoor hot tub, laundry facilities, a steakhouse restaurant, and a sunny lounge bar. Even standard rooms have king beds ($179 s or d; $10 extra for air-conditioning) and some have kitchens ($205).

Behind the Tonquin Inn, the **Marmot Lodge,** 86 Connaught Dr., 780/852-4471 or 888/852-7737, www.mtn-park-lodges.com, features 107 dynamically styled rooms, many with mountain views. On the main level is a restaurant specializing in Alberta beef, but many summer guests take advantage of a barbeque on the terrace. Some rooms and the indoor pool are fully wheelchair accessible. In summer, rates begin at $189 s or d ($225 with a kitchen).

Along Connaught Drive, a few blocks southwest of downtown is the **Maligne Lodge,** 780/852-3143 or 800/661-1315, www.malignelodge.com, which features an indoor pool, hot tubs, a sun deck, and a Western-themed restaurant. Rates for the medium-size rooms are $169 s or d ($179 beside the indoor pool), or pay $189 for a suite with a separate bedroom and full kitchen. Rates are discounted to $99–139 in May and September and as low as $55 in the depths of winter.

Near the end of Pyramid Lake Road, north from downtown, it's impossible to miss the sprawling grounds of **Pyramid Lake Resort,** 780/852-4900 or 888/852-4900, www.pyramidlakeresort.com, the only lodging away from town (besides Jasper Park Lodge) that is open year-round. Plenty of water-based activities and rentals (across the road), an interpretive program, a fitness center, and a large barbecue area make the resort a good choice for families. Summer-only cabins, with separate bedrooms, full baths, and lake views, range $175–210 s or d. In addition to lake views, motel-style units feature gas fireplaces and kitchenettes for $245 (discounted below $150 in the off-season).

Right downtown is the 35-room **Astoria Hotel,** 404 Connaught Dr., 780/852-3351 or 800/661-7343, www.astoriahotel.com, a European-style lodging built in 1924 and kept in the same family since. Rooms are brightly furnished and each has a fridge, TV, and VCR. Standard rooms are $173 s or d, while much larger Superior rooms, complete with full bath, are $189. Outside of summer, these same rooms cost $79 and $89, respectively. Note that there is no elevator in this four-story hotel.

JASPER

In a central position on Jasper's busiest corner is **Whistlers Inn,** 105 Miette Ave., 780/852-3361 or 800/282-9919, www.whistlersinn.com, one of the town's original accommodations. It features spacious rooms and a rooftop hot tub; from $195 s or d.

$200–250

On Connaught Drive southwest of downtown, **Mount Robson Inn,** 780/852-3327 or 800/587-3327, www.mountrobsoninn.com, was extensively renovated in the late 1990s and now has an air-conditioning unit in each of its 78 rooms. Other in-room features include coffeemakers, alarm clocks, and hairdryers. Rooms start at $205 s or d. The suites here are a good deal (relative to other Jasper accommodations); each holds two separate bedrooms, a full bathroom with additional outside vanity, and a fireplace for $280–325 per unit.

Jasper Inn, 98 Geikie St., 780/852-4461 or 800/661-1933, www.jasperinn.com, is a modern chateau-style lodging of brick and red cedar. Many rooms have private balconies, and more than 100 are self-contained suites with kitchenettes and fireplaces. Other features include a large indoor pool and a sundeck overlooking a Japanese rock garden dotted with outdoor settings. Rates start at $213 s or d, with kitchen units starting at $218. The Upper Loft Suites, complete with a kitchen, fireplace, and—as the name suggests—a bedroom in the loft, are a much better deal at $225 s or d (from $99 outside of summer).

The **Lobstick Lodge,** 94 Geikie Ave., 780/852-4431 or 888/852-7737, www.mtn-park-lodges.com, has 139 extra-large, simply furnished rooms and a range of modern amenities, including an indoor pool and an outdoor hot tub; $208 s or d, $223 for a kitchen-equipped unit.

Amethyst Lodge, in a central location at 200 Connaught Dr., 780/852-3394, www.mtn-park-lodges.com, is named after a lake in the Tonquin Valley. It offers large air-conditioned rooms, many with balconies, as well as an outdoor hot tub and a casual restaurant; $208–265 s or d.

The **Sawridge Hotel,** 82 Connaught Dr., 780/852-5111 or 800/661-6427, www.sawridge.

com/jasper, offers 154 air-conditioned rooms built around a large atrium and indoor pool. Also contained within the atrium is a fine-dining restaurant and lounge. Rooms overlooking the atrium are $229 s or d, outward-facing rooms are $259, or pay $289 for an extra-spacious room with a king bed. Rates are reduced up to 60 percent outside of the busiest mid-June to September period.

$250–350

Chateau Jasper, 96 Geikie St., 780/852-5644 or 800/661-9323, www.chateaujasper.com, is one of Jasper's nicest lodgings. Guest rooms are spacious and elegantly finished with maple furnishings and low ceilings that give them a cozy feel. Bathrooms are particularly well equipped, with guests also enjoying the use of plush bathrobes. Summer rates start at $325 s or d, but as you move into these higher priced places, off-season discounts become steeper—in this case, rooms throughout the winter season are just $135 s or d. The Chateau's restaurant is one of Jasper's best.

More Than $350

Jasper Park Lodge, 780/852-3301 or 800/257-7544, www.fairmont.com, lies along the shore of Lac Beauvert (meaning "beautiful green" in French) across the Athabasca River from downtown. This is the park's original resort and its most famous. It has four restaurants, three lounges, horseback riding, tennis courts, a championship golf course, and Jasper's only covered shopping arcade. The main lodge features stone floors, carved wooden pillars, and a high ceiling. The 446 rooms vary in configuration and are spread out over the expansive property. All have a coffeemaker, TV, telephone, and Internet access. The least expensive units ($549 s or d) are smallish, hold two twin beds, and offer no views. Also away from the lake, Fairmont Rooms ($549 s or d) are contained in rows of cedar-lined chalets; each has a patio or balcony. Similar in size and layout, but with water views, are Fairmont Deluxe Rooms ($559 s or d). Jasper Premier Rooms ($629 s or d) have a distinct country charm, and each has either a sitting room or patio with lake views. Moving up to the more expensive options,

Lakeview Suites ($759 s or d) overlook Lac Beauvert and are backed by the 18th fairway of the golf course. Each features a patio or balcony, fireplace, and two TVs.

Most guests don't pay the summer rack rates quoted here. The cost of lodging is usually included in one of the plethora of packages offered, such as the Grand Canadian Lodge Experience, which includes golf, meals, taxes, and gratuities and brings the cost of a standard room down to well less than $400 per night (click on the "Packages and Promotions" link on the Fairmont website for all the options). Outside of summer, Jasper Park Lodge becomes a real bargain, with rooms with lake views (remember it'll be frozen in winter) for well less than $200. The various historic cabins provide Jasper Park Lodge's premier accommodations. They are priced beyond the reach of most ordinary travelers, but are mentioned here simply because they are among the most exclusive rooms in all of Canada. They have hosted true royalty (Queen Elizabeth) and movie royalty (Marilyn Monroe, during the filming of *River of No Return*). They range from the secluded and cozy Athabasca Cabin to the 1928, five-bedroom Point Cabin overlooking the lake. The largest is Milligan Manor, an eight-bedroom, 657-square-meter (7,075-square-foot) "cottage" beside the golf clubhouse.

ALONG THE ICEFIELDS PARKWAY

Several accommodations are strung out along the Icefields Parkway close to the town of Jasper, while two lodges and two hostels lie farther south, along the parkway proper.

Less Than $50

Northernmost of these is the **Athabasca Falls Hostel,** 32 km (20 miles) south of the town Jasper and 198 km (123 miles) north from Lake Louise. It is larger than the one at Beauty Creek and has electricity. Athabasca Falls is only a few minutes' walk away. Members of Hostelling International pay $13, nonmembers $18. It's closed on Tuesday night during the months of October–April.

Beauty Creek Hostel, 17 km (10.5 miles) north of Columbia Icefield and 144 km (90 miles) north from Lake Louise, is nestled in a small stand of Douglas fir between the Icefields Parkway and the Sunwapta River. Each of its separate male and female cabins sleeps 12 and has a woodstove. A third building holds a well-equipped kitchen and dining area. Members $12, nonmembers $17. Open May–September.

Reservations can be made for these hostels by calling Jasper International Hostel at 780/852-3215. In both cases, check-in is 5–11 P.M., but the main lodges are open all day.

$150–200

Historic **Sunwapta Falls Resort,** 780/852-4852 or 888/828-5777, www.sunwapta.com, is 55 km (34 miles) south of the town of Jasper and within walking distance of the picturesque waterfall for which it is named. It features 52 units, all with televisions and some with kitchenettes and fireplaces. Rooms either have two queen beds or one queen bed and a fireplace; some have balconies. Rates are $169 s or d, reduced to $95 outside of the busy July to mid-September period. In the main lodge is a lunchtime self-serve restaurant popular with passing travelers. In the evening this same room is transformed into the Endless Chain Restaurant, featuring simply prepared Canadian game and seafood in the $18–26 range and a delectable wild berry crumble for $6. The resort is open early May to mid-October.

Columbia Icefield Chalet, 780/852-6550 or 877/423-7433, www.brewster.ca, the top story of Columbia Icefield Centre, lies in a stunning location high above the treeline and overlooking the Columbia Icefield, 105 km (65 miles) south of the town of Jasper and 132 km (82 miles) north of Lake Louise. It features 29 standard rooms, 17 of which have glacier views, and three larger, more luxurious corner rooms. All units have satellite TV and phones. Because of the remote location, dining options are limited to the in-house café and restaurant. The **Glacier Dining Room** opens daily at 7 A.M. for a breakfast buffet, reopening 6–9:30 P.M. for dinner. On the same level are a cafeteria-style café and a snack bar. All food outlets are designed around the basic needs of passing highway travelers. Rates June–Sept. range $175–195 s or d, while the last week of May and the first few days in October, rates start at $90. The facility is closed the rest of the year.

EAST OF THE TOWN OF JASPER

Two accommodations east of town but still within the park boundary are open in summer only.

$50–100

Located at the site of a once-bustling coal mining town, **Pocahontas Bungalows,** 780/866-3732 or 800/843-3372, is at the bottom of the road that leads to Miette Hot Springs, 43 km (27 miles) east of Jasper along Highway 16. Sleeping-room cabins start at $90 s or d, $100 for a kitchen-equipped unit. Motel rooms are $125, or pay $150 for the newest duplex units overlooking the pool and each with a separate bedroom. On site is a outdoor heated pool and restaurant open through the summer season for breakfast and dinner.

$100–150

Miette Hot Springs Bungalows, 780/866-3750, is within walking distance of the park's only hot springs, 18 km (11 miles) from Highway 16 and 61 km (38 miles) from town. Motel units are $125, while bungalows, each with cooking facilities, start at $145. Guest facilities include a covered barbeque area, restaurant, and laundry room.

HINTON

This medium-sized town lies along Highway 16, approximately 19 km (12 miles) east of the park gate and 69 km (43 miles) east of the town of Jasper. Staying here provides an inexpensive alternative to staying in the park. The strip of motels, restaurants, fast-food places, and gas stations along Highway 16 is the place to start looking for a room.

$50–100

The best value are the 21 newly renovated guest rooms at **Pines Motel,** adjacent to the golf course at 709 Gregg Ave., 780/865-2624, www.pines-motel.com. Each room has a microwave, fridge, and coffeemaker; $69 s, $79–99 d. The dowdy-looking **Big Horn Motel,** 780/865-1555, beside the Husky gas station, has surprisingly good rooms, some larger than others; $70 s, $75 d, kitchenettes an extra $10.

$100–150

Holiday Inn Hinton, 780/865-3321 or 800/262-9428, www.holiday-inn.com, has a restaurant open throughout the day, an outdoor heated pool, and a fitness room with a hot tub. The 104 rooms are well furnished and equipped with everything from hairdryers to Playstation games; rates start at $99 s, $109 d.

One of Hinton's newer accommodations is the **Ramada Hinton,** 500 Smith St., 780/865-2575 or 888/644-6866, www.ramadahinton.com, which offers 55 fairly spacious, comfortable rooms, each with a microwave, coffeemaker, and well-equipped bathroom. Other hotel features include a fitness room, hot tub, restaurant, lounge, and laundry room. Standard rooms are $118 s or d, two-bedroom loft suites complete with kitchens are $139, with the King Suite comes with a king bed, jetted tub, two gas fireplaces, and a private balcony with mountain views for less than $200 (about the same you'd pay for a basic, boring hotel room in the park).

OTHER LODGING OPTIONS
Tonquin Valley

Jasper's two backcountry lodges are located southwest of Jasper in the spectacular Tonquin Valley. Accessible only on foot or horseback or, in winter, by skiing, both lodges are open to hikers (with advance reservations); most guests stay as part of a package that includes horseback riding.

Dating to 1939, **Tonquin Amethyst Lake Lodge,** 780/852-1188, www.tonquinadventures.com, was extensively upgraded in the early 1990s. Private cabins have wood-burning heaters, twin log beds with thick blankets, oil lanterns, and a spectacular view. The rate, $135 per person per night, includes accommodations, three meals, and use of small boats and fishing gear. Tonquin

Adventures offers a number of well-priced packages, including riding into the lodge on horses. Rates are reduced in winter. Getting there involves a 19-km (11.8-mile) journey from a trailhead opposite Mount Edith Cavell Hostel.

Nearby **Tonquin Valley Backcountry Lodge,** 780/852-3909, www.tonquinvalley.com, offers a similar set-up, with most guests arriving by horseback on a pre-arranged ride from the nearest road. In this case, the departure point is along the Marmot Basin Road, from a parking lot at Portal Creek. Rates are $135 per person per night (discounted to $100 in winter), with a five-night package costing $775 per person.

Black Cat Guest Ranch

This mountain retreat lies on the eastern edge of the park, surrounded by mountain wilderness. All 16 rooms have private baths and views of the mountains. Horseback riding is available during the day, and in the evening, guests can relax in the large living room or hot tub. Meals are included in the rates of $135 s, $170 d. To get to the ranch, follow Highway 16 for 19 km (12 miles) beyond the east gate, head north along Highway 40 for six km (3.7 mikes), turn left to Brûlé and continue for 11 km (6.8 miles), and then turn right and follow the signs. Contact the ranch at 780/865-3084 or 800/859-6840, www.blackcatguestranch.ca.

CAMPGROUNDS

Jasper's 10 campgrounds operate on a first-come, first-served basis. When the main campgrounds fill, campers will be directed to overflow areas. These are glorified parking lots with no designated sites, but fees are reduced ($8 per vehicle). Campgrounds in Jasper begin opening in mid-June and all but Wapiti are closed by mid-October. All campsites have a picnic table and fire ring, with a fire permit costing $6 (includes firewood). For general campground information, call 780/852-6176.

Near the Town of Jasper

Whistlers Campground, at the base of Whistlers Road, three km (1.9 miles) south of town, has 781 sites, making it the largest campground in the Canadian Rockies. It is divided into four sections; prices vary with the services available—walk-in sites $17, unserviced sites $19, powered sites $23, full hookups $26. Each section has showers. Whistlers is open May to mid-October.

A further two km (1.2 miles) south along the Icefields Parkway is **Wapiti Campground,** which offers 366 sites and has showers; unserviced sites $19, powered sites $23. This is the park's only campground open year-round, with serviced winter camping $17 per night.

Whistlers and Wapiti are the only two campgrounds with powered sites, and therefore they're in great demand. A line-up usually forms well before the official check-out time of 11 A.M. Parks Canada suggests planning to spend your first night without power, after which you'll receive priority for a powered site.

Sites at **Wabasso Campground,** along Highway 93A approximately 16 km (10 miles) south of town, are set among stands of spruce and aspen; $15 per night.

East along Highway 16 from the Town of Jasper

East of town, along Highway 16, are two smaller, more primitive campgrounds. **Snaring River Campground,** 17 km (11 miles) from Jasper on Celestine Lake Rd., is $12; **Pocahontas Campground,** 45 km (28 miles) northeast, is $15. Both are open mid-May to early September.

Along the Icefields Parkway

Aside from Whistlers and Wapiti campgrounds at the top end of the Icefields Parkway (see previous entry), the next nearest campground is a further 12 miles south, and then you'll come across three facilities in a 50-km (31-mile) stretch. They are **Mount Kerkeslin, Honeymoon Lake,** and **Jonas Creek Campgrounds.** Each is $12 per site, per night.

Wilcox Creek and **Columbia Icefield Campgrounds** are within two km (1.2 miles) of each other at the extreme southern end of the park, just over 100 km (62 miles) south of the town of Jasper 105 km (65 miles) and around 125 km (78 miles) north of Lake Louise. Both are primitive facilities with pit toilets, cooking shelters, and fire rings; all sites are $12. Smallish sites at Columbia Icefield Campground are set in a stunted subalpine forest of aspen and spruce, with views extending across to the Athabasca Glacier. Immediately to the south, Wilcox Creek offers larger sites, better suited to RVs and trailers, but with no hookups.

Other Practicalities

FOOD

It's easy to get a good, or even great, meal in Jasper. Connaught Drive and Patricia Street are lined with cafés and restaurants. Considering this is a national park, menus are reasonably well priced. You should expect hearty fare, with lots of beef, game, and a surprisingly good selection of seafood.

Coffeehouses and Cafés

The **Soft Rock Cafe,** 632 Connaught Dr., 780/852-5850, occupies a sunny spot along Jasper's main thoroughfare. It is one of the most popular places in town to start the day. Seating is inside or out, and you should order at the counter. Breakfast options include omelets

© ANDREW HEMPSTEAD

dining on the terrace at Jasper Park Lodge

and skillet dishes (all less than $10). If the cinnamon buns are still in the oven, you'll have to come back later in the day—they're gigantic! The variety of coffee concoctions here is mindboggling, and all prices are reasonable. It's open 8 A.M.–10 P.M. Back toward the heart of downtown, **Mountain Foods & Café,** 606 Connaught Dr., 780/852-4050, offers a full cooked breakfast for $6 and healthy wraps, rolls, and sandwiches the rest of the day.

One block back from Connaught Drive, **Truffles & Trout,** in Jasper Marketplace, corner of Patricia and Hazel Streets, 780/852-9676, is a popular local hangout, with all the usual coffees, as well as boxed picnic lunches on offer. Across the road, **Nutter's,** 622 Patricia St., 780/852-5844, is another good prehiking stop, with a wide choice of goodies in bulk bins. **Spooner's,** 610 Patricia St., 780/852-4046, is a second-floor café with stunning mountain views and a good range of coffees and light meals. A couple of doors away, **Coco's Café,** 608 Patricia St., 780/852-4550, is another coffee-lover's meeting place.

Local bakeries include the **Pastry Shop,** tucked into the back of Patricia Centre Mall at 610 Patricia St., 780/852-2253, and, at the northern side of the downtown core, the **Bear's Paw Bakery,** 4 Cedar Ave., 780/852-3233, open daily from 7 a.m. The latter offers a great range of European-style breads as well as cakes and pastries.

Cool and Casual

For pizza, you won't be able to miss **Jasper Pizza Place,** 402 Connaught Dr., 780/852-3225. It's a large and noisy restaurant with bright furnishings, a concrete floor, exposed heating ducts, and walls lined with photos from Jasper's earliest days. Regular thick-crust pizzas are available from 11 A.M., but it's not until 5 P.M., when the wood-fired oven begins producing thin-crust pizzas with adventurous toppings, that this place really shines; expect to pay $12–15 for a 10-inch pizza.

On the same side of town as Jasper Pizza Place is one of Jasper's oldest restaurants, **Papa George's,** in the Astoria Hotel at 406 Connaught Dr., 780/852-3351. Huge east-facing windows take in the panorama of distant mountain peaks. Breakfast is $4–8, a traditional English afternoon tea served 2:30–4:30 P.M. is $9, while lunch and dinner feature burgers, pasta, and steaks; daily specials are $12–19 and include soup and salad. Hours are 7 A.M.–10 P.M.

Family-Style Dining

The ubiquitous family-style restaurant is alive and well in Jasper. One of the originals is the **L&W Restaurant,** corner of Patricia St. and Hazel Ave., 780/852-4114. It features a small outside patio and plenty of greenery that brings to life an otherwise ordinary restaurant—a good place to take the family for an inexpensive meal.

Kontos Restaurant, 622 Patricia St., 780/852-3444, is a newer addition to the Jasper dining scene. The menu is fairly standard, with especially hearty portions offered as lunch specials (ask, or you'll only be offered the regular menu) for $6–9. Dinner specials range $14–18, or choose from simple European dishes such as souvlaki for $15. (The bathrooms here are worthy of a special mention—they contain everything from sunscreen to hand cream.)

Palisades, Cedar Ave., 780/852-5222, offers several inexpensive vegetarian choices, pastas and pizza to $17, Greek specialties less than $20, a massive T-bone steak for $24, and a $5 kids' menu. Palisades is open daily 4–9:30 P.M. for dinner and in summer only 8:30–11:30 A.M. for breakfast.

Steakhouses

Most restaurants feature Alberta beef prominently, but it's a specialty at the following two places.

Tonquin Prime Rib Village, on Juniper Street beside the Tonquin Inn, 780/852-4966, has been a long-time Jasper favorite. Charbroiled steaks and hearty servings of prime rib cost $24–30, but the Prime Rib Sandwich ($18), with a plate-load of extras, will fill any carnivorous cravings for a few

dollars less. This restaurant also offers a surprisingly good selection of seafood. It opens daily at 5 P.M.

Upstairs at 640 Connaught Drive, 780/852-3920, is another popular steakhouse, **Villa Caruso,** with several open balconies offering great views across the valley. The restaurant itself has a modern, Western-style décor, with lots of polished log work and elegant table settings. The menu features a wide variety of Alberta beef dishes, including a massive 16-ounce T-bone for $31. But there's a lot more than steak on offer, including chicken, seafood, and pasta dishes from $15. Villa Caruso is open daily 11 A.M.–midnight.

Seafood

Fiddle River Seafood Restaurant, upstairs at 620 Connaught Dr., 780/852-3032, is a long way from the ocean and not particularly coastal in feel, but offers a wide variety of seafood. The striking décor matches dark polished wood with forest green furnishings, and large windows provide mountain views (reservations are needed for window-side tables). Trout, arctic char, red snapper, ahi tuna, and halibut all make regular appearances on the blackboard menu. Expect to pay about $40 per person for a three-course meal.

European

Open for dinner only (from 5 P.M.), **Andy's Bistro,** 606 Patricia St., 780/852-4559, is an elegantly casual eatery offering a wide range of uncomplicated dishes using Canadian game and produce prepared with Swiss-influenced cooking styles. Start with a plate piled high with Prince Edward Island steamed mussels ($12, but enough for two people), then chose between dishes such as vegetarian gnocchi ($18) or lake trout served with chanterelle mushrooms and a peppercorn sauce ($22). Andy's has an extensive cellar of wines but no official wine list. Instead, diners are encouraged to choose from red wines set along the bar and white wines from the fridge. At the unique *stammtisch,* a large table, up to 10 diners can be seated at once, free to come and go as they please. It's the perfect place to mingle with fellow travelers. Also notable at Andy's is the staff, who seem experienced and knowledgeable.

The best Greek meals in town are served at **Something Else Restaurant,** 621 Patricia St., 780/852-3850. Portions are generous, service is friendly, the prices are right, and you'll find plenty of alternatives if the Greek dishes don't appeal to you. Greek favorites are $14–18, pasta dishes $13–16, pizza from $13. It's open daily 11 A.M.–11 P.M.

Miss Italia Ristorante, 610 Patricia St., 780/852-4002, upstairs in the Patricia Centre Mall, features bright and breezy interior décor with tables also set on a narrow terrace bedecked in pots of colorful flowers. Cooked breakfasts (from 8 A.M.) are $6–9. The rest of the day, pastas made fresh daily average $15, a baked filet of Atlantic salmon is $16, and souvlaki with a side of salad and pita bread is just $16. Check out the daily specials before ordering—they are taken from the regular menu, but discounted a couple of bucks and come with soup or salad.

Directly behind the park information center, **La Fiesta,** 504 Patricia St., 780/852-0404, is a small eatery with a slightly Mediterranean feel. It offers a tapas menu as well as a full Canadian one. Tapas are $4–11 and include delights such as pork kebabs served with a fig and pine nut relish and mussels steamed in a tequila broth. La Fiesta is open daily 11:30 A.M.–11 P.M.

Asian

The **Cantonese Restaurant,** 608 Connaught Dr., 780/852-3559, is the place to go for Chinese; combo specials are $9–13 and set five-course menus for two start at $28. It's open daily noon–10 P.M. **Denjiro,** 410 Connaught Dr., 780/852-3780, features a traditional sushi bar and eight tatami booths for eating the Japanese cuisine; combination dinners average $19 per person. It's open 5–11:30 P.M.

Jasper Park Lodge

Jasper's premier accommodation, across the river from downtown, offers a choice of casual or elegant dining in a variety of restaurants and lounges. Across from the reception area is a dedicated dining reservation desk, staffed daily 11 A.M.–8 P.M., or call 780/852-6052. Reservations are required for the Edith Cavell, Moose's Nook, and Beauvert dining rooms.

The **Emerald Lounge** takes pride of place in the expansive lobby of the main building. Table settings of various configurations are spread throughout the room while also sprawling out and along a terrace, from where views over picturesque Lac Beauvert to distant mountains are uninterrupted. Both lunch and dinner menus feature imaginative modern Canadian cuisine, but with dinner (from 5:30 P.M.) being decidedly more expensive. At lunch, salads ranging $8–13 can be made into a full meal by adding extras such as smoked salmon and slices of chicken breast, or stick to mains such as bison burger ($15). Generous dinner mains range $18–30—the Alberta ribeye roasted in red pepper butter is typical. It's open daily 11 A.M.–10 P.M.

The **Beauvert Dining Room** is a casual 500-seat eatery across the lobby from the Emerald Lounge. It features Jasper's most extensive buffet breakfast (6–9 A.M.), with a huge selection of hot and cold dishes for $19 per person. In the evening (6–8 P.M.), diners pay $57 per person for an à la carte main—which includes a mouthwatering hickory-smoked Alberta prime rib dish—along with unlimited visits to appetizer stations and a dessert buffet.

The elegantly rustic **Moose's Nook** is a good place to enjoy traditional Canadian fare such as grilled wild boar chops, whiskey-flamed arctic char, or a chargrilled Abertan ribeye steak. Mains range $25–34. Be sure to leave room for dessert—the chestnut-crusted cheesecake smothered in maple syrup is incredible. It's open for dinner only, daily 6–9 P.M.

The **Edith Cavell Room** is the finest fine-dining restaurant in Jasper. Its dark oak walls contrast with the white linens and large, bright windows overlooking Lac Beauvert and the mountains beyond. Even though the restaurant has changed little over time, its overly pretentious atmosphere has softened and service become more comfortable. Still, this is seriously cultured dining, unequaled in Jasper. With an emphasis on local produce and Canadian game and seafood, the classic cuisine is served with a French flair. Prices for two-, three-, and four-course table d'hôte combos are a relatively reasonable $50, $65, and $75, respectively. Dinner is served 6–10 P.M. Dress code is resort casual: no t-shirts or jeans and a jacket and tie "recommended but not required." The Sunday brunch, served between 10 A.M. and 12:30 P.M. costs $27, and is especially popular.

The lodge also holds two casual eateries. From 7 A.M., light breakfasts, drinks, and snacks are served at the **1st Cup,** in the golf clubhouse opposite the first tee. Between 10 A.M. and 5 P.M., the smell of sizzling steaks served from a barbeque out front of the clubhouse wafts across the grounds. Expect to pay $7–11 for burgers, wraps, and the like. **Meadows Restaurant,** downstairs in the shopping arcade, is open for a breakfast buffet 8–11:30 A.M. and then in the evening for a dinner buffet 5:30–9 P.M.

Other Hotel Dining

Most of the larger accommodations have restaurants. In general, they open for breakfast and dinner only, with a cold or cooked buffet complimenting an à la carte menu.

Walter's Dining Room in the Sawridge Hotel, 82 Connaught Dr., 780/852-5111, is a cut above the rest and reasonably priced. Surrounded by greenery of a four-story atrium, the setting is relaxed but elegant. The cooking is contemporary, but distinctly Canadian. You could start with the venison pâté, followed by maple-glazed salmon, spending a little more than $30 for the two courses. The adjacent lounge has the same pleasant setting and a smaller, less-expensive menu (open daily from 5 P.M.).

One block back from the Sawridge Hotel is the Jasper Inn and its **Inn Restaurant,** 98 Geikie St., 780/852-3232, with a fine sheltered courtyard complete with an outdoor fireplace and heat lamps for those cooler evenings. As is usually the case in hotel restaurants, the menu is of wide appeal, presenting pastas from $14, beef dishes from $18, and seafood, such as lake trout with cucumber lime relish ($18), ranging $17–25.

Restaurants Outside of Downtown

With so many dining choices in downtown Jasper, it's easy to ignore the many fine restaurants scattered elsewhere in the park.

One of Jasper's best restaurants, **Becker's Gourmet Restaurant,** 780/852-3535, is six km (3.7 miles) out of town to the south along the Icefields Parkway, but well worth the short drive. From this cozy dining room where the atmosphere is intimate or the adjacent enclosed conservatory, the views of Mount Kerkeslin and the Athabasca River are inspiring. This restaurant is a throwback to days gone by, with an ever-changing menu of seasonal game and produce that includes a daily wild game special. A menu staple is the rack of lamb baked with Dijon mustard and fresh herbs then drizzled in a garlic butter sauce. Hot and cold starters range $9–13, while no main is more than $30. Dinner is served 5:30 A.M.–9 P.M. Becker's is also open for breakfast 8–11 A.M.; the buffet costs $11.50.

Back toward town from Becker's, on Highway 93A, is the dining room of historic **Tekarra Lodge,** 780/852-4624. It's open for breakfast (7:30–11 A.M.) and dinner (5–11 P.M.). The setting may be mountain-style rustic, but the cooking appeals to modern preferences with combinations like banana-crusted chicken breast with sweet mango curry sauce ($19). All mains are less than $30, including the fish-of-the-day, which is prepared in three different ways.

You'll probably want to eat at the **Treeline Restaurant,** 780/852-3093, just for the view—it's high above town at the upper terminal of the Jasper Tramway. Daily breakfast and lunch buffets complement the à la carte menu, while the Sunset Dinner package costs $40, including the gondola ride.

TRANSPORTATION
Getting There

Getting to Jasper by public transportation is easy, although the closest airport handling domestic and international flights is at Edmonton, 360 km (224 miles) to the east. The **VIA rail station** and the **bus depot** (used by both Greyhound and Brewster) are in the same building, central to town at 607 Connaught Drive. The building is open 24 hours daily in summer; the rest of the year Mon.–Sat. 7:30 A.M.–10:30 P.M., Sun. 7:30–11 A.M. and 6:30–10:30 P.M. Lockers are available for $1 per day. Also here are car rental agencies.

Jasper is on the Canadian route, the only remaining transcontinental passenger rail service in the country. Trains run either way three times weekly. To the west the line divides, going to both Prince Rupert and Vancouver; to the east it passes through Edmonton and all points beyond. For all rail information, call 800/561-8630. Another rail option is offered by **Rocky Mountaineer Railtours,** 800/665-7245, www.rockymountaineer.com. This company operates a luxurious summer-only rail service between Vancouver and Jasper with an overnight in Kamloops (British Columbia). The one-way fare is $670 per person, with a $150 discount for travel in May and October.

Greyhound buses, 780/852-332 or 800/661-8747, www.greyhound.ca, depart Jasper for all points in Canada (except Banff), including Vancouver (three times daily, 12–13 hours, $99.19 one-way), Edmonton (five times daily, 4.5 hours, $49.49 one-way) with connections to Calgary, and Prince Rupert (once daily, 18 hours, $132.57 one-way).

The only buses between Jasper and Banff are operated by Banff-based **Brewster,** 780/852-3332 or 800/661-1152, www.brewster.ca. Buses run May–mid-October, with buses continuing on from Banff to Calgary International Airport. Buses depart the airport daily at 12:30 P.M. ($75 one-way to Jasper), pick up passengers in Banff at 2:30 P.M. ($54 one-way) and Lake Louise at 4:15 P.M. ($46 one-way), and arrive in Jasper at 8 P.M. The return service departs daily from Jasper Park Lodge at 12:50 P.M. and from the downtown bus depot at 1:30 P.M., arriving at Calgary airport at 9:30 P.M. Brewster also runs a nine-hour (one-way) tour between Banff and Jasper, departing daily mid-April–mid-October from the Banff and Jasper depots at 8 A.M.; if the bus picks you up at your lodging, departure time is earlier. The tour costs $95 one-way, $133 round-trip. The round-trip requires an overnight in Jasper.

Getting Around

The **Maligne Lake Shuttle,** 780/852-3370, runs out to Maligne Lake May–September, 4–6 times daily ($28 round-trip) from its depot at 627 Patricia Street. Stops are made at Maligne Canyon and Maligne Canyon Hostel ($9 one-way).

Rental cars start at $65 per day with 100 free kilometers. The following companies have agencies in town: **Avis,** 780/852-3970 or 800/879-2847; **Budget,** 780/852-3222 or 800/268-8900; **Hertz,** 780/852-3888 or 800/263-0600; and **National,** 780/852-1117 or 800/387-4747.

Cabs in town are not cheap. Most drivers will take you on a private sightseeing tour or to trailheads if requested; try **Jasper Taxi,** 780/852-3600 or 852-3146. **Heritage Cabs,** 780/852-5558, has a fleet of PT Cruisers.

Tours

Brewster, 780/852-3332, offers a three-hour Discover Jasper tour taking in Patricia and Pyramid Lakes, Maligne Canyon, Maligne Lake, and Jasper Tramway (ride not included in fare). It departs April–October daily at 8:30 A.M. from the railway station; $63. **Maligne Tours,** 627 Patricia St., 780/852-3370, www.malignelake.com, schedules a variety of tours, including one to Maligne Lake ($62, includes cruise). **Jasper Adventure Centre,** in the Chaba Theatre at 604 Connaught Dr., 780/852-5595, www.jasperadventurecentre.com, operates several well-priced tours, including the following: Mount Edith Cavell (departs 2 P.M., three hours; $45), Maligne Valley (departs 9:30 A.M., five hours; $70), and Miette Hot Springs (departs 6 P.M., four hours; $49). They also offer similar-priced tours taking in historical sites and local wildlife.

INFORMATION AND SERVICES

Services

The **post office** is at 502 Patricia Street, behind the Park Information Centre. Mail to be picked up here should be addressed General Delivery, Jasper, AB T0E 1E0.

More than Mail, 620 Connaught Dr., 780/852-3151, offers a wide range of communication services including regular post, public Internet access, fax and copying facilities, a work area for laptops, international calling, and currency exchange.

The two laundromats on Patricia Street are open 6 A.M.–11 P.M. and offer showers that cost $2 for 10 minutes (quarters).

The **hospital** is at 518 Robson Street, 780/852-3344. For the **RCMP,** call 780/852-4848.

Books and Bookstores

Housed in Jasper's original Royal Canadian Mounted Police detachment building, small **Jasper Municipal Library,** Elm Ave., 780/852-3652, holds just about everything ever written about the park. It's open Mon.–Thur. 11 A.M.–9P.M., Fri.–Sat. 11 A.M.–5 P.M.

Head to the **Friends of Jasper** store in the Park Information Centre or the **museum** for a good selection of books on the park's natural and human history. A larger selection of literature, including lots of western Canadiana, can be found at **Jasper Camera and Gift,** 412 Connaught Dr., 780/852-3165; open daily 9 A.M.–10 P.M. **Counter Clockwise,** in the Jasper Marketplace at 627 Patricia St., 780/852-3152, has a similar selection. **Maligne Lake Books,** in the Jasper Park Lodge, 780/852-4779, has a good selection of coffee-table books.

Internet Access

Send and receive email and surf the Internet at the following Jasper locations:

Digital Den: upstairs at 610 Patricia Street, 780/852-9765; daily 9 A.M.–10 P.M.

Jasper Municipal Library: Elm Ave., 780/852-3652; Mon.–Thur. 11 A.M.–9 P.M., Fri.–Sat. 11 A.M.–5 P.M.

More than Mail: 620 Connaught Dr., 780/852-3151; daily 9 A.M.–10 P.M.

Soft Rock Café: 632 Connaught Dr., 780/852-5850; daily 8 A.M.–10 P.M.

Park Information Centre

The residence of Jasper's first superintendent, a beautiful old stone building dating to 1913, is now used by Parks Canada as the Park Informa-

tion Centre. It's right downtown in Athabasca Park on Connaught Drive, 780/852-6176. The staff provides general information on the park and can direct you to hikes in the immediate vicinity. Around the corner is the **Parks Canada Trail Office,** 780/852-6177, which handles questions for those going into the backcountry and issues Wilderness Passes. **Jasper Tourism and Commerce,** 780/852-3858, also has a desk in the building, and the friendly staff never seems to tire of explaining that all the rooms in town are full. As well as providing general information on the town, they have a large collection of brochures on activities, shopping, and restaurants. Beside the main Parks Canada desk is the **Friends of Jasper National Park** outlet selling topographic maps, books, and local publications. Look out for notices posted out front with the day's interpretive programs. The center is open in summer, daily 8 A.M.–7 P.M.; the rest of the year, daily 9 A.M.–5 P.M.

Other Sources of Information

Jasper's weekly newspaper, *The Booster,* is available throughout town on Wednesday. As well as newsworthy stories, it includes a list of upcoming events, trail reports, and a town map with funky little symbols highlighting the location of various "crimes".

For more information on the park, write Superintendent, Jasper National Park, P.O. Box 10, Jasper, AB T0E 1E0; website: www.parkscanada.gc.ca/jasper. For general tourist information, contact Jasper Tourism and Commerce, P.O. Box 98, Jasper T0E 1E0, or call 780/852-3858, www.jaspercanadianrockies.com. The official Town of Jasper website, www.jasper-alberta.com, with lists of current events, current weather conditions, and loads of helpful links, is also worth checking out.

Jasper National Park Radio is on the AM band at 1490. For weather conditions in the park, call 780/852-6176.

Waterton Lakes National Park

Everybody traveling to this small, rugged 526-square-km (203-square-mile) park does so by choice; tucked away in the extreme southwestern corner of Alberta, the park is not on a major highway or on the way to anywhere else. It's bounded to the north and east by the rolling prairies covering southern Alberta; to the south by the U.S. border and Glacier National Park in Montana; and to the west by the Continental Divide, which forms the Alberta–British Columbia border. The natural mountain splendor, a chain of deep glacial lakes, large and diverse populations of wildlife, an unbelievable variety of day hikes, and a changing face each season make this park a gem that shouldn't be missed on any trip to the Canadian Rockies.

The route to Waterton is almost as scenic as the park itself. From whichever direction you arrive, the transition from prairie to mountains is abrupt, almost devoid of the foothills that characterize other areas along the eastern slopes of the Canadian Rockies. Between the park gate and the small township of Waterton, two roads penetrate the mountains to the west. One ends at a large glaciated lake, the other at a spectacular canyon. The town is a smaller version of those in Banff and Jasper. Like those towns, Waterton holds a grand hotel built by the railway, a golf course, and a wide range of services, but the atmosphere here is very different.

THE LAND
Geology

Major upheavals under the earth's surface approximately 85 million years ago forced huge plates of rock upward and began folding them over each other. One major sheet known as the Lewis Overthrust forms the backbone of Waterton's topography as we

Prince of Wales Hotel

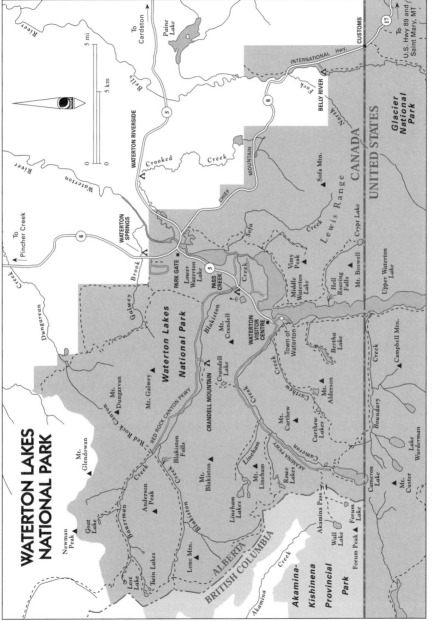

WATERTON LAKES
NATIONAL PARK

© AVALON TRAVEL PUBLISHING, INC.

WATERTON LAKES

see it today. It slid up and over much younger bedrock along a 300-km (186-mile) length extending north to Bow Valley.

About 45 million years ago, this powerful uplift ceased and the forces of erosion took over. About 1.9 million years ago, glaciers from the sheet of ice that once covered most of Alberta crept through the mountains. As these thick sheets of ice advanced and retreated with climatic changes, they gouged out valleys such as the classically U-shaped Waterton Valley. The three Waterton Lakes are depressions left at the base of the steep-sided mountains after the ice had completely retreated 11,000 years ago. The deepest is 150 meters (500 feet). Cameron Lake, at the end of the Akamina Parkway, was formed when a moraine—the pile of rock that accumulates at the foot of a retreating glacier—dammed Cameron Creek. From the lake, Cameron Creek flows through a glaciated valley before dropping into the much deeper Waterton Valley at Cameron Falls, behind the town of Waterton. The town itself sits on an alluvial fan composed of silt and gravel picked up by mountain streams and deposited in Upper Waterton Lake.

Climate

Climate plays an active role in creating the park's natural landscape. This corner of the province tends to receive more rain, snow, and wind—much more wind—than other parts of Alberta. These factors, combined with the park's varied topography, create an environment where more than half the known species in Alberta have been recorded. Wind is the most powerful presence in the park. Prevailing winds from the south and west bring Pacific weather over the divide, creating a climate similar to that experienced farther west. These warm fronts endow the region with chinooks—dry winds that can raise temperatures in the park by up to 40°C (105°F) in 24 hours.

One of the nicest aspects of the park is that it can be enjoyed in all seasons. Summer is great for the sunny windless days, fall for the wildlife viewing, winter for the solitude, and spring for the long days of sunlight as the park seems to be waking up from its winter slumber. Be aware,

PARK ENTRY

All visitors to Waterton Lakes National Park are required to stop at the park gate and buy a permit. A National Parks Day Pass is $5 adults, $3 seniors, $2.50 children up to a maximum of $8 per vehicle, and is valid until 4 P.M. the day following its purchase. If you're traveling to national parks beyond Waterton, a better deal is the annual National Parks of Canada Pass, good for entry into all 27 of Canada's national parks; $38 adults, $29 seniors, $75 families ($58 for two or more seniors). Both types of pass can be bought at the park gate; check the Parks Canada website, www.parkscanada.gc.ca, for more information.

however, that many of the park's best sights and hiking trails lie at high elevations; some areas may be snowed in until mid-June.

Flora

Botanists have recorded 1,200 species of plants growing within the park's several different vegetation zones. In the park's northeastern corner, near the park gate, a region of prairies is covered in semiarid vegetation such as **fescue grass.** As Highway 5 enters the park it passes Maskinonge Lake, a wetlands area of marshy ponds where aquatic plants flourish. Parkland habitat dominated by **aspen** is found along the north side of Blakiston Valley and near Belly River Campground, while montane forest covers most mountain valleys and lower slopes. This montane zone is dominated by a high canopy of **lodgepole pine** and **Douglas fir** shading a forest floor covered with wildflowers and berries. An easily accessible section of this habitat is along the lower half of Bertha Lake Trail; an interpretive brochure is available at the Waterton Visitor Centre.

Above the montane forest is the subalpine zone, which rises as far as the timberline. These distinct forests of **larch, fir, Engelmann spruce,** and **whitebark pine** can be seen along the Carthew Lakes Trail. On the west-facing slopes of Cameron Lakes are mature groves of subalpine trees up to 400 years old; this oldest growth in the park has managed to escape fire over the centuries. Blanketing the open mountain slopes in this zone is

© ANDREW HEMPSTEAD

Mule deer are often sighted along the downtown Waterton lakeshore.

bear grass, which grows up to one meter in height and is topped by a bright blossom often likened to a lighted torch. Above the treeline is the alpine zone, where harsh winds and short summer seasons make trees a rarity. Only **lichens** and **alpine wildflowers** flourish at these high altitudes. Crypt Lake is a good place for viewing this zone.

Fauna

Wildlife viewing in the park requires patience and a little know-how, but the rewards are ample, as good as anywhere in the Canadian Rockies. **Elk** inhabit the park year-round. A large herd gathers by Entrance Road in late fall, wintering on the lowlands. By early fall, many **mule deer** are wandering around town. **Bighorn sheep** are often seen on the north side of Blakiston Valley or on the slopes above the Waterton Visitor Centre; occasionally they will end up in town. **White-tailed deer** are best viewed along Red Rock Canyon Parkway. The park has a small population of moose, occasionally seen in low-lying wetlands. **Mountain goats** rarely leave the high peaks of the backcountry, but from Goat, Crypt, or Bertha Lakes you might catch a glimpse of one high above you.

The most common predators in the park are the **coyotes,** which spend their summer days chasing ground squirrels around the prairie and parkland areas. For its size, Waterton has a healthy population of **cougars,** but these shy, solitary animals are rarely seen. About 50 **black bears** live in the park. They spend most of the summer in the heavily forested montane regions. During August and September, scan the slopes of Blakiston Valley, where the bears can often be seen feasting on saskatoon berries before going into winter hibernation. Much larger than black bears are **grizzlies,** which roam the entire backcountry but are rarely encountered. Larger even still are **bison.** Although these prairie dwellers never lived in the mountains, they would have grazed around the eastern outskirts of what is now the park. A small herd is contained in the **Bison Paddock,** just before the park gate.

Golden-mantled ground squirrels live on the Bear's Hump and around Cameron Falls. **Columbian ground squirrels** are just about everywhere. **Chipmunks** scamper about on Bertha Lake Trail. The best time for viewing **beavers** is at dawn and dusk along the Belly River. **Muskrats** can be seen on the edges of

KOOTENAI BROWN

John George Brown was born in England in the 1840s and reputedly educated at Oxford University. He joined the army and went to India, later continuing to San Francisco. Then, like thousands of others, he headed for the Cariboo goldfields of British Columbia, quickly spending any of the gold he found. After a while he moved on, heading east into Waterton Valley, where his party was attacked by a band of Blackfoot. He was shot in the back with an arrow and pulled it out himself. For a time he worked with the U.S. Army as a Pony Express rider. One day he was captured by Chief Sitting Bull, stripped, and tied to a stake until his fate could be decided, but he managed to escape during the night with his scalp intact. Brown acquired his nickname through his close association with the Kootenay (today's preferred spelling) people, hunting buffalo and wolves with them until the animals had all but disappeared.

Brown married in 1869 and built a cabin by Upper Waterton Lake, becoming the valley's first permanent resident. Even though he had been toughened by the times, he was a conservationist at heart. When a reserve was set aside in 1895, Brown was employed as its first warden. In 1911, the area was declared a national park and Brown, age 71, was appointed its superintendent. He continued to push for an expansion of park boundaries until his final retirement at age 75. He died a few years later. His grave along the main access road to the townsite is a fitting resting place for one of Canada's most celebrated mountainmen.

Maskinonge Lake eating bulrushes. **Mink** also live at the lake but are seen only by those with patience.

Two major flyways pass the park, and from September to November many thousands of waterfowl stop on Maskinonge and Lower Waterton Lakes. On a powerline pole beside the entrance to the park is an active **osprey** nest—ask staff to point it out for you. Waterton Heritage Centre has a great little free checklist for birders listing the 250 species recorded within park boundaries.

HISTORY

Evidence found within the park suggests that the Kootenay people who lived west of the park made trips across the Continental Divide 8,000–10,000 years ago to hunt bison on the plains and fish in the lakes. They camped in the valleys during winter, taking shelter from the harsh weather. But by about 1,500 years ago, they were spending more time in the west and crossing the mountains only a few times a year to hunt bison. By the 1700s, the Blackfoot—with the help of horses—had expanded their territory from the Battle River throughout southwestern Alberta. They patrolled the mountains on horseback, making it difficult for the Kootenay hunt-

ing parties to cross. But their dominance was short-lived. With the arrival of guns and the encroaching homesteads of early settlers, Blackfoot tribes retreated to the east, leaving the Waterton Lakes Valley uninhabited.

Oil City

Kootenai Brown, the valley's first permanent settler, first noticed beads of oil floating on Cameron Creek. He and a business partner siphoned it from the water's surface, bottled it, and sold it in Fort Macleod and Cardston. This discovery created much interest among the oil-starved entrepreneurs of Alberta, who formed the Rocky Mountain Development Company to do some exploratory drilling. At this stage the park was still a Forest Reserve; the trees were protected, but prospecting and mining were still allowed. A rough road was constructed through the Cameron Creek Valley, and in September 1901 the company struck oil at a depth of 311 meters (1,020 feet). It was the first producing oil well in western Canada and only the second in the country. In the resulting euphoria, a townsite named Oil City was cleared and surveyed, a bunkhouse and dining hall were constructed, and the foundations for a hotel were laid. The boom was short-lived. Drilling rigs kept breaking down, and the flow of oil soon slowed to a trickle. A monument along the Akamina Parkway stands at the site of the well, and a little farther up the road at a roadside marker a trail leads through thick undergrowth to the townsite. All that remains are the ill-fated hotel's foundations and some depressions in the ground.

Waterton-Glacier International Peace Park

After becoming the valley's first permanent resident in 1869, Kootenai Brown began promoting the beauty of the area to the people of Fort Macleod. One of his friends, local rancher F.W. Godsal, began lobbying the federal government to establish a reserve. In 1895 an area was set aside as a Forest Reserve. Shortly after Montana's Glacier National Park was created in 1910, the Canadian government changed the name of the reserve to Waterton Lakes Dominion Park; it was later redesignated a national park. Many people followed in the footsteps of Kootenai Brown, and a small town named Waterton grew up on the Cameron Creek delta. The town had no rail link, so unlike Banff and Jasper—its famous mountain neighbors to the north—it didn't draw large crowds of tourists. Nevertheless, it

soon became a popular summer retreat with a hotel, restaurant, and dance hall. The Great Northern Railway decided to operate a bus service from its Montana rail line to Jasper, with a stop at Waterton. This led to the construction of the **Prince of Wales Hotel.**

Boat cruises from the hotel across the International Boundary were soon the park's most popular activity. This brought the two parks closer together, and in 1932, after much lobbying from Rotary International members on both sides of the border, the Canadian and U.S. governments agreed to establish Waterton-Glacier International Peace Park, the first of its kind in the world. The parks are administered separately but cooperate in preserving this pristine mountain wilderness through wildlife management, search-and-rescue operations, and interpretive programs. Peace Park celebrations take place each year, and the **Peace Park Pavilion** by the lake is dedicated to this unique bond. In 1979, UNESCO declared the park a **Biosphere Reserve,** only the second such reserve in Canada. In 1995 the park's importance was further recognized when UNESCO declared Waterton-Glacier International Peace Park a World Heritage Site.

Sights and Recreation

Make your first stop the **Waterton Visitor Centre,** 403/859-2445, on the slight rise before descending to the village. Once in town, getting around on foot is the best way to explore. The **Waterton Heritage Centre,** 117 Waterton Ave., 403/859-2624, offers a small display area, with exhibits telling the story of the park's natural and human history and a small gallery of paintings by local artists. A good variety of books are also sold. The heritage center is operated by the Waterton Natural History Association, which runs a variety of educational programs. The center is open May–September, 10 A.M.–5 P.M., July and August until 7 P.M. From the heritage center, wander south along the lakeshore to a large picnic area and the trailhead for the Waterton Lakeshore Trail (see "Hiking") or north to the **International Peace Park Pavillion** and stunning views across Emerald Bay to the Prince of Wales Hotel.

SCENIC DRIVES

Akamina Parkway

This road starts in the townsite and switchbacks up into the Cameron Creek Valley, making an elevation gain of 400 meters (1,310 feet) before ending after 16 km (10 miles) at Cameron Lake. The viewpoint one km (0.6 miles) from the junction of the park road is on a tight curve, so park off the road. From this lookout, views extend over the townsite and the **Bear's Hump,** which was originally part of a high ridge that extended across the lake to Vimy Peak (glacial action ultimately wore down the rest of the ridge). This section of the road is also a good place to view bighorn sheep. From here to Cameron Lake are several picnic areas and stops of interest, including the site of Alberta's first producing oil well, and a little farther along the road, the site of **Oil City,** the town that never was.

Cameron Lake, at the end of the road, is a 2.5-km-long (1.5-mile-long) subalpine lake that reaches depths more than 40 meters (130 feet). It lies in a large cirque carved out about 11,000 years ago by a receding glacier. Mount Custer at the southern end of the lake is in Montana. Waterton has no glaciers, but Herbst Glacier on Mount Custer can be seen from here. To the west (right) of Custer is **Forum Peak** (2,225 meters/7,300 feet), whose summit cairn marks the boundaries of Alberta, Montana, and British Columbia. Beside the lakeshore are enclosed information boards and a concession stand selling light snacks and renting canoes, rowboats, and paddleboats ($18 for the first hour; $14 for additional hours). A narrow trail leads along the lake's west shoreline, ending after two km (1.2 miles); allow 40 minutes each way. Further on, grizzlies frequent the avalanche slope at the southwestern end of the lake, so hike with someone you can outrun.

Red Rock Canyon Parkway

The best roadside wildlife viewing within the park is along this 13-km (eight-mile) road that starts near the golf course and finishes at **Red Rock Canyon.** The transition between rolling prairies and mountains takes place abruptly as you travel up the Blakiston Valley. Black bears (and very occasionally grizzly bears) can be seen feeding on saskatoon berries along the open slopes to the north. **Mount Blakiston** (2,920 meters/9,580 feet), the park's highest point, is visible from a viewpoint three km (1.9 miles) along the road. The road passes interpretive signs, picnic areas, and Crandell Mountain Campground. At the end of the road is Red Rock Canyon, a water-carved gorge where the bedrock, known as argillite, contains a high concentration of iron. The iron oxidizes and turns red when exposed to air—literally going rusty. A short interpretive trail leads along the canyon.

Chief Mountain International Highway

This 25-km (15.5-mile) highway, part of Highway 6, borders the eastern boundaries of the park and joins it to Glacier National Park in Montana. It starts east of the park gate at **Maskinonge Lake** and climbs for seven km (4.3 miles) to a viewpoint where many jagged peaks and the entire Waterton Valley can be seen. The next stop, three km (1.9 miles) farther south, provides views of Chief Mountain, which has been separated from the main mountain range by erosion. The road then passes more spectacular viewpoints, Belly River Campground, and Chief Mountain.

Hours of operation at this port of entry are mid-May to the end of May, 9 A.M.–6 P.M., June to early September, 7 A.M.–10 P.M., early September to the end of the month, 9 A.M.–6 P.M. When the post is closed, you must use the Carway/Piegan port of entry, which is open year-round, daily 7 A.M.–11 P.M. It's on Alberta Highway 2 south of Cardston (or on Montana Highway 89 north of St. Mary, depending on your direction of travel).

From the border it's 50 km (31 miles) to St. Mary and the spectacular Going-to-the-Sun Highway through **Glacier National Park.** The park's **St. Mary Visitor Center,** 406/888-7800, is open mid-May to mid-October 8 A.M.–5 P.M., and until 9 P.M. in July and August. A good source of pretrip information is the official park website, www.nps.gov/glac.

HIKING

Although the park is relatively small, its trail system is extensive; 224 km (140 miles) of well-maintained trails lead to alpine lakes and lofty summits affording spectacular views. One of the most appealing aspects of hiking in Waterton is that with higher trailheads than other parks in the Canadian Rockies, the treeline is reached quickly. Most of the lakes can be reached in a few hours. Once you've finished hiking the trails in Waterton, you can cross the international border and start on the 1,200 km (746 miles) of trails in Glacier National Park.

The eight hikes detailed as follows comprise only a small cross-section of Waterton's extensive trail system. Most of the hikes climb to alpine lakes or viewpoints. Topographic maps (one map covers the entire park) are available at various outlets in town. If you are planning to stay overnight in the backcountry, you must obtain a Wilderness Pass ($6 per person per night) from Waterton Visitor Centre or the park administration office.

Bear's Hump

- Length: 1.2 km/0.7 miles (40 minutes) one-way
- Elevation gain: 215 meters/700 feet
- Rating: moderate
- Trailhead: Waterton Visitor Centre.

This is one of the most popular short hikes in the park, and although steep, it affords panoramic views of the Waterton Valley. From the back of the visitors center parking lot, the trail switchbacks up the northern flanks of the Bear's Hump, finishing at a rocky ledge high above town. From this vantage point the sweeping view extends across the prairies and down Upper Waterton Lake to the northern reaches of Glacier National Park.

Bertha Lake

- Length: 5.8 km/3.6 miles (two hours) one-way
- Elevation gain: 460 meters/1,510 feet
- Rating: moderate
- Trailhead: south of the townsite at the end of Evergreen Ave. (near the far corner of Townsite Campground)

Bertha Lake is a popular destination with day-hikers and campers alike. For the first 1.5 km (0.9 miles), little elevation gain is made as the trail coincides with the Lakeshore Trail. Then the trail branches right and climbs steadily through a forest of lodgepole pine and Douglas fir along a well-maintained section to **Lower Bertha Falls.** Signs along this first, easier section correspond with the *Bertha Falls Self-Guiding Nature Trail* brochure available from the Visitor Centre. From here the trail passes **Upper Bertha Falls** and begins switchbacking steeply through a subalpine forest to its maximum elevation on a

ridge above the hanging valley in which Bertha Lake lies. A trail encircles the lake. The backcountry campground on the lake's edge is one of the park's busiest.

Waterton Lakeshore

- Length: 14 km/8.7 miles (four hours) one-way
- Elevation gain: minimal
- Rating: easy/moderate
- Trailhead: south of the townsite at the end of Evergreen Avenue

This trail follows the heavily forested western shores of Upper Waterton Lake across the International Boundary to **Goat Haunt, Montana,** linking up with more than 1,200 km (746 miles) of trails in Glacier National Park. Many hikers take the Wateron Cruise Company's **MV International** one-way ($14; call 403/859-2362) and hike the other. The boat dock at Boundary Bay, six km (3.7 miles) from town, is a good place for lunch. Park guides lead a hike along this trail each Saturday morning, making the return trip by boat; contact the visitors center for details. Hikers heading south and planning to camp in Glacier National Park must register at the Waterton Visitor Centre.

Crypt Lake

- Length: 8.7 km/5.4 miles (3–4 hours) one-way
- Elevation gain: 680 meters/2,230 feet
- Rating: moderate/difficult
- Trailhead: Crypt Landing; access is by boat. The **Crypt Lake Shuttle,** 403/859-2362, leaves the marina daily at 9 A.M. and 10 A.M. for Crypt Landing, returning at 4 P.M. and 5:30 P.M.; $13 round-trip.

This is one of the most spectacular day hikes in Canada. Access to the trailhead on the eastern side of Upper Waterton Lake is by boat. The trail switchbacks for 2.5 km (1.6 miles) past a series of waterfalls and continues steeply up to a small green lake before reaching a campground. The final ascent to Crypt Lake from the campground causes the most problems, especially for those who suffer from claustrophobia. A ladder on the cliff face leads into a natural tunnel that

Crandell Lake

© ANDREW HEMPSTEAD

you must crawl through on your hands and knees. The next part of the trail is along a narrow precipice with a cable for support. The lake at the end of the trail, nestled in a hanging valley, is no disappointment. Its dark green waters are rarely free of floating ice, and the steep walls of the cirque rise more than 500 meters (1,640 feet) above the lake on three sides. The International Boundary is at the southern end of the lake. A good way to avoid the crowds on this trail is to camp at the dock and set out before the first boat arrives in the morning.

Crandell Lake

- Length: 2.4 km/1.5 miles (40 minutes) one-way
- Elevation gain: 120 meters/395 feet
- Rating: easy
- Trailhead: Crandell Campground, Red Rock Canyon Parkway

This easy hike to a subalpine lake is popular with campers staying at Crandell Campground.

Alternately, the trailhead can be reached by noncampers along the Canyon Church Camp access road. The lake can also be accessed from a trailhead seven km (4.3 miles) west of town along the Akamina Parkway. This trail is shorter (0.8 km/0.5 miles) and follows a wagon road that was cut through the valley to Oil City.

Goat Lake

- Length: 6.7 km/4.2 miles (two hours) one-way
- Elevation gain: 500 meters/1,640 feet
- Rating: moderate
- Trailhead: end of Red Rock Canyon Parkway, 18 km (11.2 miles) from Waterton townsite

The first hour of walking from the trailhead at Red Rock Canyon follows the Snowshoe Trail along **Bauerman Creek** before branching to the right and climbing switchbacks through a mixed forest. The steep gradient evens out as the trail enters the Goat Lake cirque. After the uphill slog, the lake is a welcome sight, its emerald-green waters reflecting the towering headwalls that surround it. Look for the lake's namesake on the open scree slopes west of the lake.

Carthew-Alderson

- Length: 20 km/12.4 miles (6–7 hours) one-way
- Elevation gain: 650 meters/2,130 feet
- Rating: moderate/difficult
- Trailhead: end of Akamina Parkway, 16 km (10 miles) from Waterton townsite

This hike linking the end of the Akamina Parkway to Waterton townsite can be completed in one long strenuous day or done with an overnight stop at Alderson Lake, 13 km (eight miles) from the trailhead. It leads through most of the climatic zones of the park and offers some of the best scenery to be had on any one hike. Transportation to the trailhead can be arranged through the **Park Transport Company** in the Tamarack Village Square ($8 one-way; 403/859-2378), which operates a hiker shuttle service to this and other trailheads in the park. From the Cameron Lake parking lot, the trail climbs four km (2.5 miles) to **Summit Lake,** a worthy des-

WATERTON LAKES

tination in itself. The trail then forks to the left and climbs steeply to Carthew Ridge. After rising above the treeline and crossing a scree slope, the trail reaches its highest elevation of 2,310 meters (7,580 feet) at **Carthew Summit.** The views from here are spectacular, even more so if you scramble up to one of Mount Carthew's lower peaks. To the north is a hint of prairie, to the southeast the magnificent bowl-shaped cirque around Cameron Lake. To the south, the Carthew Lakes lie directly below, while glaciated peaks in Montana line the horizon. From this summit, the trail descends steeply to the Carthew Lakes, reenters the subalpine forest, and emerges at **Alderson Lake,** which is nestled under the headwalls of Mount Alderson. The trail then descends through the Carthew Creek Valley and finishes at Cameron Falls in the townsite.

Vimy Peak

- Length: 12 km/7.5 miles (five hours) one-way
- Elevation gain: 825 meters/2,700 feet
- Rating: moderate
- Trailhead: Chief Mountain International Highway, a half km (0.3 miles) from the Highway 5 junction

Vimy Peak overlooks the townsite from across Upper Waterton Lake. It was once part of a ridge that extended across the Waterton Valley and was worn down by the relentless forces of glacial action. The initial six-km (3.7-mile) stretch is along the eastern bank of Lower Waterton Lake through forest and grassland. The trail then continues along the lake to Bosporus Landing opposite the town or climbs steeply to Vimy Peak (2,379 meters/7,805 feet). The Vimy Peak trail actually ends at a basin short of the summit, which is still a painfully steep 40-minute scramble away.

OTHER RECREATION

Cruising to Goat Haunt, Montana

This is the most popular activity in Waterton. From the marina in downtown Waterton townsite, **Waterton Inter-Nation Shoreline Cruise Company,** 403/859-2362, runs sched-

Scuba diving isn't usually associated with the Rockies, but Emerald Bay holds a sunken steamer that attracts divers throughout summer.

uled cruises across the International Boundary to Goat Haunt, Montana, at the southern end of Upper Waterton Lake. The 45-minute trip along the lakeshore passes spectacular mountain scenery and usually wildlife. A half-hour stopover is made at Goat Haunt, which lies in a remote part of Glacier National Park and consists of little more than a dock and interpretive displays. You can return on the same boat or go hiking and return later in the day. If you are planning an overnight hike from here, you are required to register at the Waterton Visitor Centre before heading out on the lake. Another popular option is to take an early boat trip and walk back to town on the **Waterton Lakeshore Trail,** which takes about four hours. Boats leave the Waterton marina five times daily (from 9 A.M.) during summer. Fewer trips are made during June and September. The cruises operate until the end of September. Tickets cost $24 round-trip, $14 one-way, and you'll need to book ahead in summer. The same company operates a regular shuttle service to the Crypt Lake trailhead for $13 round-trip.

Fishing

Fishing in the lakes is above average, with most anglers chasing brook and rainbow trout, pike, and whitefish. A national park fishing license is required and can be obtained from the Waterton Visitor Centre or any of the administration offices. The license costs $6 for seven days, or $13 for an annual permit.

Windsurfing

Winds of up to 70 kph (45 mph) attract hard-core windsurfers throughout summer and into fall. The winds are predominantly south to north, providing fast runs across Upper Waterton Lake from the beach at Cameron Bay. The lake is deep, keeping the water temperature low and making a wetsuit necessary. Read the warning signs at the beach before heading out.

Scuba Diving

On any given summer day, scuba divers can be seen slipping into the frigid waters of Emerald Bay. A steamer was scuttled in the bay in 1918. It had been used to haul logs and as a tearoom but now sits on the lake's floor, attracting divers who find it a novelty to explore a sunken ship so far from the ocean. No equipment rental is available in the park. The closest is at **Anderson Aquatics,** in Lethbridge at 314 11th Street S., 403/328-5040, where you can also get your tanks filled. Full gear rental from Anderson is $50 per day, $75 for the weekend, including air fills. Through this shop, certification courses and field trips to Waterton Lakes are organized throughout the summer. Stop in on your way to the park for a rundown on all the dives, or ask at the Waterton Visitor Centre.

On any given summer day, scuba divers can be seen slipping into the frigid waters of Emerald Bay. A steamer was scuttled in the bay in 1918, and now sits on the lake's floor, attracting divers who find it a novelty to explore a sunken ship so far from the ocean.

Golfing

The rolling fairways and spectacular mountain backdrop of **Waterton Lakes Golf Course** can distract even the keenest golfer's attention. The 18-hole course, designed by Stanley Thompson and dating to 1929, is not particularly long (6,103 yards) or difficult, but the surrounding mountains and unhurried pace of play make for a pleasant environment. The course is four km (2.5 miles) north of the townsite on the main access road and is open June to early October. Its facilities include a rental shop, clubhouse, and restaurant serving sandwiches and snacks. A round of golf costs $32 during the day, or play as many rounds as you like in one day for $43. Club rentals are $7.50, and a power cart is an additional $26 per round. For tee times, call 403/859-2114.

When the Sun Goes Down

Interpretive programs are held nightly during the summer in Crandell Campground and at the **Falls Theatre** opposite Cameron Falls. Programs begin at 8:30 P.M., with special guest speakers appearing at the Falls Theatre Saturday night. Ask at the Waterton Visitor Centre or call 403/859-2445 for a schedule.

Being the biggest and most central bar in town, the **Thirsty Bear Saloon** in the Bayshore Inn, Waterton Avenue, 403/859-2211, gets crowded. It pours happy hour daily 3–6 P.M., and a band plays two or three nights a week. It's open 11 A.M.–2 A.M. If it's a sunny afternoon, relax on the lakeside deck of the inn's adjacent restaurant with a cool drink. The **Rams Head Lounge** in the Kilmorey Lodge, Mount View Road, 403/859-2334, has a rustic mountain ambience centered around a wood-burning fireplace. Outside is a deck with views of the lake. Another downtown bar is the **Wolf's Den Lounge** in Waterton Lakes Lodge, corner of Windflower Avenue and Cameron Falls Road, 403/859-2151. In the Prince of Wales Hotel, the staid **Windsor Lounge,** 403/859-2231, has panoramic views across the lake and live entertainment most nights.

Waterton Lakes Opera House, 309 Windflower Ave., 403/859-2466, shows movies daily at 7:30 and 9:30 P.M.

Wintertime

Winter is a quiet time in the park. Traffic on the roads is light, the Prince of Wales Hotel sits empty, the snowcapped peaks and abundant big game provide plenty of photographic opportunities, and a few trails are maintained for cross-country skiing. The main access road is plowed regularly, and the Akamina Parkway is cleared to allow access to ski trails. Skiing in the park is usually possible from December to March, but conditions can change dramatically. Cold arctic fronts scream down from the north, and chinook winds from the west can raise temperatures by up to 20°C (37°F) in an hour. Ski trails are set on weekends, and the ski-touring opportunities are endless. Trails in the backcountry are not marked. Groups should carry avalanche beacons, be capable of self-rescue, and register with the warden before setting out. Ice climbing, snowshoeing, and backcountry winter camping are also popular. Winter camping is possible at Pass Creek, where you'll find a kitchen shelter, woodstove, and pit toilets. Three accommodations stay open year-round and offer all-inclusive winter packages. Gas may or may not be available in winter. Obtain trail information and weather forecasts at the park administration office on Mount View Road, open weekdays 8 A.M.–4 P.M., 403/859-5133. For information regarding backcountry skiing conditions and avalanche danger, contact the **Canadian Avalanche Association,** 800/667-1105, www.avalanche.ca.

Accommodations and Camping

HOTELS, MOTELS, AND LODGES

Waterton has a limited number of accommodations. Most start opening in May and will be full every night during July and August. By mid-October many are closed, with only the Kilmorey Lodge, Crandell Mountain Lodge, and Waterton Glacier Suites open year-round. All accommodations are within the townsite, so walking to the marina and shops isn't a problem.

Less Than $50

Hostelling International–Waterton Alpine Centre is located in a wing of Waterton Lakes Lodge, one of the village's premier accommodations, at the corner of Windflower Avenue and Cameron Falls Road, 403/859-2150 or 888/985-6343, www.watertonlakeslodge.com. A total of 21 beds are spread through six rooms, with a maximum of four beds in any one room. Guests have use of all lodge facilities, including the Waterton Spa and Recreation Centre (for a small fee), tennis, and bike rentals, as well as a common lounge area, shared kitchen, and bathrooms. Beds are $21 for members of Hostelling International, $25 for nonmembers—a great deal for those travelers who are willing to share living facilities. Check-in is after 4 P.M., and it's open February to November.

$50–100

The **El Cortez Motel** is one block from the main street at 208 Mount View Road, 403/859-2366. It's an older, park-at-your-door motel with basic furnishings and no phones. Standard rooms are $75 s, $80 d, with some kitchenettes from $110.

Also in this price bracket is **Northland Lodge,** Evergreen Avenue, 403/859-2353, www.northlandlodgecanada.com, a converted house built in 1929 by Louis Hill, who also built the Prince of Wales Hotel. Backing onto wilderness, Cameron Falls and downtown Waterton are both just a short walk away. It features nine guest rooms, a large lounge with a TV and fireplace, and a large balcony. The two rooms that share a bathroom are $85 s or

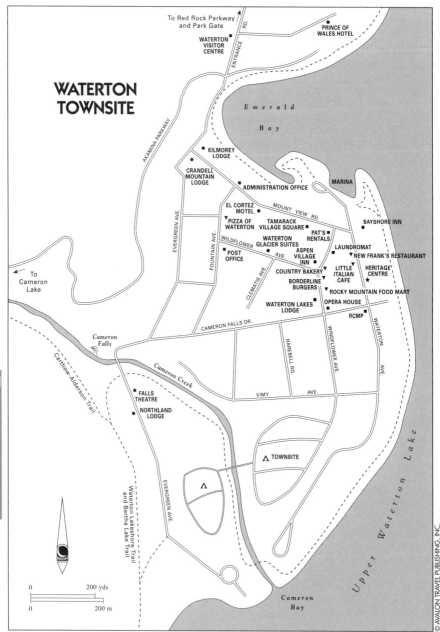

WATERTON TOWNSITE

To Red Rock Parkway
and Park Gate

WATERTON
VISITOR
CENTRE

PRINCE OF
WALES HOTEL

ENTRANCE RD.

Emerald
Bay

AKAMINA PARKWAY

KILMOREY
LODGE

CRANDELL
MOUNTAIN
LODGE

ADMINISTRATION OFFICE

MARINA

EL CORTEZ
MOTEL

MOUNT VIEW RD.

BAYSHORE INN

EVERGREEN AVE.

PIZZA OF
WATERTON

TAMARACK
VILLAGE SQUARE

PAT'S
RENTALS

WILDFLOWER

WATERTON
GLACIER SUITES

FOUNTAIN AVE.

POST
OFFICE

AVE.

ASPEN
VILLAGE
INN

LAUNDROMAT

NEW FRANK'S RESTAURANT

To
Cameron
Lake

CLEMATIS AVE.

COUNTRY BAKERY

LITTLE
ITALIAN
CAFE

HERITAGE
CENTRE

BORDERLINE
BURGERS

ROCKY MOUNTAIN FOOD MART

WATERTON LAKES
LODGE

OPERA HOUSE

RCMP

WATERTON

Cameron
Falls

CAMERON FALLS DR.

HAREBELL RD.

WINDFLOWER AVE.

AVE.

Carthew-Alderson Trail

Cameron Creek

FALLS
THEATRE

NORTHLAND
LODGE

VIMY   AVE.

Upper Waterton Lake

EVERGREEN AVE.

Waterton Lakeshore Trail
and Bertha Lake Trail

TOWNSITE

MOON

0   200 yds

0   200 m

Cameron
Bay

© AVALON TRAVEL PUBLISHING, INC.

d, while the remainder are $110–155 s or d; rates include tea, coffee, and muffins in the morning.

$100–150

Kilmorey Lodge, Mount View Road, 403/859-2334 or 888/859-8669, www.kilmoreylodge.com, a historic 1920s inn on the shores of Emerald Bay, provides an excellent value for the money. Victorian furnishings, lots of exposed timber, squeaking floorboards, and historic photographs add to the charm. From the lobby a narrow stairway leads up to 23 rooms tucked under the eaves, many of which have spectacular lake views. Each is furnished with antiques, and the beds have down comforters to ensure a good night's sleep. Downstairs is one of the town's finest restaurants, along with a lounge and gazebo for enjoying a quiet drink on those warm summer nights. Standard rooms during summer start at $113 s or d, rising to $194 for the spacious Deluxe King. Some rooms have lake views, but book in advance for these. Inexpensive packages are offered in winter. The lodge stays open year-round.

Across the road from the Kilmorey Lodge is **Crandell Mountain Lodge,** Mount View Road, 403/859-2288 or 866/859-2288, www.crandellmountainlodge.com, a centrally located country-style inn. The lodge has seen many changes since it first opened in 1940 with shared bathrooms and wood-heated water. Today each of the 17 rooms has a private bath and is beautifully finished with country-style furnishings (no phones), and out back is a private garden area. Two rooms are wheelchair-accessible. The smallest rooms are $129 s or d, most—with a choice of fireplace or kitchenette—are $159, and the largest suite is $199. Rates are reduced around 30 percent between mid-September and May.

The **Aspen Village Inn,** 111 Windflower Ave., 403/859-2255 or 888/859-8669, offers large rooms for $132 s or d ($167 with a kitchen) but is best noted for its self-contained cottages, which sleep up to eight for $188, an excellent deal for small groups. Also on the property is a barbecue area and playground. Aspen Village is open May to mid-October.

For a few dollars more, the **Bayshore Inn,** Waterton Ave., 403/859-2211 or 888/527-9555, www.bayshoreinn.com, enjoys a prime waterfront location right on the main street. The highlight of 70 nondescript rooms are the private balconies, while other on-site amenities include a hot tub, restaurant, and lounge. Rooms are $145 s or d, $155 lake view. For the first two months of the season, the Bayshore offers excellent meal-inclusive packages for the same price as their summertime, room-only rates. This lodging is open mid-April to mid-October.

$150–200

Not much ever changes in sleepy Waterton, but in the late 1990s two new accommodations, the first since the 1970s, opened. **Waterton Glacier Suites,** on Windflower Avenue, 403/859-2004 or 866/621-3330, www.watertonsuites.com, is open year-round and provides excellent value. Each of 26 units features stylish, modern décor, is air-conditioned, and offers a fridge and microwave. Two-bedroom suites are $169 s or d, units with a jetted tub and fireplace are $225, and spacious loft units are $259.

The larger of the two is **Waterton Lakes Lodge,** at the corner of Windflower Avenue and Cameron Falls Road, 403/859-2151 or 866/985-6343, www.watertonlakeslodge.com, which is set on a 1.5-hectare (3.7-acre) site in the heart of town. All 80 rooms are large and modern, and each has mountain-themed décor and mountain views. Amenities include air-conditioning, a TV/VCR combination, Internet access, and a coffeemaker. The lodge complex also holds the Waterton Spa and Recreation Centre (free entry for guests), a restaurant, a small café, and a lounge. Standard rooms are $195 s or d, while those with kitchenettes are $240. It's open February–November; check the website for steeply discounted off-season rates.

More Than $200

Waterton's most well-known landmark is the **Prince of Wales Hotel,** 403/859-2231 or 406/892-2525, www.glacierparkinc.com, a seven-story gabled structure built in 1927 on a hill overlooking Upper Waterton Lake. It was an-

The Prince of Wales Hotel is the grandest of Waterton's accommodations.

other grand mountain resort financed by the railway, except, unlike those in Banff and Jasper, it had no rail link and has always been U.S.-owned. It was built as part of a chain of first-class hotels in Glacier National Park and is still owned by the company that controls those south of the border. Early guests were transported to the hotel by bus from the Great Northern Railway in Montana. After extensive restoration inside and out, the hotel has been returned to its former splendor. Rates for the smallest (and they're small) Value Rooms are $265–276 s or d, depending on the view. Standard rooms start at $293, rising to $347 for those with a lake view. The opulence and history of this hotel is unequalled in Waterton, but don't expect the facilities of a similarly priced city hostelry: rooms have no television and some have no elevator access. The Prince of Wales is open mid-May to late September.

CAMPGROUNDS

Park Campgrounds

Waterton Lakes National Park has three campgrounds holding a total of 391 campsites. They open only in summer, with winter camping permitted at Pass Creek, along the park access road. No reservations are taken, so to ensure a site, try to time your arrival with check-out time, which is 11 A.M. **Townsite Campground,** 403/859-2224, enjoys a prime lakeside location within walking distance of many trailheads, restaurants, and shops. Many of its more than 238 sites have power, water, and sewer hookups. The campground also offers showers and kitchen shelters. Sites are available on a first-come, first-served basis and fill up by early afternoon most summer days. Open mid-April to mid-October; walk-in tent sites are $15, unserviced sites $18, hookups $24.

Crandell Campground is 10 km (6.2 miles) from the townsite on Red Rock Canyon Parkway. It has 129 unserviced sites ($14), flush toilets, and kitchen shelters. Pleasant Crandell Lake is an easy 2.4 km (1.5 miles) walk from the southwest corner of the campground. Open mid-May to mid-September. **Belly River Campground,** 26 km (16 miles) from the townsite on Chief Mountain International Highway, is the smallest (24 sites) and most primitive of the park's three developed campgrounds. It has pit toilets and kitchen shelters; sites are $12 per night. The latter two campgrounds supply firewood but charge $6 per site to burn it. Belly River is open mid-May to mid-September.

Waterton also holds 12 backcountry campgrounds. Each has pit toilets, a cook shelter, and a water supply. Open fires are discouraged and are prohibited during periods of high fire danger; check with a warden. If you are planning to camp in the backcountry, you must obtain a Wilderness Use Permit from the Waterton Visitor Centre or the administration office. Permits are $6 per person per night. Half of all sites can be reserved in advance ($10 per booking). Call 403/859-5133 for reservations. If your planned backcountry itinerary takes you over the border, ask at the information center about border-crossing regulations.

Commercial Campgrounds

Outside of the park, two private campgrounds take up the nightly overflow. **Waterton Springs Campground,** three km (1.9 miles) north of the park gate on Highway 6, 403/859-2247 or 866/859-2247, www.watertonsprings.com, has recently undergone massive renovations, including the construction of a large building holding modern bathroom facilities, a lounge, a general store, and a laundry room. Also on-site is a fishing pond stocked with rainbow trout. Tent sites are $16, trailers and RVs pay $20–24.

On Highway 5, five km (3.1 miles) east of the park gate, **Waterton Riverside Campground,** 403/653-2888, has powered sites and showers. Tent sites are $16, powered sites $20. Both of these campgrounds close by the end of September.

Other Practicalities

FOOD

Restaurants in the park offer a range of fare—from pizza and fast food to elegant dining. If you plan on cooking your own food, stock up before you get to the park. Groceries are available at the **Rocky Mountain Food Mart** on Windflower Avenue (open 8 A.M.–10 P.M.) and in the Tamarack Village Square on Mount View Road. The Food Mart sells hot chickens—an easy and inexpensive camping or picnicking meal.

Cafés and Cheap Eats

For everything from vegetarian pitas to buffalo burgers, head to **Borderline Burgers,** 305 Windflower Ave., 403/859-2284, where the indoor/outdoor tables are always busy. Next door is the **Country Bakery,** a city-style deli serving meat and fruit pies as well as a wide range of pastries. In the theater building on the corner of Windflower Avenue and Cameron Falls Drive is the **Waterton Bagel & Coffee Co.,** serving up exactly that. **Gazebo Cafe on the Bay** in the Kilmorey Lodge serves light snacks and simple meals; seating is on an outdoor deck on the waterfront. It's open daily 10 A.M.–10 P.M.

For great pizza, try **Pizza of Waterton,** 103 Fountain Ave., 403/859-2660, where they pile the dough with all kinds of meats, fresh vegetables, and a special savory sauce. It's open midday to midnight.

High Tea

Every afternoon between 2–5 P.M., the foyer of the Prince of Wales Hotel fills up as visitors descend on this historic landmark for High Tea. Scrumptious pastries, tea, coffee, and other beverages are served up on white linen at tables with the best view in town; $32 per person.

Restaurants

One of the most popular restaurants in town is the **Lamp Post Dining Room,** in the Kilmorey Lodge, 403/859-2334. It has all the charm of the Prince of Wales Hotel but with a more casual atmosphere and low prices to match. The game-oriented menu offers mouthwatering mains ranging from an East Indian–style vegetarian curry ($16) to medallions of caribou glazed in a Saskatoon and juniper berry sauce ($25.95). Leave room to finish with a delicious piece of Saskatoon berry pie ($3). An impressive wine list is dominated by Canadian offerings. The

Lamp Post is open 7:30 A.M.–10 P.M. (breakfast features delicious oatmeal with a warmed bagel on the side for $5).

The **Little Italian Cafe,** 113 Waterton Ave., 403/859-0003, is a great little restaurant serving up inexpensive Italian delights. All basic pasta dishes are priced less than $12, but worth the extra bucks is Chicken Ranchesco ($18.50), a delicious chicken dish cooked with ham and sun-dried tomatoes. The Little Italian is also the best option for breakfast, with a full cooked breakfast from just $6.50. **New Frank's Restaurant,** 106 Waterton Ave., 403/859-2240, serves inexpensive Chinese food (from $7.50) and Western food (from $9.50).

The **Kootenai Brown Dining Room** in the Bayshore Inn, 403/859-2211, overlooks Upper Waterton Lake and the mountains. Mule deer often feed within sight of diners. The food is excellent, especially the trout and beef dishes (from $17), and the view is free. The dining room is also open for a breakfast buffet ($13) and lunch. Hours are daily 7 A.M.–10 P.M.

The **Royal Stewart Dining Room,** 403/859-2231, is a formal restaurant in the Prince of Wales Hotel. Its high ceiling, views of the lake through large windows, and Old World elegance create a first-class ambience that is overshadowed only by the quality of the food. Prices are similar to any big-city restaurant of the same standard—expect to pay around $100 for two with a bottle of wine. If you are going to splurge, do it here. A large breakfast buffet every morning (6:30–9:30 A.M.; $20 per person) is worth trying if you won't be coming for dinner. Lunch is served 11:30 A.M.–2 P.M.; dinner 5–9:30 P.M. Reservations are required.

TRANSPORTATION
Getting There
The nearest commercial airport is at Lethbridge, 140 km (87 miles) away. Cars can be rented at the airport. The closest **Greyhound** buses come to the park is Pincher Creek, 50 km (31 miles) away. From the depot there, at 1015 Hewetson St., 403/627-2716, you'll need to get a cab, which will cost around $55. Call **Crystal Taxi** at 403/627-4262.

Getting Around
The **Park Transport Company,** in Tamarack Village Square on Mount View Road, 403/859-2378, operates hiker shuttle services to various trailheads within the park. Cameron Lake, the starting point for the Carthew-Alderson Trail (which ends back in town), is a popular drop-off point; $7.50 one-way. You could take one of these shuttles, then return on the bus later in the day if driving the steep mountain roads doesn't appeal to you. The company also offers two-hour tours ($25 per person) through the park and runs a local taxi service.

The **Crypt Lake Shuttle** leaves the marina regularly for Crypt landing; $12 round-trip. Reservations are necessary in summer; call 403/859-2362. **Pat's Waterton,** on Mount View Road, 403/859-2266, rents mountain bikes (from $6 per hour, $30 per day) and motorized scooters ($20 per hour, $65 per day).

INFORMATION AND SERVICES
Shopping and Services
The numerous tourist-oriented gift shops along Waterton Avenue are worth browsing through when the weather isn't cooperating. In the **Tamarack Village Square** on Mount View Road, you'll find a good bookshop, a currency exchange, and a sports store selling camping gear and fishing tackle. Waterton has no banks, but traveler's checks are accepted at most businesses, and **ATMs** are scattered throughout town, including at Pat's Waterton on Mount View Road. The **post office** is beside the fire station on Fountain Avenue. **Itussiststukiopi Coin-Op Launderette** at 301 Windflower Avenue is open daily 8 A.M.–10 P.M. The closest **hospitals** are in Cardston, 403/653-4411, and Pincher Creek, 403/627-3333. The park's 24-hour emergency number is 403/859-2636. For the **RCMP,** call 403/859-2244.

Books and Maps
The **Waterton Natural History Association,** based in the Waterton Heritage Centre, 117 Waterton Ave., 403/859-2624, offers a variety of educational programs and stocks every book ever written about the park, as well as many titles

pertaining to western Canada in general. It's open May–Sept., 10 A.M.–5 P.M.; longer hours in summer. Topographical maps of the park (one map covers the entire area) are available for $10.50 from the Waterton Visitor Centre, administration office, and Heritage Centre.

Information

On the main access road opposite the Prince of Wales Hotel, the **Waterton Visitor Centre,** 403/859-5133, provides general information on the park, sells fishing licenses, and issues Wilderness Use permits. It's open June–Aug. 9 A.M.–8 P.M., May and early Sept. 9 A.M.–5 P.M.; closed the rest of the year. The park's administration office on Mount View Road offers the same services as the Visitor Centre and is open year-round, weekdays 8 A.M.–4 P.M.; 403/859-2224. For more information on the park, write to Superintendent, Waterton Lakes National Park, Waterton Park, AB T0K 2M0. The Parks Canada website is www.parkscanada.gc.ca/waterton. For general tourist information, the local chamber of commerce website, www.watertonchamber.com, provides plenty current information and links to accommodations.

WATERTON LAKES

Lesser-Traveled Parks

The previous chapters have covered the better-known parks of the Canadian Rockies, but many other areas of special appeal are protected as provincial and wilderness parks. These parks give visitors the chance to enjoy the natural beauty and wildlife of the mountains away from the crowds associated with the national parks. They have no fancy hotels, golf courses, or shopping malls, and in some cases not even roads.

Seven provincial parks lie on the British Columbia side of the mountains. **Mount Robson Provincial Park,** west of Jasper National Park, protects the highest peak in the Canadian Rockies. The Berg Lake Trail, which climbs to a high alpine lake at the base of Mount Robson, is the most popular overnight hike in all of the mountains. **Mount Assiniboine Provincial Park** has no roads—access is on foot or by flying in by helicopter. The other provincial parks—**Akamina/Kishinena, Elk Lakes, Height of the Rockies, Top of the World,** and **Whiteswan Lake**—all have their own appeal and are well worth the effort required to reach them.

On the Alberta side of the mountains, three designated wilderness areas—**White Goat, Siffleur,** and **Willmore**—offer even more solitude. No horses or motorized vehicles are allowed within their boundaries, and hunting and fishing are prohibited, as is all construction. This, ironically, gives these lightly traveled regions more pro-

heli-hikers enjoying a heavenly view of Mount Robson

tection than national parks. The drawback, and the reason so few people explore these areas, is that wilderness really means *wilderness,* sans roads, bridges, or campsites. With one exception at Willmore, no roads even lead to the areas' boundaries; the only access is on foot.

Provincial Parks

AKAMINA/KISHINENA PROVINCIAL PARK

Bordering Glacier National Park (Montana, U.S.) and Waterton Lakes National Park (Alberta), this remote tract of 10,922 hectares (27,000 acres) protects the extreme southeastern corner of British Columbia. The park is named for its two main waterways, which flow southward into Montana from the Flathead Basin. This was the main reason for the park's creation because now, alongside Waterton Lakes National Park, entire watersheds of Glacier National Park are protected.

The landscape has changed little in thousands of years, since the Kootenay rested in the open meadows beside Kishinena Creek before crossing the Continental Divide to hunt bison on the prairies. The park supports a healthy population of grizzly bears, along with other endangered species such as wolverines, wolves, and lynx.

The only access is on foot from one of two trailheads. The longer option is from the end of an unsealed road that leaves Highway 3 at 16 km (10 miles) south of Fernie, British Columbia. The road leads 110 km (68 miles) into the Flathead River Valley, where trails climb along Kishinena then Akamina Creeks into the park.

Access from Waterton Lakes National Park

The most popular and easiest access to the park is by hiking trail from the Akamina Parkway in Waterton Lakes National Park (Alberta). The signposted trailhead is 15 km (9.3 miles) along this road from Waterton townsite. From the parkway, the trail gains 110 meters (360 feet) of elevation in 1.5 km (0.9 mile) before reaching the boundary of the park high atop the Continental Divide. After a further 700 meters (0.3 miles), the trail divides. The closest of two subalpine bodies

of water, **Forum Lake** is 2.2 km (1.4 miles) to the left up a tedious ascent of Forum Creek. Colorful meadows surround the lake's outlet, while a layered headwall provides a stunning backdrop. Allow 1.5 hours for this 4.4-km (2.7-mile) hike. Nestled below Akamina Ridge, **Wall Lake** is straight ahead from the junction, 2.7 km (1.7 miles). This trail gains only minimal elevation and passes Akamina Creek Campground.

Practicalities

The park's only facility is **Akamina Creek Campground,** 2.4 km (1.5 miles) from the Akamina Parkway along the trail to Wall Lake. Set in a forest of Engelmann spruce, each site has a picnic table and firepit; $5 per night.

Like all of British Columbia's provincial parks, Akamina/Kishinena falls under the auspices of **BC Parks,** 250/354-6333, website: http://wlapwww.gov.bc.ca/bcparks, a division of the government's Ministry of Water, Land, and Air Protection.

Fernie

The nearest town to the Flathead River Valley access point is Fernie (pop. 5,200), out on Highway 3 and a worthwhile destination in itself. It's traditionally been a coal-mining and forestry center, but the town has great skiing and boarding at **Fernie Alpine Resort,** 250/423-4655, www.skifernie.com, generally regarded as one of North America's undiscovered gems. Beside the highway, through town to the north, is **Fernie Visitor Info Centre,** 250/423-6868, www.city.fernie.bc.ca, a good source of information for those traveling to Akamina/Kishinena Provincial Park.

Least expensive of Fernie's indoor accommodations is the **Raging Elk Hostel,** in a converted motel at 892 6th Avenue, 250/423-6811, www.ragingelk.com. An associate of Hostelling International, it provides all the usual facilities, including a communal kitchen and laundry. Rates range from $16 for a dorm bed to $45 for a double room with a TV. One of the better motels along the highway through town is **Park Place Lodge,** 742 Hwy. 3, 250/423-6871 or 888/381-7275, www.parkplacelodge.com, a modern three-story hotel along the main road. Amenities include spacious and elegant rooms opening to an atrium, the Red Rock Bistro, and a pub. Summer rates are from a reasonable $99 s, $109 d, with golf and ski packages starting from $85 per person. Up at the resort, **Griz Inn Sport Hotel,** 250/423-9221 or 800/661-0118, www.grizinn.com, offers 45 kitchen-equipped suites, an indoor pool, hot tub, and restaurant. Through summer (the off-season), room rates start at a reasonable $70–85 s or d, while a condo unit is $100 for up to four people.

The best bet for campers is **Mount Fernie Provincial Park,** 12 km (7.5 miles) south of town and four km (2.5 miles) north of the Akamina/Kishinena Provincial Park access road. Facilities are basic, but it's a pleasant setting, and a short trail leads along Lizard Creek to a waterfall. Sites are $12 per night and it's open mid-May to September.

ELK LAKES PROVINCIAL PARK

This park encompasses more than 17,000 hectares (42,000 acres) of rugged wilderness along the British Columbia side of the Canadian Rockies. The park lies adjacent to the southern border of Peter Lougheed Provincial Park in Alberta (see the "Kananaskis Country" chapter), but the only road access is from Highway 3, more than 120 km (75 miles) to the south. Head north for 35 km (22 miles) from Sparwood, between Cranbrook and the Alberta border, on a paved road to **Elkford,** then take an unpaved forestry road for a further 67 km (42 miles) north into the park.

The end of the road, where you'll find a kiosk with a park map and up-to-date trail conditions, is the park's main trailhead. From this point it's an easy one km (0.6 miles) to **Lower Elk Lake** and then another kilometer beyond the end of the lake to **Upper Elk Lake.** At the lower lake, a narrow trail climbs to a lookout. Aside from the

long drive in, the ratio of effort to reward in reaching these lakes is unmatched in the Canadian Rockies. The stunningly beautiful upper lake is surrounded by steep snowcapped peaks, and several avalanche paths end right at water's edge. Fishing in the lower lake is productive for Dolly Varden and cutthroat trout.

Practicalities

The park has no facilities. The nearest town is Elkford (pop. 2,500), a small coal-mining community 67 km (42 miles) south. The community has few services, but you'll find a small **municipal campground** within walking distance of downtown ($14 with hookups). On Front Street is the **Elkford Visitor Info Centre,** 250/865-4614 or 877/355-9453, a good source of park information. For further park information before arriving in the area, contact **BC Parks,** 250/354-6333, website: http://wlap-www.gov.bc.ca/bcparks.

HEIGHT OF THE ROCKIES PROVINCIAL PARK

This long and narrow, 68,000-hectare (134,000-acre) park protects a 50-km-long (31-mile-long) section of the Canadian Rockies, including a 25-km-long (15.5-mile-long) stretch bordering the Continental Divide. The park lies entirely in British Columbia, bordered by Elk Lakes and Peter Lougheed Provincial Parks to the east and Banff National Park at its narrow northern reaches. It is accessible only on foot and is not a destination for the casual day-tripper. Mountains dominate the landscape, with 26 peaks—some of which remained unnamed until recently—rising over the magical 10,000-foot (3,050-meter) mark. They lie in two distinct ranges: the **Royal Group** in the north, and the **Italian Group** in the south. The dominant peak is 3,460-meter (11,350-foot) **Mount King George,** in the Royal Group, which is flanked by massive hanging glaciers on its north- and east-facing slopes. Mountain goats thrive on all massifs, while the remote valleys are home to high concentrations of elk and grizzly bears.

The park can be reached from two directions. Neither is signposted, so before setting out for the park, pick up a good map of the area at a local information center or Forest Service office. The following directions are intended only as a guide.

Connor Lake is the most popular destination in the south of the park. It is reached by passing through Whiteswan Lake Provincial Park (see following entry), then continuing along a rough logging road that parallels the White River to its upper reaches. (The most important intersection to watch for is 11 km/6.8 miles from Whiteswan Lake; stay right, immediately crossing the river.) At the end of the road, a tortuous 72 km (45 miles) from Highway 93/95, is a small area set aside for tents and horse corrals. From this trailhead, it's an easy walk up Maiyuk Creek and over a low ridge to Connor Lake, where you'll enjoy great views of the Italian Group to the north and Mount Forsyth to the southwest.

Small **Queen Mary Lake** lies in the western shadow of the impressive Royal Group. It is generally only the destination of those on horseback or mountaineers continuing into the Royal Group. To get there, turn off Highway 93/95 at Canal Flats and follow a logging road up the Kootenay River watershed. For the first 48 km (30 miles), the road follows the Kootenay itself. Then it turns westward and climbs along the south side of the Palliser River a further 35 km (21.7 miles) to road's end. From this point, it's a 12-km (7.5-mile) hike up a forested valley, with numerous creek crossings, to the lake.

Practicalities

Primitive campgrounds lie on the shores of **Connor** and **Queen Mary Lakes.** An eight-person Forest Service cabin sits at the north end of Connor Lake. For cabin reservations and general park information, contact **BC Parks,** 250/354-6333, website: http://wlap-www.gov.bc.ca/bcparks.

If these long approaches put visiting Mount Assiniboine Provincial Park out of your reach, there's one more option: you can fly in by helicopter from the Mount Shark Helipad.

MOUNT ASSINIBOINE PROVINCIAL PARK

Named for one of the Canadian Rockies' most spectacular peaks, this 39,050-hectare (96,500-acre), roughly triangular park lies northeast of Radium Hot Springs, sandwiched between Kootenay National Park to the west and Banff National Park to the east. It's inaccessible by road; access is on foot or by helicopter. A haven for experienced hikers, the park offers alpine meadows, lakes, glaciers, and many peaks higher than 3,050 meters (10,000 feet) to explore. The park's highest peak, 3,618-meter (11,870-foot) Mount Assiniboine (seventh-highest in the Canadian Rockies), is known as the Matterhorn of the Rockies for its resemblance to that famous Swiss landmark. The striking peak can be seen from many points well outside the boundaries of the park, including Buller Pond in Kananaskis Country and Sunshine Village winter resort in Banff National Park.

The peak is named for the Assiniboine people, who ventured into this section of the Canadian Rockies many thousands of years before European exploration. The name Assiniboine means "stone boilers"—a reference to these people's preferred cooking method. The mountain was sighted and named by a geological survey team in 1885, but the first ascent wasn't made until 1901.

Lake Magog is the destination of most park visitors. Here you'll find the park's only facilities and the trailheads for several interesting and varied day hikes. One of the most popular walks is along the Sunburst Valley/Nub Ridge trail. From Lake Magog, small Sunburst Lake is reached in about 20 minutes, then the trail continues northwest a short distance to Cerulean Lake. From this lake's outlet, the trail descends slowly along the Mitchell River to a junction four km (2.5 miles) from Lake Magog. Take the right fork, which climbs through a dense subalpine forest to Elizabeth Lake, nestled in the

LESSER-TRAVELED PARKS

southern shadow of Nub Peak. From this point, instead of descending back to Cerulean Lake, take the Nub Ridge trail, which climbs steadily for one km (0.6 miles) to a magnificent viewpoint high above Lake Magog. From the viewpoint, it's just less than four km (2.5 miles), downhill all the way, to the valley floor. The total length of this outing is 11 km (6.8 miles), and as elevation gained is only just over 400 meters (1,310 feet), the trail can comfortably be completed in four hours.

Approaching the Park on Foot

Three trails provide access to **Lake Magog,** the park's largest body of water. The most popular comes in from the northeast, starting at Sunshine Village winter resort in Banff National Park and leading 29 km (18 miles) via Citadel Pass to the lake. Not only is this trail spectacular, but the high elevation of the trailhead (2,100 meters/6,890 feet) makes for a relatively easy approach. Another approach is from the east, in Spray Valley Provincial Park (Kananaskis Country). The trailhead is at the southern end of Spray Lake; take the Mount Shark staging area turn-off 40 km (25 miles) south of Canmore. By the time the trail has climbed the Bryant Creek drainage to 2,165-meter (7,100-foot) Assiniboine Pass, all elevation gain (450 meters/1,480 feet) has been made. At 27 km (16.8 miles), this is the shortest approach, but its elevation gain is greater than the other two trails. The longest and least-used access is from Highway 93 at Simpson River in Kootenay National Park. This trail climbs the Simpson River and Surprise Creek drainages and crosses 2,270-meter (7,450-foot) Ferro Pass to the lake for a total length of 32 km (20 miles).

The Easy Way In

If these long approaches put visiting the park out of your reach, there's one more option: you can fly in by helicopter from the Mount Shark Helipad, located at the southern end of Spray Valley Provincial Park, 40 km (25 miles) south of Canmore. Helicopter access is restricted to Wednesday, Friday, and Sunday and costs $117 per person each way, including an 18-kilogram (40-pound) per-person baggage limit. Although

Mount Robson (3,954 meters/12,970 feet) is the highest peak in the Canadian Rockies.

Alpine Helicopters operates the flights, all bookings must be made through the Mount Assiniboine Lodge, 403/678-2883. If you're planning on hiking into the park, Alpine Helicopters will fly your gear in for $1.50 per pound. This same company, which also operates from a base in Canmore, charges $175 per person for a 30-minute flight-seeing trip over the park. For more information, call Alpine Helicopters at 403/678-4802, or check out the website, www.alpinehelicopter.com.

Camping and Accommodations

Lake Magog is the park's main facility area, such as it is. A designated camping area on a low ridge above the lake's west shore provides a source of drinking water and pit toilets. Open fires are prohibited. Sites are $5 per person per night. Also at the lake are the **Naiset Huts,** $15 per person per night (book through the lodge).

Built in 1928 by the CPR and now owned by BC Parks but managed privately is the **Mount Assiniboine Lodge,** 403/678-2883, www.canadianrockies.net/assiniboine. Sleeping up to 30 people in six rooms and six cabins, accommodations are rustic but comfortable. The rate of $180 per person per night in the lodge and $230 per person in the cabins includes all meals.

Information

For further park information, contact **BC Parks,** 250/354-6333, website: http://wlap-www.gov.bc.ca/bcparks. For information on the condition of trails leading into the park, drop by the Kootenay, Lake Louise, or Banff park information centers.

MOUNT ROBSON PROVINCIAL PARK

At the northern end of the Canadian Rockies, spectacular 224,866-hectare (555,650-acre) Mount Robson Provincial Park was created in 1913 to protect a vast wilderness of steep canyons and wide forested valleys; icy lakes, rivers, and streams; and rugged mountain peaks permanently blanketed in snow and ice. The park lies along the Continental Divide in British Columbia, adjacent to Jasper National Park, and shelters the headwaters of the Fraser River, one of British Columbia's most important waterways. Towering over the park's western entrance is magnificent 3,954-meter (12,970-foot) **Mount Robson,** the highest peak in the Canadian Rockies.

Highway 16 splits the park in two, and many sights of interest are visible from the highway. But you'll have to leave the car behind to experience one of the park's biggest draws; the famous Berg Lake Trail is strictly for hikers.

Flora and Fauna

The elevation differences within the park are as great as anywhere else in the Canadian Rockies, making for a great variety of flora and fauna. The main service center lies in a forested valley at an elevation of just 840 meters (2,750 feet), right in the heart of the montane. The oft-photographed view of Mount Robson from the visitors center is framed by a stand of trembling aspen across a cleared meadow, but the most common tree at this elevation is **Douglas fir,** which covers the valley floor. **Western red cedar** and **hemlock** thrive in damp sections of the park. As in the rest of the Canadian Rockies, the subalpine zone is dominated by **Engelmann spruce** and, at higher elevations, **subalpine fir.** The alpine zone in the park begins at around 2,300 meters (7,550 feet).

In spring, **black bears** are often seen feasting on dandelions by the roadside, but their larger relative, the **grizzly,** rarely makes an appearance in the busy valley through which Highway 16 winds. **Elk, moose,** and **mountain goats** are also present, as are many smaller critters. More than 170 bird species have been identified, with the rare **harlequin duck** a special joy to watch as it passes though the park each spring.

History

Local Shuswap natives called Mount Robson Yuh-hai-has-hun (Mountain of the Spiral Road) for its layered appearance. Historians guess that the peak's European name honors a member of the Hudson's Bay Company, although details of the christening have been lost to history.

Mountaineers were attracted to the challenge of climbing Mount Robson in the early 1900s; the first official ascent took place in 1913 (the same year the park as we know it today was created). Led by Swiss guide Conrad Kain, the first ascent party was made up of members of the Alpine Club of Canada. Although this was the first official summit climb, the summit had been attempted four years earlier by the Reverend

---

THE YELLOWHEAD STORY

Yellowhead is the name of a pass and lake within Mount Robson Provincial Park, as well as a highway that crosses the continent as a northern alternative to the TransCanada. The name is attributed to a blond-haired trapper of French descent, who cached furs in the area. He became known as *Tête Jaune* (Yellowhead). The French version of his name also lives on, for just outside Mount Robson Provincial Park's western boundary lies the small town of Tête Jaune Cache.

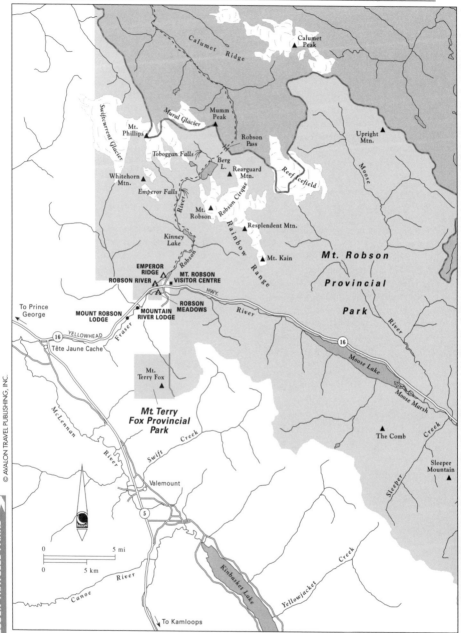

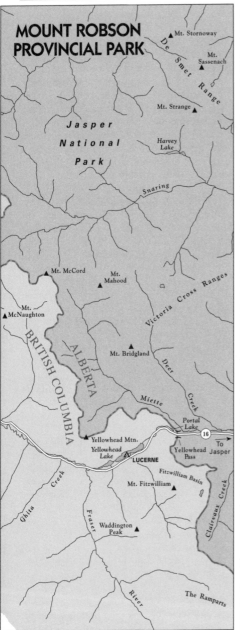

MOUNT ROBSON PROVINCIAL PARK

George Kinney and friends. Kinney thought he'd made the summit, but he was climbing the summit ridge in a heavy fog; a cairn and a message recording the names of the members of Kinney's climbing team were later found on the ridge about 100 vertical meters (320 vertical feet) from the top.

Roadside Sights

Highway 16 enters the park from the east at 1,066-meter (3,500-foot) **Yellowhead Pass,** on the British Columbia–Alberta border. It's the lowest highway pass over the Continental Divide. From the divide, it's 60 km (37.2 miles) to the park's western boundary and the visitors center. Just west of the divide, a rest area beside picturesque **Portal Lake** is a good introduction to the park.

Continuing westward, the highway passes long, narrow **Yellowhead Lake** at the foot of 2,458-meter (8,060-foot) **Yellowhead Mountain,** then crosses the upper reaches of the Fraser River. The Moose River drains into the Fraser River at **Moose Marsh,** a good spot for watching wildlife at the southeast end of **Moose Lake.** Moose often feed here at dawn and dusk, and waterfowl are present throughout the day.

Continuing west, the highway parallels Moose Lake; waterfalls on the lake's far side create a photogenic backdrop. As the road descends steeply to a wide, open section of the valley, it passes the main facility area, where you'll find a visitors center, campgrounds, a gas station, and a restaurant. On a clear day the panorama from this lump of commercialism is equal to any sight in British Columbia. The sheer west face of Mount Robson slices skyward just seven km (4.3 miles) away across a flower-filled meadow. This is as close as you can get to the peak in your car.

If you're approaching the park from the west, you'll see Mount Robson long before you reach the park boundary (provided the weather is cooperating). It's impossible to confuse this distinctive peak with those that surround it—no wonder it's known as the "Monarch of the Canadian Rockies."

LESSER-TRAVELED PARKS

Berg Lake Trail

- Length: 19.5 km/12 miles (eight hours) one-way
- Elevation gain: 725 meters/2,380 feet
- Rating: moderate/difficult
- Trailhead: two km (1.2 miles) north of Mount Robson Visitor Centre

This is the most popular overnight hike in the Canadian Rockies, but don't let the crowds put you off—the hike is well worth it. Beautiful aqua-colored Berg Lake lies below the north face of Mount Robson, which rises 2,400 meters (7,880 feet) directly behind the lake. Glaciers on the mountain's shoulder regularly calve off into the lake, resulting in the icebergs that give the lake its name.

The trail begins by following the Robson River 4.5 km (2.8 miles) through dense subalpine forest to glacially fed **Kinney Lake.** There the trail narrows, crossing the fast-flowing river at the eight-km (five-mile) mark and climbing alongside it. The next four km (2.5 miles), through the steep-sided Valley of a Thousand Falls, are the most demanding, but views of four spectacular waterfalls ease the pain of the 500-vertical-meter (1,640-vertical-foot) climb. The first glimpses of Mount Robson come soon after reaching the head of the valley, from where it's a further one km (0.6 miles) to the outlet of Berg Lake, 17.5 km (10.9 miles) from the trailhead. The first of three lakeside campgrounds is two km (1.2 miles) from this point.

While the panorama from the lake is stunning, most hikers who have come this far will want to spend some time exploring the area. From the north end of the lake, trails lead to Toboggan Falls and more mountain views, to the head of Robson Glacier, and to Robson Pass, which opens up the remote northern reaches of Jasper National Park.

Berg Lake Trail Practicalities

It's possible to traverse the trail's first section and return the same day; to get all the way to Berg Lake and back you'll need to stay in the backcountry overnight. Along the route are a total of 75 campsites in seven primitive campgrounds, including three along the lakeshore. Bookings for these sites can be made up to three months in advance by calling the BC Parks' Discover Camping hotline, 604/689-9025 or 800/689-9025; the reservation fee is $6.42 per night to a maximum of $19.26. Book early because the quota fills quickly. Upon arrival in the park, all overnight hikers must then register at the visitors center and pay a camping fee of $6 per person per night.

If the uphill walk in seems too ambitious, contact **Robson Helimagic,** 250/566-4700 or 877/454-7400, www.robsonhelimagic.com, which makes helicopter drop-offs at Robson Pass from Valemount every Monday and Friday; $175 per person (minimum four).

Other Hikes in the Park

Aside from the popular trail to Berg Lake, the park holds only two other established trails. The shortest of the two ascends the slopes of 2,458-meter (8,060-foot) **Yellowhead Mountain.** From the trailhead across the rail line at Yellowhead Lake, it's a steady climb through subalpine forest to the first viewpoint at the one-km (0.6-mile) mark. Another three km (1.9 miles) and a total elevation gain of 720 meters (2060 feet) brings you to flower-filled meadows and panoramic views extending east to the Continental Divide and west to the Selwyn Range. Allow two hours each way for this hike.

The other option is the 13-km (eight-mile) **Fitzwilliam Basin Trail,** which requires an overnight stay in the backcountry. Elevation gain is 950 meters (3,120 feet), so it's a demanding trail. From the trailhead on the south side of Highway 16, three km (1.9 miles) east of Lucerne Campground, the trail climbs steadily for six km (3.7 miles) to the confluence of Rockingham and Fitzwilliam Creeks. Although easy to follow, the remaining seven km (4.3 miles) along the northern slopes of 2,911-meter (9,550-foot) Mount Fitzwilliam are rough going. After ascending a steep ridge, the trail all but dissipates, but many camping spots can be found in the wide lake-filled basin.

Other Recreation

Mount Robson Whitewater Rafting, 780/852-4566 or 888/566-7238, runs the Class III rapids of the Fraser River, with a portage around Rearguard Falls; $65 includes lunch. Some of the Jasper rafting companies also offer this trip, with transportation from Jasper included.

Flight-seeing is available in Valemount, 20 km (12.4 miles) west then 22 km (13.6 miles) south on Highway 5 from the visitor center. **Premier Air,** 250/566-4901, offers fixed-wing flight-seeing over the area for $85 per person for 40 minutes, $145 for 70 minutes. **Robson Helimagic,** 250/566-4700 or 877/454-4700, charges $175 per person for a 36-minute helicopter flight up to and around Mount Robson.

Park Campgrounds

Within the park are four campgrounds with road access. The park operates three of these. Closest to the visitors center is 19-site **Robson River Campground,** while across the road is the much larger **Robson Meadows Campground.** Both have flush toilets and showers but no hookups; $17.50 per site. In the east of the park is the more rustic **Lucerne Campground,** where sites are $12. **Emperor Ridge Campground,** 250/566-8438, is a commercial facility right behind the visitors center; $18 per site including hot showers but no hookups. All campgrounds are open mid-May to early October.

Robson Shadows Campground, only five km (3.1 miles) west of the visitors center but outside of the park, 250/566-9190, is part of Mount Robson Lodge. It also has showers but no hookups. Sites are $14.50 per night.

Lodges

The park has no indoor accommodations, but two lodges lie just outside the park's western boundary, and motel accommodations are available 42 km (26 miles) to the southwest in Valemount.

Mountain River Lodge, four km (2.5 miles) west of the visitors center, 250/566-9899 or 888/566-9899, www.mtrobson.com, is in a delightful setting right alongside the Fraser River. The main lodge holds five rooms each with a different character, a balcony, and a private bathroom. The rates of $70–90 s, $80–100 d include a cooked breakfast. A self-contained, two-story riverfront cabin costs $125 per night.

One km (0.6 miles) beyond Mountain River Lodge is the turn-off for **Mount Robson Lodge,** 250/566-4821 or 888/566-4821, www.mountrobsonlodge.com. A variety of recreational activities, including white-water rafting, can be organized for guests, and meals are available. Rates in the free-standing cabins range $85–125 s or d.

Information

At the park's western entrance, **Mount Robson Visitor Centre,** 250/566-9174, features informative natural-history slideshows, an evening interpretive program, and trail reports updated daily. Hikers and climbers can pick up detailed trail descriptions and topographical maps ($13) at the center. Hours are mid-June to mid-September, daily 8 A.M.–8 P.M.; mid-May to mid-June and mid-September to mid-October, daily 8 A.M.–5 P.M.; closed the rest of the year. The BC Parks website, http://wlapwww.gov.bc.ca/bcparks, is another good source of information.

TOP OF THE WORLD PROVINCIAL PARK

This wild and remote 8,790-hectare (21,720-acre) park lies beyond Whiteswan Lake Provincial Park (see following entry), a rough 52 km (32 miles) from Highway 93/95 (turn off the Whiteswan Lake access road at Alces Lake). You can't drive into the park, but it's a fairly easy six-km (3.7-mile) walk from the end of the road to picturesque **Fish Lake,** the park's largest body of water. The trail climbs alongside the pretty Lussier River to the lake, which is encircled with Engelmann spruce and surrounded by peaks up to 2,500 meters (8,200 feet) high. The hike to the lake gains just over 200 vertical meters (660 vertical feet) and makes a good day trip. Trails from the lake lead to other alpine lakes and to a viewpoint that allows a good overall perspective on the high plateau for which the park is named. Fish Lake is productive for cutthroat trout and Dolly Varden.

Practicalities

Bring everything you'll need because there are no services within the park. Camping is possible at one of four designated areas for $5 per person, or you can stay in the large cabin nestled in trees beside Fish Lake ($15 per person). For park information and trail conditions, contact contact **BC Parks,** 250/354-6333, website: http://wlap-www.gov.bc.ca/bcparks.

WHITESWAN LAKE PROVINCIAL PARK

Access to this popular British Columbia park is from Highway 93/95, 50 km (31 miles) south of Radium Hot Springs and 28 km (17.4 miles) north of Skookumchuck. From a signed turnoff, an unpaved logging road takes off east into the mountains, leading first to 1,994-hectare (4.930-acre) Whiteswan Lake Provincial Park, then to Top of the World Provincial Park (see previous listing). The road climbs steadily from the highway, entering Lussier Gorge after 11 km (6.8 miles). Within the gorge, a steep trail leads down to **Lussier Hot Springs.** Two small pools have been constructed to contain the odorless hot (43°C/110°F) water as it bubbles out of the ground and flows into the Lussier River. Within the park itself, the road closely follows the southern shorelines of first **Alces Lake** then the larger **Whiteswan Lake.** The two lakes attract abundant bird life; loons, grebes, and herons are all common. They also attract anglers, who come for great rainbow trout fishing. Both lakes are stocked and have a daily quota of two fish per person.

© ANDREW HEMPSTEAD

Whiteswan Lake

Practicalities

The main road skirts the lakes and passes four campgrounds; $12 per site, no showers. For park information, contact **BC Parks,** 250/354-6333, website: http://wlapwww.gov.bc.ca/bcparks.

Wilderness Areas

SIFFLEUR WILDERNESS AREA

This remote region on the Alberta side of the Canadian Rockies lies south of Highway 11, which crosses west-central Alberta between Rocky Mountain House and Saskatchewan River Crossing, in Banff National Park. It is completely protected from any activities that could have an impact on the area's fragile ecosystems. That includes road and trail development; no bridges have been built over the area's many fast-flowing streams, and the few old trails that do exist are not maintained. Elk, deer, moose, cougars, wolverines, wolves, coy-

otes, black bears, and grizzly bears roam the area's four main valleys, while higher, alpine elevations harbor mountain goats and bighorn sheep.

The main trail into the 41,200-hectare (101,800-acre) wilderness begins from a parking area two km (1.2 miles) south of the Two O'Clock Creek Campground at Kootenay Plains (see the special topic **Kootenay Plains**). The area's northeastern boundary is a seven-km (4.3 miles) hike from here. Even if you're not heading right into Siffleur, the first section of this trail, to **Siffleur Falls,** is worth walking. Along the first section, the trail crosses the North Saskatchewan

KOOTENAY PLAINS

To appreciate them one must breathe their breath deep into the lungs, must let the soft winds caress the face, and allow the eye to absorb the blue of the surrounding hills and the gold of the grasses beneath the feet. Here the air is sweeter, drier, and softer than anywhere I know, and here the world could easily be forgotten and life pass by in a dream.

Mary Schäffer, 1905

The Kootenay Plains—a unique area of dry grasslands in the mountains—is one of the Canadian Rockies' more special spots. As Mary Schäffer noted during her historic journey north to Maligne Lake, to gain full appreciation of the plains you must leave the road and pause in their midst.

The climate on the plains is the warmest in the Canadian Rockies. Vegetation such as June grass and wheatgrass, usually associated with the prairies of southeastern Alberta, thrives here. Low snowfall and regular chinook winds make the area prime wintering grounds for elk, mule deer, bighorn sheep, and moose. For thousands of years, the Kootenay peoples would cross the mountains from the Columbia River Valley to hunt these mammals and the bison that were then prolific. Over time, the fearsome Peigans pushed the Kootenay westward and claimed the plains as their own. Today two Indian reserves can be found on the plains, but they are mostly used and protected as ecological reserves, lying at the southern end of Abraham Lake and beside Highway 93, 28 km east of Saskatchewan River Crossing (Banff National Park).

River via a swinging bridge, then at the two-km (1.2-mile) mark crosses the Siffleur River, reaching the falls after four km (2.5 miles); allow 70 minutes one-way. These are the official Siffleur Falls, but others lie further upstream at the 6.2-km (3.9-mile) and 6.9-km (4.3-mile) marks.

Once inside the wilderness area, the trail climbs steadily alongside the Siffleur River and into the heart of the wilderness. Ambitious hikers can continue through to the Dolomite Creek Area of Banff National Park, finishing at the Icefields Parkway, seven km (4.3 miles) south of Bow Summit. Total length of this trail is 68 km (42 miles), a strenuous five-day backcountry expedition. Another access point for the area is opposite Waterfowl Lake Campground in Banff National Park. From here it is six km (3.7 miles) up Noyes Creek to the wilderness area boundary; the trail peters out after 4.5 km (2.8 miles) and requires some serious scrambling before descending into Siffleur. This trail—as with all others in the wilderness area—is for experienced hikers only.

Practicalities

Two O'Clock Creek Campground lies two km (1.2 miles) from the park's main trailhead in Kootenay Plains Provincial Recreation Area. It is

a primitive facility, with 24 sites each with a picnic table and firepit, a picnic shelter, free firewood, and drinking water. Sites are $12 per night.

For more information, contact Alberta Community Development, Main Floor, 9945 108th St., Edmonton, 780/944-0313, or click on the "Preserving Alberta" link at www.cd.gov.ab.ca.

WHITE GOAT WILDERNESS AREA

White Goat comprises 44,500 hectares (110,000 acres) of high mountain ranges, wide valleys, hanging glaciers, waterfalls, and high alpine lakes. It lies north and west of Highway 11, abutting the north end of Banff National Park and the south end of Jasper National Park. The area's vegetation zones are easily recognizable: subalpine forests of Engelmann spruce, subalpine fir, and lodgepole pine; alpine tundra higher up. Large mammals here include a large population of bighorn sheep, as well as mountain goats, deer, elk, woodland caribou, moose, cougars, wolves, coyotes, black bears, and grizzly bears.

The most popular hike is the **McDonald Creek Trail,** which first follows the Cline River, then McDonald Creek to the creek's source in the heart of the wilderness area. McDonald Creek is approximately 12 km (7.5 miles) from the parking area on Highway 11, but a full day should be allowed for this section because the trail crosses many streams. From where McDonald Creek flows into the Cline River, it is 19 km (11.8 miles) to the McDonald Lakes, but allow another two full days; the total elevation gain for the hike is a challenging 1,222 meters (4,000 feet). Other hiking possibilities include following the Cline River to its source and crossing Sunset Pass into Banff National Park, 17 km (10.6 miles) north of Saskatchewan River Crossing, or heading up Cataract Creek and linking up with the trails in the Brazeau River area of Jasper National Park.

Practicalities

White Goat Wilderness Area has no services and is for experienced hikers only. For more information, contact Alberta Community Development, 780/944-0313, www.cd.gov.ab.ca (click on the "Preserving Alberta" link).

WILLMORE WILDERNESS PARK

Willmore Wilderness Park is a northern extension of Jasper National Park. It lies south and west of Grande Cache, a small town on Highway 40 between Hinton and Grande Prairie. The 460,000-hectare (1,137,000-acre) wilderness area is divided roughly in half by the Smoky River. The area west of the river is reached from Sulphur Gates. The east side is far less traveled—the terrain is rougher and wetter. The park is accessible only on foot, horseback, or, in winter, on skis. It is totally undeveloped; the trails that do exist are not maintained and in most cases are those once used by trappers.

The park is made up of long, green ridges above the treeline and, farther west, wide passes and expansive basins along the Continental Divide. Lower elevations are covered in lodgepole pine and spruce, while at higher elevations the cover changes to fir. The diverse wildlife is one of the park's main attractions; white-tailed and mule deer, mountain goats, bighorn sheep, moose, elk, caribou, and black

bears are all common. The park is also home to wolves, cougars, and grizzly bears.

Park Access and Travel

The easiest way to access the park is from Sulphur Gates Provincial Recreation Area, six km (3.7 miles) north of Grande Cache on Highway 40 and then a similar distance along a gravel road to the west. Those not planning a trip into the park can still enjoy the cliffs at **Sulphur Gates** (formerly known as Hell's Gate), which is only a short walk from the end of the road. These 70-meter (230-foot) cliffs are at the confluence of the Sulphur and Smoky Rivers. The color difference between the glacial-fed Smoky River and spring-fed Sulphur River is apparent as they merge.

One of the most popular overnight trips from Sulphur Gates is to **Clarke's Cache,** an easy 16-km (10-mile) hike to the remains of a cabin where trappers once stored furs before taking them to trading posts farther afield. A good option for a day trip for fit hikers is to the 2,013-meter (6,600-foot) summit of **Mount Stearn** from a trailhead 3.5 km (2.2 miles) along the access road to Sulphur Gates. The trail begins by climbing alongside a stream through montane, then subalpine forest, and then through open meadows before reentering the forest and forking and rejoining. The official trail then climbs steeply and continuously to Lightning Ridge (10 km/6.2 miles one-way), but an easier summit is reached by heading up through the grassed slopes to a summit knob, 6.5 km (four miles) and 1,000 vertical meters (3,280 vertical feet) from the road; allow 6–6.5 hours for the round trip.

Practicalities

Anyone planning an extended trip into the park should be aware that no services are available, most trails are unmarked, and certain areas are heavily used by horse-packers. Led by Dave Manzer, a 20-year veteran of leading trips into Willmore, **Wild Rose Outfitting,** 780/693-2296, www.wildroseoutfitting.com, offers pack trips into the park; expect to pay around $205 per person per day, all-inclusive.

More information is available by contacting the department of Community Development at

780/944-0313 or by clicking on the "Preserving Alberta" link at website: www.cd.gov.ab.ca. The book *Willmore Wilderness Park*, published by the Alberta Wilderness Association, is available in Grande Cache at **Grande Books,** in the Pine Plaza Shopper's Mall on Hoppe Avenue.

GRANDE CACHE

This town of 4,400, the most remote in the Canadian Rockies, is at the gateway to Willmore Wilderness Park and is surrounded by total wilderness, offering endless opportunities for hiking, canoeing, kayaking, fishing, and horseback riding. It perches on the side of Grande Mountain above

the Smoky River, which flows from its source in Jasper National Park through Willmore Wilderness Park, eventually joining the Peace River and draining into the Arctic Ocean.

The first Europeans to explore the area were fur trappers and traders, who cached furs near the site of the present town before taking them to major trading posts. At one point there was a small trading post on a lake south of town on Pierre Gray Lakes; its remains are still visible. Grande Cache is a planned town. Construction started in 1969 in response to a need for services and housing for miners and their families working at the McIntyre Porcupine Coal Mine. The town was developed 20 km (12.4 miles) south of the mine

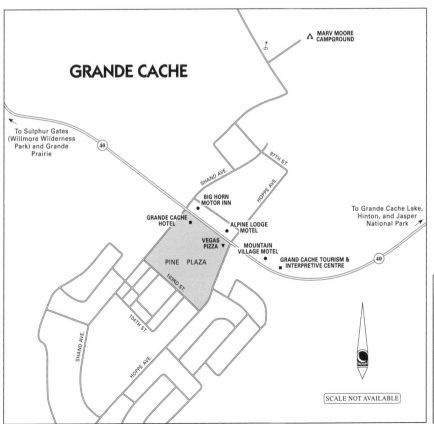

to maintain a scenic environment. The mine closed in 2000, but the population level remains stable, with many residents employed at a nearby federal penitentiary.

For great views of the surrounding area, consider climbing **Grande Mountain.** It's a steep trail, gaining 730 meters (2,400 feet) of elevation in 3.5 km (2.1 miles), but from the summit, the view across the Smoky River Valley to the Rocky Mountains is spectacular. The trail follows a power line the entire way to the peak and is easy to follow. To get to the trailhead, head northwest of town one km (0.6 miles) and turn right at the cemetery gate. Park, walk along the road to the power line, veer right, and start the long slog to the summit. **Grande Cache Lake,** five km (3.1 miles) south of town, has good swimming, canoeing, and fishing; rainbow and brook trout, whitefish, and arctic grayling are commonly caught. Many of the forestry roads are suitable for mountain biking; **Grande Cache Adventure Sports,** 780/827-3764, rents bikes.

In recent years, Grande Cache has placed itself on the calendar of extreme, ultra-marathoners the world over as host of the **Canadian Death Race** series, www.canadiandeathrace.com. Races take place three times annually along the same demanding 125-km (78-mile) course; on snowshoes in January, on foot in August, and on mountain bikes in September.

Grande Cache Practicalities

Most motels are busy in summer, so make reservations in advance. On the highway through town, **Big Horn Motor Inn,** 780/827-3744, is the best value. Each room has a fridge, some have kitchenettes, and a laundry and restaurant are on the premises; $50 s, $60 d. Also along the highway is the **Alpine Lodge Motel,** 780/827-2450, $50 s, $60 d; and the **Mountain Village Motel,** 780/827-2453, which charges the same for basic but modern rooms. Overlooking the plaza is the **Grande Cache Hotel,** 780/827-

3377, www.grandecachehotel.ab.ca, which has 44 standard rooms and four suites, a restaurant, and a lounge with country bands on weekends; $89–119 s or d.

Marv Moore Campground, 780/827-2404, has semiprivate, well-treed sites and showers, kitchen shelters, and firewood; unserviced sites $15, hookups $17. It's at the north end of town off Shand Avenue and is open May–October. Forestry campgrounds are located at regular intervals the entire length of Highway 40. Of special note is the one at **Sulphur Gates Provincial Recreation Area,** west off Highway 40 north of town, which makes a good base for exploring Willmore Wilderness Park. It's open May to October and has just 11 sites.

On a clear day, the view from **Mountainview Cafe,** in the Grande Cache Hotel, 780/827-3377, is worth at least the price of a cup of coffee. Soup and sandwich lunch specials are around $6 and pizza and pasta dishes start at $8. A dining room in the hotel opens at 5 P.M.; dinner entrées range $14–18. **Vegas Pizza and Spaghetti House,** 207 Pine Plaza, 780/827-5444, is an inexpensive place to go for a meal; portions are large and the atmosphere is pleasant.

The **Grande Cache Tourism and Interpretive Centre,** 780/827-3300 or 888/827-3790, is outstanding, not just considering the size of the town that it represents, but for the wealth of information contained within it. It's easy to spend at least an hour in the two-story complex, with displays that include the human history of the region, local industry, stuffed animals, tree identification, and one on Willmore Wilderness Park. Other features include an information desk, gift shop, and large deck from where views extend across the Smoky River Valley to the highest peaks of the Canadian Rockies. It's open in summer daily 9 A.M.–7 P.M., the rest of the year Mon.–Fri. 8:30 A.M.–4:30 P.M. The website www.town.grandecache.ab.ca is a good source of pretrip information on the town and adjacent Willmore Wilderness Park.

Resources

Suggested Reading

Natural History

The Atlas of Breeding Birds of Alberta. Edmonton: Federation of Alberta Naturalists, 1992. Comprehensive study of all birds that breed in Alberta with easy-to-read distribution maps, details on nesting and other behavioral patterns, and color plates.

Busch, Robert H. *The Wolf Almanac.* New York: Lyons & Burford, 1995. A detailed analysis of the wolf, from its evolution as a distinct species to the issues surrounding breeding wolves as pets. Includes 12 pages of color plates.

Gadd, Ben. *Handbook of the Canadian Rockies.* Jasper: Corax Press, 1999. The latest edition of this classic guide is in color, and although bulky for backpackers, it's a must-read for anyone interested in the natural history of the Canadian Rockies.

Gray, D. M., and D. H. Male. *Handbook of Snow.* Toronto: Pergamon Press, 1991. Comprehensive guide on everything you ever wanted to know about snow but didn't ask because no one else would have known either.

Hallworth, Beryl, and C. C. Chinnappa. *Plants of Kananaskis Country.* Calgary: University of Calgary Press, 1997. An incredibly detailed book, encompassing more than 400 species of flora, complete with color plates and illustrations. It could be used in the field anywhere in the Canadian Rockies.

Hare, F. K., and M. K. Thomas. *Climate Canada.* Toronto: John Wiley & Sons, 1974. One of the most extensive works on Canada's climate ever written. Includes a chapter on how the climate is changing.

Herrero, Stephen. *Bear Attacks: Their Causes and Avoidances.* New York: Nick Lyons Books, 1995. Through a series of gruesome stories, this book catalogs the stormy relationship between people and bruins, provides hints on avoiding attacks, and tells what to do in case you're attacked.

Jones, Karen. *Wolf Mountains.* Calgary: University of Calgary Press, 2002. Explores the history of wolves in the Canadian Rockies, with emphasis on the often controversial relationship between man and wolf.

Lauriault, Jean. *Identification Guide to the Trees of Canada.* Markham, Ontario: Fitzhenry & Whiteside, 1989. Makes tree identification easy through drawings of leaves, and maps detail distribution of species.

Patterson, W. S. *The Physics of Glaciers.* Toronto: Pergamon Press, 1969. A highly technical look at all aspects of glaciation, why glaciers form, how they flow, and their effect on the environment.

Rezendes, Paul. *Tracking and the Art of Seeing.* Charlottesville, Virginia: Camden House Publishing, 1992. This is one of the best of many books dedicated to tracking North American mammals. It begins with a short essay on the relationship of humans with nature.

Sharp, Robert P. *Living Ice: Understanding Glaciers and Glaciation.* Cambridge, England: Cambridge University Press, 1988. A detailed but highly readable book on the formation, types, and results of glaciers.

Slinger, Joey. *Down & Dirty Birding.* Toronto: Key Porter Books, 1996. A hilarious but practical look at the art of bird-watching, with sections of text such as "How to steer clear of people who think bird-watching is better than sex."

Vacher, André. *Summer of the Grizzly*. Saskatoon: Western Producer Prairie Books, 1985. True story of a grizzly bear that went on a terrifying rampage near the town of Banff.

Whitaker, John. *National Audubon Society Field Guide to North American Mammals*. New York: Random House, 1997. One of a series of field guides produced by the National Audubon Society, this one details mammals through color plates and detailed descriptions of characteristics, habitat, and range.

Wilkinson, Kathleen. *Wildflowers of Alberta*. Edmonton: University of Alberta Press, 1999. Color plates of all flowers found in the mountain national parks and beyond. Color plates and line drawings are indispensable for identification.

Wright, William H. *The Grizzly Bear*. Originally produced by the University of Nebraska Press in 1909 and reprinted many times since, this book was authored by a hunter turned naturalist whose change of attitude throughout a lifetime of association with bears is poignant.

Human History

Barnes, Christine. *Great Lodges of the Canadian Rockies*. Calgary: W.W. West Inc., 2000. This book delves into the history of the many famous mountain lodges—such as the Fairmont properties and Emerald Lake Lodge—and lesser-known but equally interestingly historic accommodations. Includes many historic photos.

Engler, Bruno. *Bruno Engler Photography*. Calgary: Rocky Mountain Books, 2002. Swissborn Engler spent 60 years exploring and photographing the Canadian Rockies. This impressive hardcover book showcases more than 150 of his most timeless images.

Hart, E. J. *Jimmy Simpson: Legend of the Rockies*. Banff: Altitude Publishing, 1991. Details the life of one of the most colorful of the pioneer outfitters in the Canadian Rockies.

Jenness, Diamond. *The Indians of Canada*. Toronto: University of Toronto Press, 1977. Originally published in 1932, this is the classic study of natives in Canada, although Jenness' conclusion, that they were facing certain extinction by "the end of this century" is obviously outdated.

Lavallee, Omer. *Van Horne's Road*. Montreal: Railfare Enterprises, 1974. William Van Horne was instrumental in the construction of Canada's first transcontinental railway. This is the story of his dream and the boomtowns that sprung up along the route. Lavallee devotes an entire chapter to telling the story of the railway's push over the Canadian Rockies.

McMillan, Alan D. *Native Peoples and Cultures of Canada*. Vancouver: Douglas & McIntyre, 1995. A comprehensive look at the archeology, anthropology, and ethnography of the native peoples of Canada. The last chapters delve into the problems facing these people today.

Marty, Sid. *Men for the Mountains*. New York: Vanguard Press, 1979. Written by a park warden, this book tells the story of those who lived in the Canadian Rockies and the risks and adventures involved.

Marty, Sid. *Switchbacks: True Stories from the Canadian Rockies*. Toronto: McClelland & Stewart, 1999. This book tells of Marty's experiences in the mountains and of people he came in contact with in his role as a park warden. Along the way he describes the way his experiences with both nature and fellow humans have shaped his views on conservation today.

Sandford, R. W. *The Canadian Alps: The History of Mountaineering in Canada*. Canmore: Altitude Publishing, 1990. Complete human history of the Canadian Rockies from the earliest explorers to first ascents of major peaks.

Schäffer, Mary T. S. *A Hunter of Peace*. Banff: Whyte Museum of the Canadian Rockies, 1980. This book was first published in 1911 by G.P. Putnam & Sons, New York, under the name *Old Indian Trails of the Canadian Rockies*. Tales recount the exploration of the Rockies during the turn of the 20th century. Many of the author's photographs appear throughout.

Scott, Chic. *Pushing the Limits*. Calgary: Rocky Mountain Books, 2000. A chronological history of mountaineering in Canada, with special emphasis on many largely unknown climbers and their feats, as well as the story of Swiss guides in Canada and a short section on ice climbing.

Smith, Cyndi. *Off the Beaten Track*. Jasper: Coyote Books, 1989. Accounts of women adventurers and mountaineers and their impact on the early history of western Canada.

Touche, Rodney. *Brown Cows, Sacred Cows*. Hanna: Gorman, 1990. The story of the development of Lake Louise ski area as told by a former general manager.

Whyte, Jon. *Indians in the Rockies*. Banff: Altitude Publishing, 1985. Written from firsthand experiences, this is an excellent insight into the first humans to live in the Canadian Rockies.

Recreation

Daffern, Gillean. *Kananaskis Country Trail Guide*. Calgary: Rocky Mountain Books, 1997. Two volumes cover all the official and unofficial trails in Kananaskis Country.

Eastcott, Doug. *Backcountry Biking in the Canadian Rockies*. Calgary: Rocky Mountain Books, 1999. Details more than 220 bicycling routes using simple maps, road logs, and black-and-white photography.

Kane, Alan. *Scrambles in the Canadian Rockies*. Calgary: Rocky Mountain Books, 1999. Routes detailed in this guide lead to summits, without the use of ropes or mountaineering equipment.

Kariel, Herbert G. *Alpine Huts in the Canadian Rockies, Selkirks, and Purcells*. Canmore: Alpine Club of Canada, 1986. Covers the history of all huts in the Rockies, with current access routes and status and descriptions of nearby peaks to climb.

Martin, John, and Jon Jones. *Sport Climbs in the Canadian Rockies*. Calgary: Rocky Mountain Books, 2002. Details 1,400 climbs through the Bow Valley and Banff National Park.

Mitchell, Barry. *Alberta's Trout Highway*. Red Deer: Nomad Creek Books, 2001. "Alberta's Trout Highway" is the Forestry Trunk Road (Highway 40), which runs the length of the Canadian Rockies, including through the heart of Kananaskis Country. Entertaining and useful descriptions of Mitchell's favorite fishing holes are accompanied by maps and plenty of background information.

Patton, Brian, and Bart Robinson. *The Canadian Rockies Trail Guide*. Banff: Summerthought, 2000. This regularly updated guide, first published in 1971, covers 230 hiking trails and 3,400 km (2,100 miles) in the mountain national parks as well as in surrounding provincial parks. A full page is devoted to each trail, making it the most comprehensive hiking book available.

Potter, Mike. *Fire Lookouts in the Canadian Rockies*. Banff: Luminous Compositions, 1998. This book specializes in hikes to fire lookouts. Trail descriptions are detailed, and each is accompanied by the history of the lookout and those who have staffed them.

Potter, Mike. *Backcountry Banff*. Banff: Luminous Compositions, 2001. This book's title is a little misleading, for included are many shorter trails that can be enjoyed by everyone. Includes logged distances and readable trail description of over 100 hikes in Banff National Park.

Other Guidebooks and Maps

Gem Trek Publishing. Cochrane, Alberta. This company produces tearproof and waterproof maps for all regions of the Canadian Rockies. Relief shading clearly and concisely shows elevation, and all hiking trails have been plotted using a global positioning system. On the back of each map are descriptions of attractions and hikes, along with general, practical and educational information. Website: www.gemtrek.com.

Hempstead, Andrew. *Moon Handbooks Alberta and the Northwest Territories.* Emeryville, CA: Avalon Travel Publishing, 2001. A comprehensive travel guide to the province of Alberta, including the gateway cities of Calgary and Edmonton, and the Northwest Territories.

Hempstead, Andrew. *Moon Handbooks British Columbia.* Emeryville, CA: Avalon Travel Publishing, 2002. From Vancouver to Victoria, from the Canadian Rockies to the wild northlands along the Yukon border, this book covers Canada's westernmost province extensively.

MapArt. Driving maps for all of Canada, including provinces and cities. Maps are published as old-fashioned foldout versions, as well as laminated and in atlas form. Website: www.mapart.com.

The Milepost. Bellevue, WA: Vernon Publications. This annual publication is a must-have for those traveling through western Canada and Alaska. The maps and logged highway descriptions are incredibly detailed. Most northern bookstores stock *The Milepost,* or order by calling 800/726-4707, www.milepost.com.

Periodicals

The Canadian Alpine Journal. Canmore, Alberta. Annual magazine of the Alpine Club of Canada, with articles from its members and climbers from around the world. Website: www.alpineclubofcanada.ca.

Canadian Geographic. Ottawa: Royal Canadian Geographical Society. Bimonthly publication pertaining to Canada's natural and human histories and resources. Website: canadiangeographic.ca.

Equinox. Markham, Ontario. This bimonthly publication looks at Canada's natural world and humanity's relationship with it.

Explore. Calgary. Bimonthly publication of adventure travel throughout Canada. Website: www.explore-mag.com.

Nature Canada. Ottawa, Ontario. Quarterly magazine of the Canadian Nature Federation. Website: www.cnf.ca.

Western Living. Vancouver, British Columbia. Lifestyle magazine for western Canada. Includes travel, history, homes, and cooking. Website: www.westernliving.ca.

Free Catalogs

Alberta Accommodation Guide. Alberta Hotel & Lodging Association. Lists all hotels, motels, and other lodging in the province. Available at all Tourist Information Centres or by calling 800/661-8888, www.explorealberta.com.

Alberta Campground Guide. Alberta Hotel Association. Lists all campgrounds in the province. Available at all Tourist Information Centres or by calling 800/661-8888, www.explorealberta.com.

British Columbia Approved Accommodation. Tourism British Columbia. Lists all accommodations, including commercial and provincial campgrounds in the province. Available at all Visitor Information Centres or by calling 800/663-6000, www.hellobc.com.

Reference

Daffern, Tony. *Avalanche Safety for Skiers & Climbers.* Calgary: Rocky Mountain Books, 1992. Covers all aspects of avalanches, including their causes, practical information on how to avoid them, and a section on rescue techniques and first aid.

Guide to Manuscripts: The Fonds and Collections of the Archives, Whyte Museum of the Canadian Rockies. Banff: Whyte Museum of the Canadian Rockies, 1988. This book makes finding items in the Whyte Museum easy by providing alphabetical lists of all parts of the collection.

Johnson, Leslie. *Basic Mountain Safety from A to Z.* Canmore: Altitude Books, 2000. Everything you need to know about safety in the mountains, including a large section on camping.

Karamitsanis, Aphrodite. *Place Names of Alberta.* Calgary: University of Alberta Press, 1991. An ongoing toponomy project. Volume 1 alphabetically lists all geographic features of the mountains and foothills with explanations of each name's origin. Volume 2 does the same for southern Alberta's geographical features.

Internet Resources

Accommodations

Banff Central Reservations:
www.banffreservations.com
Bed and Breakfast Online:
www.bbcanada.com
Best Western:
www.bestwestern.com
Canada-West Accommodations:
www.b-b.com
**Canmore/Bow Valley Bed
and Breakfast Association:**
www.bbcanmore.com
Days Inn:
www.daysinn.com
Delta Hotels and Resorts:
www.deltahotels.com
Fairmont Hotels and Resorts:
www.fairmont.com
Holiday Inn:
www.holiday-inn.com
Hostelling International-Canada:
www.hihostels.ca
Howard Johnson:
www.hojo.com
**International Youth Hostel
Federation:**
www.iyhf.com
Jasper Home Accommodation Association:
www.stayinjasper.com
Radisson:
www.radisson.com
**Western Canada Bed and Breakfast
Innkeepers Association:**
www.wcbbia.com

Airlines

Air Canada:
www.aircanada.ca
Air Canada Jazz:
www.flyjazz.com

Air New Zealand:
www.nzair.com
Air Pacific:
www.airpacific.com
Alaska Airlines:
www.alaksaair.com
American Airlines:
www.aa.com
British Airlines:
www.britishairlines.com
Continental Airlines:
www.continental.com
KLM:
www.klm.nl
Lufthansa:
www.lufthansa.de
Northwest Airlines:
www.nwa.com
Qantas:
www.qantas.com.au
Tango:
www.flytango.com
United Airlines:
www.ual.com
WestJet:
www.westjet.com

Car and RV Rental

Avis:
www.avis.com
Budget:
www.budget.com
C.C. Canada Camper:
www.canada-camper.com
Cruise America:
www.cruiseamerica.com
Cruise Canada:
www.cruisecanada.com
Discount:
www.discountcar.com

Internet Resources

Dollar:
www.dollar.com
Enterprise:
www.enterprise.com
Go West:
www.go-west.com
Hertz:
hertz.com
National:
www.nationalcar.com
Rent-a-wreck:
www.rentawreck.ca
Thrifty:
www.thrifty.com

Other Transportation and Tours

Banff Airporter:
www.banffairporter.com
Brewster:
www.brewster.ca
Canadian Mountain Holidays:
www.cmhhike.com
Good Earth Travel Adventures:
www.goodearthtravel.com
Greyhound:
www.greyhound.ca
Maligne Tours:
www.malignelake.com
Rocky Mountain Sky Shuttle:
www.rockymountainskyshuttle.com
Rocky Mountaineer Rail Tours:
www.rockymountaineer.com
VIA Rail:
www.viarail.ca

Tourism Offices

Banff/Lake Louise Tourism Bureau:
www.bannflakelouise.com

Canadian Tourism Commission:
www.canadatourism.com
Golden Tourism Association:
www.go2rockies.com
Jasper Tourism and Commerce:
www.jaspercanadianrockies.com
Radium Hot Springs Visitor Info Centre:
www.rhs.bc.ca
Tourism British Columbia:
www.hellobc.com
Tourism Canmore:
www.tourismcanmore.com
Town of Jasper:
www.jasper-alberta.com
Travel Alberta:
www.travelalberta.com
Waterton Chamber of Commerce:
www.watertonchamber.com

Government

BC Parks:
wlapwww.gov.bc.ca/bcparks
Government of Canada:
www.gc.ca
Citizenship and Immigration Canada:
www.cic.gc.ca
**Canada Customs and Revenue Agency
(Visitor Rebate Program):**
www.ccra-adrc.gc.ca
Government of Alberta:
www.gov.ab.ca
Government of British Columbia:
www.gov.bc.ca
Parks Canada:
www.parkscanada.gc.ca

Index

Glaciers

Index

Index

Skiing and Snowboarding

Waterfalls

Index

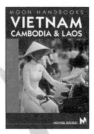

U.S.~Metric Conversion

1 inch	=	2.54 centimeters (cm)
1 foot	=	.304 meters (m)
1 yard	=	0.914 meters
1 mile	=	1.6093 kilometers (km)
1 km	=	.6214 miles
1 fathom	=	1.8288 m
1 chain	=	20.1168 m
1 furlong	=	201.168 m
1 acre	=	.4047 hectares
1 sq km	=	100 hectares
1 sq mile	=	2.59 square km
1 ounce	=	28.35 grams
1 pound	=	.4536 kilograms
1 short ton	=	.90718 metric ton
1 short ton	=	2000 pounds
1 long ton	=	1.016 metric tons
1 long ton	=	2240 pounds
1 metric ton	=	1000 kilograms
1 quart	=	.94635 liters
1 US gallon	=	3.7854 liters
1 Imperial gallon	=	4.5459 liters
1 nautical mile	=	1.852 km

To compute celsius temperatures, subtract 32 from Fahrenheit and divide by 1.8. To go the other way, multiply celsius by 1.8 and add 32.

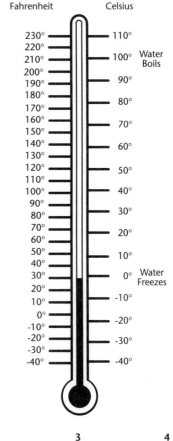

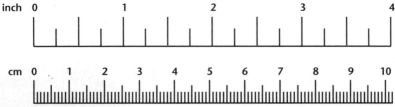